Also by Aljean Harmetz

*The Making of The Wizard of Oz:
Movie Magic and Studio Power
in the Prime of MGM—and the Miracle of
Production #1060*

Rolling Breaks and Other Movie Business

ROUND UP THE USUAL SUSPECTS

The Making of Casablanca—
Bogart, Bergman, and World War II

Aljean Harmetz

NEW YORK

Grateful acknowledgment is given to Jerry Pam for the photograph that appears on page 2; to Marvin Paige for the photographs that appear on pages 5 and 335; to Warner Bros. for the photographs that appear on pages 11, 22, 48, 58, 70, 84, 89, 91, 93, 96, 101, 104, 107, 116, 120, 125, 129, 135, 140, 156, ˑ˞ 5, 168, 171, 177, 181, 192, 206, 210, 224, 234, 247, 263, 265, 269, 271, ˑ ˑ, 311, 327, and 341; to the Gary Essert collection for the photograph ˑˑ ˑe 15; to Murray Burnett for the photograph that appears on page 34; ˑˑˑ r the photographs that appear on pages 37 and 51; to Julius and Leslie E₁ ˑˑ ˑraph that appears on page 41; to Julius Epstein for the photograph that ˑ ˑ to Saul Niremberg for the photograph that appears on page 54; to Arth ˑˑ ˑotographs that appear on pages 61, 71, and 73; to John Meredyth Lucˑˑ hs that appear on pages 65 and 122; to Turner Entertainment Co. for tˑ ˑ appear on pages 80, 98, 121, 137, 143, 152, 157, 161, 194, 202, 204, ˑ ˑ ˑ, ˑˑˑ, 296, 298, 304, 305, 306, and 337; to Jessica Rains for the photographs ˑˑ appear on pages 149 and 150; to Dorothy Blees for the photograph that appears on ˑ page 175; to Lenke Kardos for the photographs that appear on pages 189 and 209; to Peter Almond for the photograph that appears on page 212; to Harold Rader for the photograph that appears on page 256. The photographs appearing on pages 314, 319, 320, and 321 are © courtesy of the Academy of Motion Picture Arts and Sciences.

Grateful acknowledgment for permission to reprint portions of "To the Actor P.L. in Exile" by Bertolt Brecht as it appears in *Bertolt Brecht Poems 1913–1956,* translated by John Willett, is made as follows: for publication in the United States, its territories and the Philippines courtesy of the U.S. Publisher, Routledge, and for publication in the rest of the world courtesy of Methuen, London.

Library of Congress Cataloging-in-Publication Data
Harmetz, Aljean.
    Round up the usual suspects: the making of Casablanca: Bogart, Bergman, and World War II / Aljean Harmetz.—1st ed.
        p. cm.
    Includes bibliographical references and index.
    ISBN 1-56282-941-6
    1. Casablanca (Motion picture) I. Title.
PN1997.C3523H37 1992
791.43'72—dc20   92-24020
                                                                                                           CIP

First Edition
10   9   8   7   6   5   4   3   2   1

Design by Levavi & Levavi

To Friendship, imperfect but durable:

Norma Chaplain, Robin Frasier, Shirley Kiley,
Rebecca Schwaner, Anne Thompson

Contents

———◆———

Acknowledgments

———◆———

It was forty-six years after the making of *Casablanca* that I began my research. More than blue skies had disappeared from Hollywood during nearly five decades. Most of the men and women who had worked on *Casablanca* were dead. And the studio system which had shaped the movie was dead, too. But records of both remained. The history of Warner Bros. is stored in boxes of memos, letters, contracts, production reports, and scripts in the Warner Bros. Archives and the Jack Warner Collection at the University of Southern California. More subtle records are stored in the memories of those who were there in 1942. I owe a huge debt to the following people who shared their memories of *Casablanca*, Warner Bros., or the studio system during the early years of the war:

Joan Alison	Curt Bois	Katherine Dunham
Lew Ayres	Richard Brooks	Amanda Dunne
Solly Baiano	Murray Burnett	Philip Dunne
Sonia Biberman	Meta Carpenter	Julius J. Epstein
John Beckman	Meta Cordy	Rudi Fehr
Robert Blees	Owen Crump	Geraldine Fitzgerald

Bill Hendricks
Paul Henreid
Irene Heymann
Lena Horne
Lee Katz
Leonid Kinskey
Howard Koch
Lupita Kohner
Ring Lardner, Jr.
Irene Lee

Mort Likter
Sam Marx
Dennis Morgan
William T. Orr
Gilbert Perkins
Vincent Price
Tom Pryor
Bill Schaefer
Carl Schaefer
Francis Scheid

Dan Seymour
Vincent Sherman
Arthur Silver
Paul Stader
Carl Stucke
Arthur Wilde
Billy Wilder
Bob William
Frances Williams
Fay Wray

I was allowed to share other memories, too—those of the wives, children, siblings, and cousins of the men and women who played some part in the creation of *Casablanca*. For their time, patience, and graciousness, I would like to thank Lauren Bacall, Nicola Dantine Bautzer, Dorothy Robinson Blees, Stephen Bogart, Leslie Epstein, Frances Feder, Lilian Gelsey, Lenke Kardos, Pia Lindstrom, John Meredyth Lucas, Frances MacKenzie, Saul Nirenberg, Gregory Orr, Bill Rader, Harold G. Rader, Jessica Rains, Jack Warner, Jr., and Margaret Scannell Wooley.

Most of the material in this book comes from primary research. The secondary research includes Hollywood trade papers, journals, and newspapers, as well as autobiographies, oral histories, and memoirs which were, as rigorously as possible, checked against more factual sources. A list of the main archives I used and the materials available at each can be found at the beginning of the Reference Notes and Sources. I was greatly helped in my search by Howard Gotlieb at Boston University; Ronald J. Grele at Columbia University; Jan-Christopher Horak at George Eastman House; Cornelius Schnauber of the Max Kade Institute; Marta Mierendorff who made her private archive available; Mary Ann Jensen and Andros Thompson at Princeton University; Charles Bell and Mary Mallory of the Selznick Archives; David S. Zeidberg of the University of California, Los Angeles; Jeanine Basinger at Wesleyan University who unlocked doors I never could have unlocked for myself; Joan Michaels of the Burbank Public Library; Mark Locher and Harry Medved of the Screen Actors Guild; Chuck Warn of the Directors Guild of America; and Patrick Stockstill of the Academy of Motion Picture Arts and Sciences.

I owe a special thanks to Daniel Selznick who allowed me access to material from the Selznick Archives; Isabella Rossellini who made material from the Ingrid Bergman Collection available to me; and Jessica Rains who provided coffee, laughter, and thirty hours of untranscribed tape recordings made by her father, Claude Rains, during the last few years of his life.

It is impossible to exaggerate the help I received during the four or five months I trolled through the Warner Bros. Archives and the Jack Warner Collection. Leith Adams of the Archives and Ned Comstock of the USC Cinema-Television library consistently and courteously went out of their way to aid me. I would also like to thank Anne Schlosser, Stuart Ng, and Steve Hanson.

Round Up the Usual Suspects attempts to comment on the studio system and its inhabitants from the differing viewpoints of 1942 and 1992. I am indebted to the critics and specialists who helped me to look at it in both ways or who deepened my knowledge of the participants:

Forest Ackerman	Gary Essert	Stanley Kauffmann
Woody Allen	Todd Gitlin	Miles Kreuger
Peter Almond	Samuel Goldwyn, Jr.	Robby Lantz
Sam Arkoff	Cyrus Harvey, Jr.	Laurence Mark
Pat Wilkes Battle	Ronald Haver	Gerald Marks
Rudy Behlmer	Anthony Heilbut	Daniel Melnick
Al Bender	Charles Higham	Leonard Nimoy
Jack Brodsky	Joe Hyams	David Raksin
Art Buchwald	Dorothy Jeakins	Roger Richman
Larry Ceplair	Pauline Kael	David Thomson
Charles Champlin	Kathryn Kalinak	Haskell Wexler

and Yale music students Daniel Jack Becker, Arthur Bloom, Ed Harsh, Lee Heuermann, John Rogers, and Joe Rubenstein.

I am particularly grateful to Ronald Haver for generously sharing with me the materials he had collected for his own *Casablanca* project.

Warner Bros. still sits in the same place in Burbank, California, although it is now Warner Brothers. I would like to thank its chairman, Robert A. Daly, who allowed me to explore basements, storage buildings, and old files in my search for the Warner Bros. that existed in 1942; general counsel John Schulman, who is as avid a treasure hunter as I am; and office services director Dee Somers, who pointed me in all the right directions. Thanks also to Jess Garcia and Carl Samrock for their help.

I am grateful to *Casablanca*'s current owner, Turner Broadcasting System, Inc., for allowing me to use stills from the movie. I owe a special debt to Roger Mayer, president of Turner Entertainment Co.

I have other debts: to Robert Miller and Tom Miller of Hyperion; to David Freeman and my husband, Richard Harmetz, who read various drafts of the manuscript; to Hildegard D. Augustson, who helped with the research until her death in an airplane crash on February 20, 1991.

My last and most earnest thanks goes to my son, Anthony Harmetz, who organized four-foot stacks of interviews and documents into usable categories and helped create the Reference Notes and Sources. The flaws in *Round Up the Usual Suspects* are mine alone, but this would be a much inferior book if Anthony had not given it the best of his editorial skills and had not insisted that I keep rewriting long after I wanted to stop.

I raise my champagne glass to all of you.

Preface

———◆———

Cynicism is a necessary protective coat for those who come close to the film industry's seductively hot center, and I have needed a doubly thick coat. I grew up on the outskirts of M-G-M where my mother worked in the wardrobe department, and I later wrote about Hollywood for *The New York Times*. But my cynicism dissolves when Humphrey Bogart and Ingrid Bergman say goodbye at the airport; and, at least in the dark of the movie theater, I am sure that I would be capable of such a sacrifice too.

As a child of World War II, I find *Casablanca*'s blend of romance and sacrifice irresistible. As a grown-up observer of the movie industry, I am amazed that *Casablanca* survives. Like most of the other movies made under the studio system, *Casablanca* was an accumulation of accidents. Seven writers worked on the script; the cinematographer and film editor were men who happened to be available the week that the movie started production; and the movie's famous last line was written weeks after the shooting had finished.

Hundreds of forgotten movies were built in similar ways, and half a dozen other characters played by Humphrey Bogart duplicated Rick Blaine's journey from isolation to commitment. Between 1942 and 1945 while the studios burned with patriotic fervor, dozens of other movies had similar themes or were made under equivalent wartime restrictions. They were shaped by multiple forces—stars, director, censors, a government at war, the studios, and the times themselves. Few, if any, of those forces were interested in creating a work of lasting value. Yet, although it was set casually like all the other movies in the broad celluloid band of the studio system, *Casablanca* turned out to be the rarest of precious stones. How and why—the interplay between the movie and the pressures that shaped it—is the subject of this book.

ROUND UP THE USUAL SUSPECTS

1

Just Another Movie

In the old days, when the studio factories stretched across Los Angeles under a relentlessly blue sky, the end of production on one movie was almost indistinguishable from the last hours of the movie that had been finished a week earlier or the movie that would be completed two weeks later.

Casablanca ended production on August 3, 1942, eleven days behind schedule. As he had done on dozens of pictures, Al Alleborn, the unit production manager, typed a short note:

> Report for MONDAY, 8-3-42. 59th shooting day. Company opened on the French Street, EXT. BLUE PARROT & BLACK MARKET, which set was finished. Covered 1'25", 15 setups and 1¼ pages of dialogue. Working and finishing, INGRID BERGMAN. Started, worked and finished, PAUL HENREID. This production finished as of yesterday, Monday.

Nobody was unhappy that the movie was finally over. Most of the actors hadn't liked one another. The director, Michael Curtiz, had been vicious, as usual, to his crew and bit players. The war made it impossible to shoot real airplanes, so Humphrey Bogart had said

3

goodbye to Ingrid Bergman in front of a plywood plane on Warner Bros. Stage 1, with all that atmospheric fog pumped in to disguise the phoniness. The movie had started in May, and the screenwriters were still writing new speeches in mid-July. It made the actors edgy. Although Bergman always managed to hide her anxiety, Bogart lashed out. *Casablanca* was just one of the four movies he would make in 1942, and he had had much more fun on *Across the Pacific.*

Bergman had taken the part of Ilsa Lund in *Casablanca* only because she had been turned down for the role she really wanted— Maria in Paramount's film version of Hemingway's Spanish Civil War novel *For Whom the Bell Tolls.* To Bergman, who lived to work, any role was better than none, but she had been playing docile, love-torn women like Ilsa for years. Even then, Bergman was hungry for Academy Awards, and David O. Selznick, the producer who owned her contract, had assured her that Maria, the Spanish girl who had been raped by the Falangists before she joined a partisan band in the mountains, would win her one. When Bergman finished working on the French Street at noon on August 3, dancer Vera Zorina was Maria, but Paramount was having second thoughts. For days the *Los Angeles Times* had been printing rumors that Zorina's hold on the role was shaky. The movie had been in production for ten days, and Zorina seemed too much the ballerina to be believable as a peasant girl who could climb the hills like a mountain goat. "Maybe this will open the gate once again to Ingrid Bergman, who was Ernest Hemingway's own selection," said the *Times*'s film critic Edwin Schallert on July 28.

During that hot morning on the Warner Bros. back lot, Bergman was waiting for the telephone call that would tell her whether she was to replace Zorina. The call came while Bergman and Paul Henreid were posing for publicity photographs. When the phone in the Warner Bros. picture gallery rang, it was David Selznick, who said, "You are Maria," Bergman wrote in a diary long—perhaps years—afterward. "Since the day I was admitted to the acting school of the Swedish Royal Dramatic Theatre I haven't felt such heavenly joy." To Henreid, her shout of triumph was "that of a tigress who has made a kill." Henreid had been working with Bergman for nearly two months, but it was only at this last moment that he pierced her shield of sweet docility and understood "how she had managed to get ahead in Sweden and in the Hollywood jungle." Surfeited with victory, Bergman barely gave *Casablanca* another thought.

Six other movies were shooting at Warner Bros. the week that *Casablanca* ended. *Casablanca* was neither the most important nor the most expensive. Its final cost of $1,039,000 was considerably more than Warner Bros. would have spent four years earlier but relatively modest for an A film in 1942. Of the seven pictures filling the Warner Bros. stages in early August, only *Princess O'Rourke* was cheaper. *Air Force* was in production for ninety-nine days and cost $2,646,000. *Edge of Darkness,* with the studio's top star, Errol Flynn, and *The Adventures of Mark Twain* cost over $1,500,000 each. *Watch on the Rhine,* based on a play by Lillian Hellman, was to be the studio's prestige movie for 1943, the movie that would carry Warners' hopes for Academy Awards. Even *The Desert Song,* Sigmund Romberg's 1926 operetta dragged out of storage and dressed up with Nazi villains, cost $1,148,000.

   Casablanca finished on August 3, and *Edge of Darkness* took over the soundstages on August 4. "One in and one out," as Rick Blaine would say when Ilsa Lund walked back into his life. Rick Blaine said a lot of things, and college students who weren't born when he said them would shout his words back at the screen twenty years later. "The Germans wore gray; you wore blue." "We'll always have

While this picture was being taken, Ingrid Bergman was waiting for the call that would tell her if she would get the role she really wanted.

Paris." "I'm no good at being noble, but it doesn't take much to see that the problems of three little people don't amount to a hill o' beans in this crazy world."

By the time John F. Kennedy ran for President and Harvard students sat in the Brattle Theater in Cambridge, Massachusetts, and chanted Rick's words, the war that had formed the context for *Casablanca* was just another chapter in American history textbooks. The movie should have been as dead as the hundreds of other melodramas that Hollywood churned out during World War II; or, at best, Rick Blaine should have been exiled to film classes as an interesting example of The Cynical Idealist—a common film protagonist during the late 1930s and early 1940s. "But to be at the Brattle when *Casablanca* was playing was, in a small way, like being at a theater in ancient Greece watching *Oedipus*," says Cyrus Harvey, Jr., who co-owned the theater. "Some people came twenty-five and thirty times. The film was almost mythical, and audiences would repeat lines the way they did in Greek amphitheaters."

There are better movies than *Casablanca*, but no other movie better demonstrates America's mythological vision of itself—tough on the outside and moral within, capable of sacrifice and romance without sacrificing the individualism that conquered a continent, sticking its neck out for everybody when circumstances demand heroism. No other movie has so reflected both the moment when it was made—the early days of World War II—and the psychological needs of audiences decades later. It was an accident, of course, that *Casablanca* blended a theme and half a dozen actors, an old song and a script full of cynical lines and moral certainty, into 102 minutes that have settled into the American psyche. But every movie is a creature built from accidents and blind choices—a mechanical monster constructed of camera angles, chemistry between actors, too little money or too much, and a thousand unintended moments.

A gust of wind blew Maureen O'Hara's wedding veil in *How Green Was My Valley,* giving a poignant visual coda to a sad wedding and a hint of the unhappy marriage to come. "That was wonderful storytelling," said the screenwriter Philip Dunne.* "And it was just a piece of luck for us. I tried to reproduce it when I directed *10 North Frederick,* and then I realized it was a mistake to try. You can't reproduce those accidents."

---

* Interviewed a year before his death in 1992.

Casablanca was a mosaic of fortune—good and bad. The producer, Hal Wallis, was annoyed that Michele Morgan wanted $55,000 to star in the movie. "There is no reason in the world for demanding this kind of money for anyone as little known as Michele Morgan," he wrote to his director, Michael Curtiz. Wallis could—and did—borrow Ingrid Bergman from David O. Selznick for $25,000. But a choice that seems inevitable in 1992 is only clear because of hindsight. Both the young Swedish actress and the young French actress had been successful in their first American movies. *Casablanca* would have been Michele Morgan's second Hollywood film, an immediate successor to *Joan of Paris*. Bergman had followed *Intermezzo* with three mediocre movies. It was *Casablanca* that made Ingrid Bergman a star. Would it have done the same for Michele Morgan, whose Hollywood career ended after three films?

Composer Max Steiner hated "As Time Goes By" and persuaded Wallis to allow him to replace it with a love song of his own. But, lucky accident, Ingrid Bergman had already had her hair cut short for her part in *For Whom the Bell Tolls* and could not reshoot the necessary scenes. *Casablanca* also had the luck to be made early in the war, before films had to be force-fed with patriotism, stuffed to bursting like fatted European geese. And, in the Epstein twins, it had a pair of writers who tied a sting to the tail of the sentiment. Did *Casablanca* succeed because Julius and Philip Epstein and Howard Koch were bringing rewritten scenes to the set every day or in spite of it, because Ingrid Bergman was confused about what she should feel toward Paul Henreid and Humphrey Bogart or in spite of her confusion?

In later years, Bergman would get annoyed when people told her that they had loved her in *Casablanca*. "She was surprised and a little irritated, miffed by all the attention to that movie," says Bergman's oldest daughter, Pia Lindstrom. "She would always get this exasperated look. This was partly because she was terribly serious about building a character. She didn't come from the school of improvising or going with the flow. That's why she was piqued that something that seemed haphazard turned out to be everybody's favorite movie."

Bogart's response to the success of *Casablanca* was more typically sardonic. He enjoyed telling his fourth wife, Lauren Bacall, how Charles Einfeld, the studio's head of publicity, had had the amazing revelation that the actor had sex appeal. Says Bacall, "Bogie would say, 'Of course, I did nothing in *Casablanca* that I hadn't done in twenty movies before that, and suddenly they discover I'm sexy. Any time that Ingrid Bergman looks at a man, he has sex appeal.' "

It was a hot summer, although the heat wave that had choked the San Fernando Valley during July lessened in August. Landlocked, Warner Bros. was always a roasting pan. The studio's chief rivals—Paramount, 20th Century–Fox, and Metro-Goldwyn-Mayer—were on the far side of the mountains, the cool side. If you climbed high enough at M-G-M, you could even see the ocean six miles away. But Warners was all heat, metaphorically as well as physically. It was almost as though the studio were in heat: edgy, intense, feverish, throbbing with urgency. Songwriter Harry Warren described the M-G-M of that era as a garden and compared Warners to a prison, all rat-a-tat-tat machine-gun rhythm.

That was the rhythm of the studio and its movies. Dozens of Warner movies were torn from the morning headlines. Let a gangster be shot, coal miners go on strike, truck drivers or taxi drivers start a war with City Hall or crooked union officials, and Warner Bros. was there to make the news into fiction almost before the ink had dried. As late as 1942, itinerant crop pickers fought with a packing company's hired thugs in Warners' *Juke Girl*.

It is possible that one of the seven other major studios might have bought and made a movie from *Everybody Comes to Rick's,* an unproduced play about a cynical American who owns a bar in Casablanca. (One producer at M-G-M, Sam Marx, did want to buy the play for $5,000, but his boss didn't think it was worth the money.) It wouldn't have been the same movie, not only because it would have starred Gary Cooper at Paramount, Clark Gable at M-G-M, or Tyrone Power at Fox but because another studio's style would have been more languid, less sardonic, or opulently Technicolored.

Like the other studios, Warners produced melodramas, musicals, tear jerkers, and costume epics, but each studio made them on different subjects and in different styles. One effect of the war was to mash the subjects and styles together into a generic war film. Earlier, even Warner films with hoop skirts or swordplay had a rawness and social or political edge that the other studios were uninterested in copying. At the same time that Warners tackled syphilis in *Dr. Ehrlich's Magic Bullet* in 1940, M-G-M created two biographies of Thomas Edison and one of Johann Strauss.

Warner Bros. was the most frugal of the studios, and little was wasted there in 1942. World War II gave the studio's president, Harry Warner, an excuse to pick up nails dropped by careless carpenters. But he had obsessively picked up nails before the war made iron scarce. *Casablanca* moved onto the French Street created for *The Desert Song* the day after that film moved off. A few signs and two live parrots turned the French Morocco of the heroic freedom fighter El Khobar into the French Morocco of heroic freedom fighter Victor Laszlo. And half-a-dozen bit players with foreign accents got a full week's work by straddling the two films. More than half of the movies Warners made in 1942 dealt in one way or another with the war, a bonanza for actors who had fled from Berlin or Vienna. *Casablanca* was filled with those Jewish refugees, many of them playing Nazis.

Of the seven pictures being shot during the first week of August, four concerned the underground Resistance—symbolized by a Czech patriot in *Casablanca,* the American leader of the Riff tribe in *The Desert Song,* a Norwegian village in *Edge of Darkness,* and an anti-Nazi German in *Watch on the Rhine.* The real war movies would come later, when there were victories to celebrate. In the summer of 1942, there were mostly defeats. By July 22, 44,143 Americans were dead, wounded, or missing in action, and ten thousand Japanese soldiers had landed in the Aleutian Islands off the coast of Alaska.

Like all of America, Hollywood, inevitably, would be changed by World War II. Warner Bros. had already had its first death. Lieutenant Henry David Mark, the brother of two studio employees, had been killed in March on the Bataan peninsula in the Philippines. And Warners, more than any other studio, had joined hands with the government and agreed to the kind of censorship the industry had been fighting since the first nickelodeons. Eventually and grudgingly Warners would have to hire girl messengers ("Because there was nothing else to do" when "the situation became desperate," reported the *Warner Club News*). But in 1942 the unions still refused to train women as electricians and carpenters despite the fact that week by week during that first summer of the war the men—actors, directors, writers, and craftsmen—were leaving. In subtle ways, the war helped to destroy the studio system. When cameramen and actors marched home as captains and majors, they would have less tolerance for the tyranny of the seven-year contracts they had left behind.

Like most pictures, *Casablanca* ended with a whimper. The movie's troublesome climax—written and rewritten and rewritten once again—had been shot in mid-July. On that last day in early August, Bergman and Henreid spent forty minutes on the French Street, doing the silent pickup shots that are the movie equivalent of sweeping up. Curtiz filmed them from the point of view of Humphrey Bogart, who was already down in Newport on his boat. The rest of the day, Curtiz dressed the street with seventy-nine extras from Central Casting and shot refugees running from the police in the first scenes of the movie.

The other actors had scattered. Bogart had retreated into a stale and hostile marriage. During the shooting of *Casablanca,* his alcoholic wife, Mayo Methot, had accused him of having an affair with Ingrid Bergman. Mayo always prowled the sets of Bogart's movies, inventing liaisons that didn't exist. Her jealousy fed Bogart's surliness, and he spent most of his time on the set of *Casablanca* alone in his canvas dressing room, or playing a solitary game of chess. Actors had little control over their destinies. Bogart loved chess because there was no luck to the game.

Claude Rains had returned to his farm in Pennsylvania; Conrad Veidt to the nearest golf course; Dooley Wilson to a small white stucco house in Hollywood; Peter Lorre and Sydney Greenstreet to a month's vacation before they started another Warner Bros. spy melodrama, *Background to Danger.* Three weeks later Curtiz would shoot a new scene, a police official announcing the murder of two German couriers, to add some drama to the movie's first few moments. And Bogart would record a new last line. Hal Wallis wrote the line himself. Actually, he wrote two alternative lines: "Luis,[*] I might have known you'd mix your patriotism with a little larceny" and "Luis, I think this is the beginning of a beautiful friendship." Wallis was a cool and distant man, but he was admired, even by writers, as a story editor. He crossed out the more cynical line and sent the second one to Curtiz. When Bogart recorded it, he could not have imagined that the words he was reciting would become one of the most famous last lines in movie history or that, because of

---

[*] The character had originally been named Luis Rinaldo.

FORM 166

WARNER BROS. PICTURES, INC.
FOREIGN DEPT.

Camera reports USC/WB Archives

KEY LETTER ____ A ____

TITLE _Casablanca_ PRODUCTION NO. 410 DATE 8-3-42

FILM NO.	SCRIPT SCENE	Choice	SET: Blue Parrot								
731	137A	1st	1	2	3	4	5	6	7	8	9
		2nd	X	OX	OX	X	O				
			10	11	12	13	14	15	16	17	18

CAMERAS _Dolly LS Street to CU_
REMARKS: _Parrot to Susu Sign_

FILM NO.	SCRIPT SCENE	Choice	SET: Street								
732	5	1st	1	2	3	4	5	6	7	8	9
		2nd	O								
(1st Seg.)			10	11	12	13	14	15	16	17	18

CAMERAS _Man grabbed by_
REMARKS: _Police_

FILM NO.	SCRIPT SCENE	Choice	SET: "								
733	5	1st	1	2	3	4	5	6	7	8	9
		2nd	X		X	X	O	X	O		
(1st Seg.)			10	11	12	13	14	15	16	17	18

CAMERAS _(note 2 cameras for_
REMARKS: _takes #1 +2) Refugees grabbed by police_

FILM NO.	SCRIPT SCENE	Choice	SET: "								
734	5	1st	1	2	3	4	5	6	7	8	9
		2nd	O	X	O						
(1st Seg.)			10	11	12	13	14	15	16	17	18

CAMERAS _Refugees grabbed by_
REMARKS: _police._

FILM NO.	SCRIPT SCENE	Choice	SET: "								
735	5	1st	1	2	3	4	5	6	7	8	9
		2nd	X	X	OX	X	O				
(1st Seg)			10	11	12	13	14	15	16	17	18

CAMERAS _Refugees being taken_
REMARKS: _towards patrol wagon_

FILM NO.	SCRIPT SCENE	Choice	SET: "								
736	144	1st	1	2	3	4	5	6	7	8	9
		2nd	X	O							
			10	11	12	13	14	15	16	17	18

CAMERAS _Thru window and_
REMARKS: _Rick go to Renau stand, exit to cafe_

FILM NO.	SCRIPT SCENE	Choice	SET: "								
737	5	1st	1	2	3	4	5	6	7	8	9
		2nd	OX	O							
(1st Seg.)			10	11	12	13	14	15	16	17	18

CAMERAS _CU Refugee hears_
REMARKS: _police whistle, ex_

FILM NO.	SCRIPT SCENE	Choice	SET: "								
738	5	1st	1	2	3	4	5	6	7	8	9
		2nd	X	OX	O						
(1st Seg.)			10	11	12	13	14	15	16	17	18

CAMERAS _Lg CU Refugee_
REMARKS: _hears whistle, ducks_

FILM NO.	SCRIPT SCENE	Choice	SET: "								
739	135C	1st	1	2	3	4	5	6	7	8	9
8 - Best		2nd	X	X	X	X	OX	X	OX	O	
Hold only no print			10	11	12	13	14	15	16	17	18

CAMERAS _CU Native & Frenchman_
REMARKS: _talk re Ferrari_

FILM NO.	SCRIPT SCENE	Choice	SET: "								
740	135C	1st	1	2	3	4	5	6	7	8	9
		2nd	X	X	O						
alternate to 739			10	11	12	13	14	15	16	17	18

CAMERAS
REMARKS:

INSTRUCTIONS: American Print put a circle around the take O
Foreign Print put a square around the take □
Hold Print put on OX under the take
On N. G. Takes put a cross over the take X

Camera report from the last day of shooting, August 3, 1942.

Casablanca, he would replace Errol Flynn as Warners' top box-office star.

Nor could anyone at Warner Bros. have imagined that *Casablanca,* so much a creature of its time and place, defined by the sentiments of the war for which and during which it was made, would remain meaningful to audiences fifty years later. In 1942, the only reason pictures lasted a month in the theaters was because the war made it impossible to distribute a movie every week. In 1934, Warner Bros. had released 69 feature films. As audiences became more sophisticated and movies more expensive, the goal changed to one picture a week, and in 1941 Warner Bros. sent 48 movies into the theaters it owned. In 1942, as the scarcity of actors, materials, and technicians began to be felt, *Casablanca* was one of only 33 Warner films to make that journey.

The movie opened at one theater in New York on Thanksgiving Day, November 26, 1942, to take advantage of the fact that American troops had landed in North Africa and the city of Casablanca was in the headlines. In all other ways *Casablanca,* which had originally been scheduled for release the next spring, was a 1943 movie. It didn't play in any other city until January 23. The *Film Daily Yearbook* lists it as one of the 21 Warner Bros. movies released in 1943, and it competed for 1943 Academy Awards.

Ingrid Bergman had drifted into *Casablanca,* but she had fought for the role of Maria and, whatever the verdict of history, Paramount's *For Whom the Bell Tolls* was the runaway leader at the box office in 1943, selling nearly $11 million worth of tickets. 20th Century–Fox's *Song of Bernadette* was second, with ticket sales of $7 million. *Casablanca* did well financially. Ticket sales of $3.7 million put the movie in seventh place. And it did well with most movie reviewers. In *The New York Times* Bosley Crowther called it "a picture which makes the spine tingle and the heart take a leap." In keeping with the proprieties of the time, a number of reviewers praised the movie for its political correctness. "Splendid anti-Axis propaganda," said the Hollywood trade paper *Variety.* The liberal New York paper *PM* called the movie "an exciting film built around an exciting new idea . . . that leaders of Europe's anti-Fascist underground are terribly important people these days, rating priorities ahead of even millionaires and playboys in such traditional specialties of old Casablanca as stolen passports." A poll of 439 critics and commentators taken by *Film Daily* called *Casablanca* the fifth-best movie of the year—behind *Random Harvest, For Whom the Bell Tolls, Yankee Doodle Dandy,* and *This Is the Army.* *

There was some dissent, mostly in the highbrow magazines. "The 'Casablanca' kind of hokum was good in its original context in other movies, but, lifted into *Casablanca* for the sake of its glitter and not incorporated into it, loses its meaning," Manny Farber wrote in *The New Republic. The New Yorker* called the film "pretty tolerable" although not up to *Across the Pacific,* Humphrey Bogart's last picture. In *The Nation,* James Agee, one of the few reviewers who is still respected today, first offered grudging praise: "Apparently *Casablanca,* which I must say I liked, is working up a rather serious reputation as a fine melodrama. Why? It is obviously an improvement on one of the world's worst plays; but it is not such an improvement that that is not obvious." A year later Agee reappraised: "*Casablanca* is still reverently spoken of as (1) fun, (2) a 'real movie.' I still think it is the year's clearest measure of how willingly, faute de mieux, people will deceive themselves. Even *Jeannie,* hardly a movie at all, was better fun."

Howard Koch, one of the movie's three main screenwriters, has another view. In the summer of 1989, he stares out at the stream and woods that form the backyard of his house in upstate New York. At eighty-eight, he still plays croquet before cocktails, but the croquet court is not quite level and sometimes a ball gets entangled in the weeping willows. "I've got almost a mystical feeling about *Casablanca,*" he says. "That it made itself somehow. That it needed to be made and that we were all conveyers on the belt, taking it there. A woman called me up a couple of weeks ago and said, 'I tracked you down because I had to tell you that I've just seen *Casablanca* for the forty-sixth time, and it means more to me than anything in my life.' It's just a movie, but it's more than that. It's become something that people can't find in values today. And they go back to *Casablanca* as they go back to church, political church, to find something that is gone from our values today." When Koch says that *Casablanca* made itself, he holds out his hands, palms up and cupped as though he has dipped them in the stream. He has not lost the leftist

---

* Rounding out the Top 10 were *The Human Comedy, Watch on the Rhine, In Which We Serve, So Proudly We Hail!,* and *Stage Door Canteen.* Quality, in this case, was in the tenor of the time as well as the eye of the beholder. All ten movies had war themes or backgrounds. Two films that did not fit the patriotic fashions of the time and were spurned by the critics: *The Ox-Bow Incident* and *Shadow of a Doubt.*

views—he calls them "progressive"—that sent him into exile during the 1950s. *Mother Jones* and a disarmament newsletter sit on his coffee table. "I'm just part of the chain," he says. "I'm not important in it. None of us are. But we're important as links in the chain."

That chain was wound tightly around the 135 acres of the Warner Bros. First National studio in Burbank. Koch was neither the first nor the last link. With appropriate symmetry for a movie that encapsulated both the idealism that Americans brought to World War II and the forced renunciation of private lives that the war brought to them, *Casablanca* officially entered the studio system on December 8, 1941, the day after Pearl Harbor was bombed by the Japanese, and departed, draped with an Academy Award for best picture, in the spring of 1944, when the Allies were poised to invade western Europe and the studios were decisively turning their backs on the war and planning movies for the peace to come. *Casablanca* had done more than was expected. It had made money, improved careers, won awards, and given Jack Warner something to boast about. It was put in a vault and forgotten.

PRESENTS

2

The Studio: Jack L. Warner,
Executive Producer . . .
and Hal B. Wallis

———◆———

Among the many metaphors for the city-states that collectively made up the studio system, the one most commonly used by survivors is fiefdom. "Fiefdoms. Little circles of power," says director Billy Wilder. "Like in the Middle Ages, they had fortresses built on the hills and sometimes they fought but they certainly did not intermingle. You did not communicate or converse with or make bosom friends with people who were working for other studios."

The city-states are in ruins now and the barons dead, but much of the structure they invented remains. When the manuscript of *Everybody Comes to Rick's* reached Warner Bros. the day after Pearl Harbor, it became part of a process that has not changed much in fifty years.

The play was appraised by a thirty-five-year-old reader making $1.12 an hour who would leave Warners for a better-paying job in a defense plant the next October. Today, with the usual studio title inflation, readers are called "story analysts," and the job of writing a synopsis is called "coverage." But, now as then, the raw material is judged by the least powerful of studio employees.

Stephen Karnot was shrewd in his judgment of the play that would become *Casablanca*:

Excellent melodrama. Colorful, timely background, tense mood, suspense, psychological and physical conflict, tight plotting, sophisticated hokum. A boxoffice natural—for Bogart, or Cagney, or Raft in out-of-the-usual roles, and perhaps Mary Astor.

The fact that Karnot liked the play didn't matter. *Everybody Comes to Rick's* had a better advocate. Irene Lee, who headed the

```
                                        Read by:
                                        Stephen Karnot
                                        12/11/41.




                    EVERYBODY COMES TO RICK'S
                                by
                            Murray Burnett &
                            Joan Alison
```

Smart, sophisticated, luxurious Rick's Cafe is the most popular night
spot in Casablanca, French Morrocco. To the flamboyantly decorated
bar, and the gaming rooms in the rear come the wealthy French expatriates
the richer refugees, the consular officials and the French, German and
Italian military attaches. Under the cynically indifferent and watchful
eye of Rick, an American of indeterminate age, an atmosphere of strict
neutrality, both political and personal, prevails. On this warm summer
evening of 1941, the mood of Rick's cafe epitomizes the mood of Casablanca: tense, hectic, desperately gay. Rick, as usual, sits at an
out-of-the-way table near the bar, admitting or barring people from
the gaming rooms with an imperceptible nod to the major-domo, greeting
a patron here, there refusing to take the check of an imposing four-
flusher. Sam, Negro entertainer at the mobile piano, plays softly.
Ugarte, a distinguished, sleekly tailored man enters, and at a nod
from Rick is seated at an adjoining table. When the waiter brings
a magnum of champagne, Ugarte asks Rick to join him, but Rick refuses.
Poker-faced Rick evidently has little use for Ugarte, and when the
latter announces his coming departure from Casablanca, Rick remains

The first reader's report of the play.

story department at Warners, had found the play on a trip to New York and was urging Hal Wallis, who ran the studio for Jack Warner, to buy it. Later, when the movie was a hit, Wallis would say that buying *Everybody Comes to Rick's* was his idea. And Jack Warner would grab *Casablanca*'s Oscar away from Wallis because, after all, he owned the studio. Then as now, whoever was strong enough took the credit.

"But it was Irene Lee who deserved the credit," says Julius Epstein, one of the three screenwriters who got credit for turning *Everybody Comes to Rick's* into a movie. "She was much smarter than Hal Wallis. She was the one who assigned us to write it. And she has never been acknowledged." Only Julie Epstein and an unpublished memoir by a former member of the story department give credit to Irene Lee.

"When *Casablanca* came out and was that tremendous hit and I had bought it for so little money, I spoke to Hal and said, 'Don't you think I ought to have a bonus?' " says Irene Lee Diamond in the spring of 1989. "And he said, 'That's what you're here for.' A woman in those days was still sort of half accepted. You certainly didn't get the kind of pay that men did."

With Wallis's approval, Irene Lee purchased *Everybody Comes to Rick's* for $20,000 two days after Christmas 1941. For eight years Hal Wallis had been second in command to Jack Warner and had headed production of the studio's A movies. Warner was mean, charming, and suspicious. Wallis was cool and reserved, a square man with piercing dark eyes that missed very little. He was earning $5,000 a week, but the money wasn't enough to keep him from being tired of the job of overseeing eighteen movies a year. When he bought *Everybody Comes to Rick's,* Wallis had both feet out the door, and he was looking for some scripts to take with him. In a thirty-three-page contract signed on January 12, 1942, Wallis stopped being Jack Warner's employee and became Hal Wallis Productions. He would make four pictures a year for Warner Bros., and his fees would include 10 percent of the profits.* In all publicity and on the screen, "Produced by Hal Wallis" would be in type at least half as large as "Bette Davis" or "James Cagney." Section 16

---

*Wallis was to receive 10 percent of Warner Bros.' gross receipts after the gross receipts reached 125 percent of the negative cost (the direct costs of the picture plus the indirect charges arising from the studio overhead allocated to the picture) of the movie.

on page 24 gave Wallis "first call and right to use the services of any director, actor or actress, writer, unit manager, cameramen and necessary secretarial or administrative assistants who may be under contract or employed to render services to the Company." If Wallis wanted writers, directors, actors, and actresses who weren't under contract to Warners, the studio would try to get them for him. *Casablanca* was the third of the nine movies Wallis made under that four-year contract—a legal document that was in tatters two-and-a-half years later. The contract is a measure of Jack Warner's respect for Wallis. Its destruction is a measure of Warner's jealousy.

In the end, the rivalry between Warner and Wallis would turn dark and bitter, and Wallis's insistence that he was responsible for *Casablanca* would be the last straw. As the movie's producer in an era when directors were usually handed a script a few days before they were to start filming, Wallis was responsible for *Casablanca.* But he made the film at a studio where he was never more than second in command and where the movies, including *Casablanca,* were shaped to Warner's philosophy of hurry up, do it cheap, be wary, and don't trust anybody.

Both Warner and Wallis had had turn-of-the-century Jewish immigrant childhoods, Warner in Youngstown, Ohio, Wallis in Chicago. And both men had come far. Warner's father mended shoes. Wallis's father was a tailor. Wallis went to work at fourteen because his father had bolted and the family was destitute. Warner was fifteen when he left home to join his older brothers in the film buying business. But, temperamentally, the two men could have been born at opposite ends of the world. Warner was a screamer. Soft-spoken and self-restrained, Wallis never dramatized or shouted. Warner was a clown, a gambler, a pleasure seeker. When Hal Wallis's father lost the family's furniture to his gambling debts, the son took a job as an office boy, dutifully bringing the $5 he earned each week home to his mother. By 1942, Wallis, who had started in the studio publicity department, had been at Warner Bros. for nearly twenty years. Jack Warner trusted him—as much as he was able to trust anyone. But Wallis's success as an independent producer would become intolerable to the man who ended arguments by pointing to his name on the studio water tower.

Each of the fiefdoms took its tone and character from the mogul who ran it. Although they were all tyrants, their tyranny wore different garments, from L. B. Mayer's vision of himself as the stern and loving father of the Metro-Goldwyn-Mayer family to Harry Cohn's bullying imitation at Columbia of his idol, Mussolini. Even the mildest of them placed his desk at the far end of his huge office so that supplicants had to cross an acre of carpet. At Fox, Darryl F. Zanuck's office was sixty feet long, with a grand piano and heavy green shutters and drapes that were always kept closed so that no one would have the distraction of looking out a window. Zanuck's office complex also included a private swimming pool, projection room, and barbershop. Directors and producers had to look up at Mayer, whose desk was on a pedestal. And Harry Cohn told a friend: "By the time they walk to my desk, they're beaten."

Warner Bros. belonged to Jack and Harry Warner. And they hated each other. Four Warner brothers—Harry, Albert, Sam, and eleven-year-old Jack—opened a nickelodeon in 1903, began renting films to other nickelodeons a few years later, and became fly-by-night film producers by 1917. But Sam had died young, and by 1942 the quiet and unaggressive Albert (he had changed his name from Abraham, just as Harry and Jack were originally Hirsch and Jacob) had settled for running the theaters that Warner Bros. owned. So the studio was the bone over which Jack and Harry fought. As vice president in charge of production, fifty-year-old Jack made the movies and ran the studio. As president of the company, sixty-one-year-old Harry controlled the money that Jack wanted to spend on his movies.

Harry had a gift for making money. After twenty years on the fringes, he had built Warner Bros. into a major company between 1928 and 1932 by audaciously buying theaters and the First National studio in the San Fernando Valley. By 1937, *Fortune* magazine was calling Harry the second-most-important man in the movie industry. (The magazine added that the Hollywood elite, including Loew's/M-G-M, where the No. 1 man, Nicholas Schenck, resided, resented the Warners and found their success distasteful because of their bargain-basement moviemaking.)

The problems between Jack and Harry got worse when Harry moved from the New York head office to a bungalow on the studio lot during the late 1930s. Harry Warner was severe and moral, a typical oldest son, allotting punishment and rewards and passing judgment in a way that infuriated his younger brother. "My uncle was a very moral man," says Jack Warner, Jr. "In another life he would have been a rabbi or a prophet. He was a very good man, but he might have benefited by having more compassion. He strenuously disapproved of many things my father did with his life. And there was also a natural war between the home office in New York that controlled the purse strings and the studio that controlled the spending. Harry bled whenever he read the budget of a movie. He felt his brother was a spendthrift. When he moved to California, Harry brought all his hostility to spending money with him."*

"Harry was a solid fellow," says Lee Katz, who had been at Warner Bros. for ten years when he worked as an assistant director on *Casablanca*. "Jack was not too truthful and, correspondingly, not too trustworthy. If Harry said something, you could depend on it. He might not promise very much, but you could rest assured it would be forthcoming."

Despite the excesses of Jack Warner's private life—the gambling and the women—Warner Bros. was a studio without frills. That was one of the few things Harry and Jack agreed on. While Harry picked up nails, Jack turned off lights. Harry may have considered him a spendthrift, but Jack was a penny-pincher in everyone else's eyes. "I have been watching the Time Record for the Writers and have noted that they are coming in very close to ten o'clock and leaving at five," Jack Warner wrote to all his producers in 1942. "Everyone of them should arrive no later than 9:30 and stay until 5:30. . . . It is no wonder they are slow turning out the scripts when they are at the Studio for just a few hours." Once, when a picture was being filmed in Griffith Park a few miles from the studio, a prop man found an empty five-gallon water bottle that had been discarded by a crew from Paramount Pictures. Unlike Paramount, Warner Bros. did not provide its crew and actors with water, so the prop man took the bottle back to the studio and filled it with tap water. Harry Warner saw him carrying the bottle to the location the next morning and fired him because "bottled water is a ridiculous extravagance." The next day, when the situation had been explained to Harry, the prop man, Doc Solomon, was rehired and given a $2-a-week raise.

At M-G-M, L. B. Mayer once sent Joan Crawford out of the

*Eventually, Jack would have his revenge on his older brother. In 1956, he maneuvered Harry out of Warner Bros. by selling the studio, then buying control back and taking for himself Harry's title of president. When Harry died two years later, Jack stayed in the South of France, playing baccarat at Monte Carlo, instead of coming home for his brother's funeral.

An aerial view of Warner Bros., formerly the First National Pictures Studio, in the 1930s.

commissary because she was not dressed appropriately for a movie star. At Warner Bros., even major stars were wrapped in sandpaper, not ordered to dress in silk. On location for four months in 1944 for *Operation Burma,* Errol Flynn wrote a letter of complaint:

> My dressing room, as we laughingly call it, had certain novel features. I counted as many as ten holes in the canvas sides through which I found some children examining me in the act of robing and unrobing. One other quite noticeable feature was the floor. At Whittier, for instance, it consisted of a thin strip of moth-eaten matting, much torn and ratted. It only covered a minute portion of the dressing room, the rest was solid cow-dung. This undoubtedly explains the fascination the room held for ten million insects. . . .
>
> But the topper came when I discovered one day that my dressing room had been changed over night and that I was now dressing in

one that I had myself used the previous day as a toilet (in company with two or three hundred gentlemen). The only marked change between the toilet and the dressing room was that it now had a broken down chair instead of the usual receptical [*sic*]. . . .

By contrast I would refer you to the trailer dressing rooms both Fox and M.G.M. use on locations.

Jack Warner liked to make his actors angry. "Bogart will just have to stew in his own juice," he wrote gleefully in a telegram from New York. He ended another nasty telegram with "I'm a bad boy." He never liked to take the consequences of being a bad boy, so his barbs would be passed to the actor secondhand.

"They were passed through the executive chain," says Bill Orr, who started as an actor under contract to Warners before the war, married Jack Warner's stepdaughter Joy Page, and ended up running the studio for a while. One of Orr's first jobs as an executive was to make the rounds of the sets early each morning. "You tell me if Bogie or any of the others are acting up" were Warner's instructions. Says Orr, "And I said, 'Yes, Jack, as your son-in-law I have to be a squealer.' And he said, 'Well, I thought it was a good idea.' And I said, 'It's not a good idea for either of us.' "

Warner had other eyes and ears. The executive chain started with Steve Trilling, pink-cheeked and fervently loyal, plucked out of the casting department in 1942 to replace Hal Wallis as studio administrator. "Part of his job was to listen outside your door to hear if you were typing and then to open the door if you weren't," said director Richard Brooks,* who was a contract writer at Warner Bros. after he returned from the war. Brooks kept a map of the studio on his wall. Since coffee was not allowed in offices or on the sets and no young writer could leave the studio by the main gate before 5:30, Brooks, like other writers, sneaked through back exits to a drugstore across the street.

In contrast, "M-G-M didn't encourage you to work at home, but the studio allowed it," says Ring Lardner, Jr., who was at Warner Bros. in 1937–1938 and at Metro in the early forties. "And, when you went to the studio, your hours were pretty much your own. My collaborator Michael Kanin used to arrive early in the morning and get most of his work done before noon. I preferred to arrive in the late morning and stay late in the evening."

---

* Interviewed a year before his death in March 1992.

Harry Warner's effect on the movies Warner Bros. made was indirect. *Casablanca* would be the beneficiary of Harry's stubborn anti-Nazi stance and his insistence that the studio combine good movies with good citizenship. But Harry would have no hand in casting actors or approving sets. Warners, the most adversarial of the studios, was built in Jack Warner's image. Most of the moguls yearned for respectability. Almost alone among them, Jack Warner exulted in being an outsider. It is no accident that four of the studio's major stars—Al Jolson, Edward G. Robinson, Paul Muni, and John Garfield—were Jewish. During the thirties, the other studios wove fantasies around Clark Gable, Tyrone Power, Cary Grant, and Robert Taylor and eulogized the small town and the code of the West with Jimmy Stewart, Mickey Rooney, Henry Fonda, and Gary Cooper. For most of that decade, the top star at Warner Bros. was a scrappy, half-pint Irishman from New York's Lower East Side, James Cagney; and the archetypal hero of a Warner movie was a gangster. In the forties, the typical Warner Bros. hero was Sam Spade or Rick Blaine, played by Humphrey Bogart, and as wary and suspicious of emotional entanglements as the man who ran the studio.

It has been said that Warner Bros. couldn't get important, elegant stars because the studio was too cheap to pay for them. It is equally possible that Jack Warner deliberately bought actors who mirrored his own mistrust. He certainly chose actors who mirrored him physically—short, compact, and combative. Then he put them in movies where everyone was corrupt and the lower classes never got a fair shake, from *I Was a Fugitive from a Chain Gang,* in which an innocent man would be hunted for the rest of his life, to *They Won't Forget,* in which an innocent man was hanged. Warner Bros. was an underdog, and so were the shopgirls, mine workers, boxers, and condemned men who inhabited its movies.

By 1942, when Hal Wallis looked over the Warner contract list to see who could play the lead in *Casablanca,* the antisocial edges of Warner Bros. movies were beginning to be smoothed. As Ethan Mordden points out in his book, *The Hollywood Studios,* the setting and intrigue of *Casablanca* would have been at home at M-G-M in a Clark Gable picture, although M-G-M would never have let Gable give up the girl. However, there was no mistaking the fact that *Casablanca,* with its snappy dialogue, eccentric characters, witty cynicism, wary anti-hero and liberal political message was definitely a

Warner movie. *Casablanca* is a less raw and angry melodrama than the studio might have made a few years earlier, but it has the same distrust of authority and suspicion of human nature. America's entry into the war was already softening movies by requiring them to throb with patriotism, but the milieu of *Casablanca* is still corrupt, and the little people still don't get a fair shake.

Crude, cruel, and cowardly—he was the only mogul to run to the House Un-American Activities Committee and voluntarily offer up his employees—Jack Warner was a dapper man, impeccably well groomed. (His grandson, Gregory Orr, remembers wondering how a grown-up could be so perfectly shaved.) Although Warner smiled a lot and delighted in telling bad jokes, he was a shrewd administrator. The craftsmen he hired were the equal of any in Hollywood, and they banded together as a family just as the more coddled employees at M-G-M did.*

Warner could also be kind, particularly to people who were too weak to take advantage of him. He kept actors from the studio's early days on the payroll for decades, paying ex-stars $50 a week and insisting that his directors use them as often as possible. There were half a dozen of those actors in *Casablanca*. Creighton Hale, who had starred with Thelma Todd in *Seven Footprints to Satan* in 1929, and Monte Blue, the studio's biggest star during the late 1920s, played tiny roles in the black-market scenes. Only a few snippets of their dialogue remain.

Since the temptation to rewrite history is almost irresistible, autobiographies are notoriously inaccurate. *My First Hundred Years in Hollywood* by Jack Warner is no exception. But truth can often be found between the lines. "I have never owned a dog or a cat or any other kind of household pet," Warner wrote. Of the hundreds of people mentioned in the book, he spoke lovingly of only two—his brother Sam and his masseur Abdul. Over and over Warner de-

---

*Whole families worked twenty or thirty years at the same studio. Owen Marks, the film editor on *Casablanca,* had four brothers who worked in the same department at Warner Bros. From prop men to plumbers, studio employees clustered in houses outside the studio walls, with M-G-M set decorators building in Culver City and Warner electricians buying in Burbank. Stephen Karnot came back to Warner Bros. later in the war and stayed until he was laid off because of a "reduction in force" on June 23, 1967. By that time Harry Warner was dead and Jack Warner had sold the studio and the studio system was dead too, a victim of television and the government antitrust suits that forced the studios to sell their theaters and, inadvertently, gave new power and independence to top stars and producers.

scribed Sam, who died in 1927 at the age of thirty-nine, as gentle. Shy, gentle, and humble, Sam served as a buffer between his tough oldest brother and his rebellious younger brother, who played Peck's Bad Boy to the hilt. It was Sam who pushed Warner Bros. into talking films while the bigger studios lagged behind; he died, of either a cerebral hemorrhage or a galloping infection, the day before *The Jazz Singer,* the movie that would make Warners' fortune, was premiered.

Jack Warner's affection for Abdul Maljan—an ex-prizefighter who was always called Abdul the Turk, although he was really Armenian—was sadder and more complex. "I think a psychiatrist could give a better answer," says Jack Warner, Jr., who was cut out of his father's life as sharply as if his father had used a knife. "But I think he gave my father great comfort. At his core, my father always had the feeling: 'Everybody's trying to take advantage of me.' At the end of a hard day of working with people who got on his nerves, Abdul would be there with a hot shower and the sponges and the towels, and this was going home to momma."

Nearly everyone made Warner nervous. "He was scared of actors," says Geraldine Fitzgerald, who was under contract to Warners for seven years. "And of writers too." Even nineteen-year-old Lauren Bacall sensed the fear beneath his braggadocio. "He was always ill at ease, always uncomfortable," Bacall says. "He felt people were judging him all the time." And so, every afternoon, Warner fled to the steam room next to his private dining room. "Abdul was like an old faithful dog," says Bill Schaefer, who was Jack Warner's secretary for more than forty years. "If Warner told him to do something, he'd do it. If it meant bodily harm to him, he'd do it. And when he died, he left his whole estate—it consisted of a house and maybe $35,000 in stocks—to Jack Warner."

Jack Warner, Jr., remembers seeing his father standing alone at Abdul's grave. "He was terribly upset, and he looked very forlorn. It was nice to know he had that soft a spot for someone. The rest of his relationships—well, you know that saying—'Not to know him was to love him.'" Warner's son had made the mistake of not approving of his father's second wife. Even when Warner was dying there was no reconciliation. "That's a script that I would love to see rewritten," says seventy-five-year-old Jack Warner, Jr., in the spring of 1991. "But it's been shot, alas."

Warner, Jr., struggles to be both courteous and reticent. He wrote a biography of his father, but, he says, "It was not—a word that has fallen out of favor—'seemly.' So I clothed it in the strange garments of fiction." He was never tough enough to win his father's approval, yet he can appreciate his father's toughness. "Power, in a way, is a corrosive acid," he says. "But it was a tough, rough, dirty racket. And if you weren't rough and tough and sometimes dirty, you'd be down in the cellar. There's hundreds and hundreds of movie companies you've never heard of. And they were all started up by people with great intentions. The Warner brothers started on a place called Poverty Row. They rose to where they went by guts, application, knowledge. It's too easy to sit here years later and to second-guess it all."

A few months before Pearl Harbor, the head of the Army Air Corps, General Hap Arnold, asked if Warner Bros. would make short subjects to acquaint the public with the various branches of the armed forces. The relationship between the general and the mogul led to the fifty-year-old Jack Warner's being offered a commission as a lieutenant colonel in the Army Air Force in April 1942. The head of 20th Century–Fox, Darryl Zanuck, who used to work for Warner, was already a colonel in the Signal Corps, and Warner accepted with relish.

He would resign that commission a few months later, in part because he could not bear to leave his studio in the hands of another man. All the moguls identified with their studios and some put their names on their movies, but Jack Warner was the only one to make his name part of the company logo. "Jack L. Warner Executive Producer" jutted out from the Warner Bros. shield. Except for Edward Muhl, the head of production at Universal a decade later, the others were willing to let their logos speak for them. Paramount's mountain implied unsurpassable heights and M-G-M's lion, the king of the studio jungle. Columbia's lady with a torch mimicked both classical art and the Statue of Liberty. RKO's tower crackled with radio waves and electricity. Universal's globe encircled space, while 20th Century–Fox's name and futuristic design conquered time. They looked outward. The Warner Bros. shield said something different. It was offense and defense, with intimations of G-men and barricades.

Jack Warner rarely came to the studio before noon, and he spent most of the afternoon looking at the rushes of the movies in produc-

tion to make sure that nothing was out of control. "I can't understand why a fifty-four-second take must be started seven times," he
wrote to director Mike Curtiz during the filming of *Casablanca*.
"You must cut down on the amount of negative and positive film."
Keeping control of his directors also meant that Warner gave instructions to cut the outside telephone lines to Raoul Walsh's set
during the horse-racing season to keep the director from wasting
time by telephoning his bookmaker.

Jack Warner's approval was always necessary to buy properties,
assign writers, and cast actors. On February 4, 1942, in a typical
exchange, Hal Wallis's secretary let Warner know that the Epstein
twins, who were vacationing in New York, were anxious to write the
script of *Casablanca*. Did Warner approve or did he have something
else in mind for them?

Warner was most actively involved with his movies at the very
end, in the editing room, when the finished movie was in the form
of a first cut. "We'd stay until 1:30 A.M. at least twice a week," says
Rudi Fehr, who became Warner's personal editor. "One week it was
all five nights and my wife locked me out because she thought I was
cheating on her." Even Jack Warner's enemies and the people who
dismissed him as a clown gave him credit when it was time to look
at a movie whole. "He smelled a good picture," says Owen Crump,
who left Warner Bros. to head an Army Air Force film unit in 1942.
"He was a little afraid of people who had superior talent, for example writers who were famous and literate. They made him uneasy.
But he had a sense when a movie had class." He also had a gambler's
daring. "If you were able to sell him an idea, convince him it would
make a great picture," Warner would always take a chance, said
Henry Blanke, the leading associate producer at Warner Bros. during the thirties.

In the thick file of memos sent back and forth on *Casablanca*, Warner
made a creative decision only once. He suggested that George Raft
star in the movie. Hal Wallis's reply was barely polite. After saying
that *Casablanca* was being written for Humphrey Bogart, Wallis
added that Raft "hasn't done a picture here since I was a little boy,
and I don't think he should be able to put his fingers on just what
he wants to do when he wants to do it."

The other half-dozen memos sent by Warner to Wallis and
Curtiz dealt with time and money. Why were the songwriters taking

so long? When could the Epsteins be put on another script? He was counting on Wallis to bring the movie in for a reasonable price and on Curtiz to be the old Curtiz and finish the film in a maximum of seven weeks. There are similar memos on every Warner Bros. movie. Jack Warner stood at the studio drawbridge, lowering it to put this actor under contract, raising it when he let the option on that actress lapse after six months. And he expected to be besieged by employees who would waste the studio's time and money.

It was Warner's studio, and he never let his underlings forget it, but Hal Wallis was the creative force behind *Casablanca*. The French *auteur* theory, the idea that the director is the author of his film, collapses against the reality of the studio system. It is impossible to read through the hundreds of memos Wallis sent and received without understanding how thoroughly he shaped the movie, from the quality of the lighting to the exact details of the costumes to his insistence on a live parrot outside the Blue Parrot Café.

Because of Jack Warner's pervasive distrust and fear of being taken advantage of, there is a paper trail to *Casablanca* fifty years later. VERBAL MESSAGES CAUSE MISUNDERSTANDING AND DELAYS was printed on the bottom of every sheet of studio stationery in 1942. PLEASE PUT THEM IN WRITING. "Today the whole industry lives on phones," says Daniel Melnick, an independent producer who headed production at M-G-M from 1972 to 1976 and at Columbia from 1977 to 1979. "I suspect the most successful people are those who have mastered phone technique." Melnick and Laurence Mark, a producer who was a vice president of production at both Paramount and 20th Century–Fox during the 1980s, work in an era when the power once held by the studios is split among studios, stars, directors, and talent agents; and they have read through the *Casablanca* production files with a certain bemusement mixed with envy. Mark fingers a particularly blunt memo criticizing an actress. "A certain amount of murkiness serves you well today," he says. "Being too well articulated sometimes gets you into trouble."

Mark describes another memo as "kind of wonderful." On July 9, 1942, Wallis wrote to his director: "I saw the dailies last night and there is one thing I would like you to shoot . . . where Ilsa comes into the Café and asks Rick if he has taken care of everything, and Rick says, 'Everything.' At that point, if you remember, I wanted Rick to look at Ilsa a moment and then kiss her so that the audience will realize later that this was his goodbye." Says Mark, "That's not a commercial note. It's purely about adding another layer to a scene which the audience won't realize until afterwards, if then." (In the chaos of mid-July, and because of Bogart's objections, the scene was rewritten and Rick's kiss never made it into the movie.)

In his usual careful fashion, Wallis had Irene Lee send a copy of *Everybody Comes to Rick's* to several of the studio's producers on December 22, 1941. Before he bought the play, he wanted to know whether his lieutenants thought it would make a commercial movie. At Warner Bros. everything was done quickly, and they sent Wallis their reactions the next day. Robert Lord found the play "a very obvious imitation of *Grand Hotel*" with conventional and stereo-typed characters. Jerry Wald, who would become the major produc-er at Warner Bros. after Wallis left, was shrewder: "This story should make a good vehicle for either Raft or Bogart. I feel it can be easily tailored into a piece along the lines of ALGIERS, with plenty of excitement and suspense in it." (*Algiers,* a 1938 exotic melodrama starring Charles Boyer and Hedy Lamarr, was obviously in Wallis's mind when, three days after he purchased *Everybody Comes to Rick's,* he changed the title to *Casablanca.* It was also in his mind when he tried unsuccessfully to borrow Hedy Lamarr from M-G-M in Febru-ary.)

Wallis has always been underrated. The *Fortune* article puzzled over the studio's success despite its lack of "that other prime neces-sity, a producing 'genius.' " The 1937 article dismisses Wallis as Jack Warner's "methodical assistant," in contrast to the genius who preceded him at the studio, Darryl Zanuck. Why, the author won-ders, somewhat tongue in cheek, have Warner pictures been getting better, not worse, since Zanuck left?

Wallis had a remarkable batting average with the six movies he made in 1942 under his new contract: *Desperate Journey, Now, Voyager, Casablanca, Watch on the Rhine, Air Force,* and *Princess O'Rourke.* All were box-office successes. Two—*Watch on the Rhine* and *Casablanca*—were nominated for best picture by the Academy. The six movies earned a total of twenty Oscar nominations, and *Watch on the Rhine* won major critics' awards. *Now, Voyager* still makes its adherents weep fifty years later.

After Warner Bros. canceled his contract in 1944, Wallis spent the next twenty-five years at Paramount. He had three Oscar nomi-nees for best picture in *The Rose Tattoo* (1955), *Becket* (1964), and, at Universal, *Anne of the Thousand Days* (1969). He made stars of

Kirk Douglas, Burt Lancaster, and Shirley MacLaine, but he is best remembered for creating gold mines rather than art in a series of movies with Dean Martin and Jerry Lewis and several films starring Elvis Presley.

"There's no individual producer who had a greater run of important pictures than Hal Wallis," says Tom Pryor, who covered Hollywood for *The New York Times* before spending a quarter of a century as the editor of *Daily Variety*. "There was a consistency in the product Warners was turning out during the thirties when Wallis was running the show. To me, Warner Bros. then, more than M-G-M, signifies the peak. After Wallis left, Warner pictures were not what they had been. He was a cool man, a somewhat distant person, but he was the most brilliant producer this town has known. David O. Selznick was like a skyrocket, but Selznick's pride forced him to saddle himself with a big distribution apparatus and it broke him. Wallis was smart enough not to do that."

Wallis was not bold enough to gamble his future on one movie or one throw of the dice the way Selznick and Jack Warner would. He may also have been too stingy. His biographer, Charles Higham, was always amused that Wallis—who owned an exquisite collection of French Impressionist paintings—would take him to Scandia, an expensive Los Angeles restaurant, only when director Mervyn LeRoy came along and paid for lunch. When LeRoy couldn't come, says Higham, Wallis bought him a hamburger. And he grumbled excessively over the bill.

"Hal was exceedingly disciplined, under tight self-control," says Higham, who cowrote Wallis's 1980 autobiography, *Starmaker*. "Talking to him was like talking to a retired general. You had to handle him by talking only about his working achievements. Trying to write General MacArthur's autobiography would have been the same experience."

The messenger boys at Warner Bros. found Wallis the coldest and most unfriendly of the studio's executives and retaliated by inventing stories that he was having affairs with Irene Lee and with actress Lola Lane. "There were two Hal Wallises," says Julius Epstein. "Hal Wallis at the office was efficient, impersonal, cold. If you were walking across the lot and you met him, he would always say, 'When are you going to finish that script? Are you making a life career out of that script?' Then we took several trips to New York with him and he was delightful, genial, warm. We felt we'd gotten to know the real Hal Wallis. We came back to the studio and walked up to him and he said, 'When the hell are you going to finish that script?' I told him he should have been on the War Production Board. He was so efficient. The war would have been over much sooner."

Warner star Dennis Morgan never met the genial Hal Wallis. "He was a very cool sort of man, business all the time," Morgan says. "He wasn't fun to be around. Warner could be fun to be with socially. But, if you were promoting a picture and you had to be at the head table with Jack Warner, it was always a tremendous task to sit there when he got up to speak because he would ad-lib these bad jokes."

During the Korean War, when Owen Crump came up with the idea of shooting a 3-D movie about an Army patrol, he went to see Jack Warner first. Because of his World War II associations, Crump had secured the Pentagon's approval to shoot *Cease Fire* in the war zone. Warner told him to put in two or three nurses for love interest. Says Crump, "Having pretty babes running around would be the usual phony picture and spoil the whole documentary feel of the idea. So I went to see Hal at Paramount. He said, 'You really got permission to do this?' I showed him the piece of paper. We were walking to his office. He said, 'Wait here.' " Wallis made a detour to the office of Paramount studio head Y. Frank Freeman. "He came out five minutes later and said, 'Okay, we got a deal,' " says Crump. "So he agreed to the movie before we even reached his office. Hal didn't waste time or conversation."

Irene Lee worked for Wallis on and off for twenty-five years. As a young actress in the early 1930s, she had come to Hollywood from Pittsburgh to test for a part in the Fox movie *Cavalcade*. She didn't get the part, but she did get a lot of work reading scripts. Director Mervyn LeRoy brought her to Warner Bros. for a screen test, then decided that she was a mediocre actress but had too good a story mind to waste. LeRoy took her to Wallis, who gave her a job as an assistant story editor. She left after a year to go back to New York.

"I was making about $250 a week as Leland Hayward's East Coast story person, and then another producer, Pan Berman, offered me $350," Lee says. "And the first thing Leland did was to call Pandro Berman and tell him he could have gotten me for less money. So Berman told me, 'You can still have the job but I won't pay you that much.' Can you imagine? I mean, to those men the money was absolutely nothing. I called Hal Wallis, who had been very nice to me, to ask what I should do and he said, 'You'll come here as story editor.' "*

Hollywood was a man's world in 1942. But Wallis respected talent, even if the talent belonged to a woman. "I think Hal was a superb executive," says Lee. "And he was very accessible. Writers could get to him, I could get to him, the directors could get to him. He'd be the first person in in the morning and the last one to leave. I found him very decent, very untemperamental. After he became an independent producer, he was altogether different, more temperamental. There was much more ego involved. But he was easy to work for at Warner Bros."

That Warner Bros. died a long time ago. By the time that Warner and Wallis put the resources of the studio into making *Casablanca*, the studio system was well into middle age. What is hard to remember now is how young Hal Wallis was when he ran Warner Bros., how young they all were when they were building the studio system. Wallis's predecessor, Darryl Zanuck, was twenty-six when he became head of production. Wallis was thirty-three when he replaced Zanuck. The legendary Irving Thalberg was only thirty-seven when he died. The men and the system would grow old together. But a few of the movies, *Casablanca* among them, would stay forever young.

---

*When Irene Lee tells this story, as she sits in her huge New York office and fingers the double strand of pearls around her neck, her voice holds no anger, only amusement. Perhaps it's the secret joke of marrying a rug salesman and ending up as the wife of a man worth over $250 million. When her husband Aaron Diamond died in 1984, he left $200 million for his widow to give away. "Finding good projects is not unlike finding good stories," says Lee, who hands out at least $20 million a year from the Aaron Diamond Foundation. "Our priorities are minority education, medical research, and the arts. We are the biggest contributors to AIDS research of any private foundation in the country."

3

Writing Casablanca:
A Survival of the Fittest Script

In Rick's Café, Sam plays the piano. A quick shake of Rick's head and a man is barred from the gambling room. "Your money is good at the bar," Rick says to him. "You're lucky the bar's still open to you."

"Watching you just now, one would think that you had been doing this all your life," says Ugarte, a small-time crook. "What makes you think I haven't?" Rick asks harshly. Ugarte quickly agrees that he has no business thinking. He tells Rick that tonight he will sell two priceless Letters of Transit, and he will leave Casablanca forever. Because Rick despises him, Rick is the only man in Casablanca he trusts to keep the Letters—exit visas that cannot be questioned or rescinded. "I don't want them here overnight," Rick says. And he hides the Letters of Transit in Sam's piano.

The scene, the characters, and the dialogue are from *Casablanca.* They are also, intact, from *Everybody Comes to Rick's.*

Murray Burnett in Europe in 1938. His experiences with the Nazis led to his writing the play on which Casablanca *was based.*

The central myth about the writing of *Casablanca* is that all that remained of the original play was the setting and the character of Rick. But *Casablanca* also contains much of the plot of *Everybody Comes to Rick's,* in which an embittered American who owns a café in Morocco redeems himself after a reunion with the woman who has broken his heart, by arranging for her and the anti-Nazi newspaper editor who accompanies her to escape to Lisbon. Murray Burnett, who created Rick Blaine in the summer of 1940, has spent thousands of dollars and the last eighteen years trying to destroy the myth. "But it's not easy to disprove," he says. "You know the story about the man who was tried for stealing a chicken and acquitted. For the rest of his life people say, 'That's the guy who stole the chicken.' "

In 1940, Burnett was a twenty-nine-year-old English teacher at a vocational high school. Although he was married, he was still the dutiful son of an overprotective mother. Later, Theodor Reik, who psychoanalyzed Burnett, would tell him that his emotional survival was due to the scholarship from Cornell University that had enabled and forced him to leave home at eighteen. But in 1940 Burnett rebelled only in his fantasies. He wrote *Everybody Comes to Rick's* after he returned from a short but frightening trip to German-occupied Vienna. Rick—tough, morose, the man who didn't need anybody—was the man Burnett wanted to be.

If, over the decades, nobody remembered *Everybody Comes to Rick's* by Murray Burnett and Joan Alison, at least nobody publicly challenged his involvement in *Casablanca,* the thing that Murray Burnett was most proud of. Until 1973.

"The play provided an exotic locale and a character named Rick who ran a café, but little in the way of a story adaptable to the screen," screenwriter Howard Koch wrote in *New York* magazine that April.

Burnett found the article intolerable. "Koch took credit for everything," Burnett says. "He says he took this magic pencil, Eagle Number One, and he wrote it line by line. But every character in the film is in my play. Every one. Without exception."

Burnett sued Koch and *New York* for $6.5 million apiece. He lost. The court said that Koch's article had not libeled Burnett or his play. Burnett sued the Overlook Press, which published Koch's essay as a preface to the *Casablanca* screenplay. He lost. Then he sued Warner Bros. to get back the rights to his characters. He lost.

At eighty-one, Murray Burnett remains almost puppyish in his enthusiasms and his crusades. As late as the spring of 1991, he was still attacking, and Koch, then eighty-nine, had capitulated. "Having read the play more recently, I believe that the complaint was, at least to some extent, justified," Koch wrote in a letter to the *Los Angeles Times.* "After fifty years, memories can be faulty."

Actually, Koch has been apologetic for years. He didn't intentionally rob Murray Burnett, he says. But he never read the play. He was handed a script by Julius and Philip Epstein and he assumed . . . Koch is tall and thin, and his thinness makes him seem even taller. He stops abruptly and starts again. "All I saw was the work of the Epsteins that was handed to me."

It is not quite that simple. Writers of fiction embellish reality almost without knowing it. Thirty years after *Casablanca,* in the essay from which the magazine article was adapted, Koch described how he created the characters and their motivations: "I went through the

Howard Koch in 1939, recently arrived in Hollywood.

rich assembly of actors waiting to take their parts in the story and picked Peter Lorre (Ugarte) as the one to initiate the action." A nice man, people say of Koch. A decent man. There is no reason to doubt that Koch believed in the alternative reality that he was inventing.

Much of the raw material of *Casablanca* can be found in the three acts of *Everybody Comes to Rick's*. In a city where everything is bought and sold, a mysterious café owner bets a womanizing French policeman that a heroic anti-Fascist will escape. The embittered hero has a black piano-player friend who is asked to play "As Time Goes By" by a woman from the hero's past who has come to Casablanca with the heroic Resistance fighter. In the end the hero tricks the policeman and sends the woman away with the other man. The minor characters include a young couple from Bulgaria who are offered exit visas if the girl will sleep with the policeman, a black marketeer who owns a competing café and wants to buy Rick's, a Gestapo officer who must keep the Resistance fighter from leaving Casablanca, and an ex-mistress whom the hero treats cruelly.

The movie is also studded with details from the play. Rick will not drink with his customers. The leader of the Resistance, Victor Laszlo, drowns out the Germans by leading Rick's customers in the French national anthem, "The Marseillaise." And dozens of lines make the transition almost unchanged:

"For a price, Ugarte, for a price." "Call off your watchdogs." "There are a lot of exit visas sold in this café. We know that you have never sold them. That is one of the reasons we permit you to remain open." "And if he did not leave her in Marseilles, nor Oran, he will not leave her in Casablanca." "I see. Gestapo spank." "What a fool I am! Talking to a beautiful woman about another man." "Let's see, the last time we met . . . Was at La Belle Aurore . . . How nice. You remembered." "Boss, we'll take the car and drive all night. We'll get drunk. We'll go fishin' and stay away until she's gone." "We come from Bulgaria. Things are very bad there, M'sieur. A devil has the people by the throat. So Jan and I we did not want our children to grow up in such a country." "M'sieur, you are a man. If someone loved you very much, so that your happiness was the only thing in the world that she wanted and she did a bad thing to make certain of it, could you forgive her?" "No one ever loved me that much."

Yet, despite the similarities between play and movie, *Everybody Comes to Rick's* is only the bone out of which coral was made. The seven Warner Bros. writers who were assigned to *Casablanca*

changed motivations, structure, plot, and the attributes and person-
alities of three of the four central characters.

The process of finding a writer began on December 30, 1941, two
days after the play was purchased with Hal Wallis's approval by
story editor Irene Lee. No one could have imagined that the central—although serial—collaboration of two liberal, one radical, and
one conservative screenwriter would produce a script with more
memorable lines than any other Hollywood film.

As he had done with the producers and as he would do with the
studio's contract directors, Wallis circulated the play to a number of
writers. Robert Buckner sent it back in a hurry. "I don't believe the
story or the characters," Buckner wrote. "Its main situations and the
basic relations of the principals are completely censorable and messy,
its big moment is sheer hokum melodrama of the E. Phillips Oppen-
heim* variety; and this guy Rick is two-parts Hemingway, one-part
Scott Fitzgerald, and a dash of café Christ."

All the writers would struggle with the illicit sexual relationship
between Rick and the woman he had known in Paris. Fornication
was forbidden by the Production Code which the studios had set up
in an attempt to stave off government censorship. In this case the
writers hinted and implied, and the movie had less trouble with the
Code than anyone expected, although the overseers of morality were
constantly wagging their fingers. "The present material seems to
contain a suggestion of a sex affair which would be unacceptable if
it came through in the finished picture," the Code director Joseph
Breen wrote Jack Warner three weeks after the movie started production, in response to a newly written scene between Rick and Ilsa
in Rick's apartment above the café.

On January 9, 1942, Wallis chose his brother-in-law Wally Kline
and Kline's writing partner, Aeneas MacKenzie. MacKenzie had
told Wallis that he saw "the possibility of an excellent theme—the
idea that when people lose faith in their ideals, they are beaten
before they begin to fight. That was what happened to France and
to Rick Blaine." MacKenzie and Kline would work on the script for
seven weeks at a cost to *Casablanca* of $4,133, but their material
would not be used.

---

* A British author (1866–1946) who wrote over 150 novels, short stories, and plays about
international espionage and intrigue.

MacKenzie had been brought to the studio as a reader in 1935 by Dalton Trumbo, who lived in the same rooming house. MacKenzie's big break came when John Huston liked the synopsis he wrote for *Juarez* and asked him to help write the movie. After that, MacKenzie shared credit on several historical movies, including *The Private Lives of Elizabeth and Essex.* He was a $300-a-week writer, and his contract was dropped soon after he was taken off *Casablanca.* Kline stayed on, getting a new assignment every month but rarely ending up with a screen credit.

Weeks before Kline and MacKenzie finished their script, Wallis discussed *Casablanca* with Julius and Philip Epstein. If they were called by name, people always said "Julie and Phil," not because Julie was the older—they were born at home on New York's Lower East Side, and no one ever remembered which of the three-pound twins came first—but because Julie came to Warner Bros. three years before Phil. But they were rarely called by name. At the studio the identical twins were almost always referred to as The Boys or The Brothers. In 1942, they were thirty-two years old and making $1,250 a week apiece.

Nine years earlier, Julius Epstein had come to Hollywood as a ghostwriter. "I'm Julian Blumberg in *What Makes Sammy Run?*," he says with a mixture of pride and ruefulness. Jerry Wald, who has always been thought to be the primary model for the opportunistic Sammy Glick in Budd Schulberg's novel, had talked his way into a writing job at Warner Bros. Almost immediately he sent for Julius Epstein. When Wald, like Sammy Glick, was a radio columnist for a New York newspaper, Julie had been one of the press agents who wrote his column for him.

"Jerry and his partner, an old fraternity brother of mine, picked me up at the train station at ten-thirty on a Friday night," says Epstein. "By midnight I was writing, because they had to hand some pages in on Monday morning. I wrote all day Saturday. On Sunday they took me to the Paramount theater. A Bing Crosby picture was playing. As I watched the picture, they said, 'That's a fade-out, that's a dissolve, that's a cut.' I had a full-year college course in one afternoon."

In *What Makes Sammy Run?* Schulberg describes the meeting of Sammy Glick and Julian Blumberg as follows: "One day a frightened young man with an unassuming, intelligent, unhandsome face behind glasses came in with a manuscript under his arm and inquired

Julius and Philip Epstein at Penn State. As captain of the boxing team, Julius sits at center; Philip is the last player standing on the right.

for Mr. Glick in a voice quavering with inferiority." Glick puts his name on the manuscript and sells it to Hollywood. When Wald sold Epstein's first original screenplay, *Living on Velvet,* to Warner Bros. it became a screenplay by Jerry Wald and Julius Epstein. But Epstein, who had an intelligent, unhandsome face, also had several things Blumberg lacked, including a powerful left jab.

In August 1934, after the sale of *Living on Velvet,* Epstein was hired for $100 a week on a week-to-week basis. Six weeks later, Warner Bros. gave him a contract and doubled his salary. He would stay at the studio for seventeen years. After a year of coauthoring scripts with Wald, Epstein got a chance to show Warner Bros. what he could do on his own. Undaunted, Wald brought Philip Epstein to Hollywood as his new ghostwriter.

By 1938, Phil was at Warner Bros. too, and the twins were writing together as a team. They wrote the kind of dialogue that is usually referred to as sparkling, and, in addition to a full complement of screen credits *(Four Wives, The Bride Came C.O.D., Strawberry Blonde),* they were constantly being asked to add sparkle to other writers' scripts. James Cagney agreed to star in *Yankee Doodle Dandy* only if the Epsteins were assigned to liven up Robert Buckner's screenplay. "The Epstein boys are adding a little zip to the script," was a typical comment, in this case by director Raoul Walsh on his movie *Desperate Journey*.

Witty and clever, the twins impressed young screenwriter Alvah Bessie by winning every wisecracking competition during lunch at the Warner Bros. writers' table. They were also sophisticated practical jokers. They stole a piece of Jack Warner's stationery and wrote a welcoming letter to Robert Hutton, a young contract actor with whom they were friendly. It ended, "Our publicity department has decided that your name is not a good name for the box office. From now on, you will be known as Robert Rabinowitz." Forced by Jack Warner to spend eight hours a day at the studio, most of the contract writers spent part of their time playing gin rummy or working on novels and plays. After Robert Rossen and Leonardo Bercovici said they were writing a play rather than attacking the script to which they had been assigned, the Epsteins had their secretary pretend to be Wallis's secretary. She told Rossen and Bercovici to be in Wallis's office in fifteen minutes with all the scenes they had written.

The Boys always stopped the jokes in time, before Hutton timidly asked to see Warner, before Rossen and Bercovici stampeded in panic. They were as alike as two peas in a pod, balding leprechuans who played a passionate game of tennis on the studio court on Saturday afternoons—the only time Warner allowed writers to play. In tennis, as in everything else, they were a team. In 1929, the year Penn State won the intercollegiate boxing tournament, Julie Epstein was intercollegiate bantamweight champion. Phil, always a few pounds heavier, was Penn State's intramural lightweight champion. They were separated only three times, briefly, until February 1952, when they were separated permanently.

Julie Epstein has told some of the stories so often over the years that he is almost ashamed to repeat them. "One day as we were coming in at one-thirty in time for lunch, we ran right into Warner, who was in a bad mood, and he said, 'Railroad presidents get in at nine o'clock, bank presidents get in at nine o'clock, read your contract, you're coming in at nine o'clock.' We were halfway finished with a script and we sent it to his office with a note: 'Dear J.L., have the bank president finish the script.' A little while later, Warner read a scene we had written and said, 'This is the worst scene I ever read in my life.' And my brother said, 'How is that possible? It was written at nine o'clock.' "

After the war, when things got ugly and the studio asked them to fill out a two-page questionaire attesting to their loyalty to America, the twins only answered the first two questions. (1) "Have you ever belonged to a subversive organization?" "Yes." (2) "Name the organization." "Warner Bros." It was that combination of wit, bravado, and cynicism that would mark their contribution to *Casablanca*.

In contrast to Howard Koch's reverence for *Casablanca*, Julie Epstein describes the script as "slick shit." At eighty-one, he sits in the house he bought, along with two-and-a-half acres of mountaintop, in 1949, and rebuilt after he was burned out in the Bel-Air fire of 1961. A little man with big ears and a fringe of gray hair, he no longer jogs six miles a day—"Now I thank people from the bottom of my pacemaker"—but he has never stopped writing.

"Every script is concocted," Epstein says. "But *Casablanca* was really concocted. We sat down and tried to manipulate an audience." He insists that he is much prouder of the script that became his forty-third movie and won him an Academy Award nomination in 1983, *Reuben, Reuben.*

Some of Epstein's disdain for *Casablanca* is a pose. He has always masked his feelings with wit and vinegar. "Julie does care," says his nephew, novelist Leslie Epstein. "I think he went to bed for a week when Koch's book came out with that introduction."

Koch wrote that after he and the Epsteins had worked together for about ten days the twins asked to be transferred to another movie. "We never sat in the same room with him," Julie says, the words jostling against each other in an urgency to get out. "We never had one conference with him. And we never asked to be taken off the picture. But Howard is a nice man, and I think he really believed what he wrote." (In 1985, Koch sent Julie a letter apologizing for his mistaken memories and stating that a new edition of his book would make it clear that the Epsteins had done the basic work on the script.)

When Wallis discussed *Casablanca* with the Epsteins at the beginning of February, the twins were excited. "We thought the play would make a wonderful movie," says Julie. "It had a lot of juice to it. And we loved Bogart's character." But there was one complication. The Boys had agreed—had volunteered—to go to

Philip and Julius Epstein during their time with Warner Bros.

Washington to help write a series of patriotic training documentaries for Frank Capra—now Major Frank Capra—for whom they had recently adapted the Broadway hit *Arsenic and Old Lace.* (Specialists at turning plays into movies, they had also recently written screen versions of *The Male Animal* and *The Man Who Came to Dinner.*) Before they left Los Angeles on February 25, the twins told Wallis that they would start writing *Casablanca* while they were away. In order to keep from paying his employees for wasted days, Jack Warner always made sure that the actors, writers, directors, and cameramen on forty-week-a-year contracts were put on layoff as soon as they finished assignments. When he sent a note that the Epsteins were to be taken off salary, Warner suggested that the time they were in Washington be added to the end of their contracts. That way they would be bound to the studio for an extra month or two.

The Epsteins returned on March 17, 1942. They had already sent Wallis the first batch of script, and, by the time they returned, they had written about forty pages. According to Julie Epstein, Koch had written a treatment of the first section of the movie during their absence and they were shown his material on their return. There is very little of which one can be certain fifty years later. However, Koch's assignment records at Warner Bros. make it unlikely that he worked on *Casablanca* while the Epsteins were away. Koch was assigned to *The Adventures of Mark Twain* from December 1, 1941, to March 4, 1942, and the next day started four weeks of work on *Catch a Falling Star.* For most of *Casablanca,* Koch was writing behind the Epsteins and revising their work. It may be that the Epsteins were shown the MacKenzie-Kline treatment, which seems to have been lost or destroyed.

Once they were back in California, the Epsteins rewrote the material they had sent Wallis from Washington and added to it. Less than two weeks after their return, they turned in what would become the first act of the movie. On March 30, Wallis sent a note to Michael Curtiz, the man he had picked to direct *Casablanca:*

> Attached is my copy of the "CASABLANCA" script with notes. I have edited this carefully and have eliminated about 10 pages, and made other changes. I wish you would go over this in detail with the Epsteins this morning so that, when we meet this afternoon, the three of you can tell me with which of my notes you agree. . . . At the same time, you can discuss with them the next portion of the story so that when we get together this afternoon after lunch, we can proceed.

Examining this note, the present-day producer Daniel Melnick says, "It is assuming the total accessibility of everyone. Today, to deliver the note would take three-and-a-half hours. At the earliest, they would read it overnight. It would take a minimum of four days to schedule the meeting. It's the difference between an industry that regarded movies as product and today when even the toughest studio executives realize the films may not always be art, but the guys who make them think of themselves as artists." As to taking the Epsteins off salary during their trip to Washington, Melnick quips, "Today, if you took a writer off salary because he wasn't at his typewriter, there would be no scripts ever accepted."

The sixty-six pages of script, labeled PART I TEMP., were mimeographed on April 2. The Epsteins had written the first third of the movie, the section preceding the flashback to Rick and Ilsa's Paris romance. Ilsa and her Resistance-hero husband had come to Casablanca and, at the end of the Epsteins' script, Rick was sprawled drunkenly in his empty café, waiting for her to return.

"That first part was very close to the play," Epstein says. "It was with the second half that we had trouble."

Those sixty-six pages mirror the final movie. The Epsteins even begin with a spinning globe, an animated map, and a description of the refugee trail that leads to Casablanca. *Everybody Comes to Rick's* took place inside Rick's Café, and Rick was the first character to be introduced. The Epsteins start by creating the feel of Casablanca: A man whose papers have expired is shot by the police; a pickpocket warns his victims that vultures are everywhere; refugees look up longingly as an airplane brings the Gestapo captain (a few scripts later he was promoted to major) Strasser to Casablanca and lands beyond a neon sign that reads RICK'S. Inside the café, a dozen desperate refugees try to buy or sell their way to freedom. Rick is not introduced until page 15, when a hand writes "Okay—Rick" on the back of a check and the camera pulls back to a medium shot of Humphrey Bogart. And the plot is driven by an invention of the Epsteins: the Letters of Transit were being carried by two German couriers who have been murdered.

Of the four major characters in *Everybody Comes to Rick's,* only the noble Victor Laszlo remains essentially the same in the movie. Rick, who in the play is a self-pitying married lawyer who has cheated on his wife, takes on Bogart's persona of wary, hooded toughness. Says Julie Epstein, "Once we knew that Bogart was going to play the role, we felt he was so right for it that we didn't have to do anything special. Except we tried to make him as cynical as possible."

Bogart was cast in *Casablanca* in mid-February, before a word of the Epsteins' script was written. Whether the studio informed Bogart is another matter. Directors, writers, and actors belonged to the studio, which penciled them in and crossed them out with as little warning as a wind changing direction. On February 14, when Hal Wallis told casting director Steve Trilling that Bogart would star in *Casablanca,* the actor was finishing up *The Big Shot,* the first of four movies he would make for Warner Bros. in 1942. He got three weeks' vacation between *The Big Shot* and *Across the Pacific* and begged for another few weeks between *Across the Pacific* and *Casa-*

blanca. Laurence Mark, a producer who has to deal with the stars of 1992, shakes his head at "an actor like Bogart begging for a two-week vacation." Today, he says, "You're lucky if you get one picture a year from them."

In that PART I TEMP. script of April 2, Rick has already shed his wife and his profession. Captain Renault, who was an evil woman-izer called Rinaldo in the play, has become a mocking alter ego for the Epsteins. Renault's first line, as he meets Strasser at the airport, is "Unoccupied France welcomes you to Casablanca." The Epsteins' stage directions continue, "*(It is very hard to tell whether he is being servile or mocking).*" In the same vein, Renault tells Rick that "Cap-tain Strasser is one of the reasons the Third Reich enjoys the reputa-tion it has today."

The character who is most changed from play to movie is the woman in the triangle. In the stage play she is an American tramp named Lois Meredith, whose affair with Rick ended when she casually cheated on him with another man and whose renewed affair with Rick in Casablanca emasculates her current lover, Laszlo. In the film, she is Ilsa Lund, who met Rick when she thought her husband, Victor Laszlo, was dead and left him when Victor escaped from a concentration camp and lay, desperately ill, on the outskirts of Paris. It was Wallis's favorite screenwriter, Casey Robinson, who took credit for suggesting that the heroine be European. In a 1974 oral history, Robinson described how he got the idea because he was "falling in love with a Russian ballerina named Tamara Toumanova." Robinson even persuaded Wallis to test Toumanova for the part. Later, when *Casablanca* went into production, Robinson worked on the script for three weeks.

Wallis passed on to the Epsteins Robinson's idea of making the girl European. One of their letters from Washington jokes: "While we handle the foreign situation here, you try to get a foreign girl for the part. An American girl with big tits will do. Love and Kisses, Julie and Phil." But even when Lois became Ilsa, the role was not shaped to fit Ingrid Bergman. She had to wear the cloak of generic European girl and cut it to her measure. By the time she was given the role in April, Bergman would have accepted a script much worse than *Casablanca*. She had been stuck in Rochester, New York, where her husband was in medical school, since August, and she despaired of ever making another movie.

In the Epsteins' first script, Lois is still Lois and Renault's

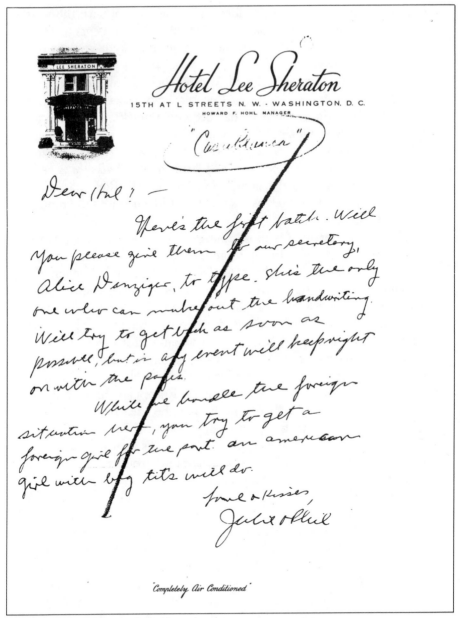

The Epsteins' note to Hal Wallis.

womanizing still has an unpleasant edge. However, the groundwork has been laid for the relationship between Rick and Renault, which may lie as close to the emotional heart of the film as the relationship between Rick and Ilsa. The Epsteins have created a bantering between equals, an admiration at the edges of the frame.

RENAULT

I have often speculated on why you do not return to America. Did you abscond with the church funds? Did you run off with the President's wife? I should like to think you killed a man. It is the romantic in me.

RICK

It was a combination of all three.

RENAULT

And what in Heaven's name brought you to Casablanca?

RICK

My health. I came to Casablanca for the waters.

RENAULT

Waters? What waters? We are in the desert.

RICK

I was misinformed.

Says Epstein today, "My brother and I tried very hard to come up with a reason why Rick couldn't return to America. But nothing seemed right. We finally decided not to give a reason at all."

In keeping with what was admired as the Epsteins' main strength, they have given the dialogue—including lines that were taken intact from the play—a twist, a kicker. In the play Renault denies that he is influenced by the Gestapo. In the April 2 script, his denial is followed by his alacrity in jumping when Strasser calls. When Renault tells Rick that the café is allowed to stay open because Rick does not sell exit visas, Rick answers, "I thought it was because we let you win at dice." Because of the importance of the murder of the couriers, says Renault, he is having his men round up "twice the usual number of suspects." Rick, in particular, has taken on some of the needling quality, the verbal aggression, for which Bogart was famous. To the thief Ugarte: "I don't mind a parasite. I object to a cut-rate one." To Yvonne, his casual mistress, when she asks, "Where were you last night?" "That's so long ago I don't remember." "Will I see you tonight?" "I never plan that far ahead." To Strasser, who asks his nationality, "I'm a drunkard."

But the Epsteins also began the process of sharpening the politics, a process that Howard Koch would complete. In the play, Rick didn't flee from the Germans. He stayed around Paris for a month, hoping to bump into Lois again. In the play, the Gestapo was chasing Victor Laszlo not only because he had written "lies" about them in his Prague newspaper but because he had $7 million. In the Epsteins' first draft, as in the film, Strasser has a dossier on Rick, and the Gestapo wants the names of the Underground leaders from Laszlo. "If I didn't give them to you in the concentration camp where you had more 'persuasive methods' at your disposal, I certainly won't give them to you now," Laszlo responds.

Almost as soon as Wallis read the Epsteins' April 2 script, he assigned Howard Koch to *Casablanca* without taking the twins off the picture. The Epsteins were to write Part II. Working from the Epsteins' April 2 script, Koch was to rewrite Part I. Up to this point, the transformation of play to film is a straight line, a map easily readable fifty years later. Now, because of the standard studio practice of using multiple writers, it becomes tangled, with unsigned and undated pages of suggestions turned into scenes in scripts that were an amalgam. In July, the pink and blue colored pages of revisions came on an almost daily basis. Much of who wrote what can only be deduced through internal evidence—whether Lois has become Ilsa, whether a scene or suggestion whose original author is known has been changed in contradictory ways.

"The major work was done by the Epsteins," says Koch. "They were on it the longest." Koch, who was making $600 a week, was on the movie for about seven weeks at a cost to the film of $4,200. The Epsteins were charged against the movie for twelve weeks, a total of $15,208 apiece.

Koch had come to Warner Bros. early in 1939, when John Huston got him a job for $300 a week. "I had slaved in New York," says Koch. "Hollywood was Utopia. The weather. Palm trees. And everything waiting for me—a nice office, a chance to lie on the

Howard Koch (at right) introduced John Huston to Huston's second wife Leslie Bloch; Huston got Koch his job at Warner Bros.

seashore, beautiful women." His friend John Huston also generously helped him get a writing credit on *Sergeant York*. Huston had starred as Abraham Lincoln in Koch's play *The Lonely Man*. And Huston and Koch were coauthors of *In Time to Come,* which reached Broadway in December 1941. A study of Woodrow Wilson and the League of Nations, *In Time to Come* got four votes from the Drama Critics Circle for best play of the 1941–42 season.*

At the time he started working on *Casablanca,* Koch's greatest notoriety had come as a $75-a-week radio writer. "John Houseman had read *The Lonely Man,* says Koch. "And he told me he and Orson Welles had an hour-long radio play to do and they needed a writer they could get very cheaply. They could get me for $75 a week, which I was glad to have, and it was my experience there, coming up with fifty, sixty pages every week according to their standards which were pretty high, that changed me from an amateur to a professional." Koch's third radio play was *The*

---

* No other play got as many votes but, unfortunately for Koch and Huston, eleven critics said that no play was worthy of the prize.

*War of the Worlds.** In his first two years at Warner Bros., Koch had written movies—*The Sea Hawk* and *The Letter*—for the studio's two biggest stars, Errol Flynn and Bette Davis. Koch has always said that his largest contribution to *Casablanca* was in making the film more political. He was never one to write froth. From the time a political satire by Koch won the $500 first prize in a national playwriting contest in 1932, his plays examined political themes. He is unquestionably responsible for providing Rick with a background of fighting for the Loyalist cause in Spain and running guns to Ethiopia. In September 1947, Koch would be one of nineteen unfriendly witnesses subpoenaed by the House Un-American Activities Committee. Fifteen of the others were or had been screenwriters. Ten, including Koch, were Jewish. But, unlike almost all of the others, Koch had never joined the Communist Party. "I wanted to keep my independence," he says. "But I was doing the same things that they were doing." Only eleven of the unfriendly nineteen were asked to testify. The ten Americans were cited for contempt of Congress and eventually went to jail, labeled the Hollywood Ten. The eleventh, playwright Bertolt Brecht, fled to Europe. The blacklist made no distinctions. Despite the fact that he had not been called to testify and that he was not a Communist, Koch was forced into exile. "My salary was cut off," he says. "From $3,000 a week to nothing." Yet, as exiles go, his was benign. He and his wife spent five years in England, both of them writing successfully under assumed names. "I don't mean to say that the blacklist was a happy period for everybody," Koch says. "It was very unhappy. Broken marriages and jobs lost forever. But we just happened to be lucky about it."

In their authoritative study of the blacklist era, *The Inquisition in Hollywood,* Larry Ceplair and Steven Englund list Koch as one of the key radicals in Hollywood, a term that means, at a minimum, people who sympathized with the Communist Party line, and that includes Lillian Hellman and Dashiell Hammett. On a parallel list of liberals, with Katharine Hepburn and Bette Davis, are the names of Julius and Philip Epstein. The twins were Jewish by birth, but their religion was Rooseveltian liberalism. Says Philip's son, Leslie, "My cousins and I were brought up as Deists, children of the Enlightenment, worshipers before the idol of FDR." When war broke out,

---

*In 1988, the fiftieth anniversary of the Halloween invasion from Mars that terrified America, Koch auctioned his copy of the script for $135,000.

Philip tried to enlist but was rejected as a premature anti-Fascist. People who spoke out against Hitler early or joined anti-Nazi organizations were seen as vaguely too far left, too liberal, even if they weren't Communists. Julius finally managed to join the Navy in 1944.

From Murray Burnett to the Epsteins to Howard Koch, *Casablanca* was shaped by Jews whose religion or politics had made them premature anti-Fascists. And, to take a step backward, the men who owned the studio were premature anti-Fascists, too. Because of Hitler's anti-Semitism, Harry Warner had begun speaking out against the dictator in 1936. In his autobiography, Jack Warner created the convenient justification that he and his brother were galvanized by the murder of one of their Jewish employees in Germany, but an exhaustive Ph.D. thesis about the studio's anti-Nazi activism says that the murder never happened.

Burnett wrote *Everybody Comes to Rick's* after a trip to Europe in 1938. "I had inherited $10,000 from an uncle, and it was one of my romantic dreams to go to Europe on a big ocean liner," he says. "My wife's family lived in Belgium. I had read headlines about Hitler, but they were meaningless until we got to Antwerp and my wife's family asked us to go to Vienna—the Anschluss had just happened—to help other relatives get money out of Austria. At that time Jews could leave if they took no money, nothing. I went to the American consulate to get a visa, and he said, 'Mr. Burnett, I don't know why you're going to Vienna and I don't want to know, but I want to warn you that if you get into any trouble in Vienna this government cannot help you.' He gave me a small American flag to wear in my lapel, and he said, 'You must never go out in the street without wearing this.'"

What he learned in Vienna, says Burnett more than half a century later, "was indescribable." He went to Austria as an American. He came back to America as a Jew. In Vienna, Jews weren't allowed to take taxicabs. When he stepped off the train with his golf clubs, tennis rackets, and American arrogance, Burnett insisted on a taxi. So his wife's relative begged the cab driver. "I don't speak German, but I'm fluent in obsequious," says Burnett. They drove past a billboard "larger than any I have ever seen and on the billboard was a caricature of a Jew, and it said in huge letters, MURDERER, THIEF. And we'd sit in the relatives' apartment and hear the marching feet outside."

Part of the scheme involved buying merchandise. "When we got on the train, I had diamond rings on every finger and my wife was wearing a fur coat in August," says Burnett. He was also running a 103-degree fever, since, as usual, he had responded to psychic stress with physical illness. And he was illegally carrying a camera, which he hid behind a pillow. When the uniformed border guards returned their passports, one pointed at the pillow. Burnett was terrified. When the guard left, his wife, who spoke German, burst into laughter. The guard had told them not to take the pillows when they left the train.

In the South of France a few weeks later, Burnett made a nuisance of himself. "I was screaming, 'Do you know what's going on?'" he says. "And finally when people saw me coming they walked away." One night he went to a nightclub with a polyglot clientele where a black man played the piano. Burnett whispered to his wife, "What a setting for a play."

Back in New York, he told his collaborator, "No one can remain neutral, God damn it, Joan. No one can remain neutral."

Joan Alison was nearly a decade older than Burnett, a divorcee with three children. She was richer and more sophisticated, and she had myriad "contacts" in the theater world. They had met a few years earlier at the Surfside Beach Club in Atlantic Beach, Long

Joan Alison, coauthor of Everybody Comes to Rick's.

Island, where middle-class New Yorkers rented cabanas and spent summer days splashing in the Atlantic Ocean. It is instructive that Burnett remembers that they met when Alison criticized his clothing as being too formal for sun and fun. It didn't happen that way at all, says Alison. "Murray came over and talked to my little boy, and I thought it was sweet of him. I always scream when he identifies himself as Rick, because he was the country boy, unsophisticated. Both my husbands were wide-shouldered and fine athletes, and Rick was my concept of a guy that I would like. Clark Gable. I hated Humphrey Bogart. I thought he was a common drunk."

Burnett had written a play that Alison helped revise and then passed on to a producer or two. After that, they began to collaborate. In the eighteen months before *Everybody Comes to Rick's* was purchased, they had submitted three original stories to Warner Bros. "Joan nourished me," says Burnett. "I went to her apartment after school, and she would give me lunch. She was a marvelous cook. She was a beautiful woman. I needed Joan. Don't for a moment think I didn't. In a way, I think she was my mother." The Letters of Transit were Alison's idea. Burnett expected someone to challenge them about the absurdity of exit visas that couldn't be canceled, but no one ever did.

Until her death in March 1992, both Burnett and Alison lived in apartments in Manhattan, but they had not seen each other for years. Something went wrong a long time ago, after *Casablanca* was a success and they were wooed by Hollywood and failed there; and each seemed embarrassed when speaking of the other. "Murray's concept of sophisticated was me," said Alison in the fall of 1989. "Lois was based on me. And he should see me now. I'm in the process of dying. Maybe this week. Maybe next. The thing that sustains me a great deal is the *Jeopardy* show, when I can yell out more answers than the contestants." Until her death more than two years later, at the age of ninety, Alison was still competing against the television-show contestants and winning.

Much of the major work on the *Casablanca* screenplay was done between April 6, when Howard Koch was assigned to the movie, and June 1, when a revised final script was mimeographed. (That "final" script was by no means final. It would be changed, sometimes daily, until mid-July.) In addition to Koch and the Epsteins, the broth was stirred by Lenore Coffee, who had started writing titles for silent films in 1919 and had become a prime adaptor of popular women's fiction, and Casey Robinson, the most expensive and deferred to of the Warner screenwriters. Coffee would be on and off the movie in a week, but Robinson would shape the love story.

"Warner Bros. was like the assembly line at an automobile plant," says Julius Epstein. "You were assigned a script, and when you were through with it, the studio would give it to another writer. And someone else would polish it, and, if you were good at a particular thing, you would do that kind of scene on one picture and another and another."

Each subsequent script for *Casablanca* became leaner and sharper, more economical, the scenes rearranged for greater dramatic effect and the speeches polished and clipped. Within the confines of a studio that both Koch and Julie Epstein describe as "a family," Koch rewrote the Epsteins to give the movie more weight and significance, and the Epsteins then rewrote Koch to erase his most ponderous symbols and to lighten his earnestness.

This kind of survival-of-the-fittest script is unlikely to happen today, when writers, director, and studio executives come insecurely and suspiciously together to make a single movie, the original writer is rarely brought back after his work is rewritten, and screen credit means that someone gets extra money from television and videocassette sales. "Everybody stakes out his territory," says Jack Brodsky, who has twenty years of experience as a producer and marketing executive. "No first draft, no matter how much it cost the studio, is considered any good today. The studio says, 'We're going to improve it.' The director has to tamper to put his stamp on it. The writers are corporations, who have no loyalty to the final movie if they have to share credit. Rarely do I see a script brought to fruition which is as good as the first draft."

At the beginning of May, the Epsteins finished the second section of the script of *Casablanca,* while Howard Koch turned in his revision of the Epsteins' first act. Earlier, in nineteen pages of "Suggestions for Revised Story," Koch had warned:

> There is also a danger that Rick's sacrifice in the end will seem theatrical and phony unless, early in the story, we suggest the side of his nature that makes his final decision in character. It would be interesting to have Renault penetrate the mystery in his first scene

with Rick when he guesses that the cynical American is underneath, a sentimentalist. Rick laughs at the idea, then Renault produces his record—"ran guns to Ethiopia," "fought for the Loyalists in the Spanish War." Rick says he got well paid on both occasions. Renault replies that the winning side would have paid him better. Strange that he always happens to be on the side of the under-dog. Rick dismisses the implication, but through-out the picture we see evidences of his humanity, which he does his best to cover up.

Koch's script of May 11 also deepened Rick's character and underlined the political tensions in subtle ways. For example, Koch makes the man Rick bars from his gambling room—who was an English cad in the play—into a representative of the Deutschbank. When the owner of the Blue Parrot offers to buy Rick's Café, Koch has added dialogue in which the character played by Sydney Greenstreet also offers to buy Sam, and Rick says, "I don't buy or sell human beings." (In their rewrite of Koch's script, the Epsteins would build on Koch's line by having Greenstreet respond, "That's too bad. That's Casablanca's leading commodity.") If Koch layered the politics rather heavily—in his version, Victor Laszlo forces Renault to toast *liberté, égalité, fraternité*—the Epsteins would remove those speeches in the script of June 1. With delicate balance, Koch managed to hold down the gags while the Epsteins managed to cut the preaching.

Although the Epsteins and Koch worked on each other's scripts, they never worked together. Hal Wallis was always the intermediary. In his nineteen pages of suggestions, Koch suggested that Renault and Rick play a chess game throughout the movie to "serve as a useful image for the chess-like intrigue which characterizes Casablanca." Says Julie Epstein, "My brother and I hated that chess game." It is Julie's memory that, when he and his brother returned from Washington, they read a chess-game scene written by Koch and replaced it with the scene in which Renault speculates on why Rick can't return to America.

Koch also suggested that the movie have a scene at the Underground meeting, where Laszlo can give a fiery speech at the end of which "this brave band of patriots rise to their feet in tribute. . . . This scene is to show Laszlo in action as the democratic leader, so that we do not have to accept his great importance to the allied cause merely by hearsay. Also, such a scene as this might enlarge the significance of the story." Like several of Koch's heaviest symbols, this method of enlarging the significance did not make it into the movie.

However, a number of Koch's ideas are on the screen. For years, Howard Koch took too much credit for *Casablanca*. Now he takes too little. He reorganized the Epsteins' April 2 script to greater dramatic effect. For example, there is more excitement and tension in Koch's version and the final film when Ugarte (Peter Lorre) is captured before Rick and the Gestapo agent meet; and the Norwegian Resistance fighter (played by John Qualen) is used to impart vital information to Laszlo. And Koch solved the play's unworkable subplot by having Rick allow the young Bulgarian couple to win at roulette.

In their script of April 2, the Epsteins had incorporated a real-life incident. Phil's wife, Lilian, had played 25-cent roulette in Palm

In this scene, which is not in the movie, Laszlo searches for Ugarte in a hotel in Casablanca's native quarter. He finds a message telling him to come to Rick's café at 10 P.M.

Springs and lost. "She was moaning and complaining about losing," says Julie. "Finally the croupier told her to put her chips on 22. She won, and he told her to get out and never come back." The Epsteins created a refugee who had been saving for three years to get enough money to leave Casablanca and was now gambling away his stake. Rick told him to put his money on 24, and he won.

In his "Suggestions for Revised Story," Koch zeroed in on this scene as a way of showing Rick's humanity.

> Why not make this a much bigger situation—for instance, it might be the way he rescues Annina and her husband from Renault? The Prefect has named a price for the visa too high for the couple to pay. In his most gracious manner, he suggests to Annina that she can pay in another way. . . . Annina comes for advice to Rick, who enables Jan to win at roulette, thus defeating the intention of his friend Renault. The Prefect, when he learns, should not resent this action of Rick's, but accept it as a sporting loss—and also as proof of his argument that Rick is a sentimentalist.

On May 6, Wallis told director Michael Curtiz to expect the Epsteins' second-act script at ten o'clock the next morning and to read it immediately so they could meet at 11 A.M. with the Epsteins, who wanted some guidance on the third act. Five days later Wallis sent a Please Hurry Up note to Howard Koch, who was to revise the Epsteins' second act as he had revised the first portion of their script. "I think this next batch of the Epsteins' stuff is for the most part good," Wallis wrote Koch. "I think almost everything of the Epsteins is useable."

Koch immediately sent back an indignant memo:

> Although the Epstein script follows in a general way the new story line, I feel it is written in a radically different vein from the work I've just finished on the first half of the picture. They apparently see the situations more in terms of their comic possibilities, while my effort has been to legitimize the characters and develop a serious melodrama of present-day significance, using humor merely as a relief from dramatic tension. I am not presuming to decide which is the better way to attack the picture, but certainly they are different from the ground up. . . .
>
> If you are in favor of the approach taken by the Epsteins, it would seem to me best that they do the patching on the few places

you don't like. Frankly, to a large extent, I've been writing, and would continue to write, a new screen play, gladly availing myself of what material I feel I could use from their script and from the original play. With the best of intentions, I would be lost trying to do anything else.

Despite Koch's pleas, he was neither allowed to write a new screenplay for *Casablanca* nor taken off the movie. He continued to write behind the Epsteins until June 5, ten days after the movie started shooting, when he was sent back to work on the screenplay on which he had spent four weeks in March. That script never became a movie.

By May 25, when *Casablanca* started production, the melodrama, the snappy dialogue, and all the characters except Ilsa Lund had been shaped and polished. But *Casablanca* still had two problems—the love story and the ending. For the next seven weeks, they would be argued and fought over as each hot summer day brought the cast and crew of *Casablanca* nearer to the day when they would have to shoot an ending that hadn't yet been written.

Warner Bros. publicist Arthur Wilde pretending to be a soldier on a date with Alexis Smith to help the war effort.

4

False Starts

———◆———

It is no accident that *Casablanca* and America's entry into World War II coincided. In Hollywood, then as now, perception is everything, and the war that had begun the day before the play reached the studio transformed *Everybody Comes to Rick's* from a standard melodrama set in an exotic land and containing a handful of interesting characters into a significant example of American ability to do the right thing and make the right choices. If the play had reached Hal Wallis's desk in August 1941, rather than December, there is a good chance it would not have been bought; certainly much less would have been seen in the sparring between Rick Blaine and the representatives of Nazi Germany and Vichy France. If it had come to the studio in 1939, it would have been perceived as an uncomfortably aggressive anti-Nazi statement. But it arrived at the exact moment when the movie industry had to change its habits to fit the realities of the war and had to change its movies to fit America's image of the war. *Everybody Comes to Rick's* would be altered both because movie audiences in a nation at war needed a less self-pitying hero and because Hollywood no longer had access to balsawood, rubber cement, and silk. To the ordinary chaos of moviemaking would be added the muddle of an industry struggling to cope with major changes.

None of that was apparent on December 7, 1941. Hollywood always played on Sunday, since the industry still worked six days a week. The director who would turn *Everybody Comes to Rick's* into *Casablanca* spent the morning on his skeetshooting range. Michael Curtiz's skeet field was just beyond his small polo field and one mile by car from the main house. The Hungarian immigrant director, born Mihaly Kertesz, had a passion for land. By 1941 he had wrapped himself in 165 acres. His twenty-five-acre grove of orange and grapefruit trees—grapefruit grew poorly on the other side of the mountains but thrived in the oppressive summer heat of the San Fernando Valley—was picked by Sunkist.

For the first few rounds of skeet shooting, December 7, 1941, was like every other Sunday at the ranch. Unless there was a polo match at one of the big fields over the hill, it was clay pigeons followed by lunch in the orange grove below the house. Mike—he had shed Mihaly as easily and quickly as he had shed Hungary for Austria and German expressionism for Hollywood eclecticism—was the money-earning workhorse in the Warner Bros. stable. Although a William Wyler might be brought in to direct an occasional Bette Davis film (*Jezebel, The Letter*), it was Curtiz whom *Variety* praised as the studio's top "money getter" year after year. When he came to Warner Bros. from Austria in 1926, Curtiz had already made sixty-two silent movies. During the decade between 1930 and 1940, he directed forty-five talking pictures. They may have been a goulash of melodramas, horror films, swashbucklers, westerns and gangster movies—he finished *The Walking Dead* and, a week or two later, was at work on *The Charge of the Light Brigade*—but his movies had three things in common. They were brought in on time, they rarely went over budget, and they almost always made money. That *Casablanca* would go eleven days over schedule was not entirely Curtiz's fault. Because *Now, Voyager* finished twenty days late, Paul Henreid did not set foot on the set of *Casablanca* until the movie had been in production for a full month.

The skeetshooters competing with Curtiz Pearl Harbor morning were two Warner Bros. stars, George Brent and Ann Sheridan; Henry Blanke who was now a full producer; and Hal Wallis. Wallis was almost always at the ranch on Sundays. Even though the two men spent the other six days a week at the same studio, they never seemed to get tired of each other. Four days earlier, they had started a musical together, *Yankee Doodle Dandy*. On Saturday nights, Wallis and his wife, actress Louise Fazenda, watched movies in Curtiz's projection room or Curtiz, his wife, and stepson watched movies at Wallis's ranch, fifteen minutes away. Most other nights, the two men talked on the phone for hours after dinner.

When Mihaly Kertesz arrived in Los Angeles in June 1926, to a city full of orange trees and air thick with the scent of orange blossoms, it was studio publicity man Hal Wallis who was sent to the train station to meet him. Their friendship began that day. It was a friendship born out of mutual interests and helped along by the fact that Louise Fazenda and Curtiz's wife, Bess Meredyth, had been close friends since long before Meredyth's marriage to Curtiz. What the two men shared, beyond movies, was physical stamina and a need to work that was close to an addiction. If Wallis—a powerfully built man with a neck so thick it seemed made of wood—came to the studio first and left last, Curtiz, before there were unions to protest, worked his actors seventeen-hour days and cursed anyone who wanted to stop for lunch. On Saturday, April 2, 1932, Curtiz, who had the constitution of an ox, worked for twenty hours, not allowing the cast and crew of *Doctor X* to go home until 5 A.M. Sunday morning. In that one day he shot 10 percent of the movie.

"Wallis was deeply admiring of Curtiz, and he wasn't admiring of many people," says Wallis's biographer, Charles Higham. "He got angry at critics who said Curtiz had no personal style. He said you couldn't mistake a Curtiz setup, that it had a stamp as clearly marked as a Matisse."

Curtiz, in turn, always gave Hal Wallis credit for *Casablanca*. To the end of his life, Curtiz told friends that Hal Wallis was the only person who had faith in the movie, that Jack Warner was convinced the movie would be a disaster.

Dozens of memos make it clear that, at the studio, Wallis was the boss. "I saw last night's dailies and, again, it is just a lot of odds and bits and reactions of people in the Café to Sam's song," he wrote Curtiz when *Casablanca* had been in production for eight days. "I don't feel yet that we have gotten into the picture."

But both the impassioned, autocratic Curtiz and the cool, efficient Wallis could be charming when they were away from the studio. Wallis usually stabled a horse or two at the Curtiz ranch, and the two men rode together. "Hal was never an elegant rider," says

Michael Curtiz and Hal Wallis at Curtiz's stable.

Curtiz's stepson, John Meredyth Lucas. "He greatly resembled a sack of potatoes, but he rode well enough." Curtiz, who had been in the Austro-Hungarian Army during World War I, rode well and with passion and kept a dozen polo ponies and riding horses. When polo was the sport of Hollywood kings, Wallis and Curtiz were part of Los Amigos, the Warner Bros. polo team, along with Jack Warner, Henry Blanke, and a ringer, a three-goal player imported from New York. Curtiz started *Casablanca* with his right hand wrapped in bandages because Snowy Baker, an Australian who rode at the Uplifters Club, had gouged his knuckles with a mallet.

"I think flirting with danger got them," says Jack Warner, Jr., who played on the Warner team in 1936 and 1937, at the same time he was on the polo team at the University of Southern California. "Now they could be the heroes in their movies."

It was twenty-year-old John Meredyth Lucas who drove down to the skeet field to break the news that the Japanese had bombed Pearl

Harbor. For the next week the bottom dropped out of the movie business, but by December 15 the *Hollywood Reporter* was announcing that the lines were normal again and, at some theaters, better than normal. Whatever else the war did, it gave the movie industry a huge audience. Warner Bros. went from a $5.4 million after-tax profit in fiscal 1941 to an $8.5 million profit in 1942. Profits totaled $8.2 million in 1943, even after the studio redeemed its preferred stock and $10 million of debentures and paid off all its domestic bank loans. Defense workers with money in their pockets and purses but no sugar, butter, automobiles, vacuum cleaners, or sewing machines to spend it on helped the industry sell 3.5 billion movie tickets a year.*

For the movie studios, the last three weeks in December were a mixture of business as usual and preparations for invasion. While *Everybody Comes to Rick's* was read and bargained over, Warner art directors drew up plans to camouflage the studio's twenty-one soundstages, which, unfortunately, resembled the airplane hangars at Lockheed down the road. There is an apocryphal story that Jack Warner had an arrow and the words "Lockheed, that way" painted on one of the roofs. It is doubtful that he would have had such confidence in the English language skills of Japanese pilots.

Within days, Warners had barred all visitors "with the exception of the always-welcome press," and 20th Century–Fox announced that it would fingerprint and issue identification cards to every employee. Metro-Goldwyn-Mayer, whose imperial ways included impassable gates and a large police force, made no changes in security. Warner Bros. bought three "surgically equipped" ambulances and a fire engine with a giant pumper and stationed airplane spotters on the roofs of Stages 7 and 21, the two tallest on the lot.

Psychologically, Warner Brothers was two steps ahead of the other studios when it came to facing the war. Unlike the other moguls, Harry Warner had been an early and fervent supporter of Franklin Roosevelt and an early opponent of Hitler. All the moguls except Darryl Zanuck were Jewish, but only Harry Warner—and, later, Jack Warner—were anti-Nazis when opposition to Hitler was unfashionable. Warner Bros. closed down its operations in Germany in July 1934. It was the first studio to leave Germany. As Hitler

---

*Since the 1950s, when television replaced movies as the mass-audience entertainment, around one billion movie tickets are sold each year.

swallowed country after country—Austria, Czechoslovakia, Poland, Denmark—Warner Bros. was almost always the first studio to withdraw, choosing principle over profit. By contrast, Paramount, M-G-M, and Fox, reluctant to lose such a good market for their films, were still operating in Germany in 1939. *Casablanca* has been used, symbolically, to illustrate many points, and one can easily compare Rick's neutrality, the blinders that allow him to keep his café open, with the other studios' willingness to look the other way.

Harry was the smartest businessman of all the Warners, and he was probably more ruthless than Jack, but his toughness was yoked to a rigid moral code. "When I first came to the studio in 1936, they had this anti-Nazi drive," says film editor Rudi Fehr. "I was from Berlin. I had very strong feelings about that, so I gave a week's salary, a big $60. About ten days after I sent the check in, I got a note from Harry Warner. 'Rudi, I just looked up the payroll. I'm hereby returning your check. Please tear the check up and give me a check for $10.' That was unheard of for the head of a company."

Born in Poland and a victim of anti-Jewish pogroms, Harry Warner was speaking out against Hitler when the rest of the industry heads were talking about European markets' being a necessary part of their fiduciary responsibility to their stockholders. In 1939, Warner Bros. made Hollywood's first overtly anti-Nazi film, *Confessions of a Nazi Spy.* And, in May 1940 Harry sent a pleading telegram to President Roosevelt: he wrote that he was worried that America's cash-and-carry policy for shipping war materials to the Allies "will work too great a hardship on these brave unfortunate nations who are, in a way, fighting our battle for us." Harry Warner also helped the British as best a private citizen could. Warner Bros. distributed two short subjects made for Britain's Ministry of Information, *London Can Take It* and *Christmas Under Fire,* and gave all the proceeds, around $35,000, to a fund to build Spitfires.

Jack, the eighth of the twelve Warner children, was born in Canada and grew up in Youngstown, Ohio. Before he was ten, he had turned his back on Hebrew school and his real name, Jacob. Harry, eleven years older, the third child and first son, spoke Hebrew as well as he spoke English. However rich and famous he might be, Harry Warner knew that he was still a Jewboy. After a Ku Klux Klan rally in Pittsburgh in October 1941, a Warner Bros. theater there was vandalized, with the word "Jew" written in red, white, and blue on the walls.

In June 1940, Harry had assembled his 3,411 employees and their wives, with stars and janitors alike sitting on folding chairs in the studio's huge crafts building. He read to them from a Nazi book, *Defilement of Race,* that detailed the German plan to rid the world of Jews and Christians. His own wife was not there, Harry said, because she was afraid that because he spoke out he would be the first one the Nazis would kill. "United we survive and divided we fall," he said. "We must unite and quit listening to anybody discussing whether you or I am a Jew or a Catholic or a Protestant or of any other faith—and not allow anyone to say anything against anybody's faith—or we will fall just the same as they did over there."

Three months later, in September, he encouraged the Warner Studio Club to form the Warvets, employees who were ex-servicemen and who pledged, "Americanism is my watchword and my creed . . . worth fighting and dying for." By November, there were 350 Warvets guarding against saboteurs, and Warner Bros. was urging other employees to get trained in the studio's Rifle and Pistol Club, Search Light Battery, or Medical Unit. "Through the foresight of Harry and Jack Warner," said an editorial in the *Warner Club News,* "every employee of this studio has been given the opportunity to prepare himself for the protection of his Home, Job and COUNTRY."

Humphrey Bogart was not a member of the Warner Warvets but he was a war veteran. As an eighteen-year-old, he had served in the Navy in World War I. During World War II, he joined the Coast Guard Reserve and patrolled the California coast.

When war came, the Warvets were ready to defend the studio against sabotage, a job Harry Warner gave them on December 8, 1941. Like most of the studios, Warners put guards around its power plants and fuel dumps. All the studios built air-raid shelters. Warners carved out four shelters—the biggest was in the basement of its craft shop—and protected them with fifteen thousand sandbags.

California, naked to the Pacific, was terrified of the dark sea. On December 11, an unidentified airplane triggered a blackout from Bakersfield to San Diego. In response, an industry that had worked around the clock shifted all thirty thousand employees to daylight hours on December 15. In anticipation of more blackouts, the cameras would start turning at 8 A.M. and, for the time being, stop at 5 P.M. Jack Warner, who usually got to the studio in time for lunch, set a good example by arriving at 7:45 A.M. the first day, according to gossip columnist Hedda Hopper.

The preparations were in earnest, even if Paramount logged some extra publicity by retitling one of its finished movies *Pacific Blackout*. Almost immediately, the studios made expensive duplicate negatives of their movies and shipped them to secret vaults in the Midwest. Southern California, with its shipyards, airplane factories, and unprotected backside, felt more at risk than any other area of the country. In a government survey taken in February 1942, 75 percent of the Southern Californians interviewed believed that "only a few" or "practically none" of the state's Japanese residents were loyal to the United States; and the same percent recommended putting the Japanese in camps. In northern California, fewer than half of those interviewed favored imprisoning the Japanese. The eventual roundup had no effect on the studios, which found, to their surprise, how few Japanese they employed and that almost all of those were easily expendable janitors, gardeners, or window washers. When the roundup began in earnest and the government pulled out the American-born Japanese actors in Warners' *Across the Pacific,* "A little indignation and some wire pulling held them at least until the picture was finished," said Mary Astor, the movie's costar. "A world-shaking tragedy comes into our lives, and characteristically all anybody was thinking of was 'How will it affect the picture?' "

Hollywood's fear was genuine. It can be measured by the fact that the overlords, jealous guardians of their castle gates, agreed to pool their production facilities if a studio was disabled by bombs. And the fear was justified. The government, afraid of panic, withheld the extent of the losses at Pearl Harbor for more than a month. Although the only attack on California came on February 23, 1942, when a Japanese submarine shelled an oilfield north of Santa Barbara without doing much damage, nine Japanese submarines lay off the coasts of California, Oregon, and Washington during the last three weeks in December. They sank tankers and waited for a signal to shell radio and navigational stations. But the signal never came, and they were withdrawn. As late as April 23, 1942, the assistant chief of staff, Major General Dwight Eisenhower, warned the Western Defense Command to expect the Japanese to retaliate for Doolittle's bomber raid on Tokyo by sending carrier-based planes against the West Coast.

Real fear or not, the studio publicity departments jumped to take advantage. When the country was switched to Daylight Saving Time

During a tour of inspection at Warner Bros. studio, Harry M. Warner shows Lynn U. Stambaugh, National Commander of the American Legion, one of the studio's four bombproof air raid shelters.

in February, Fox announced that Betty Grable was the first star to reach New York on the new war time. Asked how the first air-raid drill had gone, a Warners executive answered, "Oh, it was a great success. The *Life* photographers were there and got swell pictures." For that air-raid practice, the evacuation alarm whistle at Warner Bros. blew just before lunch on January 2—so that little production time would be lost—and reporters were invited into the biggest of the studio's shelters, to sit "on wooden benches along sand-bagged walls" with Bette Davis, John Huston, Michael Curtiz, and Dennis Morgan.

The studios had always used the press to sell their pictures. Within months, the huge studio publicity departments would shift almost seamlessly to helping the United States Government sell the

In a Warner Bros. basement, all dressed up and waiting for the bombs to fall.

war. Of the $350 billion of war bonds sold during World War II, nearly one-third was sold by movie stars or in movie theaters. The studios had always lied easily about their movies and their stars; they would lie as easily about the war. And those lies—on screen and off—would shape America's picture of what it was going through.

Warners celebrated the first Los Angeles blackout by sending out a three-page account of how the studio's stars had managed. Bette Davis and her husband stood in their garden and "watched the giant searchlights criss-cross the sky." James Cagney calmed his hysterical cook. Olivia de Havilland lit a silver candle and "took a lovely hot bath with lots and lots of bath salts," while Cary Grant, who had been loaned to the studio for *Arsenic and Old Lace,* lost his shoes on the beach, and Jane Wyman and Ronald Reagan sat in their parked car with the lights out for an hour and a half, watching "excited citizens smash neon signs and break windows" of shops that were too slow turning out their lights.

Although the blackout experiences of Ann Sheridan, who decided she might as well go to bed, and Ronald Reagan sound genuine, it is always best to be suspicious of studio press releases. "I was 4F, unfit for military service," says Arthur Wilde, who started at Warner Bros. as a seventeen-year-old laborer in 1936. "So they used to dress me up as a soldier or a sailor and photograph me out on dates with Alexis Smith to show what she was doing for the war effort. The publicity department, we had sixty people, functioned like a big newspaper. We had photo editors, downtown planters, telephone planters, column planters. One man had an absolute in with Walter Winchell, and his job was just to keep Winchell happy." (In the early 1980s, there were still a few old-timers left, old men with raspy voices who telephoned and said, "I want to plant you," before offering artificial tidbits to the wary representatives of a more sophisticated media.) There were usually only two women in those large publicity departments, one to handle the fan magazines and the other to handle fashions. "Until World War II came along, it was almost unthinkable to give a woman the responsibility of really handling a whole campaign," said C. E. ("Teet") Carle, who was the head of publicity at Paramount for years.

By the time the war came, Wilde had moved up to supplying newspapers and magazines with leg art, pictures of starlets dressed in bathing suits or shorts. "National Hardware Week is coming up next? We'd photograph the poor little things with all those hammers and saws," says Wilde. "Once, on a hot day, I took Joan Leslie, who was a sixteen-year-old girl, and filled up an old bathtub with ice cubes and photographed her in a bathing suit washing herself in ice cubes. Promoting the war effort was no different. I remember taking the young contract people to the bomb shelter and having them photographed for the press."

The name of the game was publicity. And if the war could be used to get a little extra publicity for a Warner movie, the film was, at the same time, getting a little extra publicity for the war. Warners made *Action in the North Atlantic,* Bogart's fourth movie of 1942, as a salute to the Merchant Marine. Says Wilde, "Then we promoted the public donating old furs to make vests for the Merchant Marin- ers in the North Atlantic. We asked the actors to model the stuff. The whole male and female contract list was expected to perform for the war effort."

The first publicity on *Casablanca* was planted in the *Hollywood Reporter* on January 5, 1942: "Ann Sheridan and Ronald Reagan

Nazi meets nurse on the Warner Bros. lot.

co-star for the third time in Warners' *Casablanca,* with Dennis Morgan also coming in for top billing. Yarn of war refugees in French Morocco is based on an unproduced play by Murray Burnett and Joan Alison." Two days later, the same false item was sent to dozens of newspapers as part of the studio's weekly "Hollywood News."

The studios sent out false items all the time, and the false publicity about Ronald Reagan's starring in *Casablanca* was little different from the false publicity about a star taking a lovely bath by candlelight during the first blackout of the war. "Today the press agents do the same thing," says Jack Brodsky, a producer who started as a publicist. As director of advertising and publicity for *Cleopatra* in 1963, Brodsky made up an extremely successful fiction designed to associate the names of the stars with the film. "We said the billing for Rex Harrison and Richard Burton—whose name would come first—would depend on which actor got a knighthood first," Brodsky says. *"Time* magazine printed that as fact."

There was never any chance that Ronald Reagan could star in *Casablanca.* Reagan was a second lieutenant in the U.S. Cavalry Reserve, and the studio had been writing deferment letters for him since September 1941. In November, he had been deferred because of poor eyesight, but, with the war on, the studio knew that there was no possibility of another deferment. Warners had already cast Reagan in *Desperate Journey,* which would begin production on February 2, and the studio was barely able to keep the actor long enough to finish that movie in April. Yet on March 23 the *Hollywood Reporter* published a studio handout that Warners was preparing a script called *Buffalo Bill,* which would star Ronald Reagan in the title role.

Today, nearly every actor has a private press agent, and a studio is solely interested in publicizing its movies, since the stars will be working at a different studio the next month. In 1942, the Warner Bros. publicity department tried to keep the names of its contract actors—valuable studio property—constantly in public view. Ann Sheridan and Ronald Reagan were probably teamed in the *Casablanca* press release because they had just made two movies together, *Kings Row* and *Juke Girl,* and *Kings Row* was now going into release. A successful team was always worth a few extra dollars at the box office. A few weeks earlier, the studio had planted an item in the Los Angeles *Times* that Ann Sheridan and Dennis Morgan would be starring in *Aloha Means Goodbye,* a combination romance–Japanese spy story. That movie never even got made. A few days after Warners announced the casting for *Casablanca,* the studio sent out another bulletin, this time saying that Reagan, Sheridan, Morgan, and George Tobias would star in *Shadow of Their Wings* instead of *Casablanca.* Sheridan and Morgan did co-star in that film, renamed *Wings for the Eagle,* about aircraft factory workers.

During January, casting *Casablanca* was far from Hal Wallis's mind. *Casablanca* would be the third of his independent movies to go into production, and Wallis's chief focus in January was his first movie, *Desperate Journey.* He was, however, concerned with choosing a director for *Casablanca,* and on January 5 he had his secretary send copies of the play and identical notes to Mike Curtiz, Vincent Sherman, and William Keighley: "Mr. Wallis will appreciate your

reading the attached play CASABLANCA, which we recently purchased. Please let him know what you think of it as soon as possible.
Thanks."

As soon as he read the play, Vincent Sherman told Wallis that
he wanted to direct *Casablanca.* "I thought it was great movie junk,"
Sherman says, "marvelous movie junk. I don't know who's most
responsible for the script, but I thought all the ingredients were
inherent in the material."

Sherman, who had come to Warner Bros. in 1937 on a contract
that allowed the studio to use him as a writer, director, actor, or
supervisor, remembers running upstairs to tell the story to the
Epsteins, who had written his 1940 movie *Saturday's Children.* If he
did—and Julie Epstein does not remember being introduced to
Casablanca by Sherman—nothing came of it for Sherman, who was
assigned to direct the next Ida Lupino movie, *The Hard Way.* When
Sherman found out that Curtiz had been given *Casablanca,* he was
disappointed but "I couldn't get sore," he says. "Because Mike was
a marvelous director. I used to watch Mike's pictures to learn how
to direct. He would shoot each picture in relation to the kind of story
it was. If you look at *Captain Blood* and *Robin Hood,* he was a great
action director. He could do other kinds of pictures too if you gave
him a halfway decent script. If you gave Mike a decent script, he
would do a good job of staging it. His whole life was his pictures.
I never heard of Mike having any personal or social relationships
outside that mattered."

Despite their friendship, Wallis didn't decide on Curtiz right
away. His first choice was William Wyler. Early in February he sent
the play to Wyler, who was vacationing in Sun Valley, Idaho, after
finishing *Mrs. Miniver.* What Wyler thought of it is not recorded,
only the fact that Wyler and Darryl Zanuck played gin rummy until
2:30 every morning. Wyler may never have bothered to read the
play. He had already applied for a commission in the Signal Corps.
By the time *Casablanca* went into production, Wyler had gone to
Washington and was doing research on *The Negro Soldier* for Major
Frank Capra. So Wallis turned, as he often did, to Curtiz.

Film critic Andrew Sarris has called *Casablanca* "the happiest of
happy accidents, and the most decisive exception to the *auteur*
theory." But nearly every Warner Bros. picture was an exception to
the *auteur* theory. A contract director might have a consistent style
or even a consistent point of view. Curtiz signed each film in the

1930s with coherent and exciting action within a scene that masked the fact that the heavy cameras could move only slowly and ponderously. And, if something worked in one film, it might pop up in a director's other films. "If something worked, Mike wanted to repeat it," says Julius Epstein of Curtiz. "We had a very successful birthday scene in *Four Daughters,* so Mike wanted a birthday scene in every picture we wrote. For one picture—I forget the name of it—we said, 'Forget it. It doesn't belong.' We went to the preview, and there was the birthday scene."

In the studio system, however, ultimate control lay beyond the director. With the exception of Columbia during the years when the studio was so poor that it had to gamble on giving control to creative directors, the studio system was run by executives and producers. At M-G-M, directors were not even allowed to use the executives' elevator in the administration building. Because of his relationship with Wallis and his status as a moneymaker, Curtiz, who was earning $3,600 a week in February 1942, had more power than most studio directors, but he was still assigned his stars and many of his supporting players. He could pick some members of his crew, but he could rarely choose his cinematographer and film editor, and on *Casablanca* he was assigned a sound editor, Francis Scheid, whom he disliked. The two men would be shouting at each other before the first day of shooting was over.

Curtiz asked for George Amy as his cutter on *Casablanca* and was assigned Owen Marks. Whoever had just finished a movie and already used up his twelve weeks of layoff went to the top of an assignment list kept by T. C. ("Tenny") Wright, the studio manager. On April 4, 1942, Wallis sent a memo to Wright asking him to assign a first or second assistant director to Curtiz, since the active preparation of *Casablanca* had begun.

"I would never pick someone for such a key job without the approval of the director," says today's producer, Dan Melnick. "I would come up with a short list acceptable to me and let the director pick."

Curtiz could ask, wheedle, or complain, but he could not demand. As Tenny Wright told Carl Weyl, *Casablanca*'s art director, on May 14, "You will talk sets and everything else about the picture to Mike Curtiz; from there you will go over to Mr. Wallis and get approval or disapproval." Nor did Curtiz have control over the screenwriters. Most of the writers on *Casablanca,* Curtiz's sixty-first

Warner Bros. movie, were chosen by Hal Wallis weeks before he picked Curtiz as the film's director. After he finished *Yankee Doodle Dandy,* Curtiz worked with the Epsteins, who had done four other movies with him,* but even after fifteen years at Warner Bros. the English language was not Curtiz's strong suit. Wallis had the final say on the script. Yet, within the checks and balances of the studio system, Wallis's control over the movie was not complete either. Tenny Wright, with Warner's approval, had the final say on assigning craftsmen. And Wright refused to take cameraman James Wong Howe off *The Hard Way* and put him on *Casablanca,* even when Wallis demanded that he do so.

Lee Katz has a unique perspective. He was the first assistant director on *Casablanca,* and he was vice president in charge of physical production at United Artists in 1980, when *Heaven's Gate,* the wildly out-of-control movie written and directed by Michael Cimino, wrecked the studio.

"Michael Cimino would not have lasted ten minutes in the studio system," says Katz. "Nor should he have. Cimino was a thoroughly irresponsible man, and the studio system didn't allow that."

Writers and directors alike had to play by the studio's rules of discipline and frugality. At Warner Bros. the rules included the fact that directors directed and writers wrote. John Huston broke that rule with *The Maltese Falcon* in 1941. However much Huston had to do with the scripts of his next two movies, the screenplay credits went to Howard Koch *(In This Our Life)* and Richard Macaulay *(Across the Pacific).* When director Delmer Daves tried to take credit for the screenplay of *Destination Tokyo* in 1943, Jack Warner sent a blistering telegram: "He will be director and that's all the credit he will get. This is one practice I won't stand for." And Warner continually pounced on directors who changed scripts. In a typical 1943 memo, he harangued all his directors and producers about "the continuous re-writing of scenes" on the set, which he saw as a waste of time and money.

The studio was always being combed for waste of time, waste of money. On vacation in Hot Springs, Arkansas, Warner wrote his

* *Little Big Shot* (1935) had a screenplay by Jerry Wald and Julius J. Epstein. *Four Daughters* (1938) credited Julius J. Epstein and Lenore Coffee. *Daughters Courageous* (1939) and *Four Wives* (1939) had screenplays by Julius J. and Philip G. Epstein.

assistant, Steve Trilling, and complained that Trilling used too many words in his telegrams: "A third of the words can be eliminated so in the future please see that any unnecessary words are left out thus reducing the cost of the wires accordingly." (Warner was clever and penurious enough to send his own daily telegrams to the studio collect; they sometimes included messages to be typed up and forwarded to nonstudio acquaintances, including songwriter Cole Porter.)

Rarely did a penny escape the studio's eye. In January 1942, Orry-Kelly, Warners' costume designer, was asked to pay the $1.85 he owed for telephone calls. That same month, R. J. Obringer, head of the legal department, wrote testily to Curtiz that, as he well knew, he owed the studio $26.95 for personal telephone calls. Since he had already been billed several times, would Curtiz please pay immediately. It is impossible to imagine M-G-M hounding a director who was making $3,600 a week for such a small amount of money, but Warner Bros. went after stars and directors alike. Helmut Dantine owed the studio $27.16 for one sports shirt and one T-shirt. Perhaps he had "overlooked" the bill. And Warner instructed the wardrobe department not to make any clothes for an actor's personal use until the actor or actress had signed a written agreement to pay on delivery or authorize the studio to deduct the amount from his or her salary.

Early in the New Deal, Jack Warner had been appointed an official of the NRA (National Recovery Administration) for California. "I have a poster of his, a proclamation, with the Blue Eagle," says Jack Warner, Jr. "Within a few months or so, the Supreme Court heard the case that overturned the NRA. Here we were stuck with all this stationery and letterheads and memo pads. So he had the company chop them up, and for years we used these memos, with the Blue Eagle on the back."

Beginning in the winter of 1941, the war added a layer of patriotism to the studio's parsimony. "The thoughtless waste of one hundred feet of film may cost the life of an American soldier who may be your son or your brother," went a speech delivered by Harry Warner to a group of actors, writers, directors, and cameramen. The "careless waste of material" not only costs dollars but lives and is "worse than the sabotage of enemy agents," Warner said with his usual moral passion. When a take is ruined "because a carelessly suspended microphone casts a shadow across an actor's face or a player rushes into a scene missing cues," the needlessly ruined film stock, and the waste of electricity, manpower, and machinery takes on "tremendous significance."

Jack Warner, too, used the war as a weapon for frugality. "I noticed today that there was a tremendous amount of takes of one scene on your picture," he wrote Peter Lorre on *Passage to Marseille*. "Upon investigation, I find that you did not know your dialogue, after the director had told you on Saturday you were going to have an important scene today. . . . There is a war going on, and we are trying to save film. This one scene used up many unnecessary hundreds of feet of film."

Frequent notices To Our Employees played the same tune.

"A single sheet of paper may seem an unimportant item. If 130,000,000 other Americans thought it unimportant, however, the total daily waste in stationery, copy paper, or wrapping paper would seriously handicap war production," went one. "Do not destroy paper that might be used for notes. Make large envelopes serve their purpose more than once."

Even a light bulb left on unnecessarily or a nail thrown away would lead to disaster. If nails weren't saved, said an editorial in the March 1942 issue of the *Warner Club News,* the studio would be destroyed. "Without them we cannot build sets, without sets it would be almost impossible to make pictures. When we can't make pictures there are no jobs for any of us."

This was the uneasy climate of fear, exhilaration, and the usual movie-industry hyperbole within which *Casablanca* was conceived.

5

Bogart, Bergman, and Henreid: A Date with Fate

In the summer of 1991, Curt Bois barely remembered *Casablanca*. Joy Page found it too painful to remember. Paul Henreid had shuffled the deck of his memories into new and more pleasing shapes. Leonid Kinskey occasionally thought of the accident that brought him to *Casablanca* two weeks after the movie started shooting. Dan Seymour, who had guarded the door to Rick's gambling room so long ago, lingered over his memories the most and enjoyed doing interviews at the Casablanca Restaurant, an imitation Rick's Café in Southern California.

These five—the pickpocket, the young Bulgarian girl, the heroic Victor Laszlo, Sacha the bartender, and Abdul the doorman—were all that remained of the actors who had filled Warner Bros. Stage No. 8, "INTERIOR RICK'S CAFE, main room and gambling room," in 1942. By the spring of 1992, Curt Bois and Paul Henreid had died, and there were only three.

In January of 1942, Warner Bros. had eighty-seven actors and actresses under contract. The studio divided them into nineteen stars and sixty-eight featured players. Although the featured players could hold their own against similar lists at M-G-M and Paramount, the stars could not.

"More stars than there are in heaven," M-G-M once bragged. In 1942, they included Clark Gable, Greer Garson, Mickey Rooney, Robert Taylor, Lana Turner, Judy Garland, Spencer Tracy, Joan Crawford, Katharine Hepburn, and Myrna Loy. Paramount, down from its midthirties peak, owned Claudette Colbert, Veronica Lake, Bing Crosby, Bob Hope, Ray Milland, Fred MacMurray, Dorothy Lamour, Joel McCrea, Paulette Goddard, and Ginger Rogers.

The only true stars at Warner Bros. were Bette Davis, Errol Flynn, James Cagney, and Edward G. Robinson, and Cagney would leave the studio before summer. Of the other fifteen, Ann Sheridan was wasted more often than not. Ida Lupino was given the roles that weren't good enough for Davis. Olivia de Havilland was the girl Errol Flynn always galloped back to, but she would become a major star on her own only after she sued Warner Bros., won a landmark case that limited movie contracts to seven years, and departed for Paramount in 1945. Geraldine Fitzgerald, Priscilla Lane, Joan Leslie, Brenda Marshall, George Brent, Jeffrey Lynn, Dennis Morgan, Wayne Morris, and Ronald Reagan were all serviceable actors in the right story and with the right costar. John Garfield was definitely on the way up, George Raft on the way down. And Humphrey Bogart was indefinable.

After 11 years and 42 films, Bogart, at the age of 42, had become a star three months earlier with *The Maltese Falcon*. Even if Bogart's stardom is dated from his portrayal of the doomed gangster Roy Earle in *High Sierra* in January 1941, it took him 10 years and 40 movies. Few major stars ever spent as long getting to the top. Cagney was a star in *Public Enemy* seven months and five movies after his debut in *Sinner's Holiday*. Clark Gable lit up screens in *A Free Soul* six movies and less than a year after he had his first speaking role as the villain in a western. Tyrone Power did four movies before *Lloyds of London*. *The Magnificent Obsession* was Robert Taylor's ninth film. Although Spencer Tracy had to endure five years of tough-guy roles at Fox, he had the weight of a star within months after he moved to Metro. Because of the war, Van Johnson had it easiest of all. One of the sixty-eight featured players on that 1942 Warner Bros. roster, he became a Metro-Goldwyn-Mayer treasure, the boy next door who was luckily 4F, before the year was out.

"Metro sprinkled stardust on you nicely," says Bill Orr, who as William T. Orr was the fourteenth name down in the third column of Warner featured players. "If you were an actor you didn't want to be anyplace else."

Katharine Hepburn has described M-G-M as "like a marvelous school from which you never graduated," a paternalistic kingdom where any trouble was tidied up by the publicity department and actors were not forced to make movies they didn't want to make.

Says Geraldine Fitzgerald, who spent seven years fighting with Jack Warner about movies she didn't want to make, "If you belonged to M-G-M, you were the crème de la crème. And Paramount wasn't too bad. And 20th Century–Fox wasn't too bad. But when you were at a party and said you belonged to Warners, people always tried to console you."

There are hundreds of examples, but one sums it up. The other studios sent hairdressers and makeup men to the stars' private dressing rooms. At Warners, bit players and stars alike came to the makeup department. "As far as organization of production was concerned, it was much better because there was no waste of time," said Jean Burt, who became a hairdresser at Warner Bros. in 1941 and did Ingrid Bergman's hair on *Casablanca*. "In a star's dressing room, they can do no one else but the star." Stars who came to Warners on loanout usually agreed to the system. Even Greer Garson, the queen of M-G-M, acquiesced. Only Joan Crawford refused.

Warners sprinkled sand rather than stardust. Bogart writhed and crawled and sweated as the crooked lawyer, ex-con, bootlegger, or racketeer who was killed, usually before the last reel, by Edward G. Robinson, James Cagney, or once, Errol Flynn. If the star didn't get him, a hail of police bullets did. Occasionally and with disturbing force—as Duke Mantee in *The Petrified Forest,* Baby Face Martin in *Dead End,* and Mad Dog Earle in *High Sierra*—he was the deadeyed killer at the top of the chain, the lonely anti-hero a decade before the concept was invented. Fifteen years after Bogart's death, his friend Nunnally Johnson reread Robert Sherwood's play *The Petrified Forest* and decided that the Bogie persona was actually created by Sherwood and that Bogart wore the mantle of Duke Mantee "consciously or unconsciously" ever after. Certainly Bogart's appearance on Broadway in 1935 as the brooding killer changed his future. Afterward, professionally at least, there was no trace of the young stage actor who had played a series of charming wastrels and country-club juveniles (although he never said, "Tennis, anyone?," a line that has been attributed to him).

Bogart was born in New York, at the turn of the century, into a genteel world that had more tennis than gangsters. His father, Belmont DeForest Bogart, was a doctor with inherited money and a Riverside Drive practice. His mother, Maud Humphrey, was a successful illustrator and commercial artist. The watercolor *Maud Humphrey Baby* was one of the most famous and often-used magazine illustrations during the first decade of the twentieth century. In a 1949 magazine article, Maud Humphrey's son would say that he had never really loved his mother, that he admired her but that "she was totally incapable of showing affection," even to her three children.

Educated at Trinity School, Bogart suffered through one extra year at Phillips Andover Academy in Massachusetts, which was intended to prepare him to enter Yale. He left Andover early and enlisted in the Navy, serving for the rest of World War I on the troop ship *Leviathan*. He had learned to sail on Canandaigua Lake, where his family had a summer house, and for the rest of his life the sea would represent a freedom that was not available to him on land. "He felt about the sea the way Hemingway felt about the sea," says Lauren Bacall. "When we read *The Old Man and the Sea*, Bogie would hand me those passages and say, 'This is the way I feel.' He thought the sea was pure. He thought it was one of the last few free places on earth."

When Bogart was discharged and had to get a job, he drifted into acting after working as a stage manager for a producer who was a neighbor of the Bogarts. Between 1930 and 1934 Bogart failed to make an impression in ten movies at four studios. Then he returned to the stage and was cast in *The Petrified Forest*. The myth—and in this case the myth is true—is that Leslie Howard, the star of *The Petrified Forest*, refused to make the movie unless Warner Bros. hired Bogart to re-create his role of Duke Mantee. As soon as the movie was finished and seven weeks before it was released in February 1936, the studio signed him to a seven-year contract, starting at $550 a week. He made five movies in 1936, seven in 1937, six in 1938, seven again in 1939. He didn't die or go to prison in all of them; there were a few comedies and one hillbilly farce, *Swing Your Lady*. He was also the crusading district attorney opposite Bette Davis in *Marked Woman* and a vampire in *The Return of Dr. X*.

Much has been made of the fact that Bogart won his role in *High Sierra* because Paul Muni refused the part and in *The Maltese Falcon* because George Raft turned it down. (Raft felt it was beneath him to perform for John Huston, a first-time director.) But Warner stars were always turning roles down. Claude Rains won the lead in *Mr. Skeffington* because Paul Henreid refused to play the part. In the 1940s Dennis Morgan would inherit two movies that Bogart refused, *Bad Men of Missouri* and *God Is My Co-Pilot*.

Morgan, who says he was happy to take "any script that was fairly good," is still pleased that Bogart turned down those roles. "*Bad Men of Missouri* wasn't a bad picture," says Morgan. "I still like it. And *God Is My Co-Pilot* was very well received."

By 1942, Bogart had already played, without protest, more than one part Raft had rejected, including the sympathetic gangster in *It All Came True*. Nor was Bogart accidentally assigned to *High Sierra*. He campaigned for the role. "You told me once to let you know when I found a part I wanted," he wrote to Hal Wallis.

Even before he made *High Sierra* in 1940, Bogart was beginning to be considered a valuable property by Warner Bros. Two years after Bogart arrived at the studio, his contract was torn up and replaced by one that almost doubled his salary. More importantly, starting in the fall of 1939, other studios begged to borrow him. Universal wanted him for a picture starring Mae West and W. C. Fields. Fox asked for him to star in *The Valiant*. Walter Wanger wanted him for *House Across the Bay,* M-G-M for "a very important part in the Eddie Robinson picture." By 1941, Warner Bros. was getting, and turning down, a request every few weeks.

"I remember," says film critic Pauline Kael, "my friends and I talked about when are the executives going to discover this guy. It was early in his career, when he appeared in horror movies and all sorts of stuff that Warners threw at him. We liked him years before he got the leading roles. He was small, but he knew how to use every part of himself. By the late thirties, he was quite in charge of everything in his performance. He had a tension, like a coiled spring. You didn't want to take your eyes off him."

In *The Maltese Falcon,* as Dashiell Hammett's detective Sam Spade, Bogart carried to the right side of the law the wary watchfulness, the cynicism, and the ambiguities that had infused his deadliest killers. "I think it was his very best performance," says Kael, who was twenty years old in 1941 when she saw the movie for the first time. "Because you got a sense of the ambivalences in the man, and he used all the tensions marvelously physically. I don't think he could have been as good as he was in *Casablanca* if he hadn't done the *Falcon* first, because he really discovered his powers in the *Falcon*. He created more tension in his scenes than he ever had before. And I think afterwards he drew on the qualities he had discovered in himself in the *Falcon*. So I think it was Huston who brought those things out. And Curtiz benefited from them."

Even before *The Maltese Falcon,* Bogart knew that his status had changed. Reading through his contract files, one is struck by the diffidence with which Bogart tried to turn down roles before *High Sierra* and the truculence with which he refused assignments afterward. Would Warner Bros. be very disturbed if Bogart didn't do the role in *Brother Orchid*? his agent asked in March 1940. When the studio threatened to withdraw the approval it had given Bogart to appear on two radio programs, the actor meekly agreed to play the racketeer. In March 1941, Bogart didn't give in. He returned the script of *Bad Men of Missouri* with a note that read: "Are you kidding—this is certainly rubbing it in—since Lupino and Raft are casting pictures maybe I can. . . . Regards, Bogie."

A few years earlier, Bogart had described to Geraldine Fitzgerald his philosophy as a Warner Bros. contract player. The young Irish actress, fresh from the Gate Theatre in Dublin, was offended by inferior scripts and kept turning down the parts Warners offered. "Bogart had formulated his philosophy while he was working in all those B pictures," says Fitzgerald. "He told me, 'Don't try to choose what you do because they won't let you. Say yes to everything. And eventually you'll have a body of work and you can then have a little bit of power and you can get what you want.' I didn't listen and I spent most of my seven years at Warner Bros. on suspension."

Both Lee Katz and Dennis Morgan saw Bogart's philosophy in action when, as an executed murderer, he returned from the dead in one of his worst movies, *The Return of Dr. X.* "It was a very bad script," says Dennis Morgan, who costarred in the 1939 film, "and they put a white streak down his head so he looked like a skunk. He laughed about that as much as the rest of us did. He wasn't sulky. His attitude was, 'Come on, let's get through this thing.' " Lee Katz, who wrote *The Return of Dr. X* and nearly a dozen other B movies at Warner Bros. in the late thirties, feels "particularly guilty" about that movie. "Jack Warner was p.o.'ed at Bogie for something or other," says Katz, "and he forced him to take this role as the mad doctor. And Bogart did it with as good grace as he could have done."

The arc of Bogart's career at Warner Bros. can be seen in how and when he chose to fight Warner—and with what success. Bogart was suspended for refusing to play the part of the outlaw Cole Younger in *Bad Men of Missouri.* (That skirmish was just a warm-up for battles in 1943 over *Conflict* and in 1944 over *God Is My Co-Pilot.*) His suspension ended in June 1941, when George Raft, whose career decisions at Warners were unerringly wrong, refused *The Maltese Falcon* because "it is not an important picture." And what would have happened if Raft had agreed to play Sam Spade?

The odds are high that Bogart would have made a breakthrough in some other movie. The disillusionment, stoicism, and weary aloofness that he brought to the screen fit the heroes of a new kind of movie melodrama, *film noir,* too well to have gone unnoticed. If he hadn't been working in *The Maltese Falcon* at the time, Warner Bros. might have agreed to a request from Paramount in August 1941 to borrow Humphrey Bogart to play opposite Veronica Lake in *This Gun for Hire.* That was the movie that made a star out of Alan Ladd.

Warner Bros. could overuse and misuse its actors. It could dump Van Johnson and Susan Peters in 1942 and let M-G-M build their careers. But the studio would not have remained in business if it had missed the obvious. *The Maltese Falcon* had been immensely profitable, and George Raft was becoming more difficult with every role he was offered. In January 1942, Bogart demanded $3,000 a week and the right to do ten guest radio appearances a year. He was given a new contract, starting at $2,750 a week. After six years at Warners, Bogart finally had a star's contract. Warner Bros. was stuck with him for seven years, and the studio began to look for a role that would turn him into a romantic lead.

On February 14, Wallis sent a memo to Steve Trilling: "Will you please figure on Humphrey Bogart and Ann Sheridan for *Casablanca,* which is scheduled to start the latter part of April." Six weeks later, Jack Warner wrote Wallis that George Raft was lobbying him for the role. Wallis held firm and *Casablanca* had the first of its three stars.

If it was easy to find Rick Blaine—and no one except Bogart was seriously considered by Wallis for the part—Ilsa Lund was another matter. Ann Sheridan may seem a puzzling choice for Ilsa, but in February Ilsa was still Lois Meredith, and Sheridan, who had a rough, wrong-side-of-the-tracks glamour, was the Warner star best suited to the part. The first rule at Warners was to squeeze one of the studio's contract players into the starring role, even if the part didn't quite fit. "They didn't believe that an actor should be idle for one minute," says Geraldine Fitzgerald. In turning down one of his producers who asked to borrow Shirley Temple from David O. Selznick in 1943, Jack Warner thundered, "We will not make stars for any other studio." He would agree to borrow Temple, he said, only if Selznick would let him have her for one picture each year.

In the end, Warner borrowed Ingrid Bergman from Selznick for

OFFICE OF
J. L. WARNER

To __MR. HAL WALLIS__   April 2, 1942
Confidential Correspondence

      What do you think of using

Raft in "CASABLANCA"?

      He knows we are going to

make this and is starting a campaign

for it.

              JACK

Casablanca, but that was a trade: Bergman for Olivia de Havilland. The studios were always trading their property. As part of the arrangement that brought William Wyler to Warner Bros. to direct *Jezebel,* Warner agreed to loan Humphrey Bogart to Samuel Goldwyn for *Dead End.* The position of the actor was made clear by the terminology. Bergman always described Selznick as selling her to other producers. Warner wrote about "the rental of Humphrey Bogart" to Goldwyn. Although he often did it, Warner hated to loan out his stars, particularly to more nurturing studios. Says Bill Orr, "Jack said they would come back spoiled." Renting another studio's star was always an option, but rarely the best option. As Warner put it in one of the telegrams he sent daily when he was in New York or at Saratoga for the horse racing, "See what you can do getting Dana Andrews unless we can make one our own young men a Dana Andrews. Maybe Bill Kennedy. Bill Kennedy is helluva good actor and we can make our own stars. This only way to stay in business."

One week after deciding on Ann Sheridan, Hal Wallis was negotiating for Hedy Lamarr, proof that by mid-February Wallis was exploring the idea of turning Lois into Ilsa. Louis B. Mayer, who was as stingy with his actors as Warner was, refused to loan Lamarr to Wallis.*

Once Wallis had decided on a European heroine, Ingrid Bergman was an obvious choice. At twenty-six, the Swedish actress had had a charmed career but a difficult life. Her mother died when she was three, her father when she was twelve; and the aunt who took care of her after her father's death died six months later. So shy and awkward in school that her lips and eyelids were swollen by a nervous allergy, she had no inhibitions on stage. Accepted at Stockholm's Royal Dramatic Theater School, she left after a year when she was offered a film contract. She was a star eighteen months later, at the age of twenty. After seeing her in the 1936 Swedish film *Intermezzo,* Selznick brought her to America to star in his 1939 English-language version. From that moment on it was almost as though she had hypnotized the critics. "Radiant" was one of the words that appeared in every review. "Natural" was another. As a difficult-to-please critic, novelist Graham Greene, put it, Bergman's performance in *Intermezzo: A Love Story* "doesn't give the effect of acting at all but of living." Of the response to her performance in *Casablanca,* Bergman wrote in her diary, "I was praised (as usual, I'm tempted to say) for my playing." What snared the critics over and over again is best expressed by actress Fay Wray, who worked with Bergman in the 1941 movie *Adam Had Four Sons:* "Ingrid had a quality that was spiritual and physical at the same time. She seemed not an actress. She seemed very real, not like she was performing at all."

The irony is that Bergman could not bear real life. "Having a home, husband, and child ought to be enough for any woman's life," she wrote to her friend and dialogue coach Ruth Roberts in January 1942. "I mean, that's what we are meant for, isn't it? But still I think every day is a lost day. As if only half of me is alive. The other half is pressed down in a bag and suffocated." Bergman, who had married the first man she ever had a real date with, was in agony when she wasn't working. When Selznick had no role for her after *Intermezzo,* she insisted he allow her to do a play. Selznick was terrified that a failure on Broadway would detract from Bergman's salability as a film star, but the drama critics were captivated, and

---

*Hedy Lamarr got her chance to play Ilsa in January 1944 on a popular radio show based on movie scripts, *Lux Radio Theater,* when both Bogart and Bergman were overseas entertaining the troops. Alan Ladd played Rick.

Liliom was as much a triumph for her as *Intermezzo.* In 1940–41 she made three movies in a row. Against Selznick's advice, she played a governess in Columbia's *Adam Had Four Sons* just to have something to do. She finished "Adam" at 3 A.M. and started M-G-M's *Rage in Heaven,* as the wife of the suicidal paranoid Robert Montgomery, seven hours later. Then she insisted on trading roles with Lana Turner and playing the bad girl, the barmaid, opposite Spencer Tracy in M-G-M's *Dr. Jekyll and Mr. Hyde.* When it came to acting, she was fearless, taking chances that frightened and puzzled those who saw her as a commodity. One of her chief memories of *Casablanca* was of Michael Curtiz warning her that she was ruining her career. She must, he said, simply be Ingrid Bergman and play the same role all the time. That was what Hollywood required.

"Success," she wrote in her acting diary after *Dr. Jekyll and Mr. Hyde* reached theaters in the summer of 1941. New York had laughed at the movie, she said, but audiences came. She had been praised. Yet, she added, "I wasn't even nominated for the Academy Awards. . . . Now I never want to hear the words Academy Award until I have the prize in my hand."

For Whom the Bell Tolls would bring Bergman her first Academy nomination. She would win the next year, 1944, as the wife whose

From left, Michael Curtiz, Ingrid Bergman, Hal Wallis. Curtiz treated Bergman with European courtesy.

husband tries to drive her mad in *Gaslight*. She would win again in 1956 for *Anastasia,* as a sort of "Welcome Home, All Is Forgiven" present and "We'll overlook the child you bore Roberto Rossellini while you were still married to another man." She won once more, as supporting actress for her cameo in *Murder on the Orient Express* in 1974, but this time she was displeased. She wanted prizes not to prove she was the best but because she knew she was best. In 1974 Bergman felt the best supporting performance had been given by Valentina Cortese in *Day for Night,* and, when she accepted her Oscar, she made her feelings clear to the television audience.

Bergman was elated in August 1941. In a little over six months, she had appeared in three movies. But as summer turned to fall, fall to winter, and 1941 to 1942, she wondered if she would ever work again. She wrote despairing letters to Ruth Roberts from Rochester, New York, where her husband Petter Lindstrom, who had been a dentist in Sweden, was preparing to become a neurosurgeon. "I am so fed up with Rochester and Main Street I am ready to cry," she wrote. She said she could not find the energy to talk to her three-year-old daughter Pia or take her to the park. She said that she hated David Selznick.

While the twenty-six-year-old Bergman waited for Selznick to find a movie that would not ruin his "marvelous property," Hal Wallis tried to cast Ilsa. He saw Edwige Feuillere in the French movie *Sarajevo* and thought she "would be ideal" if she "can speak any English at all." He debated not testing Michele Morgan because of her $55,000 asking price but went ahead with the test on April 9. By that time, he was already negotiating for Bergman with Dan O'Shea, Selznick's second-in-command. If one actress did not work out, perhaps the other would.

The sparring that would end with Bergman's starring in *Casablanca* began on April 1 when Wallis telephoned Selznick and suggested that he send the Epstein twins to tell Selznick the plot of the film. Wallis always thought that he convinced a reluctant Selznick to part with Bergman. In his 1980 autobiography, *Starmaker,* he tells a story of pursuing Selznick to New York because, "Knowing that I wanted and needed Bergman, Selznick avoided me and failed to return my phone calls." Julius Epstein remembers it differently: "Wallis said to us, 'Go to Selznick and tell him the story.' We said, 'What story?' He said, 'Wing it.' So my brother and I went to Selznick. He was having his lunch at his desk and he was slurping

```
FORM fo
                        WARNER BROS. PICTURES, INC.
                           BURBANK, CALIFORNIA

                    INTER-OFFICE COMMUNICATION

TO MR.____CURTIZ_____     DATE___March 31, 1942_____

FROM MR.___WALLIS_____     SUBJECT___"CASABLANCA"_____


        Dear Mike:

        I just learned that MICHELE MORGAN's salary is $55,000 for
        the picture.  Apparently she has one of those contracts at
        RKO for a number of pictures and she is permitted one or
        two outside pictures, and Feldman and Blum, of course, get
        as much money as possible on these outside pictures.  This,
        of course, does not mean that we have to pay this price
        and I am seriously questioning whether we should make this
        test, because there is no reason in the world for demanding
        this kind of money for anyone as little known as Michele
        Morgan, or who has done as little in pictures as she has.

        Talk to me about this before you make any further plans
        for the test.

                                        HAL WALLIS

           VERBAL MESSAGES CAUSE MISUNDERSTANDING AND DELAYS
                    (PLEASE PUT THEM IN WRITING)



FORM 10

                        WARNER BROS P·---
```

his soup. He never looked up. I said, 'There are refugees and transit visas and intrigue,' and I suddenly realize I've talked about twenty minutes and Bergman isn't even in the story. So I said, 'Oh, it's going to be a lot of shit like *Algiers*. And Selznick looked up and nodded to me that we had Bergman.'"

In reality, Selznick was desperate to find a movie for Bergman. Two weeks earlier he had sent a confidential memo to Dan O'Shea. Given the state of the war in Europe, Selznick wrote, there was a good chance that Sweden would be forced to join the Axis. "If this should be true Ingrid may be in something of a spot . . . there may be some fear on the part of some producers in using her, which makes all the more important our bearing down on getting a picture for her immediately."

It wasn't only that Bergman was Swedish. Her mother had been German. Bergman, who spoke German, had made the mistake of making a movie in Germany in 1938. In her autobiography, *Ingrid Bergman: My Story,* she tells of being taken to a Nazi rally and refusing to Heil Hitler. In a tougher biography, *As Time Goes By,* by Laurence Leamer, her ex-husband Petter Lindstrom says that she was taken to a Nazi rally in Hamburg and felt that Goebbels gave a "fantastic speech." Says Leamer: "In Germany as in later years, she was supremely indifferent to the political world around her." Even after Germany invaded Poland, Bergman had turned down one movie, *So Ends Our Night,* based on an Erich Maria Remarque novel, as too anti-German. Now, with America in the war, she was vulnerable. In an odd coincidence, Paul Henreid would reluctantly agree to do *Casablanca* because his Austrian citizenship made him vulnerable.

In *Starmaker,* Wallis dismissed Selznick as "an agent at heart, endlessly putting people he seldom used under long-term contracts and then farming them out at inflated prices." It was an unfair assessment of a major producer by one of his chief rivals. However, in the early 1940s, "David became virtually the agent for his stars," says film historian David Thomson, author of a 1992 biography, *Showman: The Life of David O. Selznick.* "Even Selznick's wife, Irene, said David had turned into a flesh peddler." Selznick could make money without making movies. When a studio loaned out an actor or actress it had under contract, the studio asked for more than it paid the actor and pocketed the extra money. During the seven years Bergman was under contract to Selznick, she made eleven movies, but only two of the pictures—*Intermezzo* and *Spellbound*—were for Selznick.

Between January and April, 1942, twelve possible films for Bergman were suggested by the Selznick staff or offered by other studios. Selznick put *Gaslight* on the list. But Selznick was too distracted by his business affairs to make movies himself, and he was handicapped by two psychological factors. He had been traumatized by the unduplicable success of *Gone With the Wind* in 1939, followed by another best-picture Oscar for *Rebecca* in 1940. And, even though he was overweight, nearsighted, and flat-footed, he was trying, unsuccessfully, for some important position in the armed forces. Selznick made no movies between *Rebecca* and *Since You Went Away* in 1944, so Bergman was available for *Casablanca,* the last of the suggested movies on that list. But Selznick didn't simply hand Bergman over to Warner Bros. He meddled in the photography and costuming of *Casablanca* to protect his star.

That Selznick was eager to get a movie for Bergman didn't make the mating dance with Warner Bros. any less ritualistic. Wallis "seems very eager," an underling reported on April 4. On April 6,

Wallis was still pursuing. "I think we should strike while the iron is hot," Selznick told O'Shea. And he told O'Shea to ask for top billing over Bogart.

Selznick was in the East from April 9 until late in the month. It is possible that Wallis pursued him to the Hotel Carlyle, although Selznick's datebooks show no evidence of it. Selznick may have enjoyed making Wallis beg. "That was a time when Selznick was very arrogant, cock of the walk," says Thomson. "He would have been aggressive, indifferent, tough and lordly to Wallis." In any case, the even swap of Bergman for Olivia de Havilland was made during the third week in April. Selznick would give Warners eight weeks of Bergman's time. In return, Warners would give David O. Selznick Productions eight weeks of de Havilland's time.* Each studio protected its own. Selznick refused a contract that would allow Warners to make a second movie with Bergman.† And Warners was not foolish enough to give someone else's star top billing.

It was Kay Brown, Selznick's New York story editor, who broke the news to Bergman on April 21. Brown reported to O'Shea that the actress was "so fed up with Rochester" that she wanted to leave the city immediately. Bergman's letter to Ruth Roberts described a greater passion at the news that she was going to work again. "I was warm and cold at the same time," she wrote. "Then I got such chills I thought I must go to bed and of course a terrific headache into the bargain. . . . I tried to get drunk for celebration at dinner, but I could not. I tried to cry. I tried to laugh, but I could do nothing. I went to bed three times and went down again because Petter couldn't sleep either with me kicking around in bed. But now it is morning and I am calmed down. The picture is called *Casablanca* and I really don't know what it's all about."

Wallis's choice for the third starring role in *Casablanca* was Philip Dorn. A year earlier, the Dutch actor had played the leader of Germany's anti-Nazi movement in *Underground* for Warner Bros. But Dorn was scheduled to start *Random Harvest* for M-G-M, and the timing of the two movies conflicted. In mid-April Wallis tested

---

* Selznick never used Olivia de Havilland but loaned her to RKO for *Government Girl* instead.

† Although Bergman later made *Saratoga Trunk* for Warners, it was under a separate contract and as a show of Selznick's gratitude to Wallis for the way *Casablanca* had enhanced Bergman's career.

```
FORM 10                    WARNER BROS. PICTURES, INC.
                              BURBANK, CALIFORNIA

                      INTER-OFFICE COMMUNICATION

TO MR.___WALLIS_____        DATE_____April 14, 1942_____

FROM MR.___TRILLING_____    SUBJECT___INGRID BERGMAN - CASABLANCA

    6:30 P.M. --

    DAN O'SHEA called after just speaking to David O. in Pittsburgh -- and
    the only deal they can effect on INGRID BERGMAN is an even swap for
    OLIVIA DE HAVILLAND.

    He refused to give us Bergman for two pictures but promised an
    "understanding" that should they make any outside deal -- except for
    "FOR WHOM THE BELLS TOLL" which has been pending for some time -- Warner
    Bros. would be given first consideration (which really means nothing
    but a courtesy)

    They will give us 8 weeks time on Bergman and we in turn are to give
    them 8 weeks on De Havilland on a 30 days advance notice --: services
    to be completed within the year commencing May 15, 1942. I promised
    to advise tomorrow around noon, so will you kindly give me your reaction.

                                                      STEVE TRILLING

    C.C. J.L. Warner
                  VERBAL MESSAGES CAUSE MISUNDERSTANDING AND DELAYS
                           (PLEASE PUT THEM IN WRITING)
```

Jean-Pierre Aumont, even though he was sure that the French war hero—Aumont had won the Croix de Guerre while fighting with the Free French—was too young for the role of the heroic Resistance leader. That the part of Victor Laszlo was considered inferior to the other two roles is apparent from the actors who were considered by Wallis and Curtiz. Aumont was unknown to American audiences. Carl Esmond had had sixteenth billing in *Sergeant York.* Joseph Cotten was new to the movies, although he had made a stunning debut in *Citizen Kane.* Dean Jagger, Ian Hunter, and Herbert Marshall almost defined the words "second lead."

Hunter and Marshall had English accents, a poor second-best to the continental accents of Dorn and Paul Henreid. But Dorn was beyond reach, and Wallis was sure that Henreid, his second choice, would not play the part once he read the script.

"I saw the script, and I turned it down," said Henreid in 1991. "I thought it was a ridiculous fairy tale."

Henreid was only a year older than Aumont, but at thirty-four he had a regal stolidity that the Frenchman lacked. Paul von Hernried was born into the Austrian aristocracy; his father had been knighted by Emperor Franz Josef I. Even after RKO changed his name to Henreid for *Joan of Paris* in 1941, von Hernried kept an aristocratic self-esteem that rubbed against Hollywood informality. Ingrid Bergman wrote in her acting diary that "Bogart was straightforward and devoid of prima donna behavior, something that cannot be said about Henreid." During the negotiations for *Casablanca,* Trilling called him "a bit of a ham" in his insistence on important roles and suggested that Henreid might be enticed to take the part if his ego was massaged by costar billing with Bogart and Bergman.

Fifty years later, Henreid had a courtly manner, a trace of German syntax and a bitterness about *Casablanca* that seeped into the conversation. "Mr. Bogie was nobody," he said a few months before his death. "Before *Casablanca* he was nobody. He was the fellow Robinson or Cagney would say, 'Get him.' Bogart was a mediocre actor. He was so sorry for himself in *Casablanca.* Unfortunately, Michael Curtiz was not a director of actors; he was a director of effects. He was first rate at that, but he could not tell Bogart he should not play like a crybaby. It was embarrassing, I thought, when I looked at the rushes."

Henreid said that St. Martin's Press deleted his negative comments about Bogart from his 1984 autobiography, *Ladies Man.* He winced as he said the title. "If you were to write a book about me and call it *A Ladies Man* it is all right," he said. "But for me to write a book about myself and call it *Ladies Man* is not right." Even though Henreid once shocked Viennese society by living in sin with a divorced woman from his own social class, by the time of his death he had been married to the woman for fifty-six years. The title Henreid wanted was *Naked in Four Countries,* "because I was destitute every time I moved from one country to another," he said.

His father had died when he was eight, and the money was lost soon afterward, but his mother maneuvered an excellent education for him as a scholarship student at a boarding school for young noblemen in Vienna. From 1933 to 1938 Henreid had a successful stage career in Austria. In 1936, he was offered a movie contract with UFA, Germany's top studio. According to Henreid's autobiography, as he sat in the studio offices in Berlin signing the contracts, he was handed an extra paper in which he agreed to become a member of the National Socialist Actors' Guild of Germany and to uphold Nazi ideology. He tore up the contracts and returned to Vienna, a bold gesture that left him naked in England after Hitler annexed Austria in 1938. At the time of the Anschluss, Henreid was in London playing Prince Albert in Laurence Housman's play *Vic-*

toria Regina, and he couldn't go home again. In 1947 he would make an equally brave gesture by joining the Committee for the First Amendment and flying to Washington to protest the procedures of the House Un-American Activities Committee—a dangerous thing for a newly naturalized citizen to do.

In England, a small part as a friend of Robert Donat in the movie *Goodbye, Mr. Chips* led to roles as suave Nazi villains in *An Englishman's Home* and *Night Train.* It is fate's sardonic joke that any number of German and Austrian actors who fled from Hitler found new careers playing Gestapo agents. For the steadfastly anti-Nazi Henreid, the irony continued when he was forced to register as an enemy alien.

Two years later, in 1940, he was penniless in America, since his English money was frozen and the play he had been promised in New York was canceled. Again a Nazi came to his rescue—in this

Paul Henreid, Ingrid Bergman, Humphrey Bogart. Fifty years later, Henreid was still unhappy about Casablanca.

case, Dr. Hermann Walther, the Nazi diplomat in the Elmer Rice play *Flight to the West.* "The part is played with pitiless clarity by Paul Henreid," wrote drama critic Brooks Atkinson in *The New York Times.* "His acting is brilliant, without a soft spot anywhere."

Hollywood came knocking. A leading role as a Free French pilot opposite Michele Morgan in RKO's *Joan of Paris* led to Hal Wallis's *Now, Voyager* as the married man whose love turns dowdy Bette Davis into a butterfly. It was Henreid's idea to light two cigarettes in his own mouth and then hand one to Davis. It became the romantic gesture of the year, imitated by countless high school students and parodied by Bob Hope in *Let's Face It.* Three weeks after Henreid started *Now, Voyager,* Wallis offered him *Casablanca.*

Henreid's instincts had always been good, and they told him not to accept. Said Henreid, "Then my agent Lew Wasserman said, 'You know, Paul, you have one picture a year at RKO. Since the Americans have started interning the Japanese born in America, your situation is very ticklish. You have become by the annexation of Austria a German citizen, so you are an enemy alien. The more you can fortify your position the better.' "

Henreid was offered costar billing with Bogart and Bergman. He hesitated. But there was another factor. He had been, as he says, destitute in four countries, and he was reveling in the money from *Now, Voyager.* "I had been paid by Warner Bros. $32,000 for *Now, Voyager,*" he said, his voice crackling like aging leather. "A fortune, a bloody fortune. That was enormous in those days. You could buy ten, twelve, fourteen, sixteen Cadillacs with it." With *Casablanca* and a seven-year contract at Warner Bros. he had a chance to recoup all that he had lost.

Yet he may have lost more from *Casablanca* than he gained. "*Casablanca* set Paul Henreid as a stiff," says Pauline Kael. "He was such a pompous, earnest man in *Casablanca* that you think, 'Oh God, that poor girl going back to that guy.' Before that he was sort of a romantic star in Europe and he had played villains and he was the romantic lead in *Now, Voyager.* When you play a square it doesn't do you much good. That happened with Ralph Bellamy when he started playing similar roles. Afterwards he didn't play the heroes anymore."

Irving Rapper, the director of *Now, Voyager,* thinks that Henreid was an excellent light villain and that, because of his "self-idolatry," he made the mistake of trying to be a matinee idol.

Henreid may have had his name in the same large type, but—billing obligations be damned—*Casablanca* belonged to Bogart and Bergman. In 1949, when the movie was rereleased in Los Angeles, the big Warner theaters omitted Henreid's name in their advertisements. He complained to the studio, and his name was added. In 1972, he was still fighting the same battle when United Artists, which had purchased the movie, left his name out of the ads.

Sometime in the fifty years between 1942 and 1992, Henreid reinvented the past. He spoke of a special clause in his Warner Bros. contract that ensured that he was the leading man in every movie. "I will always have the girl," he said. "That's why the ending. And it's a lucky thing they had it in the contract. It made the film one hundred percent better. It would have been such a kitsch if Ingrid Bergman had gone away with Humphrey Bogart." But neither the contract Henreid signed on February 2, 1942, for *Now, Voyager* nor the seven-year contract he signed on May 25, 1942, had any such clause.

Now, Voyager was released in October 1942. *Casablanca* opened in New York a month later. Under "Finds of the Year" in *Film Daily*'s third annual poll of newspaper and magazine critics, Paul Henreid took fifth place, behind Teresa Wright, Alan Ladd, Janet Blair, and Van Heflin. Louella Parsons, the industry's most powerful gossip columnist, went further. After viewing *Now, Voyager,* she wrote, "Within the next year, I look forward to seeing him become one of our number one stars."

He never did, of course, although he costarred in half a dozen more Warner movies before his contract was dissolved by mutual agreement in 1946. Fate and fame are tricky. It was Humphrey Bogart and Ingrid Bergman whose lives and careers were transformed by *Casablanca*.

6

The Studio System
Goes to War

In January 1942, Julius and Philip Epstein were excited about the possibility of writing the script for *Watch on the Rhine*. At Warner Bros., new movies came along almost as frequently as street-cars, and the studio's thirty-two writers hopped randomly aboard. During the first four months of 1942, Hal Wallis was assigning writers and actors to his first five movies as an independent producer: *Desperate Journey, Now, Voyager, Casablanca, Watch on the Rhine,* and *Air Force.* Wallis liked working with the Epsteins; they were experts at turning plays into movies, and Lillian Hellman's *Watch on the Rhine* might need a screenwriter, so he had suggested the idea to the twins. Dashiell Hammett, the author of *The Maltese Falcon,* was the first choice for that assignment, but Hammett, who was not under contract to Warners, said he couldn't start work for three weeks. When the studio decided to wait for Hammett, Wallis talked to the Epsteins about *Casablanca* instead. It was another lucky accident for *Casablanca.*

The decisions that Wallis made on each of his five movies meant that someone was available or not available to work on one of the other four. Paul Henreid was free to play the Czechoslovakian anti-Nazi in *Casablanca* because Wallis didn't think he was the best choice to play the German anti-Nazi whose visit to America jolts his wife's family out of their complacency and innocence in *Watch on the Rhine*. While Henreid was making *Now, Voyager,* Wallis tested him for the lead in *Rhine*. Henreid and Charles Boyer were tested secretly so that word would not get back to Paul Lukas, who had triumphed in the role on Broadway; Wallis intended to offer the part to Lukas if he couldn't find someone better. Boyer, a Frenchman, refused the part because he didn't think he could convincingly play a German. The role went to Lukas, who would defeat Humphrey Bogart for the Academy Award as best actor of 1943.

As the casts and crews of Wallis's five movies came together in the late winter and early spring, the war was beginning to cause changes in the way movies were conceived and made. Equally important, the war rubbed away Hollywood's veneer of arrogance and left the industry confused and tentative. On the crudest psychological level, the United States government was now in the censorship business and looking over the studios' shoulders. On the crudest physical level, the simplest staples of production were no longer available. Aluminum, copper, and rubber were forbidden materials. Shellac, which came from India, was diverted to coat bombs. Rubber cement—which created the spiderwebs in dozens of horror movies each year—had to be replaced by glue, which was brittle and made lopsided, sticky webs. That first spring only sugar was rationed and meat was still plentiful, but eventually actors would sit down on screen to meals of hand-painted plaster roast beef.

From the beginning, movies had been a refuge for the ingenious, so the blows to the industry's confidence came as much from the uncertainty as from the government regulations. A country that was built on individualism—as enshrined in myriad movies about lone, taciturn Westerners—was having trouble yoking its disparities together.

Typically, government agencies made a decision, then reversed or refined it. In April, the War Production Board announced a $5,000 limit on building sets, an impossible restriction since sets cost an average of $20,000 for an A movie. Weeks later, the War Production Board explained that what it really meant was that sets would be limited to $5,000 of new materials per movie; labor and the studios' large stockpiles of lumber would be excluded. Later still, the agency said that a studio could exceed $5,000 on some movies by

Brkdn Page — SET DESCRIPTION	Set No.	Constr Sets	Standby Labor	Prop. Labor	Prop. R & E	Elec. Labor	Elec. R & E	Loc	Trick	Bits	Extras	A.H. & T.	TOTAL
1-4 Int Rick's Cafe	02	9 200	8 000	4 735	2 465	12 700				5 150	33 725		76 565
4 Ext Rick's Cafe (see set C2)			500	595	225					375	166	84	1 545
5 PROC Ext Rick's Cafe		150	400	25				600		86			1 261
6 & 30 Street, Moorish Section		800	500	270	775	125				575	1 260	98	4 403
6 Mat shot " "									250				250
8 & 17 Harem Hotel	12	375	200	195	110	350				229	115	28	1 602
9 & 14 Ext Falais Justice & cor.		200	350	120	140	350				1 150	1 260	28	3 398
10 Ext sidewalk cafe		200	250	110	40	100					252		952
11 Ext Black Mkt & Parrot Cafe		300	1 000	420	750	500				1 840	2 020	140	6 970
12-13 Int Blue Parrot Cafe & Mart.Office	1	250	600	680	500	1 530				230	880		5 470
15 Int Renault Office		500	350	295	60	825					25		2 055
16 Cor. Moorish Hotel		700	100	50	105	200				230	150		1 655
18 Ext Casa Blanca Airport Location		500		140	55	1 150	1 252				475		5 272
19 PROC Renault's Car			100	50				500			25		675
19 PROC MAKE KEY on Moorish Street								200					200
20 PROC Taxi Laszlo & Ilsa			100					500					600
21 BUILD PROC EXCUR BOAT	08	225		40	10								275
21 PROC Excur boat Rick-Ilsa	14		100		10			625		75			800
22 PROC Champs Elysees Rick-Ilsa	16		100	50	10			500					660
23 Int Rick's Paris apt	10	175	100	120	45	125							665
24 Int smart Paris Cafe	18	150	100	105	50	200				370			955
25 Int Ilsa's apt	06	125	100	120	30	150							525
26-27 Ext Strand.Cafe.street	01	500	400	175	50	150		86		885			2 256
28 Int small Montmarte Cafe	04	300	250	165	25	575							1 515
29 & 32 Ext Gare de Lyon	20	400	300	80	60	350				1 260	28		2 498
31 MIN PROC AIRPORT			500					1 500					2 000
31 KEYS AND SHOOT PROC MIN AIRPORT								1 725					1 725
33 Revolving Globe		150											150
33 Animated map		150		0									150
33 Relief Map		250											250
34 stock shots		150											150
35 Int Rick's Casa Blanca Apt		750	500	440	95	650							2 435
36 Int Laszlo and Ilsa's Hotel Rm		400	250	165	50	475							1 340
37 Int office German Consulate		100	100	105	30	100							435
38 Str opposite Laszlo Hotel			300	50	10	350				65			775
Tests	90									1 980			1 980
Standins	91												1 980
Prepare Props	92		1 050	550									1 600
No Estimate Chgs	94												
Inserts, Dupes, Dissolves	96			250				1 075					1 325
No Allocation Charges	98						750					84	834
Adjustments	99												
TOTAL		18 000	15 350	10 150	6 300	20 755	750	1 252	7 475	10 551	44 978	490	136 05

FINAL SCRIPT.
Meeting May 25, 1942.
42 Shooting Days.

-BUDGET DETAIL-
No. 410 "CASA BLANCA"

June 3, 1942.

STRIKE: 7 000
Montage: -o-

The budget showed that the interior of Rick's café cost $76,565.

averaging the costs over its entire slate of films.

Constructing the complicated sets for *Casablanca* cost $18,000. Early in May, Wallis told Curtiz to find as many useful standing sets in the studio's inventory as he could; then art director Carl Weyl would revamp them. A few thousand dollars were saved because Wallis had built a $4,000 railroad station for *Now, Voyager,* which was turned into *Casablanca*'s Paris station by the addition of a sign and a piece of railing. And *Casablanca* took advantage of *The Desert Song*'s transformation of the generic French Street into a specifically Moorish street.

Uncertainty also surrounded raw film stock, the canvas on which the movie industry painted. At first, the industry was assured that savings on film stock would be voluntary; then the cutbacks were made mandatory. One week there were reports that film stock—which was made of cellulose, one of the components of gunpowder—would be cut back 25 percent. The word the next week was that supply would be cut by 50 percent. By 1943, the need to cut their appetite for film in half would force the studios to dismantle their B-movie divisions. But by that time Hollywood's allotment of raw film stock was cut not because it was needed for gunpowder but because it was needed for the training and documentary films spewed out by the competing branches of the armed services.

In the spring of 1942, conservation was more superficial. In 1941, the industry had used two billion feet of celluloid. The suggestion by the industry's Film Conservation Committee to save ten million feet of film a year by eliminating all screen credits except the main title of the movie went nowhere when only the Screen Actors Guild agreed, but the studios did stop sending out photographs of their stars. Since they had been mailing twenty thousand photos a week to fans, the savings in film, printing paper, and chemicals turned into a lot of war materials.

A few weeks after Pearl Harbor, U.S. Army regulations essentially ended location filming in Southern California and drove movie production back behind the studio walls. There were to be no crowd scenes on city streets. Who knew what saboteurs might lurk inside the crowd? Chase scenes, in vogue then as now, were banned. The tunnels used for car chases were under Army control to prevent sabotage. The dry and desolate hills used by the posses in a hundred westerns were newly topped by antiaircraft batteries. In one way, Warner Bros. was better off than most of its rivals. With America fighting a two-ocean war, pictures about submarines and battleships would be in demand, but the nearby ocean which had always been free and available, was now closed to moviemakers. A few years earlier, Warners had created a $400,000 lake with wave-making machinery and hydraulic lifts.

Although Warner Bros. sent *The Desert Song* to Arizona for its exteriors so that Dennis Morgan could lead his band of Arab horsemen across a real desert, the war would force *Casablanca* to be made entirely at the studio, except for one day and another night at a small local airport. Major Strasser's arrival in Casablanca was filmed at the Metropolitan Airport in Van Nuys, and, toward the end of production, the second unit spent a night shooting planes taxiing and taking off at the same airport. But the airport hangar where Bogart says goodbye to Bergman and the Lisbon plane being fueled in the foggy background were built on Warners' Stage 1.

John Beckman, who created the airport set, built two mockups of a real airplane. "We built two versions of scaled-down planes,"

The only scene in Casablanca *shot outside the studio walls—Major Strasser's arrival in Morocco.*

he says, "to match a real plane we borrowed from Lockheed for one shot. What I built were profiles in depth, made out of plywood and maybe some balsa. One was half-size, and the other was half of the half-size. To put them in perspective, we used lights—large lights that got smaller to give a sense of depth to the fog."

In 1942, Warner Bros. was a factory, selling its movies in bulk and guaranteeing theaters three Flynns and three Davises as though the pictures were canned tuna or string beans. The studio even saw itself as "A Leaf From the Book of Henry Ford." The Crafts Building, built in 1936, had four acres of floor space. Almost everything that was needed on the set of a Warner picture—from doorknobs to polo mallets to breakaway windows made of crystallized sugar for villains to crash through—was made there. Wood was milled, molten metal was die cast, furniture was carved and upholstered, and paper was turned into imitation marble, wood paneling, or stone. Lumber started at one end of the building as a blueprint and emerged across four hundred feet of floor as a completed set— painted, hinged, electrically wired, and with faucets ready for the studio's plumbers.

The equivalent intellectual assembly line was the B-picture unit that had been created by Bryan Foy, who kept using the same plots while giving each film a different setting. Ring Lardner, Jr.'s introduction to the studio system in 1937 as a twenty-two-year-old writer was his first meeting with Foy. "He had next to his desk several stacks of scripts," says Lardner. "As he finished shooting a picture, Foy would put its script on the top of the pile. There was more than one pile, and I don't know quite how he worked it. But when I came to see him he reached to the bottom of a pile and, with considerable dexterity, pulled out a script from the bottom without upsetting the whole pile and looked at it and said something like, 'Let's see. This one was about horse racing. Let's make it about automobile racing.' " As early as 1936, Humphrey Bogart was starring in such Foy remakes as *Two Against the World,* although he never got higher than fourth billing behind Edward G. Robinson or Pat O'Brien in more expensive movies like *Bullets or Ballots* and *China Clipper.*

Working at a movie studio had always been a choice job for craftsmen. During the Depression years of the 1930s, studio carpenters, electricians, and draftsmen were paid $5 or $6 more a week than they could get elsewhere. But the studios had started losing carpenters in 1940,

The studio reluctantly hired female messengers in 1943.

when the government offered higher wages to lure them to the new defense plants. When the war came, high wages plus patriotism accelerated the exodus of technicians. Late in January a number of RKO's best electricians left the studio, four of them for a magnesium plant in Arizona. Even laborers were being offered higher-paying jobs in defense plants. Because so many men were leaving, the *Hollywood Reporter* announced in March 1942 that the studios would begin training hundreds of women as camera assistants or sound mixers. But the unions balked and women remained secretaries. Nor did women find it easy to get jobs in defense plants that early in the war. Women who showed signs of self-reliance were rejected for a defense-plant training program at the University of California at Los Angeles. According to the Los Angeles *Times,* women who seemed indepen- dent had the wrong attitude. At the studios, too, there were few jobs for assertive women. At Warner Bros. the printed memo pads said, "From Mr. ———." Irene Lee, who headed the Story Department under Wallis, always had to cross out the "Mr." "When I left the job," she says, "Paul Nathan, who had been one of Hal's secretaries, was moved up. Paul was a very nice man, but, believe me, he really wasn't in my class as far as finding stories to buy. And he got three times as much money as I did."

Warners had always been quick on its feet and quick to change its strategy to take advantage of an opponent's weakness. That advantage eroded during the war. By mid-1943, everything had to be planned far ahead. Wigs, for example, were made by hand, and there was a critical shortage of wigmakers. Films had to be cast weeks earlier than usual to allow time for wigs to be made, since almost every movie used at least a few wigs, hairpieces for balding actors, or falls to lengthen actresses' hair.

A few weeks before *Casablanca* started production, the Screen Actors Guild and the Southern California Labor Supply Board came up with a plan to divert more than a thousand extras with factory backgrounds into jobs at defense plants. Bit parts had often been cast the same day the actor was needed. But, with actors lost to the armed services and defense plants, the casting department was de- manding nearly a week's notice. Some extras combined evening shifts in aircraft factories with movie work. Frugal as always, Warner Bros. made sure it got a full day's work from those extras, who often reported late. The studio installed a time clock in the casting office so that no one would get paid overtime until he had been at the studio eight hours.

Almost as soon as the war began, the studios started rushing movies into production in order to get completed films stockpiled before the war drained off their actors, directors, scenic artists, painters, and greensmen. By the time the war was five months old, they had 136 finished movies sitting on their shelves. Paramount had an astonishing 29 films in the can, well over half a year's supply, and Columbia had 16. "To the Point of Saturation," was the headline on a front-page editorial in the *Hollywood Reporter* in June. "There is now one of the largest pile-ups of pictures . . . that the business has ever known," the editor warned.

Jack Warner saw it differently. "Negatives are as good as money today," Warner wrote the head of his English studio, "and that is why we are hurrying to make as many as we can while good people are left. As yet we haven't been hurt much, as we have really only lost Ronald Reagan, but we will soon be in the same position as Metro, who has lost Clark Gable, Jimmy Stewart, and Spencer Tracy, and will soon be losing Mickey Rooney and Robert Taylor, according to what I read in the Trade Papers."

Because of the war, movies were playing for a month in theaters that would formerly have kept them a week. And movies that caught the mood of the audience did even better. *Mrs. Miniver,* the story of the war's effects on a middle-class English family, broke every record at the Radio City Music Hall in New York. The film played ten weeks in the summer of 1942 and would have played longer if it had not had to be withdrawn to make way for *Bambi.* With ticket prices around 75 cents, *Mrs. Miniver* grossed more than $1 million at the Music Hall.

In April 1942, General Hap Arnold, head of the Army Air Corps, summoned Jack Warner to Washington. "Jack took me with him," says Owen Crump, who had written and produced a series of historical shorts for Warners before the war. "Frankly, Jack didn't know anything about shorts. That's why he brought me along. General Arnold told Jack that he wanted his own film unit and that he'd make Jack a lieutenant colonel. Then General Arnold turned to me and said, 'Crump, you're in the Army too.'"

Crump, who started as a captain and ended as a lieutenant colonel, set up and ran the Army Air Force photographic section, which made training films. "The thing that skyrocketed my unit," says Crump, "was that the Air Force was frantically trying to train pilots, but there was a terrible problem. Since pilots had to have at least a year or two of college, the Air Force couldn't draft for them. So the Air Force needed enlistments. Could we make a picture and get it in theaters? Jack Warner said, 'Hell, yes. Anything they want.' He was a very patriotic man."

Warner Bros. made and paid for *Winning Your Wings,* a documentary that glamorized the training of an Army pilot. "When Jack returned to California, I stayed behind in Washington and got stock footage," says Crump. "I wrote the script on the plane back. Within three days we were ready to shoot. I called General Arnold. 'Can we get Jimmy Stewart to narrate?' "

Lieutenant James Stewart, who would fly twenty missions over Germany as a bomber pilot, was given orders to report to March Field with no explanation. Says Crump, "Stewart flies in, gets out of his plane, and is met by huge Warner Bros. trucks, and says, 'What the hell is going on?' The picture opened with Stewart flying in. Jack put the studio on a twenty-four-hour basis, and we got the picture finished in two weeks. They traced 100,000 enlistments to *Winning Your Wings.*"

Warner had happily accepted a commission. In one of his first gestures as an officer, he ordered John Beckman to paint a mural of the history of aviation on the walls of his office. And he was quick to educate people on how to address him. "For your information the correct military practice is to say 'Dear Colonel,' the same as you would say 'Dear General,' regardless of whether the man was a Brigadier, Major, or Lieutenant General,' " he wrote to someone who had made the mistake of calling him "Dear Lt. Colonel."

"Jack thought it was an honorary thing," says Crump. "He was running the studio. When military people came out, they had to make appointments with his secretary if they wanted to see him. Jack didn't realize what he had gotten into, that he was in the Army. The Air Force said he would have to leave the studio, so he petitioned for release."*

Hal Wallis was less naïve. Warner would resign his commission in less than six months, but Wallis never accepted his. Warner had taken Wallis with him to see Hap Arnold in April. "Jack thought

---

*It was Jack Warner, Jr., who spent the entire war in uniform, much of it as a major coordinating Signal Corps photographers in Europe. When Jackie wrote to his father, Bill Schaefer, Jack Warner's secretary, was told to answer the letters. But Schaefer forced Warner to sign the letters himself. Says Schaefer, "I felt his son deserved that much."

Hal would be a little more firepower," says Crump. During the summer while he had *Casablanca, Watch on the Rhine, Princess O'-Rourke,* and *Air Force* in production, Wallis was offered a commission as a major. "It is with deep and sincere regret that I found myself unable to accept the commission in the AAF," he wrote to Warner on August 2, the day before production ended on *Casablanca.* Wallis said that he thought he could make a bigger contribution by producing such movies as *Yankee Doodle Dandy, Air Force, This Is the Army,* and *Watch on the Rhine.* He made no mention of his other movie, the melodrama finishing up on the French Street.

It took most of that first year for the movie industry—and the country—to settle into the war. Each month brought new restrictions. When *Casablanca* was finished and the studio publicity chief was urging the New York head office to plan a major campaign for the movie, he warned that *Casablanca*'s production values and opulence could not be duplicated for the duration of the war.

From the first, rubber was a major problem. By June, the limousines routinely used to transport stars and executives were replaced by jitney buses—democracy in action, since stars were wedged next to their hairdressers. As usual, the Warners' publicity department made hay out of the restrictions, detailing how, on the first day of gasoline rationing, George Tobias arrived at the studio on horseback, Irene Manning by bicycle, and Ann Sheridan, Dennis Morgan, Mike Curtiz, and Arthur Kennedy on a bus they shared with Paramount and Universal employees who also lived in the valley. During the making of *Casablanca,* before rationing started, the studio solemnly said that Madeleine LeBeau, the young contract actress who had been cast as Rick's mistress, was preparing to walk at least five miles a day. As the months passed and no Japanese planes appeared in the skies over Los Angeles, the ban on location shooting was relaxed. When two studios were shooting at or near the same location, however, grips and prop men from both companies still shared a van.

Other things that the studio had taken for granted became difficult or impossible to get or to do. It was usual to make doubles of some of the clothes worn by actresses and actors. If the actor had a fight scene or the actress was to be splashed by mud, three copies of an outfit might be created. But the government, which had to provide socks, underwear, and uniforms for ten million draftees, cut back on the bolts of material that could be sold to each customer, so clothes that had to be doubled could only be sewn from the available stock of the few nonessential fabrics that weren't required for uniforms, blankets, and parachutes.

Just as *Casablanca* went into production, new restrictions were placed on costumes. According to Limitation Orders M73 and L75, the motion picture industry had to follow rules that eliminated pleats, lace, patch pockets, and cloth-covered buttons, trouser cuffs and lapels for woolen suits. *Casablanca* was "the first important 'all-cotton' picture of this wartime season," according to a Warner Bros. press release. Ingrid Bergman's costumes, which would normally have been made of silk or wool, were made of cotton because of the wartime restrictions. In addition, "in strict accordance with priority rulings," her clothes had no wasted pins or unnecessary zippers.

If dress materials were limited, stockings were hardly available at all—except on the black market. Actresses were required to provide their own. If an actress snagged her stockings on the set, Warners would loan her a fresh pair, but the nylons had to be turned in to the wardrobe department before the actress left the studio. In *Casablanca,* Sydney Greenstreet did an excellent traffic in American cigarettes. Publicity men at all the studios had an equally deft touch with nylons. "I supplemented my income by selling black-market nylons from a guy who had a special dispensation from Congress to make nylons for the motion-picture industry, which was a *morale industry,*" says Warner publicist Bob William. "I would meet him in the parking lot of Schwabs Drugstore at midnight, and he would give me fifty boxes of nylons for $2.20 a pair. And I would sell them to producers all over Beverly Hills for $6.60 a pair." Warner photo editor Art Wilde got his nylons from the same man through barter. "We'd photograph him with whatever stars we had under contract," says Wilde. "And he'd lay hose on all of us."

No studio that made movies as cheaply, quickly, and resourcefully as Warner Bros. could be handcuffed by physical restrictions. The psychological restrictions were a different matter. Before the war was ten days old, RKO was ordered to junk a $425,000 movie, *Call Out the Marines,* because the film poked fun at the Marine Corps. The Marines refused to allow the film to be released because "it would tend to undermine the confidence of the nation in its military services."

For the next three-and-a-half years, the movie industry would have half a dozen government masters, whose aims, goals, and ideas often conflicted. The Army, Navy, Marines, and Army Air Force wanted and got glorification of their roles in the war America was fighting. The Office of War Information (OWI) wanted to present an ideal America to its soldiers and citizens and to avoid offending the country's allies. The Office of Censorship combed movies for aerial photos of war-production plants, undue emphasis on rationing, and "labor, class, or other disturbances which might be distorted into enemy propaganda." Even the Treasury Department briefly got into the act, invoking the 1917 Trading with the Enemy Act to examine every foot of film leaving the country. And the Hays Office, which administered the studio's own Production Code and was fiercely protective of the industry's image, asked the film companies "to eliminate all scenes of destruction such as automobile wrecks, furniture breaking, and even food wasting, all the way down to pie throwing." The studios had not been filming new crashes; they had been using old stock footage of auto chases. But, said the Hays Office, audiences were responding badly to the screeching tires. "Such shots are not in keeping with the national mood of strict economy and salvage of usable objects," the Hays Office added piously.

The censorship began on December 24, 1941, as a pledge of no censorship. In a letter appointing Lowell Mellett, an ex-newspaper editor and a former presidential assistant, as the government liaison with Hollywood, President Franklin Delano Roosevelt wrote:

> The American motion picture is one of our most effective media in informing and entertaining our citizens. The motion picture must remain free, insofar as national security will permit. I want no censorship of the motion picture; I want no restrictions placed thereon which will impair the usefulness of the film other than those very necessary restrictions which the dictates of safety make imperative.

Mellett, a soft-spoken, rather gray, wispy man, who had, among other things, been coordinating government films for the preceding fifteen months, did not have a large appetite for propaganda. In *The War Lords of Washington,* Bruce Catton tells how Mellett responded, several months before the war broke out, to government officials who pressed for the kind of vast propaganda effort that Joseph Goebbels had mounted in Germany. Tired of answering that a democratic government shouldn't propagandize its own people, Mellett finally said that he would need Goebbels's two advantages:

"First, complete indoctrination of the American people for the preceding one hundred and fifty years. Second, complete, air-tight control over anything that is said anywhere in America—on the air, in the press, in Congress, from the pulpit, in the movies, or on the corner soapbox."

Yet a year later Mellett, frustrated by the kind of movies Hollywood was making, would try to force the studios to submit their finished scripts to the Office of War Information.

Airtight control did not exist during the Second World War, but it did become something of a goal. Early on, the government decided that it had to sell the war to the people rather than give them the facts and trust them to make up their own minds. Bad news was withheld. The war agencies had public-relations advisors to keep information about errors, unmet quotas, and snafus from leaking out. The War Department kept a lid on information far beyond the needs of security.

Everybody wanted to win the war. Beyond that, the senators and congressmen who hated and feared Roosevelt, the remnants of the New Dealers in the executive branch who were rapidly losing their power, the industrialists who headed the new war agencies, and Roosevelt's split cabinet had their own agendas. In June 1942, as a public-relations technique to make a divided government speak with one voice, the Office of War Information was created. Among the fragments swept into the new OWI was Mellett's blandly named Office of Government Reports, from which he cleared and planned government movies, provided informational propaganda, and tried to talk Hollywood into making the kind of movies the government wanted. Just as *Casablanca* settled into production, the OWI's Bureau of Motion Pictures opened its office in a building at the corner of Hollywood and Vine, the intersection that, to radio listeners across the country, meant Hollywood. The makers of *Casablanca* were lucky that the Bureau of Motion Pictures set up shop three weeks too late to look at the script. Evidence suggests that the bureaucrats would have tried to get Wallis and Warner to soften its portrayal of the Vichy police chief played by Claude Rains. Although the OWI liked *Casablanca*'s demonstration of underground resistance to the Nazis, it was uneasy about the movie's negative portrait of Vichy France. And both Harry and Jack Warner were eager to please Mellett.

By the time the Bureau of Motion Pictures opened, two speeches had already articulated the two major opposing views of what America should be and do after the war was won. Henry Luce, the publisher of *Time,* had called for an "American Century" in which America would exert the major economic and political influence in the world. Vice President Henry A. Wallace had called for a "Century of the Common Man." Wallace hoped that the defeat of Hitler would usher in a world of social reform, social justice, and freedom.

The OWI was clearly on the side of Wallace—the losing side. The New Dealers who ran the Bureau of Motion Pictures encouraged movies to be an instrument of social reform. In a country in which aircraft plants would only hire Negroes as janitors, during a war in which the car manufacturers made millions churning out tanks while the car dealers, with no cars to sell, were forced into bankruptcy, and at a time when wages were frozen while business profits soared, the OWI asked Hollywood to show blacks in positions of dignity and to write in scenes of labor and management shouldering burdens together. Presenting a rosy picture of America might change the reality. Even if it didn't, the sight of Americans of all colors, creeds, and classes working for a common goal would help the war effort.

The first question the OWI asked—of *Casablanca* and *The Gorilla Man* alike—was "Will this picture help win the war?" By the time both movies were released, in January of 1943, Warner Bros. had learned how to defend its films. *The Gorilla Man* was a B movie about German agents who ran an English hospital. The studio said that *The Gorilla Man* showed the tactics of Nazi espionage, while *Casablanca,* among other things, improved international understanding by portraying the Norwegians as a courageous people.

The OWI would quickly come to the conclusion that most pictures did not help to win the war but simply exploited it. However patriotic they were and however hard they tried to conform to the OWI's vision of an ideal America, the studios, as always, made the movies that they thought would sell best, including *Menace of the Rising Sun,* which advertised a huge Japanese monster with buck teeth that dripped blood. Actually, a case could be made that *Casablanca* did help win the war, that the sacrifice explicit in its ending and the idealism underlying it nudged Americans in the right direction. When *Casablanca* went into production in May 1942, Hollywood, like much of America, was still groping for ways to deal with the war. One solution was time-honored and dependable: romanticize it with a couple of stars.

FORM 96 2500 10-41 SF4276C

DAILY PRODUCTION AND PROGRESS REPORT

Day **Monday**   Date **5/#/42**

Name of Production	"CASABLANCA"	No. **410**	Name of Director **M. CURTIZ**
Number of Days Alloted **48**	Production Started **5/25/42**	Days Elapsed Since Starting **1**	Status of Schedule: **ON SCHEDULE**

Estimated Finish Date **7/21/42**	Revised Finish Date (If Ahead or Behind)	Name of Set	Location	Finished?

Company Called	9:00AM		
Lng: Up.-Reh. 'til	10:15AM	**SCRIPT REPORT**	
Started Shooting	10:15AM	No. of Scenes Original Script	**Incomplete**
Lunch Called	12:15PM	No. of Scenes Previously Taken	--
Time Started	1:15PM	No. of Scenes Taken Today	5
Dinner Called		Total Scenes Taken to Date	5
Time Started		Balance to Be Taken	**Incomplete**
Time Finished	6:00PM	No. of Added Scenes Taken	0 + 0 = 0

Int. MONTMARTE CAFE - 04
Stage 12-A

Standard Recording "As Time Goes By"

CAST				Slate No.	No. of Takes	Time of Ok Takes	STAFF		Time Started	Time Finished
S-Start W-Worked H-Held F-Finish R-Rehearse		Time Started	Time Finished							
				A-1	3	1'15"	~~Screen~~ Producer: WALLIS		AM	PM
HUMPHREY BOGART	SW	9:00AM	6:00PM	2	3		Director	Curtiz	8:00	6:00
INGRID BERGMAN	SW	9:00AM	6:00PM	3	3		Dial. Dir.	McMullan	8:15	"
DOOLEY WILSON	SW	9:00AM	3:15PM	4	2		Unit Mgr.	Alleborn		
				5	4		1st Asst.	Katz	8:00	"
				6	2		2nd Asst.	Tobin	7:30	"
				7	4		Extra Asst.			
				8	5		Script Clerk	Dwight	9:00	"
				9	2		Cutter	Marks		
				10	1	1'05"	Art Dir.	Weyl		
				11	1		Tech. Adv'r.	Aisner	8:15	"
				12	2		CAMERAMEN			
							Head	Edeson	8:00	"
							2nd	Joyce	8:30	"
							Asst.	Meinardus	8:00	"
From Music Dept.										
Bill Elfeld	W	9:00AM	3:15PM				Still Man	Woods	9:00	"
Elliot Carpenter	W	8:45AM	3:15PM				PROP MEN			
"	Rec.	10:15A	10:30AM				Head	Plews	7:30	"
"		1:15P	1:30PM				Asst.	Turner	7:00	"
								Goldman	7:30	"
Standins:				MINUTES			VITAPHONE			
BETTY BROOKS	SW	7:30AM	6:00PM	Total Today	2'20"		Mixer	Scheid	8:45	"
RUSS LEWELLYN	SW	7:30AM	6:00PM	Prev. Total			Boom	Hughes	8:00	"
				Total to Date	2'20"		Recorder	Brown	8:30	"
								Williams	8:00	"
				STILL REPORT			Gaffer	Conget	7:00	"
				Prev. Taken			Best Boy	Studeman	7:00	"
				Taken Today	4		Grip	Dexter	7:30	"
Bits on Day Check				To Date	4		Makeup	McCoy	7:00	"
				ORCHESTRA (W) (R)						
				Total						
JOHN BARTON	SWF	9:00AM	5:00PM	Called			Hair Dr.	Burt	7:15	"
				Dismissed						
				Setups Today	12					
				Pages Today	2½		Wdrbe.	Pickering	7:30	"
				Pages to Date	2½			Robert	7:30	"
								Dunn	8:00	"

EXTRAS	ANIMALS	LUNCHES	Script Scenes Taken	115	116	117	117A	117B
8 C.C.								

STAND-INS	ANIMAL HANDLERS	AUTOS	Added Scenes Taken
Day 1		Stand by— 1	
		In Scenes—	

Remarks

PRODUCTION STARTED TODAY - 5/25/42

2310
2310

NOTE: Kindly indicate above: If any artist delays director starting work or arriving later than time called, state reason, or any mechanical delay:

7

The First Day
of Shooting

The daily production report for Monday, May 25, 1942—the first day of shooting on *Casablanca*—shows that Humphrey Bogart and Ingrid Bergman started work at nine A.M. At Warners, the studio system didn't tolerate actors arriving late, but, even if it had allowed stars to demonstrate their power by public tardiness, neither Bogart nor Bergman would have taken advantage of it. Bogart clung to the idea that acting was a profession. Consciously at least, he had none of the embarrassment that made most male stars grumble that acting was a silly way for a grown man to make a living.

Bergman might have preferred to stay at the studio twenty-four hours a day instead of returning to her rented apartment in Beverly Hills. She was most comfortable in the artificial world of whatever movie she was making, whatever character she was creating. And she was happiest when the emotions she was feeling on the screen could spill over into real life. Bergman's first husband, Petter Lindstrom, told a biographer that his wife worked best when she was in love with her costar or her director. Whether the love was chaste or carnal, it never lasted beyond the last scene. Of his affair with

Bergman on *Saratoga Trunk,* a bemused Gary Cooper told one journalist, "In my whole life I never had a woman so much in love with me as Ingrid was. The day after the picture ended, I couldn't get her on the phone."

Bergman projected an innocence and purity that enraptured men. The movie critic of *The New York Times,* Bosley Crowther, met her boat when she returned from Europe in 1940 and wrote: "Picture the sweetheart of a Viking, freshly scrubbed with Ivory soap, eating peaches and cream from a Dresden china bowl on the first warm day of Spring atop a sea-scarred cliff, and you have a fair impression of Ingrid Bergman." That aura of purity—as though her underlying sexuality was something of which she was ignorant until, a sudden wave, it drenched her unaware—enabled Bergman to make audiences sympathize with the women she portrayed who cheated on their husbands or seduced married men. Audience response to Ilsa Lund would have been very different if the character had been placed in the knowing hands of Hedy Lamarr. But eternal virginity has its disadvantages. The purity that made people joke about Saint Bergman when she played Joan of Arc made both audiences and United States senators feel betrayed when they learned of her affair with Roberto Rossellini.

"When she was in all that trouble with Rossellini, I called her and said, 'I don't want to ask you any questions but could I read your mail?' " says columnist Art Buchwald. "Oh, that mail was bad, ten, twelve, fourteen huge mail bags. 'Dirty whore.' 'Bitch.' 'Son of a bitch.' And they were all Christians who wrote it," Buchwald says.

Saint and sinner. The irony is that the real-life sexuality of Bergman and Bogart was almost reversed on screen. The tough guy who could sleep with a woman and then turn her over to the police in *The Maltese Falcon,* the user of women who could throw his girlfriend out of his Café Americain when he was bored with her in *Casablanca,* despised deceit in any form, including sexual deceit. He warned Lauren Bacall, whom he married when she was twenty and he was forty-five, that the occupational hazard for an actor was playing love scenes with attractive people. He lectured her about adultery, insisting that a quick romance was almost never worth the risk. Surely Bogart was not as much of a knight-errant as he seems in Lauren Bacall's autobiography, and he may have had a few quick romances. But, in a town where everyone's secrets were public gossip, he never had the reputation of being a chaser. "I never saw

Bogart play around with anybody on the set or even flirt with women who came on the set," says Meta Carpenter, who was the script supervisor on several of his movies. Even his drinking buddy Peter Lorre said, "He has very set ideas about behavior and morals in that respect." Forced by his character into serial monogamy, Bogart was stuck in an unhappy marriage to an alcoholic wife—Mayo Methot, the third of the four actresses he married—while he was making *Casablanca*.

Casablanca started on Stage 12A with the flashback to Rick and Ilsa's romance in Paris. It was an accident that Bogart was required to make love to Bergman almost before he was introduced to her. Originally, production was to start in Rick's Café on Stage 8, but the intricate clockwork that matched actors, scripts, stages, and sets had been thrown off because Irving Rapper was two weeks behind schedule on *Now, Voyager*. Claude Rains didn't finish his role as the wise psychiatrist in *Now, Voyager* until June 3. Paul Henreid was not free until June 25. So the Curtiz movie began with the scene in the Montmartre café. That first day, a lovestruck Richard Blaine—*"His manner is wry but not the bitter wryness we have seen in Casablanca,"* say the stage directions—pours champagne for himself, Ilsa, and Sam while the Germans march toward Paris and Sam plays "As Time Goes By."

According to Geraldine Fitzgerald, Bogart and Bergman had lunch together a week or ten days before *Casablanca* started production. "I had lunch with them," she says. "And the whole subject at lunch was how they could get out of the movie. They thought the dialogue was ridiculous and the situations were unbelievable. And Ingrid was terribly upset because she said she had to portray the most beautiful woman in Europe, and no one would ever believe that. It was curious how upset she was by it. 'I look like a milkmaid,' she said. I knew Bogart very well, and I think he wanted to join forces with Bergman, to make sure they both said the same things. He had had such a bad time for years at Warner Bros."

For whatever reason there was a lack of empathy between Bogart and Bergman; the lunch did not create an alliance, and their relationship never went further than politeness required. "There was distance between them," says Dan Seymour, who spent four weeks as the guardian of the door to Rick's gambling room. From almost the first day, it was different with Lauren Bacall on *To Have and Have Not*, Seymour says. "Bogart would give Bacall trouble. One time he had the prop man put handcuffs on her. He cuffed her to the portable dressing room. Then he came back and unhooked her and took her to lunch. But from the beginning Bogart and Bergman were not too friendly."

Between scenes, Bogart played chess or disappeared into his spartan canvas dressing room—four walls, a sofa, a makeup table, and a chair. "Almost nobody wanted to go into those dressing rooms if they didn't have to," says Curtiz's first assistant director, Lee Katz. "But Bogie, despite his reputation, was not an easy man to get along with. Not that he was a bad fellow. But he was kind of a loner."

There was a bottle in the dressing room, but in his years at Warner Bros. Bogart was too drunk to show up for work only once. That was when he was making *The Big Sleep,* and drowning himself in alcohol was the easiest solution to being torn between his obligation to Mayo and his love for Lauren Bacall. When Bogart was making *Casablanca,* everyone knew of his nightly battles with Mayo, whom he had nicknamed Sluggy in the early days of the marriage, when her drunken rages were infrequent enough to be cute. Eight months earlier, when he was filming *All Through the Night,* Bogart

Bogart and Mayo Methot on their wedding day.

had walked the edge of being unprofessional. "We had a few days on the picture when he came in in the morning with a terrible hangover," says the director, Vincent Sherman. The actor had pulled himself together and apologized. One Saturday night Mayo showed up. "She had been drinking quite a bit," says Sherman. "She was crying and said, 'He doesn't love me anymore.' " An angry Bogart refused to comfort her. "I went through a few days like that," Sherman says.

"Bogie was very unhappy," says Francis Scheid, the sound mixer on *Casablanca.* "I had a boom man who would see Bogie talking to a girl on the set and say, 'Watch me shake him up.' He'd go over and say, 'Mayo just came in.' And Bogie would jump."

Mayo was suspicious enough to prowl the set of *Casablanca,* but she had no reason to be jealous of Ingrid Bergman. When Bogart fell in love with his leading lady two years later, it was with a nineteen-year-old from New York with a sharp tongue who could take his kidding and toss it back.

"I kissed him but I never knew him," Bergman would often say of Bogart after *Casablanca* became an artifact that demanded explanation and explication.

In her autobiography, *My Story,* Bergman admits to only one extramarital affair—with war photographer Bob Capa—before she ran away with Italian movie director Roberto Rossellini. Her biographer Laurence Leamer lists a dozen more. But there was no one to fall in love with on *Casablanca.* Bogart was wary of her. She found Paul Henreid dull. And she was too canny to become emotionally or physically intimate with Mike Curtiz. Curtiz had as great an appetite for women as he had for land, horses, and movies. Sometimes he didn't even bother to find a vacant dressing room.

"He was always going behind a flat," says Katz, who was an assistant director on nearly a dozen Curtiz movies. "On *Casablanca* as on every other picture. The girls were always extras. There were a couple of girls who were always on call because they were famous for their behavior. You were asked to put them on the list of extras to be called whenever you needed people. And if you didn't have room on your set you went to a friend who was an assistant director on another picture and said, 'I wish you would call Jane Doe.' "

Curtiz had been married once in Europe, to Lucy Doraine, who starred in many of his Austrian films. His contract file shows that, when he came to America, he also left behind an illegitimate son. After Curtiz stopped paying child support, the thirteen-year-old boy's mother pursued him to California in 1933 and wrote a heartbreaking letter to Jack Warner asking the studio to intervene. There is no evidence that it did.

By 1942, Curtiz's second wife, Bess Meredyth, was spending most of her time in bed. They had met when he was just off the boat from Europe and she was an important and well-paid writer of silent films at M-G-M. Most of the best and highest-paid writers of scenarios for silent films were women, and Bess Meredyth shared the top of the list with Frances Marion, Lenore Coffee, and June Mathis. She was a jolly blonde woman who had written the screenplays for *Ben-Hur* and *A Woman of Affairs*.

"When they were married, it was unbalanced," says John Meredyth Lucas, who was nine when Michael Curtiz became his stepfather. "Mike was just the new director Warner Bros. had brought

Bess Meredyth with Michael Curtiz.

over. Then the balance, of course, went the other way. By the late thirties my mother was no longer working. I think now that my mother was depressed and that her depression took a hypochondriacal form. There was the constant stress of Mike's extracurricular activities. She was very well aware of them."

Bess Meredyth left Curtiz once, early in 1941. But she had returned by Pearl Harbor. And even after she took to her bed she worked on his scripts, including *Casablanca*. When a movie was in production, Curtiz telephoned Bess at least once or twice a day. "Bogart would say, 'Why do I do it this way?' and Mike would walk away and call Bess," says Francis Scheid. Even the stuntmen on his movies knew that Curtiz had a smart wife. "If he was stuck in any predicament on the set, Curtiz would always say, 'I'll be back in a minute' and go call his wife," says Paul Stader, who dressed up as an Arab and jumped out of the way of the French police car in the first scenes of *Casablanca*.

"When we had a story conference and Mike came in the next day and made criticisms or suggestions, we knew they were Bess Meredyth's ideas and not his," says Julius Epstein. "So it was easy to trip him up. We'd make a change and say, 'What do you think, Mike?' and he'd have to go back to Bess."

To the end of his life, after thirty-six years in America, English was a foreign language to Curtiz. "He spoke five languages," says his stepson, "and I am told he spoke all of them equally badly."

Curtiz threw himself on the language, wrestling with English and continually being defeated. David Niven entitled a memoir *Bring on the Empty Horses*. That was Curtiz's way of asking for horses that had lost their riders during a battle scene in *The Charge of the Light Brigade*. Vincent Price watched Curtiz fume on the set of *The Private Lives of Elizabeth and Essex* when a gofer didn't return quickly with a soft drink. "Next time I send some dumb son-of-a-bitch for a Coca-Cola, I go myself," he said. That was a construct that he used fairly often. When he was acting in *Black Fury,* John Qualen remembers Curtiz shouting the variation, "The next time I send some big damn fool to get something, I go myself."

Everyone who worked with Curtiz has at least one story. For Lee Katz, it was when the poor white trash in the script of *Cabin in the Cotton* were called peckerwoods and Curtiz made a speech telling the actors how to act like woodpeckers. Hal Wallis thought that the fractured English was caused by Curtiz's mind working faster than his tongue. "There're more words milling around in his brain than he can get out in the usual way," Wallis said. Louise Randall Pierson, the author of *Roughly Speaking,* which Curtiz turned into a movie in 1945, thought that Curtiz felt no need to use words precisely but used them "approximately, like Gertrude Stein." Almost no one felt that Curtiz's bludgeoning of English was deliberate, the way some people saw Samuel Goldwyn's malapropisms as a publicity trick.

Casablanca was not a typical Curtiz set. Curtiz was still an autocrat, striding the set in his boots and riding britches. But the war had put him on a choke chain and kept him from flogging his actors into working longer hours. Because of the war, the summer shooting day ended at 6:30 P.M. so that everyone could get home before dark. The lead story in the *Los Angeles Times* the Monday morning that *Casablanca* began production said that unidentified airplanes had caused Los Angeles to be blacked out the night before. The planes had turned out to be friendly, but, two days later, a nightly dimout began in some parts of the city, in order to reduce the danger of American freighters' being spotlighted for Japanese submarines. Rains and Henreid, who lived in Brentwood, would not have been allowed to drive to their homes after dark.

Screenwriter Philip Dunne, who loathed Curtiz, calls him a bully, a description with which many of his crew members would have agreed. Francis Scheid, for one, would have seen the symbolism in a memo from Hal Wallis while Curtiz was making *The Sea Hawk.* Wallis complained about the glee with which Curtiz was having overseers whip the galley slaves. "In almost every scene you have these men going up and down in long shots, medium shots, and closeups, with the whips coming in and hitting the men as they are rowing," Wallis protested.

Fay Wray describes the malicious way Curtiz fired an extra: "He kept saying, 'Move to your right. More. More. Now you are out of the scene. Go home.' " In one picture, says Katz, the producer had asked Curtiz to cast his current girlfriend. "She had one line and she could not get it out," Katz says. "This was one of those nights when we were obliged to shoot until midnight, but we did not want to go beyond it because we had to start again at eight o'clock the next morning. And finally, about one A.M., Mike said the immortal line: 'Goddamn it, René, you fuck to get in my picture and now you fuck my picture.' "

Curtiz was particularly cruel to actresses. Bette Davis hated him

Jack Warner, Michael Curtiz, and Hal Wallis read the script of Casablanca. *Note the signed photograph of Roosevelt along with the two Oscars behind Jack's desk.*

so much that, rather than work with him again, she turned down *Mildred Pierce,* which won Joan Crawford an Academy Award.

On *The Unsuspected,* Curtiz badgered Joan Caulfield until she became hysterical. "Mike kept insulting her and insulting her until he got her to break down," says John Meredyth Lucas, who was his stepfather's dialogue director on the movie. "But he had a reason. There simply wasn't a performance there. When she broke down, that was the scene he wanted." And Lauren Bacall, who was by then Bogart's wife, remembers Curtiz screaming at her when she made *Bright Leaf* in 1950. Bacall says that Curtiz was angry at Gary Cooper, who had come to work late. Since the director didn't dare to take his rage out on Cooper, he chose a weaker target. "I think he resented actors," Bacall says. "Actors got in his way."

Curtiz's behavior toward the stars of *Casablanca* was less spiteful. Bogart was a match for any director. And, like most men, Curtiz was deferential to Bergman. "I greatly enjoyed Mike Curtiz, who really taught me quite a bit," Bergman wrote in her acting diary.

"With Bergman, he oozed continental charm," says Scheid, who automatically eavesdropped on everything that went on. The sound mixer kept an earpiece in one ear, and most fights and liaisons were within range of some microphone. "Not the way he was with Bette Davis when we were making *Cabin in the Cotton*. God, Mike hated her. He'd say, 'Who the hell is this Davis? Jesus, she's not going anywhere.' "

Says Lee Katz, "Mike called Bergman 'Christmas baby.' I have no idea why." Curtiz may not have been saying "Christmas baby" at all. When he was an executive at Warners, Bill Orr never did understand what Curtiz meant by "devil up," a phrase he used in every conceivable context.

"He was not crude or rude," says actress Fay Wray, who starred in two Curtiz movies, *Doctor X* in 1932 and *Mystery of the Wax Museum* in 1933. "But I felt that he was not flesh and bones, that he was part of the steel of the camera. He did not seem to have any tenderness. Oddly for a man who was extremely thick-skinned, he actually had the thinnest skin I've ever seen. On his cheeks and his lips, it was like the blood was on the surface."

That hot blood boiled over before *Casablanca* was a day old. And Francis Scheid was the target.

"Curtiz was a miserable bastard to work for," said Fran Scheid in the summer of 1990. Most of the early sound technicians came from the telephone company. They had no artistic experience but were hired because they knew how to wire equipment. Scheid is a college graduate. If he hadn't worn glasses, he says, he would have been an actor instead of a sound man. "But I was blind without them, and in those days a movie actor couldn't wear glasses. Three years ago I had an operation and now, at eighty-two, I don't need glasses anymore."

Scheid had acted in plays with the mother of Lloyd Bacon, and he asked the Warner Bros. director to get him past the gates of the old Warner studio in Hollywood. The year was 1929. Every day Scheid waited in the room where they stored the rugs for someone to call for a laborer or need a man to carry props. It was a perfect vantage point from which to observe the dynamics of the studio. "I decided not to go into the production department because it was full of the executives' relatives," Scheid says. "I thought, 'I can't fight the cousins and uncles.' I watched the sound men when I stood in the rafters and dropped microphones down. And I thought, 'These guys aren't too smart. So that's where I'll go.' "

Francis Scheid had not wanted to work on *Casablanca*. And Curtiz had not wanted him. "I was a peasant to Curtiz," says Scheid. "But they always put me with him. I had done six pictures with the bastard. At Warners, if a director didn't like you, it didn't make a bit of difference. They put you on the picture anyway."

Even before he set foot on stage 12A, Scheid made a decision not to be humiliated by Curtiz. The war had already changed things. Scheid had applied for a commission in both the Air Force and the Navy, and he was waiting to see which came through first. Nearly every branch of the service had a film unit, and men who knew how to handle cameras or sound equipment were fought over. Scheid, who took his sound equipment onto the Normandy beaches on D day plus seven, would end the war as a captain in a combat camera unit of the 9th Air Force.

After lunch on May 25, Curtiz did rehearsal after rehearsal of the four-page love scene in La Belle Aurore, the Paris café.

Francis Scheid (right) in The Petrified Forest. *The sound editor for* Casablanca, *he started his career as an actor.*

"With the whole world crumbling we pick this time to fall in love," says Ilsa.

"Yeah, it's pretty bad timing. Where were you, say, ten years ago?"

"Ten years ago? Let's see. Yes, I was having a brace put on my teeth. Where were you?

"Looking for a job."

"It was a real difficult scene because there was a low-beamed ceiling, and Curtiz played the scene right under the beams," says Scheid, who, as sound mixer, was head of the sound crew. "I told him there was no way to put a mike in. He said, 'Oh shut up, you dumb sound man.'"

Earlier in the day, the filming had been complicated by the fact that the music was not prerecorded but was being recorded on stage. Dooley Wilson was pretending to play "As Time Goes By" to Bogart and Bergman while the song was actually being played by Elliot Carpenter, who sat at a piano out of camera range where Wilson could watch his hand movements.

Curtiz may not have been in the best of moods to begin with. His right hand was wrapped in bandages, a memento of the weekend's polo match. But finally, after a dozen rehearsals, he was ready to shoot the love scene. After four lines, Scheid killed the tape. "She sounds lousy," he told Curtiz.

"He got red in the face, completely red in the face," Scheid says. He said, 'To hell with you, to hell with you, to hell with you.' I said, 'To hell with you.' You could have heard a pin drop. In the silence, I said, 'To hell with you' once more."

Scheid went home and told his wife he was going to be fired. He drank a pitcher of Tom Collins and waited for the phone to ring. By morning, no one had called. "Jesus, I'm not going to phone to find out if I'm fired," Scheid said, and went to work.

That morning, Wallis sent a long memo to the sound department:

> The major portion of our day's work was a four page scene which was carefully lined up, lighted, and rehearsed late yesterday afternoon. Mike Curtiz told me that he had twelve different rehearsals, with lights on and everything in readiness and he had no objection or comment from the mixer during any of these twelve rehearsals.
> Then, as they started their first take the actors spoke about four of their lines at which point the mixer's voice called out and said,

It was the open-beamed ceiling of this set that caused the sound problems on the first day of shooting.

"Cut," and explained that there was a noise from the sun arcs which he picked up. The time after that required to replace the offending lamp made it impossible for us to get the take yesterday.

My question to you is, why didn't the mixer hear the hum of the sun arc during the twelve rehearsals? Why didn't he speak up at that time, which would have given the company plenty of opportunity to replace the lamp while other rehearsals were taking place? As I understand it, the mixer's argument was that there were too many other noises for him to have heard the sun arc during the rehearsals, but this was not the case as the scene was a very tender, delicate one and Mike called for absolute quiet on the set.

The memo is the version Curtiz told to Wallis fifty years ago, and Scheid's own face grows red as he challenges it. "Why didn't the mixer hear the sun arcs? It wasn't quiet enough. 'No complaint!' That's a lie! I said, 'I can't do it.' Yelling and screaming at me, he said, 'You will do it. Sit down.'"

When Scheid walked onto Stage 12A Tuesday morning, Curtiz looked at him and said, "I'm sorry you got mad at me."

"Mike was gutless," says Scheid. "If anyone challenged him, he would back down. Let a little guy be docile and he'd chew him up."

Jack Warner wasn't at the studio when *Casablanca* started production. Dressed in his uniform as a lieutenant colonel in the Army Air Force, Warner had taken the Super Chief to Chicago and then the Twentieth Century Limited to New York for the May 27 premiere of Michael Curtiz's previous movie, *Yankee Doodle Dandy*. One of the paradoxes at Warner Bros. was that the studio's stinginess was counterbalanced by generosity when it came to the war. The price of admission to the premiere was the purchase of a war bond. It was the first time that a premiere had been used to sell war bonds, and the Treasury Department raised $5.5 million. Later, at the Los Angeles premiere of *Yankee Doodle Dandy,* another $5.8 million worth of war bonds were sold.

Warners was almost always first and most enthusiastic in raising money, making films, and donating blood for the government. When the Red Cross opened a Hollywood blood bank, 504 Warner employees gave blood during the first month. Reading the *Warner Club News* makes it clear that there was a certain amount of coercion. "A high-ball a day, a pack of cigarettes a day, or two or three 'cokes' a day will win the war if that money is put into BONDS," a typical editorial admonished. (The writers managed to resist such exhortations. When 100 percent of the studio's actors and janitors were buying war stamps and bonds through paycheck deductions each week, and even 52 percent of the laborers were giving, only 50 percent of the writers had enrolled.) In April 1942, five weeks before *Casablanca* began shooting, Warner Bros. proudly became the first studio—and one of the first companies in the country—to win the United States Treasury flag for the purchase of war bonds and stamps by its employees.

There was nothing halfhearted or cynical about Jack and Harry Warner's response to the war. The studio had already lost more than a million dollars on a series of fourteen patriotic shorts it produced and distributed before America entered the war, but Harry Warner said he would continue producing such shorts because they safeguarded America's future. In December 1942, Harry met with all the studio department heads and told them that he didn't want to make "a single dollar of profit" on the four to five hundred reels of training pictures Warners would make for the government during

1943. If Warner Bros. had to spend more than government regulations allowed, Harry said that the studio would take the losses. Warners had gotten the movie rights to Irving Berlin's musical play *This Is the Army* by promising to give half the profits to Army Emergency Relief. The studio gave away all the profits, $7 million.

When *Yankee Doodle Dandy* was premiered, the director was left behind. And, since Jack Warner never liked sharing the spotlight, Hal Wallis, who had been Warner's coproducer on the movie, had made the decision to stay home to launch his new film. It was a wobbly launch. Very little went right on the set of *Casablanca* that first day.

Of the stars, Bergman had the more difficult job. Bogart had only to play a man in love. Foreshadowing without giving away too much, Bergman had to let the audience know that love wasn't enough.

ILSA
And I hate this war so much. Oh, it's a crazy world. Anything can happen. If you shouldn't get away, I mean, if, if something should happen to keep us apart. Wherever they put you and wherever I'll be, I want you to know that I—Kiss me! Kiss me as though it were the last time.

And Bergman had to hold the audience even when she was saying dialogue that was so richly romantic that it was almost a parody, including "Was that cannon fire? Or was it my heart pounding?"

Her voice and her face could make almost anything believable. In 1947, several top sound men agreed that Bergman had the sexiest voice of any actress. "The middle register of her voice is rich and vibrant, which gives it a wonderfully disturbing quality," said Francis Scheid. "It's sexy in a refined, high-minded way." "The face is quite amazing," says Pauline Kael. "I think she had a physical awkwardness on the stage and in her early films, but I think somehow that the beauty of her face obviated it. Even in *Casablanca,* her physical movements are not very expressive. But you didn't really care."

As usual, Bergman was radiant and placid, giving no hint of whatever inner turmoil she was feeling. She may not have felt any disquiet, since she had played a woman tormented by love in a dozen films, Swedish and American, by the time she made *Casablanca*. And, with her usual diligence, she had gone to see *The*

Maltese Falcon several times so that she could get used to Bogart, "so that when I met him I wouldn't be so frightened."

It was different for Bogart; he was snappish and moody. Love scenes were uncharted waters for him. "I've always gotten out of my scrapes in front of the camera with a handy little black automatic," he told a journalist who visited the *Casablanca* set during production. "It's a lead pipe cinch. But this. Well, this leaves me a little baffled." The interview is typically frothy and insubstantial as Bogart plays with the idea of becoming a sophisticated lover or a caveman lover. But, even as he jokes about it, his uneasiness is obvious. "I'm not up on this love stuff and don't know just what to do."

According to a memoir by Bogart's friend Nathaniel Benchley, before *Casablanca* began shooting, a mutual friend, Mel Baker, advised Bogart to stand still and make Bergman come to him in the love scenes. Bogart appears to have taken the advice, but his reticence may have been as much innate as calculated. Nearly a dozen years after *Casablanca,* Bogart told a biographer that love scenes still embarrassed him. "I have a personal phobia maybe because I don't do it very well," he said.

"What the women liked about Bogey, I think," said Bette Davis, "was that when he did love scenes he held back—like many men do—and they understood that." Miscast as an Irish horse trainer in *Dark Victory,* Bogart had tried to make love to Davis, who played his rich employer. Said Davis, "Up until Betty Bacall I think Bogey really was embarrassed doing love scenes, and that came over as a certain reticence. With her he let go, and it was great. She matched his insolence."

However distant Bogart and Bergman may have been from each other in real life, and however uneasy Bogart may have been with Bergman in his arms, their love scenes have the poignancy and passion that Hollywood calls chemistry. "I honestly can't explain it," says Pauline Kael, "but Bogart had that particular chemistry with ladylike women. He had it with Katharine Hepburn in *The African Queen* and he so conspicuously had it with Lauren Bacall—who pretended to be a tough girl but really wasn't—in *To Have and Have Not.* But he didn't have it with floozy-type girls."

Critic Stanley Kauffmann explains the match between Bogart and Bergman as the resonance of a relationship between brash America and cultured Europe. "She was like a rose," he says. "You could almost smell the fragrance off her in the picture, and you could feel his whiskers when you looked at the screen. It was intangible. Movies put things together expecting things to happen that don't happen. Put a fine actor like Robert De Niro in a picture with Meryl Streep, a fine actress, and nothing happens."

That first day—while Bergman waited patiently and Bogart grew more surly—Arthur Edeson fussed for nearly an hour and a half before he was satisfied with the lighting for the love scene in La Belle Aurore. Wallis had wanted James Wong Howe, but Edeson brought his own strengths to the photography of *Casablanca*.

By the time he filmed *Casablanca,* Edeson—who was making $500 a week—had been a cameraman for thirty years and a portrait photographer before that. He turned the crank on his first movie camera in 1913 when movies were one reel long and made in New Jersey. In 1942, Edeson still liked to load and handle the camera himself, even though the American Society of Cinematographers frowned on cinematographers doing the pushing and pulling. But then Edeson had been one of the fifteen cameramen who founded the society in 1919.

Edeson, who was little more than five feet tall and whose nickname at Warner Bros. was "The Little Napoleon," had been a cameraman in the days when every movie was an experiment. In 1924, he had had lenses designed that gave an otherworldly distortion to Douglas Fairbanks's *The Thief of Bagdad,* and in 1925 he was putting cardboard in front of the camera so that Constance Talmadge could play a dual role in *Her Sister from Paris.* "I spent weeks testing and experimenting to get the illusion necessary to make the scenes of the Flying Carpet realistic," he said of *The Thief of Bagdad.* "In those days we knew nothing of projective process and these scenes had to be made by double exposure. Some scenes in the picture had as many as eleven exposures on a single strip of film."

Edeson's greatest work in silent films may have been on Fairbanks's *Robin Hood,* for which he covered the forest with blue gauze sixty feet high and one hundred feet long to give a diminished perspective and yet retain sharpness. "Arthur Edeson's photography makes such magnificent use of Buckland's incredible sets that each new shot has an almost physical impact," Kevin Brownlow wrote in *The Parade's Gone By.*

Edeson had told Fairbanks that *Robin Hood* cried out for dramatic photography but that such photography would overwhelm the picture unless the story and characters were strong enough to support it. Unlike most cinematographers, who were only interested in images, Edeson was continually aware of the story that he was photographing. "The principal factors are always the story and the actors," he said. "The picture *The Maltese Falcon* called for strong, modernistic, eye-arresting camerawork. Other pictures require that the camerawork be as inconspicuous as possible to heighten the illusion of realism and perhaps keep it from overpowering a weak story. The best thing I think is to strive to always keep things as simple as possible photographically speaking. And if lighting and composition are kept simple and the accent is placed on the story and actors rather than on the camera, we can't go very far wrong."

Edeson's emphasis on the actors and the story would add an extra dimension to *Casablanca*. Haskell Wexler, who won an Academy Award for his photography of *Who's Afraid of Virginia Woolf?* in 1966 and another in 1976 for *Bound for Glory* has seen *Casablanca* many times. Recently he sat down and looked at nothing but the photography. "The photography bears out what Edeson said," says Wexler. "He really works on making the photography part of the story. The opening scenes were rather documentary for those days. People were dark in the foreground. It set the film in the time and place. When he got into the romantic sections in Rick's Café, and Ingrid Bergman came in, he actually caressed her face. He put net filters on her. It was like looking through your panty hose. And he delicately shadowed her forehead so your eye would go into her eyes and eyebrows and her forehead didn't seem as long as it really was."

After he saw *Casablanca,* David O. Selznick would tell Wallis of his gratitude for Edeson's "superb photography of Ingrid." But in photography as in other things *Casablanca* lurched to a start. During the first two weeks Edeson worked on the movie, his work would be criticized several times by Wallis, and he would break into tears. The first memo from Wallis came on Tuesday morning, May 26:

> I understand that the setup took an extraordinary length of time yesterday and that the little Montmartre Café scene which Mike lined up yesterday afternoon but did not shoot, took about an hour and a half to light. This was a very small set involving only two people and, if it is true that it took an hour and a half to get the lighting set, I must say that it is unreasonable.
>
> I, too, want a beautiful photographic job on this picture, which

Although Arthur Edeson had been a cinematographer for almost thirty years, nothing went right on the first day of shooting.

offers a great deal of background and color for a cameraman, but you were present at all the meetings we had about all the war emergencies and the necessity of conserving money and material, and I must ask you to sacrifice a little on quality, if necessary, in order not to take these long periods of time for setups.

Edeson, who tended to strut across his sets, was not a man to sacrifice quality, and lighting had always been his specialty. He said that in 1914, when movies used flat lighting, he introduced the softer lighting he had used in portraits—"a suggesting of modeling here, an artistically placed shadow there"—ideas that, he said, "were completely out of line with what was considered good photography in those days." In the early thirties, Edeson had been noted for his bold effect lighting in a series of horror movies—*Frankenstein, The Old Dark House, The Invisible Man.* George Pratt of Eastman House considered Edeson's work on *The Invisible Man* the finest trick work since Georges Melies at the turn of the century.

No matter how upset Edeson was when Wallis wrote him about taking too much time, he was more upset a week later when Wallis complained about the look of the first scenes in Rick's Café. Wallis asked for more contrast and sent Edeson to examine the tests of Michele Morgan and Jean-Pierre Aumont, which had the look he wanted. "I am anxious to get real blacks and whites, with the walls and the backgrounds in shadow, and dim, sketchy lighting," Wallis wrote in a memo to Edeson on June 2. Two days later Wallis was still complaining that Rick's Café was not dark enough.

"They wanted it kind of shadowy, mysterious," Scheid says. "It pierced Arthur through the heart. He cried. 'What are they doing to me?' Arthur was always suffering. He was kind of a weak sister."

Says Katz, "He cried, but he knew what he was doing. Arthur would not have stood up to Hal or Mike. But he wasn't a bad guy."

In this case, cinematographer Wexler sides with Hal Wallis. Wexler is amazed to find a producer who understands visuals, just as musicians who have examined Wallis's music notes are impressed by his understanding of music. "Wallis's memo of June 2 is intelligent, cogent, helpful, respectful, and also true," Wexler says. "When Edeson went into the closeups, his work was great. But the wide shots at Rick's Café gave it away as a set and didn't have the gutsy look of the other stuff. I think Wallis's criticism was pretty damn good."

It would take weeks for *Casablanca* to settle into a rhythm and a style that satisfied Wallis. And, even then, there was the script to contend with. Wallis summed up his feelings about May 25 in his memo to the sound department: "We had a very poor day for our first day's work on CASABLANCA." An uneasy Humphrey Bogart, an angry Michael Curtiz, and a frustrated Arthur Edeson would have agreed.

But, says Francis Scheid, who was angrier than anyone that Monday night, "All the pictures I worked on where everybody was lovey dovey ended up lousy."

8

The Usual Suspects: Rains, Veidt, Greenstreet, Lorre, and Wilson

———

Except for Dooley Wilson as Sam, none of *Casablanca*'s featured players were needed during the first few days of production. Yet even before *Casablanca's* three stars were set, Hal Wallis had worried about the supporting roles. In the stew of the studio system, stars were the meat and potatoes; character actors were the gravy that held things together. The surprising thing about the casting of *Casablanca* is how few of the actors in the movie were under contract to Warner Bros. Studios always wanted to get their money's worth out of the 85 or 150 actors to whom they owed a weekly paycheck. *The Hard Way,* the next A movie that Warners released after *Casablanca,* was stuffed with Warner contract players: Ida Lupino, Dennis Morgan, Joan Leslie, Jack Carson, Faye Emerson, Ray Montgomery, and Julie Bishop. But Wallis took full advantage of the contract he had signed in January 1942. Warners was required to try to provide him with the actors he wanted, and he filled *Now, Voyager* and *Watch on the Rhine* with such noncontract players as Claude Rains, Paul Henreid, Bonita Granville, Ilka Chase,

Gladys Cooper, Paul Lukas, Lucile Watson, and George Coulouris. Of the actors in *Casablanca,* only Bogart and Sydney Greenstreet were on that January 1942 contract list.*

The freedom Jack Warner had given Wallis quickly became irritating. Giving up any control over his studio rubbed Warner raw. On February 2, 1942, the day Wallis's new contract went into effect, Warner told Jake Wilk, his New York story editor, that all of Wallis's requests to purchase stories and plays must be sent back for approval "by air mail and I will in turn tell you if we should go any further." The chafing continued, and by March 1943 Warner was aggressively trying to remove Wallis's control of actors. "I personally want to okay the actor or actress before you agree to terms and conditions," he wrote his casting director. "This goes especially for pictures that Hal Wallis is producing."

On *Casablanca,* Wallis's first casting idea was almost perversely wrong. He decided to change Sam to a woman. Making Rick's best friend a woman would have unraveled the movie emotionally. Imagine Bogart crumpling into the comforting arms of Hazel Scott as he reads Ilsa's goodbye letter at the Paris train station. But Wallis had seen and admired Scott's act at the Uptown Café Society club in New York. Early in February he had Trilling check on the availability of Scott and of a singer who had been recommended to him, Lena Horne, who was described as a light-skinned colored girl.

The words sound derogatory today, but in 1942, "colored" and "Negro" were the polite appellations, and they were interchangeable. It was a time when black actors were required to be race ambassadors, and the newsletter of the Negro Actors Guild said that Bill Robinson, Ethel Waters, and Duke Ellington had "endeared themselves to thousands" by "their well-bred behavior." Lena Horne—who was not available for *Casablanca* because she had just been placed under contract by M-G-M—was at the center of a storm that erupted during the war over the kinds of roles Negroes should play in movies. Horne's father refused to allow her to sign a contract until L. B. Mayer promised that she would not have to play menial roles. "My father said that he could afford to get a maid

---

* After Madeleine LeBeau won the role of Rick's mistress, she was given a twenty-six-week contract at $100 a week, but she was terminated before the movie was released. Paul Henreid signed a long-term contract the day *Casablanca* started production. And twenty-three-year-old Helmut Dantine so impressed Warner and Wallis as the silent but burning-eyed young husband that he was put under contract while he was working on the film.

FORM 11

WARNER BROS. PICTURES, INC.
BURBANK, CALIFORNIA

INTER-OFFICE COMMUNICATION

TO MR. WALLIS

DATE February 7th, 1942

FROM MR. TRILLING

SUBJECT COLORED GIRL FOR "CASA BLANCA"

Re memo on the colored girls for "CASA BLANCA".

LENA HORN, the singer at the Little Troc, Felix
Young's new place, is signed to a
term contract at MGM starting next
month. She is an excellent talent --
a very pretty light colored girl. Do
not know if she will fit your requirements as she is a stylist, singing soft,
throaty rhythm and torch numbers in a
very intimate manner (no microphone).
Her voice is reminiscent of Florence
Mills, but with the Ethel Waters style
and she does such numbers as "I Cried
For You", "Blues In The Night", "Sweet
Embraceable You", "St. Louis Blues",
etc. She made a test for Universal
about a month ago and I will try to get
it, as there is always a possibility we
can borrow her for a specific role. I
have no idea why MGM would want to sign
her for a term -- unless they have several musicals to use her in. You probably
saw her in New York over the past few years
as she was at the "Cafe Society" in the
Village, and drew attention last year at
the Jam Session at Carnegie Hall when she
sang with Count Basie.

ELLA FITZGERALD is going to appear at the Trianon here
starting April 30th for a run -- and might
be a suggestion as she is a more exuberant
colored stylist. Of course, neither of these
girls are pianists -- strictly singers. I will
therefore try to get a check on HAZEL SCOTT'S
possible availability after I get some indication from you when "CASA BLANCA" might go
into production.

ST:vj   STEVE TRILLING

VERBAL MESSAGES CAUSE MISUNDERSTANDING AND DELAYS
(PLEASE PUT THEM IN WRITING)

for his daughter, and so his daughter shouldn't play maids. I don't think Mayer had ever been approached by a gorgeous black man with all that chutzpah," says Horne, who could have passed for Spanish but refused.

The National Association for the Advancement of Colored People and such militant actors as Paul Robeson insisted that no black actors should play menial roles. A number of black actors, including Clarence Muse, who almost played the part of Sam, told the NAACP to keep its nose out of Hollywood. They said that without old plantation mammies and Uncle Tom parts, there would be no roles at all for Negro actors. The Office of War Information was also trying to get the studios to upgrade Negro characters, and the OWI's attitude was largely responsible for all those war movies in which a black man fights next to a farm boy from Iowa and a fast-talking New Yorker. Those integrated platoons existed only in Hollywood. The real Army was segregated, the Navy used blacks as kitchen help, and the Marine Corps didn't accept blacks in any capacity until six months after the war started. After the OWI encouraged Hollywood to be sensitive about showing Negroes as servants, parts for black actors were often simply eliminated. By the end of the war, the Negro Actors Guild had lost 50 percent of its members.

The role of Sam in *Casablanca* was one of a handful in the early 1940s in which an African-American was allowed some dignity. Since Sam was Rick's employee as well as his friend, he could not match the character played by Leigh Whipper who objects to lynching suspected cattle rustlers in *The Ox-Bow Incident* or the Negro clerk played by Ernest Anderson in *In This Our Life* (written by Howard Koch) who resists bribes and threats and refuses to lie about Bette Davis's automobile accident. But for 1942 Sam was a sympathetic and restrained character, partly because of the way the role was written and partly because of the sweetness that was brought to it by Dooley Wilson. For a comparison with the roles black actors were usually given, one has only to look at Wilson's previous film, *Night in New Orleans,* which was released in July while Wilson was making *Casablanca.* In that film, Wilson played Shadrack Jones, described by *The New York Times* as the "inevitable colored servant who makes sounds of appropriate comic alarm when the lights go out or a body suddenly splashes off a fogbound wharf."

How or by whom Wallis was talked out of turning Sam into a woman is not recorded, but Curtiz directed a test of Dooley Wilson on April 20. Wallis's criticism of the way Curtiz chose to characterize Sam is one more example of how Wallis shaped the movie.

Dear Mike:

The test of Dooley Wilson is pretty good. He isn't ideal for the part but if we get stuck and can't do any better I suppose he could play it.

I didn't particularly like the way the scene was played however, and I think we should have a talk about this so that we are in agreement in the manner of characterization. I didn't like the flip, bouncy manner of the man and it was always my impression that he would be really worried about 'Rick' and that when he said: "Come on, boss. Let's go fishing. Let's get out of here—we'll go for a long drive," etc., that he was pleading with the man, knowing what the results would be if he left him there for 'Lois.'

What happened to the test we were going to make of Clarence Muse?

Hal Wallis

Clarence Muse, who was one of the founders of a black theater company in Harlem, had been playing the usual submissive movie roles since 1929 and was comfortably well off because of it. He owned a thirty-eight-acre chicken farm in the San Fernando Valley. Muse tested for Sam, as did William Gillespie, Napoleon Simpson, Fred Skinner, and Elliot Carpenter, who would play the piano for Sam in the movie. (Dooley Wilson was a professional drummer, but he didn't know how to play the piano.) Curtiz found Carpenter unsuitable and cut his test short. Wallis made it clear that he preferred Muse, but a contract was never signed and Muse ended up instead as a house servant in Wallis's *Watch on the Rhine,* which started production fifteen days after *Casablanca.*

"Clarence Muse wouldn't have been right at all," says Katherine Dunham, who costarred with Dooley Wilson on Broadway in 1940 in *Cabin in the Sky.* "I think Clarence Muse had gotten to a point where he couldn't move from under the stereotype."

Dooley Wilson had tried to resist stereotyping. Born Arthur Wilson, Dooley got his nickname because he specialized in Irish roles, which he played in whiteface. He began singing for his supper at churches in Tyler, Texas, when he was seven, the year his father died. By the time he was eight, he had graduated to tent shows and tear-jerking ballads like "I'm Only a Bird in a Gilded Cage," and he

Dooley Wilson, who played Sam. Wilson got his name from singing Irish songs in whiteface.

was making $18 a week. His contract at Paramount Pictures lists his birthdate as 1884, but he may have been born as late as 1887. He was the youngest of five children of a laborer, and no one kept careful records.

By 1908 Wilson was a member of the Pekin Theatre in Chicago, the first legitimate black theater in the United States. It was at the Pekin that Arthur Wilson earned his nickname, when he put on white makeup and pretended to be an Irishman as he sang the song "Mr. Dooley." During the next decade, he was part of most of the early attempts at theater for black actors, including the Anita Bush Company in New York City in 1914 and Charles Gilpin's Lafayette Players Stock Company in Harlem in 1915. He also formed a band and sang in cabarets. After the First World War Europe seemed more hospitable than America. Dooley formed a new band—he sang and played the drums—and went overseas.

Back in the United States during the Depression, he starred in *Conjur' Man Dies* for John Houseman's Negro Theatre wing of the Federal Theatre Project, the play that preceded the Houseman–

Orson Welles Negro *Macbeth.* Then, in 1940, Wilson got the break that eventually brought him to Hollywood, the role of Little Joe in *Cabin in the Sky.* Little Joe was a lazy rascal and gambling man whose soul had to be saved by his wife, Ethel Waters, from the devil's sexy emissary Katherine Dunham.

Dunham, whose Katherine Dunham dance company was already prominent, had been recruited by the choreographer George Balanchine. "I was absolutely green," she says. "I had never sung in a Broadway show. Dooley helped me carry the rough edges of Ethel Waters, who was always mad at somebody and particularly at me. She used rough language I wasn't accustomed to then. Dooley was essentially a gentle person, honest and straightforward. And modest."

The Communist *Daily Worker* described *Cabin in the Sky* as "a show which is shameful in its maltreatment of the Negro," with "cardboard figures cut to fit the white man's assumed ideas," but Dooley got good enough reviews elsewhere. He was signed by Paramount, where he made $350 a week playing Pullman porters. Since *Cabin in the Sky* was bought by M-G-M, Katherine Dunham and Dooley Wilson lost the movie roles to Lena Horne and Eddie ("Rochester") Anderson.

Lena Horne speaks of Dooley Wilson as "sweet" and "dear." In addition to having exquisite looks, Horne was lucky. It was courtesy of the government that two all-Negro musicals, *Cabin in the Sky* and *Stormy Weather,* were available for her to star in. According to *The New York Times,* the Roosevelt Administration felt that putting Negroes in important movies would help a government effort to get them hired by war industries. Manpower was a problem, and black manpower was being wasted by industries that balked at hiring Negroes. Dooley Wilson also benefited, playing the small role of a drummer in *Stormy Weather.* Of course, there were no blacks in the movie hairdressers' union and M-G-M's white hairdressers refused to work on Horne, so the head of the department, Sydney Guillaroff, did her hair himself.

In May 1942, Warner Bros. borrowed Wilson from Paramount for a guaranteed seven weeks at $500 a week to play "Sam the Rabbit" in *Casablanca.* Paramount pocketed the extra $150 a week. The studios either made a profit when they rented their actors or laid off the salary of a contract player who would otherwise have been idle for a few weeks. Since Sam was a minor role and Wilson a minor actor, there was no argument over or even a mention of billing, a relief from the complicated contracts of the other featured players.

Claude Rains had to receive "first featured billing on all positive prints and paid publicity issued under the control of the Producer." Conrad Veidt who played Major Strasser was "to be billed in fifth position, not less than second feature and the same size type as Claude Rains." Because the role of the owner of the Blue Parrot was so small, the studio enticed Sydney Greenstreet into playing it by giving him a special contract at $3,750 a week—his regular contract called for two movies a year at $1,500 per week—and promised him featured billing on the movie screen and in the paid publicity. Peter Lorre had to be given featured billing on screen, although his name did not need to be mentioned in the advertising. In mid-July, when *Casablanca* was getting further behind schedule every day, Greenstreet's $3,750 a week became irksome to Wallis, who was already complaining about the movie's large and expensive cast. Greenstreet's role would only take five days to shoot, but he sat around the set for most of July, affably doing nothing. Greenstreet would end up being paid more than $13,000 for his few scenes.

Movies today are bigger, brighter, technically dazzling, awesome in their computer-generated special effects. But they are also thinner. They lack the thick layers of character actors who brought depth to the background and refracted the star's light so that it formed a different and more complicated image. At Warner Bros., there was Alan Hale as Little John challenging Errol Flynn's Robin Hood, then riding beside Flynn into *Dodge City* and *Virginia City* and standing on a wooden deck beside him in *The Sea Hawk*. There was Gene Lockhart—treacherous, oily, not to be trusted. There was the all-purpose heel, Jack Carson, who could turn into the hero's clowning best friend if the movie was a comedy, and the proletarian standard-bearer George Tobias, who seemed to be in two dozen Warner war movies. Frank McHugh brought his Irish charm and high-pitched laugh to a half-a-dozen Warner movies a year. And there were character stars with the weight and authority of Raymond Massey, who moved from Abraham Lincoln to the abolitionist John Brown to the captain of Humphrey Bogart's ship in *Action in the North Atlantic*.

These actors, two paces behind the stars and a few steps to the left, filled in the blank spaces. Carroll O'Connor might have had such a career at Warner Bros. in the 1930s. But neither the scripts nor the times allow it now. Films today tell private, not public, stories. There are few movies of social observation that require half-a-dozen character actors to bring richness and depth to their subplots. In most movies, the subplots are nonexistent, and the camera is continually pointed at the $6 million star, or, sometimes, at the $10 million star and his $3 million best friend or girlfriend. And, before Frank Morgan, Thelma Ritter, Reginald Gardiner, Basil Rathbone, Flora Robson, or Donald Crisp could build the audience goodwill that comes from familiarity, they would—like Carroll O'-Connor, Ed Asner, and Charles Durning—be starring in a television series.

By most definitions, Conrad Veidt and Claude Rains were character actors. By others, they were stars, including the fact that Warner Bros. paid them $5,000 a week and $4,000 a week respectively for *Casablanca*. Veidt had been a major star in silent films in Germany (*The Cabinet of Dr. Caligari*) and Hollywood (*The Man Who Laughs*) before Hollywood demanded that he play Nazis. Rains's career was of a dual nature. He moved easily between title roles—the phantom in *Phantom of the Opera, Mr. Skeffington,* Caesar in *Caesar and Cleopatra*—and worldly-wise villains, urbanely corruptible politicians, and the psychiatrist every patient would like to have in *Now, Voyager.*

Bette Davis always thought that *Now, Voyager* ended wrong. In her mind, she wrote a new ending for the film. Instead of spending the rest of her life pining for Paul Henreid, Davis's Charlotte married Rains's Dr. Jacquith. Davis and Rains admired each other for thirty years. When she arrived for a visit at his farm in Pennsylvania after they costarred in *Deception,* her first words were "You son-of-a-bitch, you stole the picture." He could steal a picture from anyone. It was partly because of his charm and the way he filled out a role and made the character more sardonic, suave, cynical, or on the edge of madness than the script implied. It was partly because of his voice—wry, insinuating, seductive, cultured. "That voice was one of the great actors' voices that I have ever heard," says *New Republic* critic Stanley Kauffmann. "It was easy, warm, and had a tremendous range. He could make it do whatever he wanted. His voice by itself was an attraction, something that was true of James Mason and Rex Harrison too."

It was his voice that got Rains his first movie role in 1933. Rains, who was forty-four years old, had been brought to Hollywood by Universal for a test. The test, Rains always said, was awful. Having spent his life on the stage, the actor stormed the camera. He was sent back to the New York theater, where he was a leading actor with the Theatre Guild. A few weeks later his test was being run along with other rejects. In the screening room next door, director James Whale listened and said the equivalent of "I don't care what he looks like. That's the voice I want." Rains's voice starred in Whale's *The Invisible Man*. He played the role covered with bandages, his face seen only at the moment of his death.

The joke was that the urbane Claude Rains, like the similarly elegant Cary Grant, was self-created. "He didn't go to school past the second grade," says his daughter, Jessica. "He was one of twelve children. All but two died. He had a very serious cockney accent and a speech impediment."

At ten, Willie Rains was selling newspapers and singing in a church choir for packets of sweets. The next year, 1900, he played a ragged street urchin in *Sweet Nell of Old Drury* at the Haymarket Theatre in London's West End. Then he became a call boy, knocking at the dressing rooms of Sarah Bernhardt and Ellen Terry to tell them the time until curtain. Sir Herbert Beerbohm Tree saw an actor in the boy who called himself Willie Wains because he couldn't say the letter "r." Tree gave him the money for elocution books and lessons, and Willie spent eighteen months practicing in front of a mirror. He was with Tree seven years, as call boy, prompter, stage manager, and actor. Near the end of his life, when he was reminiscing for an autobiography that was never written, Rains said that he had never had any ambition to be an actor, that success was thrust upon him.

During the First World War, Rains was gassed at Vimy Ridge. He was almost blind in one eye after that, but few people ever knew it. "When we walked down the street, he would switch me from side to side," says his daughter, "because he didn't want anybody to know." Rains had turned a cockney boy with a speech impediment into an officer and a gentleman, and there were to be no flaws in the new creation. He had done what was almost impossible in the class-bound British society: he had entered the Army as a private and emerged a captain. With his stage-created confidence and upper-class accent, he had acted himself into the role.

Rains was on his way to reenlist when he passed a theater where a friend offered him a job. By the mid-1920s an English theater critic listed him as one of the "Twenty Hopes" of the English stage. Among the twenty were Somerset Maugham, Noel Coward, Gordon Craig, and Edmund Gwenn. Rains used to say that in his career he had played everything but a woman and the hind part of a horse. Even as a young man he was good at what one British critic called "degenerate characters." But he also found a home in the stinging socialist comedies written by George Bernard Shaw. Rains treasured copies of Shaw's plays which the author had inscribed: "To my favorite actor" and "To my favorite interpreter."

In 1942, Rains was happy. He was married to the fourth of his six wives, and at fifty-two, he was the father of a four-year-old daughter, his first and only child. "Women always served on him," Paul Henreid said in a 1972 oral history. Ingrid Bergman called Paul Henreid a prima donna. Henreid applied the same words to Rains. "He was the kind of man who was like a big baby. An unbelievable prima donna," Henreid said. "Everybody served on him because he played the role of being helpless. I always say to my wife, 'I wish I'd started in our marriage to play the role of being helpless.' " Henreid and Rains acted together in four movies. They had just finished *Now, Voyager* when they began *Casablanca,* and would later appear in *Deception* and *Rope of Sand.* "Claude had this attitude of let everybody do everything for me. I'll just sit back and let them do it," said Henreid. "Otherwise, I think he would have in his career been probably as important as Leslie [Howard] or Ronnie Colman, because he certainly was a superb actor."

Casablanca was Rains's thirty-second film. He had already created a portrait gallery that ranged from the ambitious district attorney who gets an innocent man hanged in *They Won't Forget* to the petulant Prince John in *The Adventures of Robin Hood,* from the corrupt senator in Frank Capra's *Mr. Smith Goes to Washington* to the lovable father in *Four Daughters, Four Wives,* and *Four Mothers. Four Daughters* had brought Julius Epstein his first Academy Award nomination for screenwriting and, after that, he thought of Claude Rains as his good-luck piece. Yet Epstein wasn't happy when he was told that Rains would play Captain Renault. Says Epstein, "We told Wallis and Curtiz, 'There are so many good French actors. Why get an Englishman?' " But Wallis, who had chosen to work with Rains on everything from *The Prince and the Pauper* and *The Adventures of Robin Hood* to *Now, Voyager* never seriously considered anyone else.

Claude Rains, above, with Merle Oberon; his daughter, Jennifer (who later changed her name to Jessica), and his wife, Frances.

And Rains never considered turning down the meaty and well-written role of the amused cynic for whom compromise is an art.

Under contract at Warner Bros. a few years earlier at $30,000 per picture, Rains was willing to accept a guaranteed $20,000—five weeks at $4,000 per week—to be in *Casablanca*.* He finished his role in *Now, Voyager* on June 3 and did his first scene in *Casablanca* at 10:30 the next morning. Rains's bigger compromise was spending the summer in Los Angeles. He found Southern California "bare, cold, and brown." His heart belonged to a 380-acre farm, Stock Grange, in Pennsylvania. He sat on the set of *Casablanca* and read brochures on fertilizer and soybeans. In 1941, Rains had raised eighty tons of hay, eleven hundred bushels of barley, and thirteen hundred bushels of corn. "When he talked about his estate, talked about the farming, you had the feeling that he was talking about something that he loved," says Rick's bartender, Leonid Kinskey.

---

* Rains actually worked seven weeks and made $28,000.

"Otherwise, you couldn't squeeze a word out of him."

The difference between character actors and stars was more than salary and status. Although they had screen personas as strong as the stars whom they accompanied—and sometimes stronger—character actors did not trigger adoration. Because almost no one in the audience wanted to be Charles Coburn or Marjorie Main, or to be their lovers, or to destroy them, the actors were more or less able to keep their work separate from their lives, to make acting a job in a way that audiences would not tolerate from Humphrey Bogart or Ingrid Bergman. Audiences invested their dreams in stars and expected to be repaid, with interest. Since the real Bogart and Bergman were somewhat, but not entirely, like the reel Bogart and Bergman, the celluloid cloaks they wore complicated their ordinary

Claude Rains at his beloved farm in Pennsylvania.

lives. Bogart dressed in his screen persona offscreen and was always being attacked in bars. Bergman left her innocence on screen and shocked America when she ran away with Roberto Rossellini.

There was freedom in being a successful character actor. If stars had to be perfect, or at least heroic, Claude Rains could indulge himself by being a villain. He elaborated on the pleasures of villainy in a number of interviews. "We spend a good portion of our lives stifling impulses to be bad," he told Hedda Hopper, and added that it was delightful to get paid for being a heel. "You can get rid of all your nastiness on the stage," he told his biographer.

Conrad Veidt was probably tired of being nasty by the time he was cast as Major Strasser in *Casablanca*. Former casting director Steve Trilling had suggested Otto Preminger, who was thirteen years younger than Veidt, for the role of Strasser, who was then a Gestapo captain, and Preminger was tested on April 27. It wasn't necessary to test Conrad Veidt. He had been playing smart, malicious Germans since the mid-thirties. Including *Casablanca*, Veidt played Nazis in three movies that reached theaters in 1942. In M-G-M's *Nazi Agent* he not only played the evil Nazi spy but his loyal-to-America twin brother. In Warners' *All Through the Night*, he loaded a speedboat with explosives and drove it at a battleship in New York harbor but was foiled by Humphrey Bogart. Just a month before Veidt was given the role of Major Strasser in *Casablanca*, director Herman Shumlin refused to have him play the Nazi sympathizer in *Watch on the Rhine*. "Veidt, I think, is too immediately sinister," Shumlin wrote Wallis. "I am afraid he would be too much the villain on first sight." Shumlin's resistance was another of the accidents that benefited *Casablanca*. If Shumlin had been pressured into accepting him, Veidt would not have been available.

Born in Berlin in 1893, Veidt had started out as the hero, not the villain. Exceptionally handsome, he had become a star overnight in 1919 as the sleepwalker in *The Cabinet of Dr. Caligari*. In 1926, John Barrymore insisted that Veidt come to Hollywood to costar with him in *The Beloved Rogue*. Veidt was under contract to Universal for two years at $1,500 a week before the innovation of talking films and his imperfect English sent him back to Germany in 1929. He chose to leave despite his huge success a year earlier as the tragic clown whose face is twisted into a perpetual smile in *The Man Who Laughed*.

Veidt was not Jewish, but his second wife, Lily, was. They

married in 1933 and left immediately for England. "Veidt would never have moved away from his adored daughter, Viola, unless it was absolutely necessary," says Patricia Battle, who is writing a biography of the actor. "But he made sure his daughter and his first wife were safe in Switzerland before the war began. There is a story—which may not be true—that when Veidt left Germany for good and had to fill in a form asking religious affiliation, he wrote 'JEW.' "

When he was interviewed by Carl Combs, a Warner publicist assigned to *Casablanca,* Veidt denounced Strasser. "This role epitomizes the cruelty and the criminal instincts and murderous trickery of the typical Nazi," he said. "I know this man well. He is the reason I gave up Germany many years ago. He is a man who turned fanatic and betrayed his friends, his homeland, and himself in his lust to be somebody and to get something for nothing."

Veidt became a British citizen in 1938. By that time he was playing grand villains like the Grand Vizier in Alexander Korda's *The Thief of Bagdad.* When war came, he loaned the money he had in the bank to the British government. After he came to America in

Conrad Veidt was a fervent anti-Nazi, who ended his life playing Nazis. He would be the first of the major participants in the making of Casablanca *to die.*

1940, he donated most of his salary from his American films to the British War Relief. He was, after all, only forty-nine years old, under contract to M-G-M, with years of good movies ahead of him. But he would be the first of the major participants in *Casablanca* to die. He dropped dead on a golf course less than a year later.

"Connie must have thought he had fifteen, twenty years more of work," says Robbie Lantz, Veidt's friend and fellow immigrant. A talent agent, Lantz brought Lily Veidt to New York to work in his agency. She survived her husband by more than forty years. "In the most touching and unsentimental and wonderful way, Lily carried the torch to the end," says Lantz. "There was no man after Connie. And she never talked about Connie. Up to the end, it was too painful for her."

In late May, Warner Bros. borrowed Conrad Veidt from M-G-M for $25,000, five weeks at $5,000 a week. By the time Warners borrowed Dooley Wilson from Paramount and Veidt from Metro, the war had caused the studios to cooperate in ways that would have been unthinkable six months earlier. When Conservation Order L-41 limited the cost of sets to $5,000 per movie, the studios coped by borrowing and leasing used sets from each other. In a plan that the *Hollywood Reporter* called "just short of a general pooling of all studio resources," the studios agreed that they would exchange actors and technicians. Although the swapping of contract personnel remained more an abstract idea than a reality, it was a response to a sudden draining of actors and craftsmen into the armed services. By mid-March of 1942, fifteen hundred or 5 percent of Hollywood's thirty thousand employees had enlisted or been drafted. By 1944, that number would reach 22 percent.

On April 29, a month before *Casablanca* went into production, the studio's tentative cast list included Humphrey Bogart as Rick, Ingrid Bergman as Lois Meredith, Claude Rains as Renault, Conrad Veidt or Otto Preminger as Strasser, and Peter Lorre as Ugarte if *Casablanca* didn't conflict with a commitment Lorre had at Universal. Victor Laszlo was still to be selected. Clarence Muse was tentatively scheduled to play Sam. Curt Bois was, equally tentatively, to be Carl the waiter, the role played in the movie by S. Z. Sakall. Fydor, Rick's bartender—whose name was later changed to Sacha—was to be played by Mikhail Rasumny, Michael Delmatoff, or the reliable George Tobias. All the other parts were open.

Wallis and Curtiz did not feel under pressure with the smaller roles. American actors might be in short supply, but Hitler had made sure that Hollywood was full of German, Austrian, Hungarian, Polish, and French actors whose accents and mannerisms seemed interchangeable to the studio casting directors. Wallis wanted Sydney Greenstreet as the black marketeer, but he was willing to accept J. Edward Bromberg if Greenstreet couldn't be persuaded to play the small role. Still, to entice Greenstreet, Wallis had the part enlarged: in *Everybody Comes to Rick's,* the character only appears in the scene where he offers to buy Rick's Café. And the stingy Wallis offered Greenstreet the bait of nearly $4,000 a week. Although the part was still small, Greenstreet was worth the money. Greenstreet's bulk made him one of the few actors who could stand up to Bogart. He had proved it in *The Maltese Falcon* and *Across the Pacific,* and he would prove it again in *Passage to Marseille* and *Conflict.* Greenstreet's affable malignancy made Casablanca more dangerous.

Sydney Greenstreet and Peter Lorre had no scenes together in *Casablanca.* But the mind's eye pairs them, remembering back to *The Maltese Falcon* and ahead to *Background to Danger, Passage to Marseille, The Mask of Dimitrios, The Conspirators, Three Strangers,* and *The Verdict.* They are complements of evil, yin and yang—the huge man, monstrously fat and monstrously corrupt, rolling into a scene like some landlocked ship, and, at his side, the dainty little man whose evil was not of will but of madness.

Greenstreet made his film debut at the age of sixty-one as The Fat Man, Casper Gutman, in *The Maltese Falcon.* From then on, fan mail kept arriving at Warner Bros. addressed simply to "Fat Man." And when Greenstreet died in 1954 at the age of seventy-four, many of his obituaries were headlined "The Fat Man Dies." Just as *Casablanca* was being released, Jack Warner announced that he intended to give Greenstreet the star buildup, and, indeed, Greenstreet was added to the studio's star roster in 1943.

"To some acute Hollywood eye, Greenstreet represented a niche that needed to be filled," says Stanley Kauffmann. "There were other fat men in pictures, but not with that suavity or the depravity underneath the jolly smile."

And fill the niche Greenstreet did. Making up for lost time, he acted in twenty-four movies between 1941 and 1949. In most of them he was greedy—for money, for food, for power—but his corruption was always urbane and often disguised by good manners. By the time he made his first movie, Greenstreet had spent forty years on the stage, almost all of them as a comedian. The story Greenstreet told is that when he left England at the age of nineteen to work on a tea plantation in Ceylon, he discovered that his mother had tucked the complete works of William Shakespeare into his trunk. With nothing else to do during the evenings, he memorized the plays.

Two years later he was back in England, working for a brewery. His mother gave him the money for the Ben Greet Academy of Acting in London. By 1904, Greenstreet was touring America with Ben Greet's Shakespearian Repertory Company. By 1909, he was permanently settled in the United States. For more than two decades, he went back and forth between Shakespeare—Sir Toby Belch in *Twelfth Night,* Dogberry in *Much Ado About Nothing*—and modern plays, in which he usually got the only good notices. A review of *Junk* in 1927 lamented that Greenstreet was so good that the reviewer had no heart to report how bad the play was. "Someone, perhaps, should take his weight and measure and tailor a play for him as good as he deserves."

But it was left to the movies to do that. During the 1930s Hollywood came calling several times. Greenstreet always shook his head. By then, he was working with Alfred Lunt and Lynn Fontanne at the Theatre Guild. And the plays were better too, including Robert Sherwood's *Idiot's Delight.* In the summer of 1941, the Lunts' tour of Sherwood's *There Shall Be No Night* closed down for a while so the stars could take a vacation. The last stop on the tour was Los Angeles. Greenstreet could hardly refuse to do one movie, *The Maltese Falcon,* while he waited for the tour to start up again.

There is a story that may be apocryphal. Greenstreet told the story many times, but the details varied. He was crossing a New York street, he said, when he was run down by a horse and cart. He was uninjured; the horse was so badly hurt that it had to be destroyed.

"Greenstreet was made by his bulk," says Pauline Kael. "And he used his bulk marvelously. That was his chief characteristic as an actor. You can't imagine Sydney Greenstreet being thin. But Peter Lorre was something else. Lorre had a beauty when he was thin that he lost when he ballooned up and became a caricature. If you see

*Sydney Greenstreet
with Ingrid Bergman in
a publicity shot.*

him in one of his thin roles, you're amazed by what an elegant creature he is."

Greenstreet was, by and large, a happy man. Lorre was a tragic one.

An intellectual, a pupil of Sigmund Freud, an actor of delicacy and depth, Lorre was betrayed by his body and, in turn, betrayed it back. He was short. Most of the press releases said five feet five, but he was probably at least an inch shorter. His moon face was described as pasty, his body as squat, his eyes as frog eyes, soft-boiled eggs, Ping-Pong balls, popping out of his head, hanging down his cheeks like eggs.

"This is an absolutely true story," says Stanley Kauffmann. "Lorre had had some theater experience in Vienna when he went for a job in Berlin. The manager of the theater said, 'What can I do with you, you pop-eyed, funny-looking little fellow? But go see my stage manager, and maybe he'll find a place for you.' The stage manager happened to be Bertolt Brecht, and he said, 'You're what

I want for my hero.' It's my belief—you can't find this in any books—that Brecht had a lot to do with Lorre's performance in *M* and with the script of that movie."

Lorre's performance as the child murderer in Fritz Lang's *M* in 1931, a man struggling against his compulsion even as he lured little girls to their deaths with toys and balloons, was one of the great film debuts. It is impossible to watch Lorre's performance without feeling both sympathy and revulsion. Lorre turned down dozens of horror films after that. "I am a young man," he said in a 1934 press release from Columbia Pictures. "I was only 28 then. After playing villains of 50 for a year or two, I would have been through. I want to act forever."

Lorre followed *M* with several German comedies before his satirical sense of humor got him into trouble with the new Nazi regime and sent him—via the usual Vienna-Paris route—to England, where he played the villain in Alfred Hitchcock's *The Man Who Knew Too Much*. He was a Jew, born Laszlo Lowenstein in Hungary on June 26, 1904, so he would have had to leave Germany anyway eventually. He accepted a contract with Columbia because he had been assured that it was not like other big studios. He was

Peter Lorre and Sydney Greenstreet in a scene from The Verdict.

told that Columbia gave freedom to actors and to such directors as Frank Capra, whose *It Happened One Night* Lorre admired. But Harry Cohn didn't know what to do with Lorre, and the actor sat around for months before he was loaned to M-G-M to play a doctor who has become insane from unrequited love in *Mad Love*. A *New York Times* film critic, Andre Sennwald, complained, "Peter Lorre's American film debut should have been one of the important events of the season. Yet the producers were content to arrange a vehicle called *Mad Love* for him, apparently under the delusion that the distinguished Hungarian actor was a rival of Bela Lugosi."

Lorre was, despite himself, the poet of the damned, a tour guide to the dimly lit interiors of the brains of madmen. He would end his life playing in Roger Corman horror films. "Gothic tales," says his costar, Vincent Price. "We prefer to call them 'gothic tales.' Peter had an extraordinary personality, and it seemed to blend into a kind of strangeness about him. In a picture called *The Comedy of Terrors* or the one called *Tales of Terror,* in a dream sequence we cut off Peter's head and played basketball with it. And he could hardly stand to watch us kicking his rubber head around. I think Peter resented having to be in those pictures more than most of us did." "Oh yes," says Sam Arkoff, who produced most of those gothic tales. "Peter was the only horror star who thought horror was beneath him."

In 1934, the Columbia publicity release described Lorre as "on fire with acting." By 1937 he was the invulnerable Japanese detective Mr. Moto, judo expert and master of disguises, in 20th Century–Fox's *Think Fast, Mr. Moto*. Lorre had taken the role to get away from playing madmen. But he was so good at it—turning himself into a Japanese without any physical tricks except slicked-down hair and wire-rimmed glasses—that he was stuck as Mr. Moto for three years and eight movies.

"Even as Mr. Moto he was a wonderful actor," says Billy Wilder. "What made his Mr. Moto so good was that there was this spark of ridicule. Once, he was in a dark house infested with deadly enemies and, through the door, came a man with an enormous knife. Mr. Moto in one movement whacks him on the neck, grabs the knife, and kills the guy. Then he turns back and says, 'So sorry. Explain later.' One of my favorite lines, which I use constantly in conversation with my wife."

"At lunch one day somebody brought in a can of rattlesnake

```
FORM 11                          WARNER BROS. PICTURES, INC.
                                    BURBANK, CALIFORNIA
                              INTER-OFFICE COMMUNICATION
         WARNER-WALLIS-CURTIZ
TO MR.   WRIGHT-ALLEBORN                        DATE  April 29, 1942

FROM MR. TRILLING                               SUBJECT


                         "CASABLANCA"
                        Tentative Cast


         RICK .................. HUMPHREY BOGART

         LOIS MEREDITH ......... INGRID BERGMAN

         VICTOR LAZLO .......... To Be Selected

         LUIS RENAULT .......... CLAUDE RAINS
           (Prefect Police)

         SAM, THE RABBIT ....... CLARENCE MUSE(?)
           (Colored Pianist)

         STRASSER .............. CONRAD VEIDT or
           (Nazi Legation)       OTTO PREMINGER

         UGARTE ................ PETER LORRE
                                 (If works out with
                                  Universal commitment)

         CARL .................. CURT BOIS (?)
           (The Waiter)

         FYDOR ................. GEORGE TOBIAS
           (The Bartender)       or
                                 MIKHAIL RASUMNY
                                 or
                                 MICHAEL DELMATOFF



                         STEVE TRILLING

         js

         VERBAL MESSAGES CAUSE MISUNDERSTANDING AND DELAYS
              (PLEASE PUT THEM IN WRITING)
```

meat," says Amanda Dunne, who, as Amanda Duff, had a small part in *Mr. Moto in Danger Island* in 1938. "With great Hungarian disgust, Peter asked, 'Who would eat anything like that?' Someone else at the table said, 'Oh, the same people who like Peter Lorre movies.'"

Dunne remembers arguing with Lorre, who insisted that one must live as far from the studio as possible, so that one could drive home and be out of range. Long before the end of his life, Lorre would distance himself further with alcohol and drugs. When Victor Sherman was directing Bogart and Lorre in *All Through the Night* in 1941, Lorre balked at retaking a scene in which, revolver drawn, he ran down a hallway with Judith Anderson. Says Sherman, "Peter said, 'That's all, Brother Vince. I can only do this kind of crap once a day.' So I said, 'You've done crap before. How the hell did you do all those Mr. Motos?' He said, 'I took dope.' Everybody roared with laughter because we thought he was making a joke. Two months later, I discovered it was true."

In 1941, Lorre was teamed with Greenstreet for the first time, as the dainty and gardenia-scented—but no less deadly for it—Joel Cairo in *The Maltese Falcon.* The role of Ugarte, who kills two German couriers for their Letters of Transit and sets the plot of *Casablanca* in motion, might have been created for him: an odd little man too eager to be liked to seem dangerous. For *Casablanca,* he was paid $1,750 a week, with no minimum guarantee. He worked six days in the small role, spoke less than four hundred words, and was, as always, memorable. On the set he occupied himself, as always, with practical jokes. One of his favorites was to drip water from an eyedropper on Mike Curtiz's lighted cigarette whenever the director wasn't looking.

By mid-May, when Greenstreet and Lorre were added to the cast of *Casablanca,* the movie was less than a week away from starting production. There were a dozen or more minor roles still to be filled, but that was hardly unusual. And Wallis had to be satisfied. He had gotten his first choice for most of the roles, his second choice for a few. And if he had had to compromise once or twice, it was, after all, just another movie.

9

Love and Censorship

———◆———

Six days before *Casablanca* started production, Jack Warner received a letter from the Production Code Administration, the moral overseer that the industry had set up in an act of self-censorship. Joe Breen had read Part I of the script and was happy to report that—except for a few lines of dialogue—the script met the Code requirements.

Naturally, all the unacceptable lines had sexual implications:

> Page 5: "Of course, a beautiful young girl for M'sieur Renault, the Prefect of Police."
> Page 6: "The girl will be released in the morning."

The Production Code reflected Roman Catholic morality overlaid by conservative Protestantism. It had been written in 1930 by a Jesuit priest and the Catholic publisher of a movie trade paper. And it began to be enforced in 1934 after Catholic bishops formed the Legion of Decency and threatened to bar American Catholics from seeing all movies. For good measure, it was enforced by a Catholic, although the power in the Code Administration belonged to Will Hays, an elder in the Presbyterian church.

Joseph Ignatius Breen objected to two other lines in the incomplete *Casablanca* script. A woman who has no money says, "It used to take a Villa at Cannes, or the very least, a string of pearls—Now all I ask is an exit visa." And after Renault watches Rick send Yvonne home, he says, "How extravagant you are—throwing away women like that. Some day they may be rationed."

In 1942, movies had no free-speech protection,* so the industry felt vulnerable to censorship from dozens of cities and states. Locked in a mutually advantageous embrace (the Code defined public purity while partially shielding the industry from more excessive local censors) the industry and the Code usually accommodated each other. The beautiful young girl remained in the final movie—with no indication of how long she would be held. The woman who was willing to trade her body for an exit visa was eliminated. And, instead of saying that women might be rationed, Claude Rains said they might be scarce.

There was more substantial trouble with the second and third sections of the script. Breen was particularly disturbed by the character of Renault. "Specifically, we cannot approve the present suggestion that Capt. Renault makes a practice of seducing the women to whom he grants visas," Breen wrote to Warner on May 21. He also found it unacceptable that Ilsa was married when she fell in love with Rick in Paris. A month later Breen was warning Warner that the script made it appear that Rick and Ilsa slept together when she came to his apartment to get the Letters of Transit. In the stilted Code language, which always had a slight air of embarrassment, the words used were "suggestive of a sex affair"; and Breen urged the studio to take "great care" to avoid such a suggestion.

The Production Code served and served up the mainstream morality and conservative political attitudes of America's small towns and small cities. The American court system must not be shown as unjust. Religion and the flag were to be treated with respect. The Code insisted that "The sanctity of the institution of marriage and the home shall be upheld," with the corollary that "Impure love must not be presented as attractive and beautiful." Sexual perversions, white slavery, and lustful kissing were not to be

---

*In 1915, the Supreme Court had said that movies were purely a business. In 1952, a unanimous court extended to movies the guarantees of free speech in the case of *Burstyn* v. *Wilson,* which concerned an Italian movie, *The Miracle,* that had been banned by New York censors, who considered it sacrilegious.

shown. Adultery was to be punished. There was to be no nudity. Obscenity and profanity were forbidden. Obscenity and profanity included such words as *nerts, nuts, cripes, fanny, Gawd, hell,* and *hold your hat.*

The studios could—and did—finagle and maneuver. After a meeting between Breen and Wallis, a number of lines that referred to Renault's womanizing were removed from the script, but Claude Rains's performance left no doubt that Renault traded exit visas for sex. Warner Bros. followed Breen's suggestion and made sure that no bed was visible in Rick's apartment. Audiences were allowed to decide what, if anything, happened during the dissolve that followed Rick's passionate kiss. (Breen insisted on a dissolve rather than the fade-out in the script, since a fade-out signals the passage of time. Of such circumventions was the Code built.)

The marriage of Ilsa and Victor Laszlo was important to the plot, and the studio left in Ilsa's offending line that she had been married "Even when I knew you in Paris." The fact that when she met Rick Ilsa thought her husband was dead may have been a good enough excuse.

The studio also refused to take out a line that was not at all important to the plot. Breen felt that when Rick lashes out at Ilsa by telling her that he has heard a lot of stories that "went along with the sound of a tinny piano in the parlor downstairs," it was a "quite definite reference to a bawdy house." No movie was allowed to show or refer to a brothel. A few years earlier, in the Bette Davis–Humphrey Bogart movie *Marked Woman,* Warners had had to turn call girls controlled by gangsters into "hostesses." But each side knew which battles were worth winning, and Breen did not further attack *Casablanca*'s oblique reference to a house of ill repute. Although the Code was obsessive about language, the Code's guardians often let the subtle slip by. When *Casablanca* was finished, it earned Production Code Certificate of Approval 8457. The movie's summation page in the Production Code files lists "Much Drinking," a little gambling, two killings, and no illicit sex.

One reason that the studios accommodated themselves so easily to the Code—and, during the war, to the often conflicting demands of the Office of War Information—is that they were constantly censoring themselves. The writers were censored by the expectations of the audience and by the expectations of the studio. No anti-Roosevelt picture would have gotten beyond a first draft at

MOTION PICTURE PRODUCERS & DISTRIBUTORS OF AMERICA, INC.
HOLLYWOOD OFFICE
5504 Hollywood Boulevard
HOLLYWOOD, CALIFORNIA
GLadstone 6111

WILL H. HAYS
PRESIDENT
CARL E. MILLIKEN
SECRETARY

JOSEPH I. BREEN, DIRECTOR
PRODUCTION CODE ADMINISTRATION

May 19, 1942

Mr. J. L. Warner,
Warner Brothers,
Burbank, Calif.,

Dear Mr. Warner:

We have read Part I of the incomplete script
for your proposed picture CASABLANCA. While of course
we cannot give you a final opinion until we receive the
balance of the script, we are happy to report that, with
the exceptions noted below, the present material seems
to meet the requirements of the Production Code.

Going through the material so far submitted, we
call your attention to the following:

Pages 5 and 6: The following lines seem unacceptably sex suggestive, and should be changed:

Page 5: "Of course, a beautiful young girl
for M'sieur Renault, the Prefect
of Police".

Page 6: "The girl will be released in the
morning".

Page 14: Please submit all lyrics to be used
throughout this production.

Also the following lines seem unacceptably sex
suggestive:

"It used to take a Villa at Cannes, or the very
least, a string of pearls - Now all I ask is an exit visa".

Page 28: The following dialogue seems unacceptable:

"How extravagant you are - throwing away women
like that. Some day they may be rationed."

Warner Bros., while L. B. Mayer would have turned down scripts
that showed the President favorably. Since America in 1942 was a
more homogenous and repressed country, the censors also had the
two potent weapons of shame and good manners.

Today, the basic censorship is that of the box office. It is not that
modern moviemakers have no awareness of ideology, and a few,
including Oliver Stone, ride their hobby horses into whatever thick-
ets they wish. But for those who choose to be socially or politically
correct, such correctness is often simply another way to sell tickets,
since certain incorrect stands—deferential black mammies fussing

over golden-haired white children, for example—won't sell. With movies protected by the Constitution, anything that promises to make a buck, no matter how derivative or tasteless, will be filmed by some producer, while scripts that seem difficult to sell to audiences, no matter how brilliant or tasteful, will rarely find buyers. The studio factories, cushioned by the ability to sell movies to theaters they owned, sometimes found it easier to mix a little art into their commerce.

How was *Casablanca* affected by the Production Code? The writers and director were forced to be subtle, to use language, pauses, and camera angles as sexual metaphors. The scene when Rick and Ilsa first see each other again and talk of Paris in front of Laszlo and Renault—"I remember every detail. The Germans wore gray; you wore blue"—is pulsing with sexual tension. Today, any movie that didn't show Rick and Ilsa sweatily grappling with each other's naked bodies in Rick's apartment above the café would be considered old-fashioned. But graphic sex wipes out ambiguity, and the ambiguity in *Casablanca*—the uncertainty about events and motives—is one of the things that still entices us.

Casablanca was censored by the Production Code, the Office of War Information, and the studio itself. At the same time that Warner Bros. was arguing with Breen, the studio's head of foreign publicity, Carl Schaefer, was suggesting changes that would make the movie easier to sell abroad. To avoid offending any friendly country, Schaefer suggested that two unpleasant characters—the pickpocket and Peter Lorre's Ugarte—be Italian. Since the character played by Sydney Greenstreet appeared to be Spanish—he was still named Martinez as he had been in the play—he must have a distinguished appearance. The South American entertainer played by Corinna Mura "could flatter Latin America if given dignity and if her artistry is top-notch." And Wallis must be very careful with the allusions to the Mohammedan religion in several early scenes.

"We didn't want to offend anybody," says Schaefer, laughing at his memo fifty years later. "We wanted to be able to show pictures anyplace. I'm surprised we didn't get around to the Pope."

Wallis took Schaefer's suggestions seriously. The pickpocket and the murderer were turned into Italians. So was the head of the black market in Casablanca, Sydney Greenstreet, who became Signor Ferrari. And all references to Mohammedanism were cut out. Wallis had a second reason for eliminating what he called the "Allah, Allah business." As he wrote Curtiz, "It does seem to be a little on the operetta, *Desert Song* style and I would much prefer to keep these opening scenes realistic."

During the few weeks just before and after *Casablanca* began shooting, Wallis made dozens of such decisions. "Hal was a great producer," says his story editor, Irene Lee. "I worked for two years for Sam Goldwyn, and they were two of the unhappiest years of my life. I had been told what marvelous taste Goldwyn had, but I sat in a projection room with him for hours and never heard him say a creative word. Hal knew every aspect of pictures and, when he was at Warner Bros., he okayed every single thing—every costume, every script, every set."

With the larger problem of an unfinished script looming over his head, Wallis shaped *Casablanca* in a hundred small ways. He kept insisting on "sketchy, interesting lighting." During Rick's drunken reverie that led into the flashback, Wallis wrote Curtiz, "The general lighting in the Café should be turned out when we dissolve into the room from the Ext. Sign, and the Café should be almost in darkness with the exception of a couple of lamps on the bar [and] two or three lights on tables."

Wallis wanted Humphrey Bogart to wear as few hats as possible. Bogart was definitely to be hatless throughout the flashback except at the train station. He preferred the way Claude Rains looked in the photograph labeled Moustache B and Paul Henreid with a white streak in his hair. He did not want Sydney Greenstreet to wear the Moroccan shoes and seminative outfit outlined on the wardrobe plot. At all times Greenstreet must wear a white single-breasted suit and, possibly, a cummerbund. The young couple from Bulgaria, played by Helmut Dantine and Joy Page, must look as if they escaped "with just the clothes on their backs."

The clothes for *Casablanca* were designed by Orry-Kelly, who was the major costume designer at Warner Bros. from 1932 to 1943. Born in Australia, Orry-Kelly was openly and flamboyantly homosexual and famous for his tantrums. His personal style didn't bother Bette Davis. She said that when Orry-Kelly left the studio in 1944 after a fight with Warner she felt as though she had lost her right arm. "His contribution to my career was an enormous one," she wrote. "He never featured his clothes to such a degree that the performance was overshadowed."

Wallis threw out the costume Orry-Kelly had created for Bergman's entrance into Rick's Café. On page 25 of *Everybody Comes to Rick's,* Lois Meredith enters the café wearing "a magnificent white gown, and a full-length cape of the same fabric. Her jewels are fabulous." The Epsteins had incorporated the same costume into their script. But if Helmut Dantine and Joy Page have escaped with just the clothes on their back so have Paul Henreid and Ingrid Bergman. The "evening formal attire" listed in the wardrobe plot and tossed out by Wallis was changed into a simple white two-piece dress.

Wallis had tried to keep David O. Selznick from looking at Ingrid Bergman's costume tests. Selznick was always obsessive about his actresses and would be sure to write one of his famous long memos. But Selznick managed to see the tests two days after the movie started production and was appalled. "In order for her to look smart, she doesn't have to be dressed up like a candy box," he

Half of Ilsa's costumes were thrown out before the movie began.

```
                              "CASABLANCA"

                 Curtiz        -        #410
                                                  5/21/42
                 WOMEN'S WARDROBE PLOT (Part I)
                 (Final Script  Part I & II 5/19/42)

        PART OF: "ILSA"              PLAYED BY:  INGRID BERGMAN

  Costume #1 - Street attire - small hat - veil (tropical)
      WORN   - EXT. HOTEL - Sc. 27


  - - - - - - - - - - - - - - - - - - - - - - - - - - - - - -

  Costume #2 - Evening formal attire - wrap
      WORN   - INT. CAFE - Sc. 80-81-83-85-86-88-91-92-99-100
             EXT. CAFE - Sc. 103
             INT. CAB (PROCESS) - Sc. 104


  - - - - - - - - - - - - - - - - - - - - - - - - - - - - - -

  Costume #3 - Street attire - automobile - hat - gloves - purse
      WORN   - EXT. AUTOMOBILE (PROCESS) - PARIS     RETROSPECT "A"


  - - - - - - - - - - - - - - - - - - - - - - - - - - - - - -

  Costume #4 - Street outfit - hat - purse - coat
      WORN   - EXT. EXCURSION BOAT (PROCESS)         RETROSPECT "B"


  - - - - - - - - - - - - - - - - - - - - - - - - - - - - - -

  Costume #5 - Dinner gown
      WORN   - INT. RICK'S APARTMENT                 RETROSPECT "C"


  - - - - - - - - - - - - - - - - - - - - - - - - - - - - - -

  Costume #6 - Evening gown
      WORN   - INT. PARIS CAFE                       RETROSPECT "D"


  - - - - - - - - - - - - - - - - - - - - - - - - - - - - - -

                                              (CONTINUED)
```

wrote in his memo. Most of the hats were hideous, he complained. She "shouldn't wear white shoes because they make her feet look simply titanic." The evening dress with the striped skirt and sheer blouse was hideous too, Selznick said, and made Bergman look big in the rear.

Most of the costumes that dismayed Selznick had already been thrown out by Wallis. And Bergman assured Selznick that she would be wearing low-heeled blue shoes in the only scenes where her feet would be seen.

Paul Henreid always ridiculed the idea of Victor Laszlo, a "fugitive leader of the resistance," running around the world "in an immaculately clean white suit," but Wallis did tone the costumes down, while still allowing for the flourishes and designing skills that always highlighted the stars. He eliminated the tuxedo that Henreid was scheduled to wear in Rick's Café and settled for a "very well tailored" tropical suit.

Verisimilitude was more important than truth anyway. The most powerful political metaphor in *Casablanca*—Victor Laszlo leading the patrons of Rick's Café in the French national anthem and drowning out the German officers who are singing "Watch on the Rhine"—was deliberately phony. The Nazi anthem was the "Horst Wessel" song. But the copyright to "Horst Wessel" was controlled by a German publisher. If Warner Bros. used the song, the studio would be able to show *Casablanca* in countries at war with Germany, but copyright restrictions would make it impossible to show the film in neutral countries, which included most of South America.

Lee Katz wrote Wallis on May 27 that the music department had found that it was against the principles of the Nazi Party to sing "Watch on the Rhine." "Horst Wessel" and "Deutschland Über Alles" were the only two songs approved by the Nazis.

Wallis left that decision in Curtiz's hands. "If we want to be technically correct, we should not use this," he wrote Curtiz as soon as he received Katz's memo. "I doubt if many people know that this song is not in favor with the Nazi Party but, if you feel that we should be accurate, I would suggest that we use 'Deutschland Über Alles.' " Curtiz, as always, chose the dramatic over the correct.

Movies, then as now, were a blend of implausible stories and background details that were as accurate as the studios' research libraries could make them. The first thing Aeneas MacKenzie did when he was assigned to write *Casablanca* was to request pictures of Casablanca. He was sent "Picturesque North Africa." By April, the research department had created the movie's bible, two ten-inch-thick leather-and-linen volumes with pictures of city walls and gates, native shops, camels, details of arches, sand dunes, trails across the Sahara Desert, Moroccan telephones, police uniforms from every French west and north African country, and a map of Casablanca drawn from memory by Robert Aisner, the movie's technical advisor, who had escaped from a German prison camp and made his way to Morocco. The bible, which was shared with *The Desert Song,* was sent to Carl Jules Weyl, *Casablanca*'s art director, when he began to design the sets in mid-April. Like many art directors in that era, Weyl was an architect. One of the West Coast's leading architects during the 1920s, Weyl had designed the famous Brown Derby restaurants, which were shaped like derby hats.

By the time *Casablanca* began production, the research department had provided the appropriate pictures of 1940 French license plates, excursion boats on the Seine River, and Montmartre cafés for the early scenes. The accuracy of the background didn't ease Wallis' unhappiness with the first week's work on the movie. "While I know you have been under a handicap because you didn't have your actors you now have Rains and I would like to get into some more solid material and really get some work done," he wrote Curtiz on June 4.

Nor was Humphrey Bogart comfortable. In addition to making love to Bergman on the movie's first day, he had to dance with her two days later. Bogart was taught the rhumba but had trouble with it. He had trouble with Bergman's height too.* Selznick wanted Bergman to explain to Warner Bros. how he had compensated for the difference in height between the actress and Leslie Howard in *Intermezzo* by having the actor stand on blocks. Bergman reassured him that Curtiz was already building Bogart up on blocks and pillows and was careful only to shoot her best side.

What made Hal Wallis particularly unhappy was Leon Mostovoy, the actor Curtiz had chosen to play the Russian bartender,

---

* Bergman was probably two inches taller than Bogart. There may be definitive records of the actors' heights somewhere, but certainly not in studio biographies. Warner Bros. always tried to make Bogart taller (his official studio height was 5'9") while Selznick always tried to make Bergman shorter. As she became an important star she was allowed to grow—from 5'5" to 5'9".

An uncomfortable Bogart being taught to rhumba.

who was then named Fydor. "I don't think he is at all funny and I want to give him as little to do in the picture as possible," Wallis wrote. "We can forget the scene of 'Fydor' where he crosses and kisses Bogart after Bogart lets Jan win at roulette."

Curtiz, who wanted as much comedy as possible to leaven the melodrama, decided to recast the part. On June 9, Leonid Kinskey signed a contract for a guaranteed two weeks at $750 a week.

Kinskey says that it was Bogart who got him the role of the bartender, renamed Sacha. "We used to drink together—Bogart, Ralph Bellamy, and myself—at Mischa Auer's house. At least three times a week," says Kinskey. "We were all good drinkers. Ralph

Bellamy was a good-looking guy. We thought he was the one who was going to be a star. And I said to myself about Bogart, 'He's short. He speaks with a lisp. And he's not a good-looking guy, so what chance does he have?' "

As Kinskey remembers it fifty years later, "Bogart said, 'Leonid, do us a favor.' I knew I was replacing an actor who had already been chosen. He was too heavy, speechwise, and they wanted to have something very light." Kinskey had played an informer in *Algiers* and a coward in *So Ends Our Night,* but he was best known as a comic actor—usually playing a caricatured Russian—from his first movie role in the Ernst Lubitsch comedy *Trouble in Paradise* in 1932 to the Marx Brothers' *Duck Soup* to *On Your Toes* and *Down Argentine Way.*

Kinskey was in Hollywood almost by accident. Born in Saint Petersburg, he was seventeen when his mother sent him out of Russia. "It just happened to be that I belonged to a group of people that was not wanted after the Revolution," he says. He had reached New York with a South American theater troupe. When the Firebird Theatre failed on Broadway—the American public was not into paying to watch famous paintings brought to life by dancers—he was stranded in New York. He eventually learned English and came west.

The thing Kinskey remembers best about *Casablanca* is that, without his noticing it, his drinking companion had already become a star. "I didn't see many pictures," he says. "I didn't know that Bogart had grown into an important star. But on the set, I saw the way he was treated by everybody. I saw that he is the show."

By June 12, when Kinskey stepped into Rick's Café on Stage 8, *Casablanca* had been in production for almost three weeks, and there was still trouble with the screenplay. Eight months later, when Jack Warner wanted to complain about out-of-control scripts, he had Steve Trilling send a memo to all the studio's producers. *Casablanca* was his major example of scripts so out of control that the writers had to rewrite while the movie was shooting and, thus, were not available for any other work.

The most important decision Wallis made during those early weeks was to assign his favorite writer, Casey Robinson, to the movie. At $2,500 a week, Robinson was the highest paid of Warner Bros. writers. His status at the studio is made clear by his contract.

Bogart got Leonid Kinskey, his drinking companion, a role in the movie.

Unlike all but a few major stars and directors, Robinson was not laid off for three months a year. Instead, he was given eight weeks' vacation. And the studio had to pay him during four of those weeks.

After finishing the script for *Now, Voyager,* Robinson had started to write the script that would become *Passage to Marseille.* But it is likely that he was looking over the shoulders of Howard Koch and the Epstein twins long before he was pulled off *Marseille* and officially assigned to *Casablanca* the day the movie started production. Five days earlier, on May 20, Robinson had sent Wallis seven pages of NOTES ON SCREENPLAY "CASABLANCA." The notes began: "Again, as before, my impression about CASABLANCA is that the melodrama is well done, the humor excellent, but the love story deficient." In the five days before shooting started, Robinson would write at least one version of the flashback.

In addition to his regular salary, Robinson was paid $9,000 extra for his three weeks' work on *Casablanca.* What he did during those three weeks, working against the inexorable clock of a movie in production, was to sculpt the love story, using bits and pieces from the play, the Epsteins, Howard Koch, and his own imagination. Descended from Mormon pioneers, Robinson was as conservative as the other writers were liberal. He was a member of the Screen Playrights, the conservatives who had left the Screen Writers Guild to form the equivalent of a company union. Robinson was one of the few Screen Playrights at Warner Bros. The Screen Playrights' guild was created and dominated by the elegant, highly paid writers who worked at M-G-M, while Warner Bros. was a studio that provided a temporary home for a number of writers besides Koch who ended up in front of the House Un-American Activities Committee, including Dalton Trumbo, Ring Lardner, Jr., John Howard Lawson, Albert Maltz, and Alvah Bessie. Robinson used to call M-G-M the graveyard of writers, but he went there eventually for $5,000 a week.

Looking back in 1974, Robinson said that Warner Bros. was the great studio for screenwriters, despite the fact that Jack Warner despised writers. But, Robinson said, just because Warner was stingy and resented having to give money to writers, "He wouldn't pay for rewrites or reshooting, so your stuff got shot as you wrote it." Robinson had started his career writing titles for silent films. During the thirties, he wrote three or four pictures a year at Warner Bros. After the war, he moved from studio to studio. In his view, "the two greatest organizations that ever were in Hollywood" were M-G-M when Thalberg was alive and Mayer took care of the actors while Thalberg made the movies and Warner Bros. when Jack Warner took care of the contracts and Hal Wallis was his strong arm. Because Wallis recognized and trusted talent, Robinson said, Warner Bros. collected "the greatest staff of writers that ever existed in any studio in the history of motion pictures."

Robinson had a gift for handling emotionally difficult material and solving censorable situations. He was able to make a movie out of Henry Bellamann's steamy novel *Kings Row* by turning the heroine's incest into an inherited predisposition to insanity. (Incest—like abortion, venereal disease, and birth control—was unacceptable to the Code.) During the days when cancer was almost unmentionable, he helped make *Dark Victory,* a stage play about a woman who has brain cancer, into a box-office winner by playing it as a love story of a woman who rebels against her fate. The sexual and doubly masochistic relationship between Rick and Lois in *Everybody Comes to Rick's* was impossible to put on the screen in 1942. Robinson made the characters nobler and more romantic.

In *Everybody Comes to Rick's,* Lois was a tramp who jumped into bed with Rick the first night she came to his café in Casablanca. Except for writing a love scene between Rick and Lois on a beach, the Epsteins kept the contours of the characters and their relationship. In their first version, Lois still bedded Rick immediately. Then the twins and Koch dressed up the characters without making them more sympathetic. In various suggestions and scenes, Renault knows about the renewed affair between Lois and Rick, Renault offers Lois an exit visa if she will agree to his "usual arrangements," and Lois confesses her affair with Rick to poor Victor Laszlo.

Robinson defined and sharpened the romantic relationship between Rick and Ilsa and also the romantic relationship between Ilsa and Laszlo. It is less that he wrote new scenes than that he acted as an editor of previously written material. Wallis trusted Robinson as an editor and often used him in an unusual way. Early in May, during the production of *Now, Voyager,* Wallis had asked the writer to look at the scenes that director Irving Rapper had already shot. Robinson suggested closeups and reshooting that would make the audience better understand the motivations and terrors of the char-

Casey Robinson in 1942. He was brought in to shape the love story between Rick and Ilsa.

acter played by Bette Davis, and Wallis incorporated most of his suggestions.

One unexpected by-product of Robinson's restructuring of the love story in *Casablanca* was to make Sam more important. In his seven pages of notes on May 20, Robinson suggested heightening the interplay between Ilsa and Sam, and later between Sam and Rick. Almost all of those suggestions survived into the final movie.

> Play the stuff at the piano where she asks Sam to play some of the old songs, and then insists on "As Time Goes By." Play up very strongly Sam's trying to avoid playing this. I'm sure this material will tell the audience that there is something of great significance to this music, and something of romantic significance.

Howard Koch had written a scene that is not in the final script in which Rick and Ilsa talk privately while Laszlo and Renault are away from the table. Robinson suggested eliminating it.

> In place of this scene, I would play the scene where Ilsa tries to find out from Sam where Rick is. Think a minute of the facts of the love story and you will see why this scene is necessary. The girl has just one thing in mind, that she must get to Rick and tell him why she didn't catch the train in Paris. Loving him as she does, and suspecting what he thinks about her, she must clear this up. Now, she need not disclose this motive to Sam, in fact, shouldn't but the audience will realize it later. In the meantime, this business serves as a very good buildup for the love story and will pique the audience's interest and make the first meeting between Ilsa and Rick tremendously effective.

As Robinson's notes clearly indicate, he built on scenes and dialogue that Koch had created and scenes that the Epsteins had taken from the play and sharpened:

> Scene between Rick and Sam about Ilsa is weak. You must heighten here the great fear that Sam has, the almost superstitious darky fear, and also heighten his pleading with Rick to get out of town until this woman is gone. The audience will get from this the fact that this woman has done terrific damage to Rick, but also that this woman is of terrific importance to Rick, and is a very effective lead-in to the flashbacks.

2.

MED. SHOT   AT OPEN WINDOW.

as Rick and Ilsa come into the scene. The loudspeaker
is blaring in German.

                    RICK:
          My German's a little rusty --

                    ILSA:
               (sadly)
          It's the Gestapo. They say they expect
          to be in Paris tomorrow. They are tell-
          ing us how to act when they come marching
          in.

They are silent, depressed.

                    ILSA:
               (smiling faintly)
          With the whole world crumbling we
          pick this time to fall in love.

                    RICK:
               (with an abrupt
                laugh)
          Yeah. Pretty bad timing.
               (looks at her)
          Where were you ten years ago?

                    ILSA:
               (trying to cheer up)
          Ten years ago? Let's see --
               (thinks)
          Oh, yes. I was having a brace put on
          my teeth. Where were you?

                    RICK:
          I was looking for a job.

Pause. Ilsa looks at him tenderly.

                    ILSA:
          Rick -- Hitler or no Hitler, kiss me.

Rick takes her in his arms, kisses her hungrily. While
they are locked in an embrace the dull boom of cannons
is HEARD. Rick and Ilsa separate.

                    ILSA:
               (frightened, but
                trying not to
                show it)
          Was that cannon fire -- or just my
          heart pounding?

                              (CONTINUED)

A close-to-final version of one of the Paris love scenes.

Robinson also added a number of small touches, including having the bartender kiss Rick to top off the scene where Rick lets the young couple win at roulette. And he kept suggesting emotional underpinnings for the characters to play. When Rick sends Ilsa away with Victor, Robinson wrote:

> He is not just solving a love triangle. He is forcing the girl to live up to the idealism of her nature, forcing her to carry on with the work that in these days is far more important than the love of two little people.

Robinson also gave Paul Henreid something more intimate to play than the heroism and determination that the script provided him. Robinson stressed that, in the relationship between Laszlo and Ilsa:

> (1) Victor must have done something wonderful for her in the past. She must be under some strong spiritual obligation to him.
>
> (2) Victor must need her. A man in this position, doing this kind of work, does need someone, does need some place to lay his head when the dangers and troubles are overwhelming.
>
> (3) Victor must absolutely worship Ilsa and be lost without her.

Robert Blees, Robinson's brother-in-law and a junior writer at Warner Bros. in 1942, feels that the scenes between Victor and Ilsa were easy for Robinson to write. "Remember that Casey had just finished making Paul Henreid into a romantic leading man in *Now, Voyager,*" says Blees.

During the first few weeks in June, Robinson and the Epsteins were not swept by the urgency that Koch would feel in July as he rewrote *Casablanca*'s ending. There was time to fiddle with the love story because Curtiz was concentrating on the scenes that established Bogart's relationships with Peter Lorre, Claude Rains, Dooley Wilson, and Madeleine LeBeau. Between June 1 and June 15, Ingrid Bergman only worked three days, although she was waiting on the set for another nine days.

Few memories are trustworthy thirty years after the fact. In his oral history, Robinson claims that he persuaded Wallis to buy *Everybody Comes to Rick's,* which he misdescribes as a play whose only relationship to the movie was that it was set in Casablanca and "There was one gimmick or 'weenie,' as we sometimes call it in writer's terms, in it: namely, there is one exit visa and two who want to use it." Robinson says that the story was totally unrelated to World War II and that he intrigued Wallis by hinting at a new plot which would have refugees, a European girl, and the war.

The play—with characters who include a Gestapo captain, a Czech resistance leader, and a young couple fleeing from Bulgaria— speaks for itself. But dusty story files and production records support Robinson's claim that he made the heroine European because he wanted the role for Tamara Toumanova with whom he was infatuated. Long before Robinson was assigned to the script, he wrote a seven-page scene for Toumanova to play in the screen test Wallis made of her in April. (Wallis sent Curtiz a note complaining about the length of Robinson's scene.) At that time, the Epsteins had only turned in Part I of their script; it ended with Rick waiting for Ilsa to return to the Café without Victor Laszlo. In Robinson's scene, Ilsa comes back to see Rick that first night in order to tell him what happened in Paris, but his bitterness disillusions her. Robinson later reworked the scene for the movie. Two years later, Toumanova became Robinson's second wife, and he did write a movie for her. He wrote and produced *Days of Glory,* in which Toumanova and the unknown Gregory Peck played Russian patriots who earned their glory by dying heroically. The marriage lasted ten years.

One cannot give all the credit for the love story to Robinson just as one cannot give all the credit for the politics to Koch or credit every funny line to the Epsteins. Each of the writers won and lost, was rewritten and rewrote.

Julie Epstein maintains that he and Phil rewrote much of the flashback that Casey Robinson had rewritten from their earlier draft. "Only one line remained and we couldn't get it out," says Epstein. 'A franc for your thoughts.' And we fought it. But we couldn't get it out."

Howard Koch had argued against having a flashback at all. He felt it would drain tension from the melodrama. "I was wrong," he says today. But it was Koch whose suggestions included a new scene in which Ilsa comes to the café as soon as her husband leaves for the Underground meeting. She begs for the Letters of Transit. When Rick won't give them to her, she points a revolver at him.

> For a moment a look of admiration comes into Rick's eyes. He walks over to the place where the Letters are concealed. He has them in his hand, facing her. . . . 'You'll have to kill me to get them. If

you're sincere, if the cause means so much, you won't stop at anything." . . . Her finger holds on the trigger. She can't go through with
it. She drops the revolver on the table. No, she can't kill him, not for
the cause, not for Laszlo, because she loves him. She tried not to let
him know, keep faith with her husband, but it wasn't any use.
. . . She is in his arms when we dissolve.

And many of Robinson's suggestions did not end up in the film.
In his notes, he wrote that "the love story suspense and the melodrama suspense are all mixed up in a hodge-podge." He argued that
the two things must be separated by having Ilsa enter the movie and
Rick's Café without Laszlo. Wallis rejected the idea. Robinson also
insisted that Rick and Ilsa must not meet until late at night when she
returns to the café after the flashback. But the movie contains the
effective scene—which was taken by the Epsteins almost intact from
the play—in which Rick and Ilsa speak of Paris in front of Renault
and Laszlo, and Rick breaks two precedents by drinking with a
customer and picking up the check.

By mid-June the love story was straightened out and the Epsteins were off the picture, although they would unofficially keep
coming back. That still left the problem of the ending, but all the
tensions of shooting the ending wouldn't have to be faced for
another month. On June 25, one month to the day after Casablanca
started production, Paul Henreid entered Rick's Café for the first
time. With six weeks to go, Mike Curtiz finally had all his major
actors.

10

Directed by
Michael Curtiz

O n Friday, July 3, 1942, there was a party on the set of
Casablanca to celebrate Michael Curtiz's fifteen years at Warner
Bros. Shooting stopped more than half an hour early, and Jack
Warner and Hedda Hopper, the industry's second-most-important
gossip columnist, were among the guests. Five years later, to com-
memorate Curtiz's twentieth anniversary, Warner published a "For
the Love of Mike" letter in the Hollywood trade papers. The adver-
tisement praised Curtiz's decision to spend a second twenty years at
Warner Bros. It was illustrated with two entwined hearts labeled
"W.B." and "M.C." Six years after that, Curtiz had a bitter fight
with Warner Bros. over money and left the studio.

At the height of his success, Curtiz had foretold his fate. "In
Europe, if an actor or director establish himself, he live forever," he
said just before he signed the contract that led to his ruin at Warner
Bros. "Here, if he doesn't make dough, they kick him out. Hollywood is money, money, money, and the nuts with everything else."

What did Curtiz bring to *Casablanca*? Technical skill, of course.
Says Lee Katz, "His camera movement was as good as anyone's I've
ever known." Even in the early days of sound when the noisy

cameras were tied down inside soundproof booths and scenes were shot through glass, Curtiz could make the camera seem to move by the way he used his actors. "Mike taught me that when you don't have enough people to make a crowd, by lining them up on opposite sides and having them deliberately run into one another, you create such confusion that it looks like a crowd," Katz says.

Says Jack Lucas, who worked with his stepfather as dialogue director on such movies as *The Unsuspected* before he became a television writer-producer on his own, "Mike had an instinct for camera movement. The one great thing I learned from him was that any camera movement must be motivated, that the camera couldn't just move for the sake of showing off."

The camera never shows off in Casablanca, never preens and calls attention to itself, although, as always, Curtiz carefully composed each shot. It was Curtiz's ability to compose exciting action that made a star of Errol Flynn. From Flynn's first major role in *Captain Blood* in 1935 through *The Charge of the Light Brigade, The Adventures of Robin Hood,* and *The Sea Hawk,* Curtiz created a huge canvas tailored to the limited talents of the actor.

Curtiz also brought to *Casablanca* a ravenous single-mindedness. Jack Lucas does a good imitation of his stepfather's Hungarian accent. "Mike would tell the actors and the crew to be 'On the camera like a tiger, fighting for the picture,'" Lucas says.

Hal Wallis told his biographer that Curtiz was the most cantankerous of the Warner Bros. directors, that he fought with everyone, and that a day on a Curtiz set seemed to be nothing but quarrels and irascibility. And yet, Wallis said, when he sat and watched the rushes from each quarrelsome day, he discovered that an alchemy had taken place.

"I think that every director must admire Curtiz because there was no big fancy talk, no deep searching for the reason for certain actions," says director Billy Wilder. "He was a good soldier. He clicked his heels and did it, and he did it as well as anybody in the world could have. In *Four Daughters,* John Garfield decides to commit suicide, and it was one of the very best suicides ever in a picture. He's driving a car, and it's snowing. And he puts on the windshield wipers. Then he decides to shut them off and start speeding, and you know he's going to hit a tree. It's a wonderful, wonderful pictorial invention."

Curtiz's vision of any movie, including *Casablanca,* was almost totally a visual one. The exasperation that he caused in Warner executives comes across clearly in the sheaves of memos sent to and about him during dozens of movies.

"I don't understand what you can be thinking about at times," Wallis wrote Curtiz on *Captain Blood.* With important information to be gotten across and the need for the audience to see the crafty look in Errol Flynn's eye, Wallis complains that Curtiz has played the scene in a long shot: "so that you can get the composition of a candlestick and a wine bottle on a table in the foreground, which I don't give a damn about."

On *Charge of the Light Brigade,* Jack Warner complained to Wallis: "All he [Curtiz] talked about were the sets and that he wants to build a fort someplace else, and all a lot of hooey. I didn't hear him say anything about the story. In other words, he's still the same old Curtiz—as he always will be!"

And Wallis warned Henry Blanke, his associate producer on *The Adventures of Robin Hood,* "There is one thing that we will have to watch with Mike. In his enthusiasm to make great shots and composition and utilize the great production values in this picture, he is, of course, more likely to go overboard than anyone else, because he just naturally loves to work with mobs and props of this kind."

Casablanca did not lend itself to bravura directorial touches, although Curtiz is responsible for ending the love scene in Paris by having Ingrid Bergman's fist knock over the wineglass. And Curtiz created the effective swirl of cigarette smoke that leads into the flashback. The Epsteins' original idea was to have Rick's whiskey glass turn into an hour glass with liquid rather than sand flowing through it. There are also two character-revealing gags that cannot be found in any of the scripts: Sydney Greenstreet gleefully swatting flies and Claude Rains dropping the bottle of Vichy water into a wastepaper basket when he decides to become a patriot. "Curtiz, of course, was a comedian," says comedian Leonid Kinskey. "He had a wonderful eye for what's good comedy."

But *Casablanca* benefited most from Curtiz's need to hurl himself on his movies, to attack them as though he were a real tiger and the camera was raw meat. There is very little action in *Casablanca,* but there is a tension that gives the illusion of action in almost every scene. And on that phony French Street around the corner from the commissary, there is all the confusion and terror of Casablanca circa 1941.

Most of the actors thought that *Casablanca* was a ridiculous, overripe story. But Curtiz was an expert at misdirecting the audience's eye. He could disguise the absurdities of a story by rushing the audience past them.

"Once," says Lee Katz, "and I've forgotten what picture this was on, the master shot had a grand piano prominently in the foreground. And when Mike moved into a reverse shot, he said, 'Take out the piano.' And I said, 'Mike, isn't somebody going to say, Where's the piano?' And he said, 'Believe me, if anybody asks, Where's the piano?, they're not watching the picture.'"

Howard Koch wrote several movies for Curtiz, and whenever he complained that Curtiz was making a character behave illogically, Curtiz would brush him off with "Who cares about character? I make it go so fast nobody knows." On *Casablanca,* says Koch, "Mike was a little bit over his head politically and socially. But he made the Paris scenes more romantic than we wrote them."

Peter Lorre once described Curtiz as not only eating but excreting pictures. Yet, although he lived for movies, Curtiz was not immune to real life. Many Jewish refugees played bit parts in *Casablanca,* and Curtiz was as much an immigrant Jew as the refugees he cast in his movie. He was a holiday Jew from an Orthodox family. Says Lucas, "Mike used to say, 'Christ, Buddha, Confusion is all the same.'" But Curtiz knew that his secular status didn't matter to Hitler. He brought his mother to America in 1938, but he could only get his two brothers as far as Mexico, where they spent a year waiting for visas. His sister survived Auschwitz, but her husband, her daughter, and two of her sons did not.

At his anniversary party on July 3, Curtiz told Hedda Hopper that he had talked to a number of the refugees who played small roles in *Casablanca* and had worked their experiences and escapes into the film. *Yankee Doodle Dandy,* Curtiz's biography of George M. Cohan, was the big movie that summer, artistically and commercially, and Hopper wondered how Curtiz could successfully make such an American picture. He answered that maybe because he had seen so many people without liberties he loved to do American stories.

Curtiz and his boyhood friend Alexander Korda had both fled from the counterrevolutionary, anti-Semitic Horthy regime in Hungary in 1919. The two men spent hours fighting over the merits of England, where Korda had settled, and America. "Alex was violently British; Mike was the patriotic Yank," says Lucas, who would sit and listen to the two filmmakers screaming at each other. An American-born director of *Casablanca* would probably have accepted the offscreen presence of the United States as a necessary plot point. But the movie exudes Curtiz's intoxication with America.

Their fervor for America gave Curtiz and another boyhood friend, S. Z. Sakall, something to talk about in Hungarian. Sakall, who played Rick's headwaiter and bookkeeper, was the son of a stonecutter who specialized in tombstones. Born Eugene Gero, Sakall took the pseudonym Szoke Szakall—blond beard—at eighteen, when he became a gag writer for a Budapest comic. He went from gag writer to playright, then started acting in his own plays. It was visiting the set of Curtiz's famous movie, *Sodom and Gomorrah,* in 1922 that made Sakall want to try acting in films.

After the German comedian Felix Bressart turned the role down, Curtiz insisted on Sakall for the part of Carl, the headwaiter. When it came to casting the small parts, Wallis wanted to hire cheap actors and use them as few days as possible. Most of those roles had not been cast by May 25 when *Casablanca* began production, and Wallis and Curtiz argued over the director's plan to keep minor actors on salary for several weeks. "There is no point in carrying unimportant characters like Heinze, Ferrari,* Casselle and the overseer who have absolutely nothing to do and paying them salaries $500 and $750 per week," Wallis wrote. "We have a terrifically expensive cast as it is, and I am not going to put on anybody for longer than they are needed."

Wallis lost most of those battles. Once the cameras started rolling, Curtiz had an edge that he lacked during the weeks of preproduction. Wallis agreed to Sakall's $1,750 a week salary, but only for a maximum of two weeks. Sakall held out for his regular guarantee of four weeks. Curtiz, who was desperate to have Sakall to add comedy relief to the melodrama, convinced Wallis to offer and Sakall to accept a three-week guarantee. Bustling over the customers, giving Major Strasser the best table—"knowing he is German and would take it anyway"—and bringing Paul Henreid to safety after the Underground meeting, Sakall, omnipresent in Rick's Café, had a bigger part than either Peter Lorre or Sydney Greenstreet.

---

* The "Ferrari" mentioned in the memo is not the Sydney Greenstreet role but the bit part of an Italian officer.

In another early squabble, Wallis blasted Curtiz for shooting the first scenes of the Bogart-Bergman romance in Paris without dialogue. "The transition from driving down the Champs-Elysées to the country road means nothing because you left out the dialogue," Wallis wrote on May 28. "The dialogue was from the girl, and to the effect that 'When I am driving with you, I don't know if I am in the city or on a country lane' and, at that point, we dissolve to the country lane . . . For the balance of the picture I will greatly appreciate it if you will call me on the telephone when you drop dialogue out of a scene, or make changes, as it will be far simpler, and considerably less expensive for us to discuss these things before you do them than to go back and retake the scenes later." But the short shots of Bogart and Bergman together in Bogart's convertible remained without dialogue in the movie.

The Paris love scenes—the flashbacks known as the Retrospect—had been the first scenes shot on *Casablanca*. But, on the afternoon of July 3, during the hours before Curtiz's anniversary party, Bogart and Bergman returned to the Montmartre café for some retakes and a few new speeches. This time, Bogart toasted Bergman with, "Here's looking at you, kid." Did Humphrey Bogart create that quintessentially Bogart line? There is a certain amount of evidence that he did. According to the unit publicist's notes, Bergman's hairdresser and her English coach taught the actress poker during the long waits on the set, using hairpins as chips. Bergman's command of English did not extend to slang, and Bogart, who observed the game now and then, added "Here's looking at you" to her poker repertoire. Unit publicists are deft at making things up, but the incident seems too odd to have been invented. And "Here's looking at you, kid" does not appear in any of the mimeographed scripts. It is penciled into the cutter's script—the final record of dialogue and shots after a movie has been finished. So it was created on the set that early July day.

By the beginning of July, actors and director knew what to expect of themselves and each other. After the early fights, they had settled into a more or less placid routine. During the lunch break, Curtiz dosed himself with aspirin and muttered, as he always did, about "lunch bums." He insisted that actors who ate lunch had no energy in the afternoon. If Curtiz's energy ever flagged, no one knew it. His spartan lifestyle included hour-long horseback rides at dawn and long cold showers. "We were in New York once, in a big suite at the Sherry Netherland Hotel that we were sharing with Henry Blanke," says Lucas. "And one morning, Henry ran in and said, 'Jack, come quickly. I think Mike is dead.' I went into the bathroom with him, and Mike was slumped down in the shower with the water on. That wasn't unusual. He loved to sleep under the cold water."

Except for Sakall and Sydney Greenstreet, there were no lunch bums—no full bellies—on *Casablanca.* Claude Rains usually brought two or three apples for lunch. Even after more than two dozen movies, Rains was still "terribly tense" on a movie set and unable to work on a loaded stomach. Ingrid Bergman loved American ice cream, but David Selznick was always warning her to watch her weight. To Bogart, food was simply a necessary fuel. He ate to live, except on the days when he met Mayo for lunch at the Lakeside Golf Club and found his lunch in a glass.

Greenstreet, who had little to do but eat during most of the weeks he spent on *Casablanca,* was a serious cook. Geraldine Fitzgerald calls him "a great, great gourmet." When Fitzgerald, Greenstreet, and Peter Lorre were starring in *Three Strangers,* Greenstreet would cook dinner for them one night and Lorre would cook the next. Greenstreet was the epitome of the jolly fat man, light on his feet and, despite his 280 pounds, a dancer and a golfer. Like the Fat Man he played in *The Maltese Falcon,* he was fond of antiques, and his collection included a silver soup ladle once owned by Napoleon.

Sakall, a sunny, sweet-tempered man who looked like a dumpling, always ate with his wife. She accompanied him to the studio every day and sat reading or knitting in his dressing room. "He was one of the happiest married men I've ever met," says Leonid Kinskey who acted with Sakall in other movies, including *Ball of Fire.* Bozsi Sakall always brought their lunch from home—heavy, rich Hungarian food because, much as he loved America, Sakall refused to eat anything else. The Sakalls were childless. Around the time he went to work on *Casablanca,* they remedied that by buying a German shepherd puppy. "The dog cost them thousands of dollars," says Sakall's sister-in-law, Lenke Kardos. "Yani wouldn't go on tour unless the hotels would take the dog. When he worked, if the housekeeper was off, they hired a baby-sitter so Flame wouldn't have to be alone. When his agent Paul Kohner brought them caviar, they shared it with the dog." Sakall died of heart disease in 1955, and Flame had a heart attack and died within a month. Bozsi Sakall always said that the dog died of a broken heart.

Sakall got along with Curtiz, as he did with everybody. And Curtiz never wavered in his courtesy toward Bergman. In later years, Bergman would describe Curtiz—with whom she never made another movie—as "very sweet and nice to me." Curtiz, who was contemptuous of actors, would pay her a bigger compliment. She was a great help to him on *Casablanca,* he said. "Finest and most intelligent actress—terrific story sense," with patience like an angel.

Curtiz was also extremely polite to Joy Page, Jack Warner's seventeen-year-old stepdaughter, who had the small role of Annina, the Bulgarian girl who catches Captain Renault's eye. Page, who was still in high school, had been taking acting lessons from Sophie Rosenstein, the studio's drama coach, and Rosenstein suggested her for the part. Page was tested on May 8. The day the movie began, Warner sent a telegram telling Curtiz to hurry up and make up his mind. Page was hired for two weeks at $100 a week but, because the schedule was constantly being changed to finish the more expensive actors, she was on the set for two months.

Claude Rains also got along well with Curtiz, with whom he made eight movies, from *Stolen Holiday* in 1937 to *The Unsuspected*

S. Z. Sakall with his dog, Flame.

in 1947. Rains, whose first screen test had been a disaster, credited Curtiz with teaching him the difference between stage and film acting. As Rains put it, Curtiz taught him "what not to do in front of a camera." Later, Rains passed that advice on to his daughter. "My father only gave me one piece of advice about movie acting," says Jessica Rains, who now produces low-budget movies—*To the Devil a Son, Bloodspell, PsychoCop*—that go straight to videocassette. "My father said, 'Don't ever do anything. Just think. Because the camera picks up what you are thinking.'"

The following story may be apocryphal. Rains told it several times, but never to his daughter. The actor said that Curtiz kept demanding that he use more energy when he entered Rick's Café for the final showdown. After entering the café half a dozen times without being able to please the director, Rains finally rode in on a bicycle.

Humphrey Bogart's feelings about Curtiz were mixed. "He thought the way Curtiz used a camera was brilliant," says Lauren Bacall. In the aftermath of *Casablanca,* when Bogart signed a fifteen-year contract in 1946 that gave him director approval, Curtiz was one of five directors Bogart preapproved.* But Bogart, who had ended up dead as a crooked fight promoter, a crooked lawyer, and a gold thief in his three previous Curtiz movies—*Kid Galahad, Angels with Dirty Faces,* and *Virginia City*—also resented Curtiz's lack of interest in actors. Lee Katz remembers Bogart and Bette Davis stopping in the middle of a scene during the filming of *Kid Galahad.* Says Katz, "They were furious as hell because Mike was not watching what they were doing. He was watching the movements of the dolly. Mike was sometimes more entranced by camera movement than by what was in front of the camera."

Acting, Curtiz once said, "is fifty percent a big bag of tricks. The other fifty percent should be talent and ability, although it seldom is."

Under the Warner Bros. system, the job of coaching the actors was left to a dialogue director. Often, as with Irving Rapper, who was dialogue director on many Curtiz movies, the job was a first step to becoming a director. The dialogue director on *Casablanca,* Hugh McMullen, left for a commission in the Navy before the movie was

---

* The other four directors preapproved by Bogart were John Cromwell, Delmer Daves, Howard Hawks, and John Huston.

finished. McMullen's qualifications were slightly grandiose for a dialogue director. A Phi Beta Kappa from Williams College, he had a B.Litt. from Oxford University, wrote novels, and translated medieval Latin poetry. But what was important to the studios was that moving pictures move, and Hollywood could buy men like McMullen cheap to shore up a director's weaknesses. Directors did not have to rely on their dialogue directors, but Curtiz always did.

In the late forties, Curtiz formed a corporation to make movies for Warner Bros. He would put up 30 percent of the production costs and get 30 percent of the profits. But Curtiz had lost his box-office touch. Warners claimed that only one of Curtiz's eleven films, *I'll See You in My Dreams,* had made a profit and that the others—including *Lady Takes a Sailor, Bright Leaf,* and his remake of *The Jazz Singer*—had lost a total of $4.6 million.

"I never dreamed I would be battling . . . in a court action against the studio with which I spent twenty-six years and for whom I made eighty-seven pictures," the sixty-four-year-old Curtiz wrote to Jack Warner in January 1954. According to Curtiz's letter, the studio's lawyer, Roy Obringer, had said that the director should be ashamed to have caused the studio such a big loss.

"I was always faithful to Warners in doing my very best with whatever material the studio entrusted to me," Curtiz wrote. "You know in your heart, Jack, that whatever story you assigned to me, I worked my heart out without any regard to whether it was a 'big' or a 'little' picture or whether the story should ever have been purchased in the first place."

Curtiz's career went downhill after *Mildred Pierce* in 1945 and *Life With Father* in 1947. After a postwar boom that brought the studios peak profits in 1946 and good revenues in 1947, the movie industry went downhill, too, a victim of television and the government antitrust suit that forced the studios to divorce themselves from their theaters and to sell their movies on a picture-by-picture basis.

Curtiz had worked best in the caldron of the studio system, in which a new movie bubbled up each week and no one picture mattered too much. But the studio system, even though it would linger for a while, was fatally ill. And Curtiz was not suited to making for himself the decisions that Hal Wallis had once made for him. When Wallis left Warner Bros. for Paramount in 1944, he asked

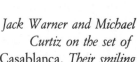

Jack Warner and Michael Curtiz on the set of Casablanca. *Their smiling relationship dissolved once Curtiz's pictures stopped making money.*

Curtiz to come with him, as his partner. Loyalty to Warner Bros or, perhaps, the promise of his own film unit made Curtiz refuse. It may not be a coincidence that both Wallis and Curtiz ran into trouble at Warner Bros. after they were promised a share of the profits. Jack Warner did not share easily with anyone.

"I thought these eleven pictures would be like life insurance for me," Curtiz wrote Jack Warner in that 1954 letter. How could he have predicted that *The Jazz Singer,* perhaps because of the Jewish theme or because it was a remake, wouldn't be a financial success? How could he have foreseen of *The Story of Will Rogers* that "the American public was no longer interested in this great man, once their most popular hero?" How could he have known that the downbeat tale of *Jim Thorpe—All American* would not be to the audience's taste? He prefaced his defenses of his movies with "It wasn't my fault."

Curtiz died of cancer in 1962. The cancer had been diagnosed six or seven years before he died, but the family doctor did not tell him the truth. "Mike found out after he fell when he was directing his last movie, *The Comancheros*," says his stepson, John Meredyth Lucas.

"When he was x-rayed, the bone looked like lacework. That was maybe six months or a year before he died. When Mike went to the doctor and asked why he hadn't been told, the doctor said, 'How many pictures have you made since your operation?' Mike said, 'Seven or eight.' 'How many do you think you would have made?' And Mike said, 'You're right.' "

When he died in 1962, Michael Curtiz was, according to most of the obituaries, seventy-two years old. He may have been older. "Mike would never tell us his age," says his stepson. When they went to get passports and my mother saw Mike's age, she said, 'But it says you're ten years younger than I am.' And Mike said, 'Darling, it's simple. You lie.' " By the time he died, he had directed more than 150 movies.

11

Working Relationships: On the Set and Off

A movie set can be compared to a cruise ship, a desert island, or a long coach journey in an eighteenth-century novel. The actors are marooned together and must make it through the days as well as they can. At best, a burst of emotion in front of the camera is followed by an hour of waiting. At worst there is nothing but tedium. (One has only to look at the daily production reports on *Casablanca* to see how often Joy Page was held on the set but not used.) Alliances spring up. So do animosities. Sexual dalliance is a way to make the time pass. When the movie is over, the castaways usually disappear into their private lives as if they had never met.

Ingrid Bergman made no alliances on *Casablanca,* but she had her language coach, Ruth Roberts, with her as she did on all her other movies. And she was protected by the aura she exuded that made men want to treat her chivalrously. "I must say Ingrid was marvelous," says Lee Katz, who usually looks back with a jaundiced eye. "Of all the people I ever worked with, she was the only one of whom I ever said, 'By God, there is really a wonderful, wonderful woman.' When the Rossellini thing happened, I was as disillusioned as everyone else."

As Bergman wrote in her acting diary, "I made many friends at Warner Brothers. Apparently they weren't used to kind and decent people." Bergman has been called a calculating woman, and she certainly used people shrewdly to build her career. But there is no way a calculated charm could have worked as dependably as hers did—on men and women alike. "The glow that comes through was in her person," says Howard Koch. "She wasn't acting that."

What are usually referred to as "the little people" on a movie—hairdressers, wardrobe women, electricians, assistant directors—are quick to detect sham and insincerity. Not even the best actress can disguise her true nature day after day for two months from the women who dress her. At least part of Bergman's aura was a lack of artifice that shocked people who spent their days creating the artificial. "She always looked so clean and well-scrubbed," said Jean Burt, Bergman's hairdresser on *Casablanca* and *Saratoga Trunk*. "It seemed ridiculous and a waste of time to shampoo her hair, because it always looked so clean." Twenty years after *Casablanca,* Burt remembered how unusual Bergman was, with her refusal to wear makeup and her lack of concern about whether her socks matched.

Jean Burt once tried to explain the sea change that turns actresses into monsters: "It would be very difficult for anyone to keep his perspective and still be a motion picture star. Take a woman player. The first thing, she comes to the hairdresser in the morning. . . . The hairdresser has to say nice things to her. . . . You can't say, 'My heavens, you look horrible today. What's the matter with you?' You don't dare do this. So you say, 'Hi, how are you? Gee, you know that is a pretty pair of slacks you have on, today.' " Burt described a routine day, with makeup man, wardrobe mistress, cameraman, and director exclaiming, "My, you look pretty, today. Oh, isn't she pretty?" and the vast apparatus of the studio concentrating on—lying to—the actress, with the publicity department telling the biggest lies of all. "We have the expression in the studios: 'They believe their own publicity,' " said Burt. "I don't see how they can help it. It's almost as if they were brainwashed to make them narcissistic."

It is obvious that Burt counted Bergman among the few who did not succumb. In the class-conscious studio system, Bergman demanded no privileges. "She was wonderful to work with because she was patient," Burt said. Bergman wore four different wigs in *Saratoga Trunk,* elaborate period wigs full of hairpins. Her own hair was tightly bound underneath, and the pressure was painful. Stoic,

Bergman would never pull at the wigs or even touch them. The closest she ever came to complaining was when the last wig was taken off at night and she said, "Oh, it's so good to get that off."

That same stoicism saw her through the months when she kept on working in *A Woman Called Golda* while she was dying of cancer. "'Trooper' is a lousy word," says Leonard Nimoy, who played Golda Meir's husband in the television miniseries. "But she was staunch. We knew she had to lie with her arm elevated, and her dresses were designed with long sleeves because of her swollen arm. But she gave no indication that anything was wrong."

Although Bergman lacked star temperament, she was immovable in demanding whatever she thought was necessary for her character. On *Casablanca,* she refused to allow Burt to set her hair or even to use bobby pins or hairpins. "And that was during the days when hair was quite contrived," Burt said. "That was during the pompadour period, and we used rats* or crepe wool in the hair to pile it up; Bergman had none of that. When you see *Casablanca* on TV now, her hairdo, because it was simple, looks as right now as it did then." Such simplicity had a cost, at least for the hairdresser. "I had to be combing that hair almost constantly. Because I wasn't allowed to put one pin in her hair, not even hide a hairpin."

On July 10, Bergman celebrated her fifth wedding anniversary. Petter Lindstrom was in Rochester, New York, with their daughter. He would not have come to the studio even if he had been in California. "I never visited the studio," he says. "I think she made nine films, and I never visited her at any studio. I never saw any of the people that she worked with. I was not informed about anything that was going on."

If Bergman appeared to slip through the July days like a shallow-keeled boat through calm water, Bogart—who was concerned about the script, the love scenes, his marriage, and what he felt to be self-pity at the core of his character—stirred up a whirlpool. There are few actors about whom opinions are so divided as Humphrey Bogart. It was not that people saw him differently but that they reacted to the same stimuli—his needling, his verbal defiance, his irascibility—with either admiration or disgust. Bogart was almost a Rorschach test.

To Billy Wilder, who directed him in *Sabrina* in 1954, Bogart was

*Rats were small pads used to make hair look thicker.

an "evil man," a lazy but competent actor who took "tremendous joy in being a troublemaker," and who got his greatest pleasure out of inciting other people to fight.

Sure, agreed writer-producer Nunnally Johnson approvingly. "Bogey thinks of himself in the role of Scaramouche, the mischievous scamp who sets off the fireworks and then nips out."

To Tom Pryor, who was a reporter at *The New York Times* when he matched Bogart and Mayo Methot drink for drink during a four-and-a-half-hour liquid lunch at 21, "He was a real guy, not one of these false fronters, actors who try to impress you all the time. He wasn't playing to the crowd."

Ezra Goodman of *Time* magazine saw that same individualism as superficial. "There was something a little hollow, dull and not entirely honest about what was going on," he wrote in *Bogey: The Good-Bad Guy,* a book based on unused background interviews Goodman did for a *Time* cover story on Bogart in 1954. In 1942, Goodman had had a less pleasant liquid lunch with Bogart and his wife. During the shooting of *Casablanca,* Goodman met Bogart for the first time at the Lakeside Golf Club, a few blocks from Warner Bros. Newly hired in the studio publicity department, Goodman had been sent to interview the actor so that he could write special features on him. Bogart was in no hurry to get back to the set, and Wallis had to send a limousine to pick him up. Goodman was accused of pumping Bogart full of alcohol. Instead of defending the young publicist, Bogart gleefully agreed that it was all Goodman's fault.

Of course, Goodman could not allow his anger and embarrassment to leak into his work. "Exit the 'Bogey'-Man. Bad Man Bogart Becomes Humphrey the Hero" was sent to newspapers—"Exclusive in Your City"—across the country in September.

"Sadistic" is the word Goodman and Billy Wilder use for Bogart. Writer-director Richard Brooks saw the same behavior as fun and games. "Bogart was the kind of guy who would invite Hedda Hopper to lunch at Romanoff's and then invite me without saying she was coming," said Brooks in 1991, a few months before his death. "Then he would say something like, 'Oh, this is Richard Brooks. He's the guy who hates you columnists. He thinks you're all full of shit.' "

"Teasing," said Peter Lorre, "is his great entertainment."

Yet Bogart was basically well-bred, said Philip Dunne. "He had manners when he chose to exert them."

Bogart was always happy to tweak the noses of studio executives, and his files are full of their wounded bellows. One letter from Obringer, the studio lawyer, responded to an interview the actor gave to Hedda Hopper after the studio refused to loan him to Hal Wallis at Paramount for *Come Back, Little Sheba*. Bogart, who was seven years into his fifteen-year contract, said that it would serve Warner Bros. right when he had no teeth or hair but the studio would still have to put him in movies.

"We are at a total loss to understand your attitude . . ." Obringer wrote. "When we entered into our existing contract with you there was no understanding or intention on our part that a part of the deal would involve an obligation on our part to accept your uncooperative services and be limited in the time when you would render such services to when you have no hair or teeth."

Such a letter, carefully sent by registered mail, delighted Bogart, who saw himself as a general in the fight against Hollywood pomposity and insincerity. Errol Flynn was almost universally well-liked at Warner Bros. because he saved his mischief for people who were important enough to fight back. Unlike Flynn, Bogart didn't reserve his needling for his betters. Bogart would sneer at anybody. "Sneer" is the word used by publicist Arthur Wilde, who was assigned the task of picking the actor up at 4 A.M. on Easter Sunday. "I was to take him to the Hollywood Bowl, where he was going to read the Lord's Prayer to the assembled multitude as the sun came up," says Wilde. "But, at midnight, Mayo called to say that Bogart was out on the town. I spent hours going from place to place and finally I found him at a friend's house, drunk as a skunk and unshaven and filthy and smelling badly. The chauffeur and I got him in the car and beat it over to the Hollywood Bowl and he pulled himself together and went out on the stage and read the Lord's Prayer movingly. And all the ministers and priests backstage—I was backstage—had tears in their eyes. When he came off the stage, they crowded around him to congratulate him, and all he said was 'Where can I puke?' To me, that summed up Bogart."

There is something in that tale of the drunken star and bitter press agent that echoes Fredric March and Lionel Stander in the 1937 movie *A Star Is Born*. Year after year on Christmas Eve, after his marriage to Lauren Bacall, Bogart would run *A Star Is Born* in his Benedict Canyon house and, later, his Holmby Hills mansion and cry as he watched it. "I was over there many Christmas Eves," said Richard Brooks. "And every year he wept in the same places. After three or four times, I asked him what made him cry. He said, 'I don't know. Maybe I'm looking at myself.' "

In *A Star Is Born,* the fading, alcoholic movie star commits suicide to keep from ruining the life of the young actress he has married. Pop psychology provides no easy parallel. Alcohol never ruined Bogart's career. John Huston said that when Bogart drank and played the roughneck he was always half acting. And Bogart's last years were his happiest ones. He didn't drink as much after he married Bacall, and he became a father for the first time at the age of forty-nine. It may have been some feeling of having reached a safe port that allowed Bogart to drop his guard each year. It may have been the symbolism of his birthday, which, according to his widow and friends, was Christmas Day 1899, although some accounts say he was born on January 23, 1899, eleven months earlier.

According to Brooks, who cowrote the screenplay for *Key Largo* and later directed Bogart in *Deadline U.S.A.* and *Battle Circus,* Bogart needled him into writing his Hollywood novel, *The Producer.* The title character is based on Mark Hellinger, but Bogart—as the actor Steve Taggart—is prominent.

"Steve Taggart did not need much scotch in his drink to make him tight," Brooks wrote of his Bogart character. "Few, however, mentioned it to him." When a policeman flags Taggart down for drunk driving and escorts him home, the actor taunts the cop for not having the guts to book him. Taggart becomes bored and surly whenever he is "obliged to act any way other than he felt like acting." He destroys one of the producer's parties, beginning by greeting one of his ex-wives with, "That lace collar you're wearing is just perfect. Hides all the wrinkles, doesn't it?" Taunted into it, he chews up a champagne glass, then stumbles through the house, "kissing the maids, acting rough to all the male guests, looking under the gowns of the female guests." The next day he telephones all the guests. "He was sorry if he had done anything wrong. No, that was all right. What was it he had done? 'Tell me.' And so each of the guests recounted the incidents of the party, the ones featuring, naturally, Steve Taggart. They all forgave him."

Bogart thought it was a fair portrait, said Brooks. And, whatever Bogart's behavior during fun and games, Brooks added, "He behaved well when things got tough."

During the year that Bogart was dying from cancer of the esophagus, even his enemies admired his gallantry. The last time that

Brooks saw him, in January 1957, the director had come over to play a few moves of chess. By then, a week or so before his death, even an attempt to eat made Bogart queasy and, as his nurse fed him, Bogart began to have trouble breathing. "Let's make it tomorrow night," Brooks said. "Maybe you'll feel better tomorrow." Bogart shook his head, despite the fact that he was obviously in pain. Brooks watched a while longer, then said, "I'm going to go. I'll see you tomorrow." Bogart motioned for the nurse to help him up so he could talk. "What's the matter, kid?" he asked. "Can't you take it?"

In her autobiography Lauren Bacall lashes out at Brooks because he did not visit often enough. No one, she says, wanted to face the fact that indomitable, indestructible Humphrey Bogart no longer had any physical strength. But he still had fortitude. Bacall paints a picture of a dying man who insists on being dressed and shaved and taken downstairs in the dumbwaiter when he can no longer walk, to hold court for close friends two hours each afternoon. In his eulogy at Bogart's memorial service, John Huston said, "No one who sat in his presence during the final weeks would ever forget. It was a unique display of sheer animal courage. After the first visit—it took that to get over the initial shock of his appearance—one quickened to the grandeur of it, expanded, and felt strangely elated, proud to be there."

Was Bogart acting during those last months, cloaking himself in the Bogart persona? Or had the persona become the man?

The alliances on *Casablanca* were between Bogart and Claude Rains, who had never worked together before and would never work together again, Bogart and Peter Lorre, and Dooley Wilson and pianist Elliot Carpenter. For Bergman, says her daughter Pia Lindstrom, "there were no cozy relationships on that set. So it was somewhat of a surprise to her that people who saw the movie felt undercurrents of warmth, passion, and deep caring."

Since an actor's ability to draw audiences was more important to the movie industry than skin color, Hollywood was less prejudiced than the rest of America during the forties. (The studios paid Eddie "Rochester" Anderson $25,000 a picture in 1942, enough to buy a few racehorses.) But Wilson and Carpenter were still the only blacks on the set of *Casablanca,* and they became and remained friends. "Elliot and his wife, Dooley and his wife, and my husband and I

Rick and Ilsa in love in Paris.

would get together for dinner, drinks, laughs," says Wilson's friend actress Frances Williams. "Whenever you were with Dooley, you had a good, warm time." Williams, who came to California the same year as Dooley Wilson, wasn't working much because, she says, "That was the heyday of Hattie McDaniel and I refused to wear bandanas." Wilson, who played a Pullman porter in *My Favorite Blonde,* his first movie under his Paramount contract, was afraid that his movie *career* would be over almost as soon as it had started. He decided that if he could get three more film roles it would be a good omen, and he and his wife would stay in Los Angeles. "We waited 'til after I got my fourth role before we bought a house," he told the unit publicist on *Casablanca.* "We just wanted to make sure." *Casablanca* was Wilson's fifth movie.

What alliances Paul Henreid made are not ascertainable. In his autobiography, which was published forty-two years after *Casablanca,* Henreid describes the tricks he watched Lorre play on Curtiz and cinematographer Arthur Edeson. But, just as Victor Laszlo never met Ugarte in Rick's Café, Paul Henreid never saw Peter Lorre on the set of *Casablanca*. Henreid started his role at the end of June; Lorre had completed his small part three weeks earlier.

It is difficult enough to differentiate truth from embroidery at the time, much less decades later. And the written accounts—by Henreid, Wallis, Bergman, Koch, Robinson—contradict each other on every page. What probably can be trusted are the feelings of the participants. The portrait of Mike Curtiz—his volcanic outbursts, his fawning courtesy to his stars, his belittling of bit players—is remarkably consistent, whether the teller is Paul Henreid or Jean Burt.

Joy Page has been a recluse for years. "When she was younger, she was very torn by success," says her son, Gregory Orr. "She was raised very strongly Catholic, and success was unseemly, not a proper thing to achieve." All that is left of his mother's career is a leather scrapbook. The tattered clippings show a career that began in a blaze with *Casablanca* and her second movie, *Kismet,* in which she played Ronald Colman's daughter. Two-thirds of the scrapbook is empty.

Almost all that Page can remember of her two months on *Casablanca* is how "sweet" and protective Humphrey Bogart was. May 29 was Page's first day of work on her first movie, and the emotional scene required her to find out from Rick if a man could ever forgive his wife for sleeping with another man. "If someone loved you very much, so that your happiness was the only thing in the world that she wanted and she did a bad thing to make certain of it, could you forgive her?" Annina asked. Page waited, frightened, in her dressing room for the call from Curtiz. "Don't worry," Humphrey Bogart said from the doorway. He came in and, patiently and kindly, went over the scene with her. In Page's memory, Bogart protected her from then on.

With Peter Lorre, it was a different Bogart. Lorre played Loki to Bogart's Puck—or vice versa. Lorre told Ezra Goodman that he once won a $100 bet that he could goad Bogart and Mayo into a fist fight within five minutes. He succeeded simply by saying, "General MacArthur," a man Mayo admired and Bogart loathed.

Bogart and Lorre were friends before *Casablanca,* and after. When they were making *Casablanca,* they lived a few blocks away from each other at the foot of the Hollywood Hills and, after a weekend night of drinking, would stagger arm in arm into the steam

Bogart with Helmut Dantine and Joy Page.

baths. Warner cinematographer James Wong Howe used to join them at the baths occasionally. "I couldn't keep up with them," he said. "They would steam out their hangovers and go straight to the bar across the street and start drinking again."

Bogart and Lorre had had the good fortune of working together on two of Bogart's last four movies, *The Maltese Falcon* and *All Through the Night*. Encouraged by John Huston, who shared the same nasty sense of humor, they embarrassed any visitors the publicity department brought onto the set of the *Falcon* with practical jokes that included Bogart's calling Sydney Greenstreet a fat old fool and Lorre's coming out of Mary Astor's dressing room with his fly unfastened. Curtiz was too intense to share Huston's fondness for practical jokes, and it is likely that at least some of the stories of Bogart and Lorre ganging up on him—refusing to work unless Curtiz laughed at their jokes—are true. But it's equally possible that those things occurred a year later on *Passage to Marseille*, when Bogart was an unassailable star and Lorre had a longer part. Lorre provided diversion for Bogart on *Casablanca* for barely a week. He started work in Rick's Café on Stage 8 on May 28 and finished his last scene on June 2.

Since Bogart didn't use his dressing room for the usual male-star sexual acrobatics—Errol Flynn sometimes managed four starlets a day and Fredric March's reputation was such that Jean Burt says she had to be accompanied by a makeup man before she was allowed to go into March's dressing room to fit his wig for *The Adventures of Mark Twain*—he concentrated on liquor and chess. The solitary chess game Rick is playing when the camera first focuses on him in *Casablanca* was a real game Bogart was playing by mail with Irving Kovner of Brooklyn. Bogart would play chess with anyone at any time, and, when he was making *Casablanca,* he was also doing his patriotic duty by playing a number of mail games with sailors in the U.S. Navy. How good a player Bogart was is debatable. His friend Nathaniel Benchley said that, as a young actor in New York, Bogart used to make money by beating the experts who sat in the park and took on all comers at a dollar a game. But the owner of Romanoff's, Mike Romanoff, one of Hollywood's best players, belittled Bogart's game. "He wouldn't have a chance against a third- or fourth-class player," Romanoff said. "I usually win when I play with him, but it is no distinction for me." Once, when Romanoff was home sick and Bogart and Richard Brooks were having dinner at his restaurant, they jointly played a telephone game with him. After the fifth or sixth move, said Brooks, "We knew we were in trouble. So Bogie calls the chess expert from the *Los Angeles Times* and asks what our next move should be. Then he calls Mike and gives him the move. In less than a minute, Mike called back and said, 'Who's there with you?' "

Whatever the quality of his game, Bogart loved chess. In a business full of gamblers, he hated gambling. "I enjoy chess because there's no luck to it," he told Ezra Goodman. He would undoubtedly be amused by the fact that the postcard on which he sent his fourteenth move to Kovner—14-P-Q5—recently sold for $1,750.

Bogart and Rains admired each other, and that admiration comes through in their scenes together. What seems to be a genuine friendship between Rick and Renault takes the sting out of the ending of *Casablanca.* "My father loved Humphrey Bogart," says Jessica Rains. "He told me so." The cockney who turned himself into a gentleman was unexpectedly compatible with the gentle-born son of a doctor and a famous illustrator who turned himself into a rowdy. "Professional" is the word the people they worked with pin, like a badge, to both men. "Bogart never missed a cue," says script supervisor Meta Carpenter. "He was completely professional." Rains, says assistant director Lee Katz, "was very professional altogether." To the Warner hairdressers, said Jean Burt, Bogart and Bette Davis were "the real pros. They were on time; they knew their lines; they knew their craft."

Rains was nearly ten years older, but both men were born in the nineteenth century—Bogart described himself as a last-century boy—and they shared a quaint morality, which made them uncomfortable when they didn't marry the women they slept with. Bogart met his fourth wife, Lauren Bacall, when she was nineteen and had

Stuck in Rick's Café, the actors forged alliances and animosities.

his first child when he was forty-nine; Rains met his fourth wife, Frances Propper, when she was nineteen and had his first child when he was forty-eight. Bogart's fourth marriage lasted until his death. Rains and Frances were married for twenty years. Bogart and Rains also shared a taste for alcohol. Rains was a heavy drinker, but a discreet one. He never showed the effects of drowning an actor's insecurities in booze until his liver collapsed.

What did they have in common, the voyagers on the cruise ship *Casablanca*? Most importantly, a professionalism that barely exists today, when stars make $10 million a movie and sometimes agonize for years before committing to a film, when self-indulgence is considered proof of a director's brilliance, and the title of producer goes to anyone who buys film rights to a novel or raises some money. It is a mistake to confuse *old* with *golden,* a word within which those letters are often trapped, but the old Hollywood studios did have a golden era when art and commerce and hard work fitted comfortably together. Whatever their deficiences as people or however messy their private lives, Curtiz, Bogart, Bergman, Rains, Wallis, Lorre, Henreid, and Jack Warner were at the heart of it during the summer they made *Casablanca*.

12

The Refugee Trail: Europeans in Hollywood

The dozens of minor performers in Casablanca were described in the daily production report as "Bits on Day Check." Some had a line or two, some only a gesture. Many of them were refugees from the war in Europe who would play refugees from the war in Europe. And, for most of them, Warner Bros. was an exotic land at the end of the earth.

The refugee trail described in the opening moments of *Casablanca* was "Paris to Marseilles. Across the Mediterranean to Oran. Then by train or auto or foot across the rim of Africa to Casablanca in French Morocco," where the lucky or wealthy could get a visa to Lisbon, and "from Lisbon to the new world." Of all the refugees who played a part in *Casablanca,* only Robert Aisner, the technical advisor, had followed that trail.

The usual path for film artists was from Berlin to Vienna to Prague in Czechoslovakia to Paris, then England, and, finally, Holly-

A photograph taken the day S. Z. Sakall and his wife, Boszi, became American citizens, December 13, 1946. He said, "Mama and I are happy, happy people today."

208

wood. "Naked in four countries" was Paul Henreid's description of himself. Like the others he had to leave behind not only his furniture and his bank account but also his language. Yet Henreid was one of the lucky ones. Henreid, Conrad Veidt, and Peter Lorre were "Saint Bernards," actors whose starring roles in European films gave them a chance for success in Hollywood. The designation comes from an émigré joke retold by Lotte Palfi. There were some émigrés, she said, who embroidered on their former imagined successes in Europe. "And so the story came about that one émigré-Dachshund

On June 17, 1942, the "Bits on Day Check" included Lotte Palfi.

asks another: 'Were you, too, a Saint Bernard over there?' "

Palfi had one line in *Casablanca*—"But can't you make it just a little more, please?"—as a woman selling her jewels in Rick's Café to a man who answers that diamonds are a drug on the market. Palfi titled a rough draft of her memoirs "I Never Was a Saint Bernard." But, like more than a dozen of the other refugees who sat in Rick's Café for a day or two or ran down the French Street in the California sunshine, she had left on the far side of the Atlantic Ocean a celebrity and esteem that could never be reclaimed.

Lotte Palfi had played leading ingenue roles at the prestigious theater in Darmstadt. Trudy Berliner—the woman at the baccarat table who asks if Rick will have a drink with her—was a well-known cabaret performer in Berlin. Curt Bois, the pickpocket, was a child acting prodigy, a leading comedian under the direction of Max Reinhardt, and, in his biggest success at the Josefstad Theater in Vienna, the man who dresses as a woman and pretends to be *Charley's Aunt.* Wolfgang Zilzer, who was shot in the opening scenes of *Casablanca* and died with his fingers curled around a Free French pamphlet, was a cabaret star who had been a successful actor since 1917. Ilka Gruning, who spoke thirty words in *Casablanca* as an old lady on her way to America, had played Strindberg and Ibsen for Max Reinhardt and had run the second-most-important drama school in Berlin. Her *Casablanca* husband, Ludwig Stossel, had been a character actor for both Reinhardt and Otto Preminger. In *Casablanca,* they would practice their English: "My dear, what watch?" "Ten watch."

Not all of the German-speaking refugees in *Casablanca* were Jewish. Hans Twardowski, who made a fine-looking German officer, had fled because he was a homosexual. The desperate young husband, Helmut Dantine, was the leader of the anti-Nazi youth movement in Vienna. The son of the head of the Austrian railway, Dantine was only nineteen when Hitler marched into Austria in March 1938. He was rounded up with a few hundred other enemies of the Third Reich and sent to a concentration camp outside Vienna. He spent three months there before influence, and a doctor who swore that the young man needed to be released for medical treatment, unlocked the gates. Dantine was released in June, and his parents immediately sent him to Los Angeles, to the custody of the one friend they had in America. Afterward, Dantine made use of the days he had been forced to spend standing in a room—stripped of paper, books, games, and conversation—staring at the other prison-

Lotte Palfi and Wolfgang Zilzer, who later changed his name to Paul Andor. As with many refugees, their careers in Hollywood never equaled their careers in Europe.

ers and the German guards. He was one of Hollywood's best young Nazis. His breakthrough came in the small role of a downed German pilot in *Mrs. Miniver.* And in 1943 he told an interviewer that he had based his portrayal of Captain Koenig in *Edge of Darkness* on the commandant of Rosserlaende camp.

Of the seventy-five actors and actresses who had bit parts and larger roles in *Casablanca,* almost all were immigrants of one kind or another. Of the fourteen who were given screen credit, only Humphrey Bogart, Dooley Wilson, and Joy Page were born in America. Some had come for private reasons. Ingrid Bergman, who would lodge comfortably in half a dozen countries and half a dozen languages, once said that she was a *flyttfagel,* one of Sweden's migratory birds. Some, including Sydney Greenstreet and Claude Rains, wanted richer careers. But at least two dozen were refugees from the stain that was spreading across Europe. There were a dozen Germans and Austrians, nearly as many French, the Hungarians S. Z. Sakall and Peter Lorre, and a handful of Italians.

"If you think of *Casablanca* and think of all those small roles being played by Hollywood actors faking the accents, the picture wouldn't have had anything like the color and tone it had," says Pauline Kael.

Dan Seymour remembers looking up during the singing of the Marseillaise and discovering that half of his fellow actors were crying. "I suddenly realized that they were all real refugees," says Seymour.

Marcel Dalio, Rick's croupier, had starred for Julien Duvivier as the informer in *Pepe Le Moko,* and for Jean Renoir in two classic French films—as the Jewish prisoner of war in *La Grande Illusion,* and, in the role of a lifetime, as the benevolent aristocrat in *The Rules of the Game.* Like Richard Blaine, Dalio left Paris hours ahead of the invading German army. Like the most fortunate of the refugees in *Casablanca,* the forty-year-old actor and his seventeen-year-old second wife, Madeleine LeBeau, eventually reached Lisbon. Then it was another two months before they could get visas to Chile. They didn't know that their visas were forgeries until their Portuguese

Croupier Marcel Dalio in the gambling room. The refugees in Rick's casino were mostly real refugees.

steamer docked in Mexico, stranding two hundred passengers with fraudulent visas. Dalio and LeBeau were eventually able to get temporary Canadian passports. At forty, the actor whose photograph had been used on Nazi posters to demonstrate the features of a Jew began English lessons. Dalio and LeBeau had met when she played a small role in a play in which he starred, and the marriage lasted long enough for them to play adjoining small roles—croupier and discarded mistress—in *Casablanca.* On June 22, while LeBeau rushed into Rick's Café on the arm of a German officer, Dalio was at a Los Angeles courthouse filing for divorce on the grounds that his wife had deserted him.

Acting is what actors do. It is not necessary to be a murderer to portray one. But a dozen good actors, cast adrift, brought to a dozen small roles in *Casablanca* an understanding and a desperation that could never have come from Central Casting. After the Germans occupied Austria, Ludwig Stossel was imprisoned several times before he was able to escape from his country. Dalio's mother and father died in a concentration camp. Palfi begged her mother to emigrate, but, until it was too late, her mother continued to believe that a "nation of poets and philosophers was incapable of committing the crimes" her daughter feared. Sakall's wife lost her brother and sister-in-law, her sister and her sister's daughter. Not one of Sakall's three sisters survived the concentration camps. On the French Street, on May 27, an extra broke into tears as Rick and Ilsa sat at a sidewalk café and wondered how soon the Germans would reach Paris. "We went through that awful day," her husband said.

In Europe everyone knew their names. In America they would play roles that were defined by occupation—Baccarat Dealer, News Vendor, Policeman, German Officer, or, even more simply, Refugee, Woman, and Civilian.

Curt Bois was the Dark European in *Casablanca,* the pickpocket. "I have such a small part," he says in 1990. "If one of the audience coughed while I was stealing from a man his money and then he stopped coughing, he didn't see me anymore. It was such a small part. It was no part at all."

He apologizes for his English. It is rusty, he says, "since I'm in Germany already for forty years now." Like many of the German-speaking refugees, Bois went home when the war was over. The bitterness of his regret at the choice he made is tangible, even over the telephone from Berlin. They went back, most of them, to reclaim their language, just as all but a reckless few had first gone to Austria or Czechoslovakia in a futile attempt to avoid being stripped of speech. Bois is typical of the Germans. An atheist with Jewish parents, he left Germany soon after Hitler became chancellor in January 1933. He went to Vienna, where applause had bumped the rafters when he had turned *Charley's Aunt* into a dapper flapper. "Already in 1933," Bois says, "my fellow colleagues didn't greet me anymore." When Vienna became too uncomfortable, he went to Prague. But in Prague, too, he heard "the awful voice of the murderer of all times."

By 1935, Bois was in America. Others stayed in Austria until the Anschluss in the spring of 1938, then crowded into German-speaking Czechoslovakia until the Nazis occupied the Sudetenland in October. Many of them made it no further. Billy Wilder, then a young screenwriter, was one of the few who dared to discard his language immediately. He was on a train to Paris on February 28, 1933, the day after the Nazis burned the Reichstag and blamed it on the Communists. "For the rest of that year, people were stupid enough to go to Austria or the German part of Czechoslovakia," Wilder says. "They thought they would be safe there. Mostly writers or actors, they were afraid that being deprived of language they would have to die of hunger."

Wilder, whose six Academy Awards for *The Lost Weekend, Sunset Boulevard,* and *The Apartment* testify to his success in Hollywood, never quite starved in Paris, but there were days when Wilder, Peter Lorre, and Lorre's wife, Celia Lovsky, shared a single can of tomato soup for dinner. When he reached Los Angeles, Wilder avoided the restaurants and living rooms where refugees met to drink coffee, eat pastry, and speak German. Instead, he lay on his bed and listened to the radio. Each day he learned twenty new English words. It was years before he was willing to speak German again.

"Most of the refugees had a secret hope that Hitler would be defeated and they could go back home," Wilder says. "I never had that hope. This was home. I had a clear-cut vision: 'This is where I am going to die.'"

Bois learned his English by listening to the burlesque comics on New York's Forty-second Street. Leonid Kinskey, who tended Rick's bar in *Casablanca,* came to New York equipped with such textbook phrases as "My good kind sir." Kinskey expanded his vocabulary by working as a waiter in Manhattan. He got the job because a friend remembered his dashing performance in a French play, *The Singing Waiter*.

Marcel Dalio was lucky enough to have his friends Charles Boyer, René Clair, and Jean Renoir to introduce him to the intricacies of the language. S. Z. Sakall never really did learn English despite English lessons seven days a week. Which was all to the good since audiences found his jolly mangling of the language irresistible. And, when Warner Bros. wanted to sign him to a long-term contract in 1943, Sakall was able to see what the studio was trying to get away with by having a friend translate the contract into Hungarian.

It was the émigré writers and actors who struggled the hardest and the longest. Directors spoke with their eyes. With the aid of dialogue directors to coach the actors, Fritz Lang, Henry Koster, Robert Siodmak, and Douglas Sirk slipped easily into the industry. Producers had assistants to translate their thoughts. And the musicians, including Franz Waxman, Hanns Eisler, and Miklos Rozsa, didn't need words at all.

Lotte Palfi didn't anticipate trouble. "America was called a melting pot because the great majority of the people there had emigrated from other countries," she wrote. "So my German accent shouldn't be any hindrance to my acting career. Of course I couldn't have been more wrong."

Some of the refugees who acted in *Casablanca* were luckier than Palfi. Ludwig Stossel was upgraded to Sakall's job as Carl the headwaiter in the *Casablanca* television series in 1955 and then found his own role of a lifetime, and fame, as the little old winemaker in Italian Swiss Colony television commercials. And nothing could keep audiences from loving S. Z. ("Cuddles") Sakall.

It was Jack Warner who called Sakall "Cuddles" and insisted, despite Sakall's protests, that the nickname be used as part of his screen billing. If there was ever a Cuddles, it was Sakall, who played flustered, endearing fussbudgets in thirty movies between 1940 and 1950. Sakall refused to loan money because he didn't want a borrower who couldn't repay him "to see me coming and run to the other side of the street." Instead, he told people who asked for money, "I'll give you as much as I can. Pay me back if you can." Says Sakall's sister-in-law, Lenke Kardos, "In Berlin there were a few part-time actors who practically lived off Yani—Mr. Sakall. Once, one was embarrassed to take Yani's money, and Bozsi, Mrs. Sakall, said, 'If you don't take the money, I'll call the police.'"

On stage in Vienna, Sakall's ignorance of German made audiences laugh the same way his fractured English would two decades later. He was a popular comedian in early German talkies before the brown shirts and black shirts on the streets of Berlin sent him back to Hungary. A *New York Times* reviewer wrote in 1936, "Since that excellent Hungarian comedian, Szoke Szakall, once so familiar a sight in German films, is banned from working in Nazi Germany under Hitler's racial dispensation Budapest producers are profiting by the situation."

Movie producer Joe Pasternak, a relative by marriage, brought Sakall to America in May 1939. A few weeks later, Bozsi wrote to relatives that Sakall was depressed because, in America, "He draws no crowds." He missed "being feted, applauded, celebrated." Sakall's first two movies, *It's a Date* and *Spring Parade,* both starring Deanna Durbin, remedied his anonymity. By April 1940, Bozsi would be writing: "People begin to recognize him on the street."

On the set at Universal, Sakall said, "I didn't did it," and jerked his head up, causing his jowls to shake and the director and crew to laugh. When he buried his face in his hands, the laughter grew longer and louder. Sakall laughed with them. A Hungarian on the set told him not to be happy, that now he would have to wiggle his jowls for the rest of his life.

"Everything happened as he had foretold it—with the difference that later they weren't satisfied with the trembling of my jowls," Sakall wrote in his autobiography. "They demanded that they should quiver and shake in a bigger and better way. . . . Later the writers made no attempt to put any humour or wit into my roles. They merely added as a piece of business: 'Here Sakall shakes his jowls and slaps his own face!' "

Curtiz didn't make the actor shake his jowls, but he used Sakall to leaven *Casablanca*'s melodrama. In a wordless gag, the pickpocket bumps into Sakall, who responds by frantically touching all his pockets. Sakall, whose mother died before he was of school age and whose father died before he was grown, loved America with all the passion of the dispossessed. He kept his citizenship papers on the mantel in the living room. "He had lived in so many parts of the world, and he never felt at home except here," says his sister-in-law.

Books about Southern California during the 1940s use the metaphor of Paradise. The literary refugees—Thomas and Heinrich Mann,

Lion Feuchtwanger, Bertolt Brecht—fill the pages of *Strangers in Paradise* by John Russell Taylor and *Exiled in Paradise* by Anthony Heilbut. Alvah Bessie titled his memoir of the blacklisting *Inquisition in Eden*. There is intentional irony and unintentional envy in the metaphor. In addition to blue skies and sunshine, Hollywood provided freedom from formal modes of behavior. But the loose culture was worn more uncomfortably than the light clothing by Middle European refugees used to a tighter fit. It is one reason why Paul Henreid seemed fussy and self-important and Leonid Kinskey was greeted with "I ain't got no change" when he tipped his hat and tried to ask directions of a man standing next to him on the street.

Many were horrified by the provincialism of the desert oasis in which they now lived surrounded by palm trees. Others marveled at mountains that rolled gently down to a huge calm ocean. When Kinskey saw Palm Springs for the first time, he "visualized the famous painting of Michelangelo of God's finger stretched, because God's finger had touched this spot, it was so incredibly beautiful."

For the most successful of the émigrés, Southern California was close enough to paradise. For others, it was Eden after the fall. In his poem "Hollywood Elegies," Brecht wrote that the heaven of Hollywood "Serves the unprosperous, unsuccessful as hell." The movie industry was an aristocracy based on success. When Ingrid Bergman bought her first house and planned a housewarming party, Irene Selznick told her that her guest list was impossible since it included writers and cameramen as well as producers. Within a few years, most of the émigrés who had found success in the movie industry didn't associate with the others. Marta Feuchtwanger, the widow of Lion, remembered Thomas Mann waiting for invitations that never came. "I can't understand that they ignore us always," the German novelist complained to her.

The émigrés were divided by status, by nationality, by politics—the Feuchtwanger-Brecht circle were Marxists while Salka Viertel's salon was more interested in film art—and by geography. Those who lived in Santa Monica and the Pacific Palisades were almost an hour's drive away from those who clustered in Beverly Hills or Hollywood. And, if they were Germans, they were divided from the rest by the curfew. As enemy aliens, the Germans were not allowed to leave their houses between 8 P.M. and 6 A.M. Among those under the curfew was the German novelist Erich Maria Remarque, who had been stripped of his German citizenship and had his books, including *All Quiet on the Western Front,* burned by the Nazis. To Marta Feuchtwanger, the 8 P.M. curfew was only a humiliation. To Lotte Palfi's best friend, Meta Cordy, it meant that "From one day to the next we lost our livelihood. We were singers—my husband had been engaged to sing the tenor solo in the Ninth Symphony by Beethoven when the curfew came—and you could not sing only in the morning."

The curfew went into effect in June, just after *Casablanca* started production. It caused the most trouble for the day players, the actors and actresses who had to move from studio to studio in search of work. Because their country had been occupied by Hitler, the Austrians on *Casablanca*—Paul Henreid, Helmut Dantine, Ludwig Stossel—were exempted. Austrians were even allowed to roll bandages for the Red Cross.

Although many of the successful émigrés had little to do with the others socially, they supported them financially. The European Film Fund was formed in 1938 to provide clothes and a place to live. That August, Charlotte Dieterle, the wife of director William Dieterle, sent out the first begging letter:

> They are desperately unfortunate human beings, and you are a human being too . . . and so HELP with a more or less big check . . . or baby clothes that your little ones no longer need or kitchen utensils or whatever seems to you not good to use anymore. They can use every little rag, they are poor beyond imagination.

The purpose of the fund, which was incorporated as a nonprofit organization in November 1938, changed after England and France went to war with Germany in 1939. Paul Kohner, the talent agent who was the soul of the fund, received frantic letters from writers who were stranded in Marseilles, Toulon, and Casablanca. Kohner went to successful screenwriters, including the Epsteins, and asked them to sponsor the writers. "We signed to assure that they would not be the financial responsibility of the government," says Julius Epstein.

Born in Bohemia but an American citizen since the early twenties, Kohner had spent three years in Berlin as head of Universal's European operations, and he knew the Nazis' work firsthand. "I was there when they burned all the books," says Kohner's widow, Lupita Tovar, herself a famous Mexican film star, who was tested for the role of Rick's mistress. "We used to make the trip to Paris to smuggle money for people. Somebody denounced us because we so often made trips out of the country. We were pulled off the train. My husband was carrying ten thousand marks. He was always terribly quick. He realized what was happening, so he said, 'There is one piece of luggage missing.' As though he was looking through the compartment, he bent down and threw the money under the seat, and said, 'No, it is not here.' We were taken off, and the train went away. It was terrible and cold, on the border between Germany and Czechoslovakia. They took off all our clothes. In Paul's briefcase, they found a publicity picture taken at Universal when the Zeppelin came and all these Germans were guests at a luncheon at Universal. And there is the picture of Paul shaking hands with the war minister. And so they let me dress and offered me a cigarette. All my clothes, my brassieres, my panties, were on the floor. And they said, 'Will you have your wife sign this affidavit that she has been treated with the utmost courtesy?' And I said, 'I want my ambassador.' And they said, 'You better tell your wife to sign.' And Paul said, 'Darling, sign.' And we never put our feet in Germany again. We went by car over the mountains to Czechoslovakia."

After the war began in 1939, Kohner asked Ernst Lubitsch to call a meeting of all the important members of the European film colony; he proposed that they get the playrights, novelists, and philosophers into the country by having the studios hire them at minimum salaries. Kohner was chosen to approach the studios. The first mogul he approached—the man he felt would be easiest to sell—was Jack Warner. He told Warner that most of the stranded writers were Jews, and Warner agreed to hire four of them at $100 a week each. Kohner was not a successful agent for nothing. Since Warner had bought four, L. B. Mayer took six, and Harry Cohn at Columbia took ten.

The contracts were for a year. Week after week, the writers sat in their studio offices, bewildered and ignored. Few learned English well enough to be assimilated; few kept their jobs beyond a year. Until the fund ran out of money in 1945, the immigrants who had jobs supported those who didn't, giving one percent of their salaries to the fund. Almost all of those who helped and were helped were German, Austrian, Hungarian, and Czechoslovakian, the Middle Europeans to whom German was a first or second language. According to the Deutsches Film Museum in Frankfurt am Main, fifteen hundred German film-industry exiles ended up in Southern California. Jan-Christopher Horak of George Eastman House, who has written a Ph.D. thesis on that emigration, says that fifteen hundred fled and more than half of them came to California. In either case, there was no way Hollywood could make room for everyone.

From the money that they earned for *Casablanca,* Michael Curtiz, S. Z. Sakall, Paul Henreid, and Peter Lorre contributed to the European Film Fund. At one time or another in 1942, Curt Bois, Ilka Gruning, Lotte Palfi, Ludwig Stossel, Hans Twardowki, and Wolfgang Zilzer were receiving money. So was Louis Arco, born Lutz Altschul, who played an almost wordless refugee in Rick's Café. When he first arrived in California, Zilzer lived in a cheap rooming house provided by the fund. "One could stay there until one got back on his feet," Zilzer said. "Until one could earn money oneself and give some money back for the next people who had to come."

The careers of those little-remembered actors can be read in the filmography of one of them, Richard Ryen, a round-faced little man who was fifty-six years old when he greeted Conrad Veidt at the Casablanca airport: "It is very good to see you again, Major Strasser." As Heinze, the chief Nazi official in Casablanca, Ryen, who had Americanized his name from Revy, had a windfall. Because he trailed after Veidt in several scenes shot weeks apart, he made $1,600, four weeks of work at $400 a week. Ryen's best year was 1943. He was in eight movies, including *Hostages, Hitler's Madman, The Strange Death of Adolf Hitler,* and *The Cross of Lorraine.* Then Hollywood went on to other things. Ryen's sole credit for 1944 was *The Hitler Gang.*

Finding it harder and harder to get work when the war ended, many of the refugees in *Casablanca* left for home, or what used to be home. But it was too late. Marta Mierendorff, whose husband died in Auschwitz, has been documenting the émigrés since 1970, trying to build a testament of their brief hour in the sun. In her files, there are form questions: Was the original persecution racial or political? If the actor returned to Europe after the war was he fully reintegrated?

Louis Arco was partly reintegrated. Ilka Gruning went to Berlin in 1950. "But 1950 was an unfortunate year for exiles who tried to return," Mierendorff wrote on Gruning's form. "The end of denazification and the cold war brought former Nazis back—and they had not much interest in reintegrating former colleagues."

Gruning came back to California, where she died in 1964 at the age of eighty-seven.

His fare partly paid by the European Relief Fund, the successor to the European Film Fund, Curt Bois also returned to Berlin in 1950—to East Germany and Brecht's Berliner Ensemble, for which Bois created the leading role in Brecht's play *Mister Puntila and his Farmhand Matti* on the stage and on the screen. But Brecht died, and Bois's stay in East Berlin cost him his American citizenship. What Bois remembered best about America, and missed most, was Red Label scotch whiskey. A few years ago the *Guinness Book of World Records* listed Bois as the actor having the longest screen career, seventy-eight years. He made his film debut in 1909, when he was nine years old, in *Mutterliebe,* and he played Homer, an aging story-teller, in Wim Wender's *Wings of Desire* in 1988.

The German newspapers were full of praise on his ninetieth birthday. "But, madame," said Bois six months before his death on Christmas Day, 1991, "after what happened, Germany is not what I thought it would be."

Others, too, heard the call. In 1950, Brecht wrote a poem, "To the Actor P. L. in Exile," to summon Peter Lorre home:

> *Listen, we are calling you back. Driven out*
> *You must now return. The country*
> *Out of which you were driven flowed once*
> *With milk and honey. You are being called back*
> *To a country that has been destroyed.*
> *And we have nothing more*
> *To offer you than the fact that you are needed.*
>
> *Poor or rich*
> *Sick or healthy*
> *Forget everything*
> *And come.*

And Lorre came. For years he had wanted to direct. In 1943, "as bait" to get Lorre to sign an exclusive contract, Warner Bros. had cynically suggested that "if sometime later on in his career he showed proclivities as a director, we might be interested." In Germany in 1951, Lorre cowrote, directed, and starred in one movie, *Der Verlorene.* A bitter movie about a good German scientist who becomes a murderer under the Nazis, the film was intensely unpopular. *Der Verlorene (the Lost One)* was finally shown in America, at one theater in New York, in 1984, twenty years after Lorre's death. "Lorre's carefully controlled, intense performance is far more impressive than the movie that surrounds it," wrote Vincent Canby in *The New York Times.*

After the failure of *Der Verlorene,* Lorre left Germany. Resettled in California, he grew fatter and fatter and parodied himself in movie after movie. Estranged from his third wife, he died of a stroke at the age of fifty-nine in March 1964.

For even the most successful of them, exile cast its shadows. Young and handsome, Helmut Dantine had a good career in Hollywood. He was grateful to America for taking him in but full of rage and frustration at what he had lost. "That's what made him difficult to live with," says Nicola Bautzer, Dantine's third wife and the mother of his three daughters. "He should have been an ambassador." The marriage ended in divorce, and Nicola married entertainment attorney Greg Bautzer, but Nicola and Helmut remained friends until his death in 1982.

Dantine had been the president of his class at Austria's consular academy, passionate about politics in a way that he was never passionate about movies. "His friends—Herbert Schober, Otto Eiselsberg—became ambassadors," says Nicola. "I didn't learn that Helmut had organized the youth riots from him. He didn't discuss any of this easily. I found out through our visits to Vienna. All the important people in Austria were in awe of Helmut. He thought of returning once. After the children were born. But being a successful actor is very alluring. It's not easy to go back. He was a brilliant young man. His whole life was diverted."

To most of the refugees in *Casablanca,* the film was just another anti-Nazi melodrama, and their unrewarding roles were just another's day's work. Hans Twardowski was lucky enough to be given a full week's salary when his one-day bit as the German officer who picks up Madeleine LeBeau took four days to shoot.

They were grateful for any job. "I played a Frenchie, this Free Frenchman, in the beginning. When they asked about his papers, he ran away and they killed him," said Wolfgang Zilzer. "Michael Curtiz said, 'Do your phony dying.' I played it and we didn't do it over, so it must have been right."

Helmut Dantine

Zilzer, who later changed his name to Paul Andor, had an advantage his fellow refugees lacked. Raised in Germany, he had been born in America to a pair of German actors touring Ohio. He didn't know he was an American citizen until he fled to Paris in 1933 and applied for a quota number to emigrate to the United States. His first Hollywood role was in *Bluebeard's Eighth Wife* for Ernst Lubitsch. When he was honored by the Deutsche Kinemathek in Berlin in 1983, Zilzer told an interviewer that working for Lubitsch had made him haughty. After that, he waited for good roles until another actor took him aside and told him it was unwise to be choosy. It was hard to get work, the American said. So you took what you could get.

What Zilzer could get included *Confessions of a Nazi Spy, Hotel Berlin,* and *Hitler's Madman.* The male refugees could always play Nazis, although, as the war went on, there were few intelligent and icy Major Strassers and more Nazi monsters. "I am not acting people; I am playing caricatures," Helmut Dantine complained a year after *Casablanca.*

It was harder for the women. "Following my arrival I was able to get tiny parts in the anti-Nazi films made in those days, sometimes as a villainess, other times as a victim," said Lotte Palfi. "But between jobs there were month-long, even year-long, pauses."

Zilzer and Palfi married in 1943, and when the war was over and Hollywood no longer needed foreign accents, they moved to New York. They lived a long time there, with Palfi playing occasional roles in soap operas and Zilzer, who had become Andor, also working off and on in television. Palfi had one memorable bit part, in 1976, as a concentration-camp survivor in *Marathon Man* who pursues Laurence Olivier down a New York street screaming that he is the death-camp doctor who did medical experiments on the Jews. They divorced a few years ago when Andor's Parkinson's disease grew worse. He wanted to die at home in Germany. She never wanted to live in Germany again. "Lotte knew she couldn't take care of him forever, and he would end up in a home, which neither of them wanted," says Peter Almond, for whom they starred in a short film that used material from their lives. "The divorce was done in friendship." Andor married his nurse. "Lotte and I were the witnesses at the wedding," Almond says.

Paul Andor died at the age of ninety in Berlin in June 1991. Two weeks later, eighty-seven-year-old Lotte Palfi died in New York.

Fifty years ago, on the set of *Casablanca,* Lotte Palfi and Wolfgang Zilzer were in love but not yet married. "I was not there," says Billy Wilder. "But it must have been a kind of heartbreaking reunion for the people who worked in the movie. Like meeting on the Alexanderplatz old pals, friends who were in the theater with you for years." Wilder was working at a different factory then, Paramount, where writers had to turn in eleven pages every Thursday. As a writer and director, to whom story and characters are everything, he dismisses the relevance of the refugees to *Casablanca.* "It didn't mean a damn thing to the movie," Wilder says. But he immediately changes his mind. "First you have to believe the main character and the story. But that there were in the background all these minor players did help it."

Don't forget, says Pauline Kael, "Our image of the Nazi was formed by the Jewish refugees."

Anthony Heilbut, the author of *Exiled in Paradise,* takes the idea even further. "Certainly *Casablanca*'s cynical nihilistic amoral vision is foreign to America," the historian says. "It would be exciting to think of *Casablanca* as helping to translate the émigré sensibility to an American audience."

13

At the Airport: The End of Production

———◆———

The uncertainty of victory shaped *Casablanca* in subtle ways. These were the darkest days of the war, said the Los Angeles *Times,* days that needed "an exceptional dose of courage." German Field Marshal Erwin Rommel was advancing in Egypt, and Nazi armies were moving deep into Russia. If Russia collapsed, Hitler could turn all his attention to England. As *Casablanca* moved toward its climactic scene at the airport, the theme of duty became stronger, especially in the last rewrites by Howard Koch. So did the theme that honor required early resistance to tyranny.

Both Koch and Julius Epstein remember carrying newly written pages of *Casablanca* script down to the set. It was rare for writers to pass out words fresh from the typewriter. That they did points up the anxiety of Wallis and Curtiz. The pages made an almost floral bouquet—blue, pink, salmon, and green. "The pages were colored so you could keep the changes straight," says Carl Stucke, who had the formal job of bringing change pages to the *Casablanca* set.

One of a thousand unnoticed spokes in the Warner Bros. wheel, Stucke worked at the studio for forty-four years. The house he lived in, just behind the Warner lot, is visible in an aerial photograph of the studio. To make sure what year he retired, Stucke looks at the back of his gold watch: "With deep appreciation. Warner Bros. 1978." Stucke started in the story department as a clerk in 1933. Almost immediately, he began collecting and making files of the production information and memos that were sent on every movie. Stucke and David Matthews, the story editor, would sometimes spend two or three hours a day in the vaults, trying to piece the records together. It is Stucke's production files, dating back to movies made in 1933, that are preserved at the University of Southern California.

It was during the July heat wave that Wallis, Curtiz, and Koch fought out the ending of the script. The temperature in Burbank hit 104 on July 7 and didn't dip below 90 for most of the month. The heat and the grim war news were tinder for the arguments. Ordinarily, Wallis, who trusted Curtiz, would have left the director alone. In any case, Wallis also had *Watch on the Rhine, Air Force,* and *Princess O'Rourke* in production during July. "But Hal came down more frequently to the set of *Casablanca* than I'd ever known him to come down on any other picture," says assistant director Lee Katz. "Largely, I think, by reason of the unfinished script."

The second-most-popular myth about *Casablanca* is that nobody knew how the movie would end. Rick sends Lois to Lisbon with Victor Laszlo in *Everybody Comes to Rick's,* just as he sends Ilsa to Lisbon in every version of the script and in the suggestions of all but one of the writers. (Lenore Coffee, who had recently finished *The Gay Sisters* for Barbara Stanwyck and *Old Acquaintance* for Bette Davis, wrote a six-page "suggested story line" in which Lois was killed by one of Major Strasser's men. Coffee was on and off the picture in less than a week.)

Even people who didn't like the play agreed with sending the girl away. Wally Kline, Hal Wallis's brother-in-law, called it "the only dramatic situation worthy of survival." Before being assigned as cowriter on the movie in January, Kline wrote Wallis:

> In taking this apart I find that when the highly censorable situations, relationships and implications are removed, we have left an American ex-lawyer in Casablanca who owns a café—the reasons for which are lacking. A mild plot about selling exit visas illegally. A millionaire Czech who must get to Lisbon for reasons not supplied

and his very beautiful paramour who once had a lengthy affair with the American but who leaves for Lisbon with the Czech—if the original ending is to be preserved—and it should be as it is the only dramatic situation worthy of survival.

Both Koch and Epstein remember a number of conversations about whether to go for what Koch calls "the sacrifice ending" or the more conventional romantic ending. Ingrid Bergman said that when she asked Curtiz and the writers which man she was to go off with, she was told that they would let her know as soon as they knew. But, although having Ilsa stay with Rick was often discussed, everyone kept agreeing on the sacrifice ending. And the Production Code would never have allowed Ilsa to desert her husband and stay in Casablanca with her lover.

The difficulty was in making the sacrifice ending work. There were two major problems: how to make Ilsa's leaving the man she loved seem believable and what to do with Rick after she leaves. In the play, Rick was arrested, but movie audiences wouldn't tolerate a Gestapo victory.

As late as May 20—five days before *Casablanca* started shooting—Casey Robinson wrote Wallis:

MISCELLANEOUS NOTES ON ILSA'S EXIT FROM THE PICTURE
It has always struck me as pretty weak that she just turns and runs out of the room, that an argument has convinced her. Either it has to be a better argument, or it has to be something more. I am frank to say I don't know just what. The best thing I can come up with is that Rick clips her on the jaw and lets her husband carry her out.

If the ending of *Casablanca* hadn't worked, the movie would have long since been forgotten. But the ending wasn't solved suddenly or dramatically. Like a portrait made of mosaic tiles, little chips eventually formed a larger picture.

In *Everybody Comes to Rick's,* as in *Casablanca,* Rick tricks Renault into calling off his watchdogs, then pulls a gun on him in order to allow Laszlo and Lois to escape with one Letter of Transit. (In the play, each Letter was good for two people, so Rick gave the other Letter to the young Bulgarian couple he had been hiding in his café.) Just as the Lisbon plane is taking off, Strasser rushes into the café.

Rick holds the gun on Strasser as long as necessary, then throws it contemptuously on the table. As he walks out, under arrest, Renault (then named Luis Rinaldo) asks, "Why did you do it, Rick?" Rick reminds the policeman that he has won his bet that Laszlo would escape.

> RICK (pausing)
> For the folding money, Luis, for the folding money. You owe me five thousand francs.

Julie Epstein has always said that the ending was solved when he and his brother, while driving to the studio one day, turned to each other and said in unison, "Round up the usual suspects." Rick would kill Strasser, and Renault would protect him.

The twins were always finishing each other's sentences. They often worked in the library of Phil's Pacific Palisades home, and Leslie Epstein remembers lying on the floor and listening to their laughter through the closed door. "One of them would start a joke and the other would finish it and it seemed like they were having the greatest time," Leslie says wistfully. In some ways, the relationship between Julie and Phil made even their wives and children seem to be outsiders.

Actually, the Epsteins's three-page outline of the last section of the movie shows that they came up with the idea of "Round up the usual suspects" early in May. Although having Rick shoot Strasser took care of one part of the problem—how to keep Rick from getting arrested—it didn't touch the major issue of how to make Ilsa's departure with Laszlo believable.

In the play a thoroughly disagreeable Lois insisted on staying with Rick. "That, my dear, is entirely up to you," a humiliated Laszlo answered. "Get her out of here, Victor, for God's sake," said Rick. To add to the unpalatability, Laszlo was grateful to Rick for giving him a woman who didn't want to be with him.

In their outline, the Epsteins avoided a three-character conversation or confrontation. They simply eliminated Lois from the movie's climax by sending her off to the airport alone. After Renault is tricked and Laszlo is sent to join his wife, the Epsteins wrote:

> Strasser comes in, because Renault has called him. The fight between Strasser and Rick follows. Strasser is shot. (Perhaps Rick,

too.) Renault informs his gendarmes that Strasser has been shot and "to round up the usual suspects." At the tag, Rick, watching the plane leave with Lois and Laszlo, informs Renault that he owes him five thousand francs.

Koch's nineteen pages of suggestions take a different tack. Where the twins eliminated Lois, Koch eliminated Strasser. In Koch's version, Rick tricks Lois into leaving by pretending that he has really betrayed Laszlo. Koch created a long scene in which Lois breaks into a "fury of denunciation" of Rick. "Does Rick imagine that she is going to run away with him after his conscienceless betrayal of her husband? . . . Never will she leave Laszlo." Then Laszlo persuades his wife to go to the plane because "In America she can serve France." It is only after Lois has left that Rick pulls a gun on Renault and sends Laszlo to join her.

RENAULT

I'll have to arrest you, of course.

RICK

When the plane leaves, Luis.

The two men sit down to finish their chess game. After two moves, Renault says, "There is no move. The Kings can't get out. We're checkmated." Rick answers grimly, "I guess the game's finished." As the plane roars over the roof of the café, Renault responds, "Ricky, I was right. You are a sentimentalist." And the movie ends.

All of these endings took place in the café. The last scenes of the movie were not shifted to the airport until the PART I REV. FINAL script of June 1. In a script mimeographed ten days earlier, the PART II TO END TEMP. script of May 21, the ending was obviously written by the Epsteins. It follows their suggestions. And the twins have managed to remove Koch's hated chess game. By that script of May 21, several more bits of the mosaic have been glued into place. When Rick points a gun at Renault's heart and tells him to call the airport, Renault responds, "That's my least vulnerable spot" and dials Major Strasser. In that May 21 ending, Strasser bursts into the café while there is still time to stop the plane.

"Strasser, in desperation, throws a lamp at Rick, then leaps at

him. The gun goes off harmlessly. The men struggle," the Epsteins
wrote. After Rick shoots Strasser, deliberately shooting bullets into
him until the gun is empty, the gendarmes rush in, and Renault tells
them to round up the usual suspects. Rick and Renault stand on the
terrace, watching the airplane soar above their heads. Rick's final
line is "It doesn't make a bit of difference, Luis. You still owe me
five thousand francs."

That ending, mimeographed four days before the movie started
production, is the one about which Casey Robinson complained. In
it, Ilsa tells Laszlo that she is staying with Rick. Rick talks her out
of staying. She belongs "to a fighter, not a saloon-keeper." And he
is no longer the man she knew in Paris. "I serve drinks. I run a
crooked gambling table. Every morning I lock myself in a room and
drink myself dizzy." Once again, Ilsa is simply handed over to Laszlo
by the screenwriters. "If I had any pride I'd walk out and leave you
here," says Laszlo. "But I'm asking you, Ilsa, come with me." And
Ilsa goes.

In no version did Ilsa (or Lois) play an active part in her destiny.
Even when she decided to stay, she was sent away. Similarly, Ingrid
Bergman could only watch the contortions through which Curtiz,
Wallis, the Epsteins, Koch, and Robinson put Ilsa Lund. The stories
that Bergman told afterward differed in details, but the psychological
center was always the same. She went to Curtiz or to the writers,
begging to know which man she loved. She was told to "play it
in-between." She protested that "there is a little bit of difference in
acting towards a man that you love and another man for whom you
may just feel pity or affection." Her questions unanswered, she
"didn't dare to look at Humphrey Bogart with love because then I
had to look at Paul Henreid with something that was not love."

For as careful an actress as Bergman, not knowing the heart of
her character was painful, but she only showed small cracks in her
equanimity. Bogart responded to the uncertainty by getting angry or
sulking. As usual, he retreated to his dressing room. When Bogart
spoke to Lauren Bacall about Casablanca afterward, it was always
about how he had fought to make the script better. "I wasn't there.
I was in high school at the time," says Bacall. "But he said he kept
fighting to make the dialogue and the scenes better. I think he was
very pleased the movie was successful, but, mind you, it wasn't the
success in his lifetime that it is now."

It was Koch whom Bogart invited to his dressing room. "We
never had any quarrels," says Koch. "And he was always noncha-

lant. It was 'Come in and have a drink.' Most of the talk centered around the lack of an ending. That was mostly what Bogart was concerned about."

Koch had been taken off the movie early in June, after a new script was handed out, the PART I REV. FINAL script of June 1. During June, the final script of June 1 was revised by Casey Robinson and the Epsteins. Unfortunately, since there was never an entirely new version of the script, the old pages were simply discarded when new ones replaced them. If a scene was written two or three times, usually only the final version remains. Wallis was away during the last week in June, when another revision of the ending was handed out on June 25. That was Paul Henreid's first day on *Casablanca,* and he worked from 9 A.M. to 6:30 P.M., filming the scenes when Laszlo meets Captain Renault and the Norwegian Resistance fighter Berger in Rick's Café. For some unrecorded reason, Jack Warner ordered the new pages recalled the next day. Since so many early scenes with Paul Henreid remained to be shot, the script problems could wait until Wallis returned on June 30.

Internal memos make it clear that, almost as soon as he returned, Wallis brought Koch back to write yet another ending. In a memo to Curtiz on July 6, Wallis wrote:

Dear Mike,
    I see that tomorrow you are shooting in the Cafe with Laszlo and Ilsa arriving and with Renault putting Laszlo under arrest. All of this in the new rewrite on which we are working with Koch is the same as in your present Revised Final Script, with the exception of scene 245 where Ilsa asks Rick if he has arranged everything. I am attaching the new dialogue to take the place of this scene. Everything else remains the same.
    I am also attaching the new ending as Koch and I have finally worked it out. I think you will find that it incorporates all of the changes you wanted made, and I think we have successfully licked the big scene between Ilsa and Rick at the airport by bringing Laszlo in at the finish of it.
    It was practically impossible to write a convincing scene between the two people in which Rick could sell Ilsa on the idea of leaving without him. No arguments that Rick could put up would be sufficient to sway her from her decision to remain, and that, I think, is why we always had so much trouble in trying to write such a scene between the two people.
    However, by bringing Laszlo in for the additional few lines, it

makes it impossible for Ilsa to protest further and in this way the scene can be finished convincingly.

Casablanca moved to the airport on Stage 1 on July 17, and the ending was completely shot by July 23. So Ingrid Bergman knew exactly how Ilsa Lund felt about Rick and Laszlo before she played several earlier scenes, including the scene in the black market with Bogart, the scene in the Blue Parrot where Ilsa and Laszlo refuse Sydney Greenstreet's offer of a single exit visa, and some of the conversation between Ilsa and Laszlo in their hotel room before Laszlo goes to the Underground meeting. Those scenes were shot during the last week of July.

Although Wallis's memo of July 6 states that he and Koch had licked the ending, new speeches were being written—sometimes every day—through July 16. "Wallis was not a subtle man," says his biographer, Charles Higham, who thinks that *Casablanca*'s ending, like much else in the movie, reflects Wallis's personality. "The film

A scene in which Rick makes arrangements with Laszlo in a prison visiting room was cut out of the movie.

reflected his precision in looking at life as a series of blacks and whites. The crisp, clear-cut approach to a moral dilemma was Wallis."

One of Koch's late additions that helped make the ending credible was Rains's comment to Bogart that Ilsa was only pretending to believe him.

RENAULT

. . . that fairy tale you invented to send Ilsa away with him. I know a little about women, my friend. She went, but she knew you were lying.

So that the other actors, who were being held on the set, would have a chance to learn new dialogue, Curtiz changed the schedule on June 16 and shot a scene in their hotel that only involved Bergman and Henreid. It was another page of new dialogue that triggered Bogart's tantrum on Friday, July 17. As July 17 was described by the unit production manager Al Alleborn:

During the day the company had several delays caused by arguments with Curtiz the director, and Bogart the actor. I had to go and get Wallis and bring him over to the set to straighten out the situation. At one time they sat around for a long time and argued, finally deciding on how to do the scene.

There were also numerous delays due to the cast not knowing the dialogue, which was a rewritten scene that came out the night before.

In front of the camera, Bogart was rarely difficult. "He was only interested in the truth of the character," says Geraldine Fitzgerald. "He didn't care what he looked like, and he didn't care how he sounded. He lacked any kind of personal vanity." Cinematographer James Wong Howe said that Bogart never caused trouble for a cameraman. Unlike more narcissistic stars, he didn't care how he was photographed. "He didn't have a good side or favorite side," Howe said. He just went out there and played his scene the way he played it."

And few of his directors, except Billy Wilder, complained about him. Wilder said that on *Sabrina* Bogart never studied complete scenes but learned only the bits and pieces that were being photographed.

For Richard Brooks, who directed Bogart in two movies, the actor was always prepared and never difficult—except once. In a situation that may have parallels to July 17 on *Casablanca,* Bogart kept arguing with Brooks and demanding to know why his character was moving around a table in a pivotal scene with Ethel Barrymore in *Deadline U.S.A.* (1952). After Bogart had stopped the scene four or five times, said Brooks, Miss Barrymore said, "Why don't you just do what the man says and get it over with?" But the scene wasn't completed until just before the lunch break. During lunch, Brooks went to Bogart's dressing room and said, "What the hell's the matter with you? You've never done anything like this before." Bogart answered, "Listen, kid, I didn't know the lines." "Bogart said the Rat Pack* had been over the night before and kept him up until two in the morning," said Brooks. "So, on the set, he was just learning his lines."

One can speculate that on *Casablanca,* too, Bogart attacked in order to avoid the embarrassment of being seen as unprepared. And the speeches that he had to deliver were the heart of an ending that had caused trouble for months. The new dialogue that day included Rick's "We'll always have Paris" speech.

As Koch fiddled with the language, both the romance and the need to do the right thing were heightened. In one speech, written on July 14, Rick told Ilsa:

RICK

Last night we said a good many things. We meant them then— just as we meant them once in Paris. But the minute that plane leaves the ground and you're not with him, you'll regret it.

In the same speech as changed on July 16, Rick told Ilsa:

RICK

Last night we said a good many things. You said I was to do the thinking for both of us. Well, I've done a lot of it since then and it all adds up to one thing. You're getting on that plane with Victor where you belong.

---

* The original rat pack was a group of friends, most of whom lived near each other in Holmby Hills. It included Bogart and Bacall, Frank Sinatra, Dean Martin, and Judy Garland.

Bergman has talked about an alternative ending—which she said was never shot—in which she would stay with Bogart. But all the changes of mid-July, page after page of dialogue, built to the sacrifice ending. By that time, the other ending would have made no emotional sense. And the dark days of the war demanded renunciation. It was a time when the problems of three little people didn't amount to a hill of beans. However, the camera reports for July 18 show that there was one alternative scene. It was a version of the scene, in which Rick tells Laszlo why Ilsa came to see him and what had happened between them in Paris. That scene was written and shot in a long and a short version.

It was just before the airport scenes were shot that assistant director Lee Katz got his great inspiration. "We were not allowed to leave the lot," he says. "So this airport was built on a stage with a cutout airplane. And, obviously, we fogged in the set not so much to give it an atmosphere but because we had to conceal the fact that everything was so phony. We finally positioned the plane, which was, I thought, a pretty bad cutout, as far away as we dared. And we had no way to give it any perspective. And it occurred to me to hire a bunch of midgets to portray the mechanics. To give it a forced perspective. And it worked."

Few people can see how well it worked, however, since, during the editing of the movie, most of the shots of the mechanics swarming over the plane dropped out.

No matter how final the script, no matter how many times it was rewritten, there were always accidents and changes on the set. In the last scene of the final script, Renault sent Rick off to the Free French garrison at Brazzaville, and Rick reminded Renault, as always, that he had lost the bet—which had somehow, inexplicably, been raised to 10,000 francs. Renault's decision to go along—"And that 10,000 francs should just about pay our expenses"—was not in the script. The line does not appear until it is penciled into the cutter's script, a record of shots, camera angles, and dialogue that is always recorded after the fact. Who decided that Rains should accompany Bogart on the journey is lost in the vaporized fog of fifty years ago, while a miniature airplane flies overhead.

July 22 was *Casablanca*'s last day on Stage 1. The major work had been done, and July 22 was used for added closeups and retakes. Wallis had watched the rushes of the airport scenes several times. He was not yet feeling dissatisfied with the ending; he wouldn't write a new last line for the film until August. Wallis asked Curtiz for a few additional shots and retakes, but he told the director that he felt that, in general, "the stuff will cut up all right." Wallis told Curtiz to reshoot Bogart's dialogue with Rains after Ilsa and Laszlo leave. "This should be delivered with a little more guts," Wallis said, "a little more of the curt hard way of speaking we have associated with Rick. Now that the girl is gone, I would like to see Rick revert to this manner of speaking."

There was one other problem. When Bogart shot Strasser, the actor had improvised a line, "All right, Major, you asked for it," which would have to be removed, Wallis said. Otherwise, it would appear that Conrad Veidt had reached for his gun in self-defense. Wallis told the director to do it over, using the line in the script: "I was willing to shoot Renault, and I am willing to shoot you." Conrad Veidt had finished his role in *Casablanca* two days earlier, but on June 22 he came back to die again.

This time the dirty Nazi drew his gun first. When Howard Koch speaks of people today returning to *Casablanca* as to "political church," he calls it a hunger "for political, social and human values that are missing today." It is also a hunger for simplicity, for an era when black and white rarely shaded into gray and for a war when the good guys were firmly distinguishable from the bad guys.

14

"Our Ism
... Americanism"

———◆———

On July 18, on Stage 1, Victor Laszlo welcomed Rick
Blaine back to the fight. "This time," he said, "I know our side will
win."

The credentials with which *Casablanca* supplied Rick—his record of running guns to Ethiopia and fighting against Franco in
Spain—would have gotten a real Rick Blaine into serious trouble in
1947, when the House Un-American Activities Committee (HUAC)
went looking for Communist subversion in the motion-picture industry. Humphrey Bogart, whose milder record included supporting Franklin Roosevelt for President and giving a few dollars to
striking lettuce pickers in Salinas, California, in 1936, got into
enough trouble.

Bogart may not even have given money to the farm workers. The
accusation that he did is one of the lumps of raw and undigested
information in an FBI file that runs hundreds of pages. The right-
wing fervor that swept America from 1947 to 1957 can be read in
the files of Bogart, Peter Lorre, and even Ingrid Bergman. From this
distance, those FBI reports create a world like the one in *Alice in
Wonderland* where the Knave of Hearts is guilty of writing a letter

he swears he didn't write because, if he were an honest man, he would not have disguised his handwriting and refused to sign his name.

In one summary, Bogart is suspect because his movies included *Passage to Marseille,* which "followed the Party Line with rigid adherence," and *Action in the North Atlantic,* a World War II movie about the Merchant Marine, which was written by one of the Hollywood Ten, John Howard Lawson. In addition, say the files, although Bogart was mentioned infrequently by the Communist newspaper the *Daily Worker,* he was always mentioned favorably.

The 173 pages of material released from Lorre's file have a single obsession. Lorre was a friend of a suspected Communist, Bertolt Brecht, and had even read some of Brecht's inflammatory poems at a public dinner. Like all the files, two-thirds of Lorre's is unreadable because all but two or three words on a page have been blacked out to protect the informer or the internal practices of the FBI. Conrad Veidt's files manage to have their cake and eat it too. Veidt is accused of having pro-Axis leanings and of being associated with fervent anti-Fascists.

The day that Veidt finished work on *Casablanca,* July 20, 1942, he had plans for the evening. According to FBI file No. 100-3514, Veidt was to be a speaker at the Free Peoples' Dinner held at the Beverly Hills Hotel under the auspices of the Joint Anti-Fascist Refugee Committee and the Council on African Affairs. Guests included the mayor of Los Angeles, the vice-consul of the USSR, Charles Laughton, Major William Wyler, and an FBI agent who detailed the pro-Russian sentiments of the guest of honor, Paul Robeson. Although Veidt's name was on the program, he never showed up. He may have gone out to celebrate the end of his role in *Casablanca* or simply gone home to bed. But the fact that he was expected to appear is on file forever.

The files are a garbage dump of rumors, innuendo, and heavily edited non sequiturs. In 1940, Bogart, Fredric March, James Cagney, and screenwriter Philip Dunne were accused of being Communists by an FBI informant. Despite the fact that they were cleared immediately by Martin Dies, the chairman of HUAC, and that the informer was later called a pathological liar by a judge, the disproven charges were resubmitted to HUAC when the inquisition began seven years later.

Anyone could accuse anyone of anything. Bergman's slim files include an accusation by Gerald L. K. Smith, a rabble-rousing anti-Semitic zealot, that she had been doing "some pretty clever stuff for the Reds" because in December 1945 she participated in a banquet for the American Youth for Democracy. Since FBI director J. Edgar Hoover had called that organization a successor to the Young Communist League, Smith asked HUAC to investigate Bergman. (He also asked for investigations of Frank Sinatra, Eddie Cantor, Edward G. Robinson, the War Writers Board, headed by mystery writer Rex Stout, and the Anti-Defamation League.)

There were Communists in the movie industry, of course. Most of them were writers, and several of those were writing movies at Warner Bros. during World War II. But the industry's emphasis on box-office success served as a wall against subversive ideas. Beyond vague references to brotherhood and a certain speechifying about social inequalities and the meaning of the war, there is little to differentiate movies written by Reds from anyone else's films. In Warners' *Destination Tokyo,* written by one of the Hollywood Ten, Albert Maltz, submarine skipper Cary Grant makes a speech describing the difference between Americans and Japs: a sailor who has just died bought his five-year-old son roller skates while the Japs buy their five-year-olds daggers. We are fighting so that the next generation of children, including Japanese children, will get roller skates. Alvah Bessie, another member of the Ten, wrote the original story for *Objective, Burma!* for Warner Bros. Bessie argued against a "racist statement" in the movie's script that called for the Japanese to be "wiped off the face of the earth." In a letter to producer Jerry Wald, Bessie warned that "Wiping people off the face of the earth is the private idea—and policy—of Fascists." He praised *Destination Tokyo* for having Cary Grant point out that "people can be trained from childhood to be brutes . . . or decent human beings."

The decisions that came back to haunt the movie industry—to make movies praising our noble ally Russia during World War II—were not made by Communists but by Jack Warner, Sam Goldwyn, and even the conservative Republican L. B. Mayer. Among the most embarrassing of those movies was Warners' *Mission to Moscow,* based on a book by American Ambassador Joseph E. Davies, in which Russia is full of happy faces in happy factories. They are well-fed, smiling workers who have learned English in night school. Walter Huston as Ambassador Davies is convinced that the victims of Stalin's purge trials were guilty and that their confessions were not forced. As to Russia' invasion of Finland, it was necessary because Finland was being ruled by one of Hitler's puppets.

Howard Koch, who has screenplay credit on the movie, did not want to write *Mission to Moscow.* "I had done three pictures in a row and I wanted a vacation," he says. I said, 'How about getting another writer who's maybe been to the Soviet Union?' Hal Wallis said, 'All right, if you don't want to.' And then I got a call from Jack Warner's office to come up. And there was Jack Warner and Harry Warner who hardly ever saw writers. He just talked to bankers and Jehovah. So I knew something was up. Jack, who was the talker, said, 'Look, we've just had lunch with President Roosevelt and he had *Mission to Moscow* on his desk. He said it's very important to get a better understanding of the Soviet Union. It's part of the war effort.' I said, 'Well, under the circumstances, I'll do it.' "

Mission to Moscow—which was directed by Mike Curtiz—was released in May, 1943. There is no separate FBI file on Curtiz, although his name appears in a thick file written in July 1943 and titled "Communist Infiltration of the Motion Picture Industry." *Mission to Moscow* is listed as one of the pictures containing "alleged Communistic propaganda." The paragraph on Curtiz contains enough misinformation to make a reader uneasy about the FBI's fact-gathering ability. Investigation reveals, says the report, that Curtiz (who actually came to Hollywood seventeen years before the report was written) had been in the United States for five years and had "very little experience as a director of pictures." Therefore, *Mission to Moscow* was really directed by Jay Leyda.*

While *Mission to Moscow* was in production, Jack Warner wrote to Ambassador Davies that ". . . there's no reason why we will not have one of the most important documents that has ever been filmed." How Warner must have squirmed four years later. His humiliation, and the fear beneath the humiliation, can partly explain if not excuse the rapidity with which Warner offered up a dozen of his employees, including Koch and the Epsteins, to HUAC in May, 1947.

Even if he had refused to write *Mission to Moscow,* Koch would have ended up in front of the committee. He was not a Communist, but he had joined too many organizations and signed too many

---

*Leyda, the technical advisor on *Mission to Moscow,* was an alleged Trotskyite who had worked with the great Russian director Sergei Eisenstein in Moscow during the 1930s.

documents. Humphrey Bogart—a mildly political man who was resolutely for the underdog—is a more subtle object lesson.

A report in Bogart's FBI file notes that he wrote an article that had appeared in November 1944 in a suspect publication, *Fraternidad,* in which he denounced "race bunk" and insisted that prejudice against Negroes and Jews was wrong. Lena Horne lived across the street from Bogart when he was making *Casablanca.* "I didn't know anything about him except I'd hear him fighting with Mayo Methot who he was married to at that time," says Horne. "Because I was black, I had to be put in that house secretly. The house was signed for by Felix Young, a white man that I got a job with, singing at his club. He pretended to rent the house, and I was sneaked in with my two babies and my aunt. When the neighbors found out, they passed around a petition to get rid of me. And Bogart raised hell with them. He and Mayo made a great stand about the neighbors leaving me alone. Then he sent word over to the house that if anybody bothered me, please let him know."

In 1947, Bogart joined the Committee for the First Amendment, which was founded by his friend John Huston, screenwriter Philip Dunne, and director William Wyler to protect free speech and protest against the growing censorship and intimidation. Julius Epstein was on the steering committee. Bogart was one of a planeload of celebrities who flew to Washington in October 1947 at the same time that Koch and the others were being called before HUAC.

"John Huston and I were very careful all the way through to be the only spokesmen for the committee," said Philip Dunne. "If the actors were asked a question, we answered it. The actors were outraged by the business of congressmen picking on people and the blacklist and all that. They were decent, honorable people, but they were innocents. I think Huston got Bogart into the plane ride. Bogart caved in eventually."

The moguls caved in first. In November they jettisoned the Ten,* all of whom were or had been members of the Communist Party, something that was not illegal. It was the beginning of years of blacklisting and graylisting in the movie industry, during which the pursuit of Communists turned into the hounding of liberals.

---

*Writers Alvah Bessie, Lester Cole, Ring Lardner, Jr., John Howard Lawson, Albert Maltz, Samuel Ornitz, and Dalton Trumbo, producer Adrian Scott, directors Edward Dmytryk and Herbert Biberman.

Careers were ruined simply because one had been too active in a union, had given money to the wrong causes, or had a name which was spelled the same way as that of someone who had been subpoenaed by HUAC. And being controversial became as bad as being a Communist. Or maybe it was the same thing.

"We went to Washington because we felt the Bill of Rights was being attacked," Bogart said with all his tough-guy cockiness on a radio program with the other celebrities, including Paul Henreid, Gene Kelly, and Danny Kaye, on October 29. By December, he was giving newspaper interviews apologizing for the trip: "I went to Washington because I felt fellow American citizens were being deprived of their constitutional rights. I see now that my trip was ill-advised, foolish, and impetuous." Bogart had to keep making stronger and stronger apologies. He had been duped, he admitted in an article, "I'm No Communist," published in *Photoplay* magazine in March 1948. He had been a dope. But he was no Communist. He was an American dope.

The set of *Casablanca,* like Warner Bros. in general, skewed liberal. "We might as well question why we breathe," Victor Laszlo answers when Rick asks him, "Don't you sometimes wonder if it's worth all this? I mean what you're fighting for?" Says Laszlo, "If we stop breathing, we'll die. If we stop fighting our enemies, the world will die." Jack and Harry Warner were perfectly happy with a social order that let them own a studio, make money, and pay as little of it as possible to their employees. But, in the context of studio moguls, they reigned from the left. Harry's sense of Jewish identity, the pleasure Jack took in rebellion, and a patriotism that can't be doubted by anyone who reads their letters and speeches led them to stands that weren't duplicated by the other moguls. Their cowardice later on does not erase the boldness of their early positions.

The first public anti-Nazi gesture by a Hollywood mogul was made by Jack Warner in March 1938, when he held a fund-raising dinner at his home for the Hollywood Anti-Nazi League. The Warners refused to be cautious and allow the powerful German-American Bund and the conservatives who ran the Production Code to threaten them out of making such early anti-Nazi movies as *Confessions of a Nazi Spy* and *Underground.* The overseers of the Production Code considered *Confessions* to be dangerous to the long-term interests of the movie industry. "Although the script is *technically* within the provisions of the Production Code, it is questionable," Joe Breen wrote to Jack Warner, because it treads on another country's national feelings. After reading the script, which was based on a true story, an angry Code reviewer was less diplomatic: "Hitler and his government are unfairly represented in this story, in violation of the Code. . . . To represent Hitler only as a screaming madman and a bloodthirsty persecutor and nothing else is manifestly unfair, considering his phenomenal public career, his unchallenged political and social achievement, and his position as head of the most important continental European power." Fritz Kuhn, head of the German-American Bund, sued for $5 million. The Warners were delighted to have another way of exposing the Bund. A year later the libel suit was dropped.

Harry Warner's hatred of Communism equaled his hatred of Nazism. For years, "OUR ISM . . . AMERICANISM" headed the editorial page of the *Warner Club News*. But, in the late thirties, the Warner brothers supported the Hollywood Anti-Nazi League, even after the other producers withdrew because the league's leaders included Communists. "Harry Warner in particular had refused to yield to the arguments," said Donald Ogden Stewart, the upper-class, Yale-educated, Communist screenwriter of light comedies who was president of the league. "Hitler was the enemy and Harry was willing to use any help, even from Reds, to fight him." Sonja Biberman, executive secretary of the Anti-Nazi League, remembers that "Jack and Harry Warner were the studio chiefs who were the easiest to get money from."

Early in 1939, Harry had some kind of mild breakdown, and Jack warned an executive in the New York office not to worry Harry with "any of the Jewish or world social problems as he is starting to become a nervous wreck again"; the worrying was "a very definite threat to his health." Harry and Jack, like most of their writers and actors, supported Roosevelt. They also made the mistake of allowing that support to seep into their movies. Critic James Agee uses the words "sacred treatment" to describe the way the President was treated in *Mission to Moscow*. Said Agee: "The man whom Ambassador Huston faithfully calls 'Boss' . . . is here accorded almost the divine invisibility of good taste which Jesus Christ rated in Fred Niblo's *Ben-Hur*." Roosevelt was treated no less admiringly in *Yankee Doodle Dandy, Princess O'Rourke,* and half-a-dozen other movies made by Warners during the war. In a rave review of *This Is the*

Army, Time magazine's only reservation was "to Warner Bros.' continued public rumbleseating with the President of the United States. It is still any gossip's guess whether the engagement is official or whether they just like each other very, very much."

It is no wonder that Harry Warner found himself in front of a Senate subcommittee as early as 1941. In those months before America entered the war, the committee was investigating "war mongering" by Hollywood, and seven of the twenty-five films it questioned had been made by Warner Bros.* Timing is everything, and *Casablanca* would also have been denounced by the subcommittee if it had been made before—instead of after—America's declara-

---

* *The Inquisition in Hollywood* gives a list of the movies of the thirties that most impressed Communist writers: *I Am a Fugitive from a Chain Gang, Juarez, The Story of Louis Pasteur, The Life of Emile Zola,* and *The Grapes of Wrath.* All but one, 20th Century–Fox's *The Grapes of Wrath,* were produced by Warner Bros.

tion of war. One of the movies that raised the wrath of the committee was *Sergeant York,* which starred Gary Cooper in the true story of a pacifist farm boy who turned into a World War I hero when it became necessary to fight. Warner told the committee that the proof that Warner Bros. had no ulterior propaganda motive was that *Sergeant York* would make more money than any other movie the studio had released in recent years. Pearl Harbor cut those Senate hearings short, but the Warner brothers were vulnerable when HUAC gathered strength six years later.

Except for Bogart, who was denounced by right-wing columnists, and Koch, who was dropped by Warner Bros., the liberals on *Casablanca* managed to avoid the HUAC spotlight. The OSS, the precursor of the CIA, had a file on Peter Lorre because of his membership in an organization, The Council for a Democratic Germany, that it considered a Communist Front, but the government seems to have more or less lost interest in Lorre after Brecht testified before the committee and fled the country.

The Epsteins—despite their activism in the Screen Writers Guild, an organization that HUAC considered little better than the Communist Party—had always been outspokenly anti-Communist. And, like most men, HUAC member J. Parnell Thomas refused to believe ill of Ingrid Bergman. At a time when any accusation carried the weight of truth, Thomas challenged Gerald L. K. Smith to prove that Bergman had given financial assistance to a Communist group.

On the Committee for the First Amendment's airplane and radio program, Paul Henreid had once again played the second lead, overlooked in the newspaper reports. But, according to his autobiography, Henreid's plane trip was not overlooked by the major studios. He maintained that he was blacklisted by the majors for four years. It is Henreid's contention that Bogart, Judy Garland, Frank Sinatra, and others who had been part of the Committee for the First Amendment avoided punishment because the studios to which they were under contract protected them. Henreid said that he had bought himself out of his Warner Bros. contract and, against the advice of his agent, Lew Wasserman, had refused to sign with M-G-M. Henreid continued working in independent films, so he must not have been a target of the most virulent Red hunters. But he said that his only work at a major studio came because—very early but still "in defiance of the blacklist"—his friend, director William Dieterle, and producer Hal Wallis hired him to play a villain in *Rope of Sand.* Even from the perspective of forty-five years, Philip Dunne thought that what Paul Henreid did was brave. "It takes particular courage to take a stand if you're a naturalized citizen," said Dunne in 1991. "Paul Henreid was absolutely a straight arrow, wonderful fellow."

In the less grim days when the Epsteins were working on *Casablanca* and communism could still be joked about, Julie and Phil played one of their finest practical jokes on several of their left-wing colleagues, including John Garfield and director Vincent Sherman.

"We played the same thing on a lot of people," says Julie. "My brother had a wonderful dialect. He would call on the phone and say, 'I'm here from New York. I've been asked to contact you. Take care of me. I have no place to live. I'm walking downtown like a wild animal. I'm sure you have an extra room.' He pretended to be a member of the Communist Party or the very far left. He had been assured that he would be taken care of when he came to Hollywood. Phil would leave it vague. 'I'm sure you understand why I'm calling you. . . .' And whoever we were calling would have all types of excuses. They would say, 'Unfortunately, I have people visiting me.' And Phil would hang up and let an hour go by and call again. This time he was the manager of a bachelor hotel. 'Mr. Garfield,' he would say, 'There's this man in the hotel who gave you as a reference. He's eating. He said you'd pay the bill. He's eating a magnificent dinner and he wants kosher food.' And Garfield would say, 'No, no. I didn't give my permission.' And Phil would keep calling being different people. Finally, he would call up from Warner Bros., from the entrance. 'Mr. Sherman, there's a man here coming to see you.' And Vincent would say, 'Call the security!' And then my brother would wind up, saying, 'The trouble with you, Mr. Sherman or Mr. Garfield, is that you are ashamed of being a Jew.' "

Right and wrong were so simple on the set of *Casablanca,* with the picture dramatizing an enemy who was obvious to every right-thinking American in 1942. Outside, keeping one's footing was more difficult. When the Epsteins went to Washington in February 1942 to help write a series of films that would tell American soldiers and sailors why they had to fight, they took with them their secular religion of belief in the ideas of Franklin Delano Roosevelt. Frank Capra called his seven Hollywood writers "my seven little dwarfs" and found them a place to sleep and cubbyholes to work in at the Library of Congress. They didn't stay long. The volunteer civilians were Hollywood's best. Like most screenwriters, they were liberals; and one, John Sanford, was a member of the Communist Party. As Capra, a conservative man who became more and more conservative, told the story in his autobiography, he thought the treatments they turned in for the seven movies in the "Why We Fight" series "were larded with Communist propaganda." Capra sent the writers home.

Some drifted into the net of political entanglements and were caught. Curt Bois would go to East Berlin and lose his American citizenship because of it. More than forty years after he left America, Bois said, "I was never political minded until I was invited, through a friend, to Bertolt Brecht's house."

And some escaped. Claude Rains was friends with two members of the Hollywood branch of the Communist Party, Herbert Biberman, who had directed him in plays, and Biberman's actress wife, Gale Sondergaard. Biberman asked him to give money to various causes, but Rains, who was scarred by years of poverty, never got around to it. "I hedged and didn't do anything," he said when he was reminiscing for that never-written autobiography. "If I had, I might have found myself up before the committee. Frightening."

Biberman invited Rains to his house to meet a Chinese actress. "I knew nothing about Herbert's politics," Rains said. "The large living room had been fixed up with a stage at the end and rows and rows of seats. The Chinese actress got up on the platform. And, brother, she was a Chinese Communist." Rains looked at the woman he was with. "She said, 'Get out fast.' And we got out. And I never went to that house again."

Some thirty years later, remembering his terror, Rains said, "I was frightened to death. And I had reason to be."

Rains's fear was justified. The winds of political fashion shifted abruptly after the war, leaving much of Hollywood chilled. Free speech in America has always been more accepting of some ideas than of others, and the premature anti-fascists of 1937 were labeled fellow travelers and pinkos in 1947. But, however unpopular their ideas had been five years earlier and whatever pain the organizations they had joined or the money they had donated would cause them five years later, few people on the set of *Casablanca* were ashamed of being liberals in the summer of 1942.

15

Play It, Sam

W hen Lois Meredith enters Rick's Café in Act I of *Everybody Comes to Rick's,* she asks Sam to play "As Time Goes By." By the time Murray Burnett wrote that ballad into his play, he was nearly a decade older than the Cornell University senior who had fallen in love with the song and had played Frances Williams's recording over and over until his fraternity brothers were sick of the words. But he had never forgotten the song. "It struck a chord," is all that Burnett can say now about his passion for "As Time Goes By." "I feel the same way about 'Send in the Clowns.'"

By 1942, "As Time Goes By," like most briefly popular songs, had been forgotten. No one could have imagined that its resurrection would far exceed its original success. "As Time Goes By" was written by Herman Hupfeld for a 1931 Broadway show, *Everybody's*

Welcome. Hupfeld wrote more than a hundred songs, but he never wrote a complete show. He was brought in to write specialty songs to fill in the gap when a show sagged. The plot of *Everybody's Welcome* had something to do with an unmarried couple who lived together in Greenwich Village. The dead spots were filled with jokes and dancing by the Ritz Brothers and the velvety liquid crooning of Frances Williams.

" 'As Time Goes By' was the big hit of the show," says Ann Sothern, who hadn't yet changed her name from Harriette Lake when she played the ingenue in *Everybody's Welcome.* "And Frances Williams sang it wonderfully. She was a long skinny lady with a low husky voice. I always wished I could be the one to sing it."

With heavily discounted tickets, *Everybody's Welcome** limped through 139 performances. And Rudy Vallee made a successful record of "As Time Goes By" before the song disappeared.

Eleven years later, on July 11, 1942, Hal Wallis pushed Leo Forbstein, who ran the music department at Warner Bros., for an answer to a request he had made earlier. Could he count on having Max Steiner compose the score for *Casablanca*?

Steiner, who wrote over three hundred film scores, preferred not to see a movie until it was edited and ready to be scored. When he watched *Casablanca* in a Warner Bros. projection room, he decided to dump "As Time Goes By" and replace it with a theme of his own.

"None of us likes having to use somebody else's schmucky song," says David Raksin, whose scores include *Laura* and *The Bad and the Beautiful*. "Otto Preminger wanted to use 'Summertime' for *Laura*'s theme, but Ira Gershwin wouldn't let him have the rights. Then he wanted to use Duke Ellington's 'Sophisticated Lady.' I argued against it on a Friday afternoon, and Preminger gave me until Monday morning to come up with something better."

What Raksin came up with was *Laura*'s haunting theme, which became the hit song "Laura." When Steiner, who wrote as many as six scores a year at Warner Bros., sat down to watch *Casablanca*, he had just finished the score for *Now, Voyager* that would win him the 1942 Academy Award. He had written the song "It Can't Be Wrong," which served as *Now, Voyager*'s love motif, and he was sure he could do the same thing for *Casablanca*. "He told me he didn't

---

*Burnett may have unconsciously taken his title, *Everybody Comes to Rick's,* from *Everybody's Welcome,* as well as consciously taken the song.

think 'As Time Goes By' was appropriate," says Al Bender, director of the Max Steiner Music Society. In 1943, a few months after *Casablanca* was released, Steiner told an interviewer that he still didn't much like "As Time Goes By," but he guessed the tune must have something.

Jack Warner knew the song had something. From now on, he told Leo Forbstein, he wanted to use well-known theme songs for the love motifs in Warner movies. Since Warner music companies owned hundreds of songs to which people remembered the words and music, "We should be able to do the same thing that we did in CASABLANCA" on other movies, Warner said.

Short and balding, Steiner was a fast talker and an incessant cigar smoker. Before he started a score, he always watched the movie twice. With her hair cut short for her role in *For Whom the Bell Tolls,* Ingrid Bergman couldn't lean against Sam's piano and hum the first few bars of a Steiner love song. Since he was stuck with "As Time Goes By," Steiner did more than give in gracefully. He proceeded to make "As Time Goes By" the centerpiece of his score. The song was not only Rick and Ilsa's love theme but Steiner's main connecting device. The song linked Rick and Ilsa, present and past, the source music to the underscoring, and the audience to the characters in the movie.

"The song is a main character, not mere music," says Arthur Bloom. Bloom is one of a group of masters and doctoral candidates at the Yale University School of Music who sat down in the spring of 1992 with pizza and beer to spend an afternoon examining the movie on videocassette. "It functions in the plot. It ushers in the past. And, to some extent, it implies humanity in a world thrown out of kilter."

Steiner may not have liked the song, but he gave Herman Hupfeld a gift. He enriched and enlarged "As Time Goes By." From the moment Ilsa asks Sam to play it, the song is omnipresent in the movie. During one minute and forty-six seconds of underscoring, when Rick is saying goodbye to Ilsa, "As Time Goes By" is transformed emotionally from a tone of tragic loss to romantic love to bittersweet resignation to a tragic and final climax as Ilsa and Laszlo turn their backs and walk toward the Lisbon plane.

Today, Hupfeld's other songs, which include "Sing Something Simple," "When Yuba Plays the Rhumba on the Tuba," and "Let's Put Out the Lights and Go to Sleep," are remembered vaguely, if at all. But "As Time Goes By," permanently entwined with *Casablanca,* has increased the fame and longevity of the movie that, in turn, ensured the fame and longevity of the song. After *Casablanca* was released, Hupfeld tried to get a contract at Warner Bros. It would be a natural tie-up, said his agent. But nothing came of Hupfeld's request.

Hupfeld died fairly young, but he lived long enough to savor "As Time Goes By" on the *Hit Parade* radio program for twenty-one straight weeks in 1943. It's ironic that he should be remembered for a love song. He may never have been in love. In fact, he may never have had any adventures at all except the ones he composed. Even his World War I service consisted of playing in a Navy band a few hundred miles from home. Herman Hupfeld was born in Montclair, New Jersey, in 1894 and died there, on the same street, in 1951.

"I always thought it was rather a sad life," says Margaret Scannell Wooley, the daughter of one of Hupfeld's three first cousins. "He had an alcohol problem and he never married and he had no children."

Hupfeld, who was never called anything but Dodo by the family, was an only child whose father had died young. Dodo left his mother

Herman Hupfeld.

only once. When he was a young man, his grandfather sent him to Germany for a while—the family had come from Germany—to study the violin. "His mother, a pianist and organist, helped him to some degree in creating his songs," says Hupfeld's cousin Harold Rader. After Hupfeld began to make money, he built a house next to the house where he had grown up. It had separate apartments for himself and his mother; Frediricka Rader Hupfeld outlived her son by many years.

Although Steiner used "As Time Goes By" in many ways—romantically, ominously, militarily, tragically, joyously—the song is only one strand in a complicated score. "The Marseillaise" is used almost as much and is similarly a song that means something to the characters and also creates a mood in the underscoring. The hope for victory over the Nazis is expressed in the continual musical dueling between "The Marseillaise" and both "Watch on the Rhine" and "Deutschland Über Alles." In the end, "Deutschland Über Alles" falls to "The Marseillaise" as the fatally shot Major Strasser falls to the floor of the airport hangar.

"The function of music in the movie was way beyond creative wallpaper," say the Yale students. One of them, John Rogers, notes that an instant before Rick gets Ilsa's letter at the Paris train station the sound track plays a snatch of "The Marseillaise" and that when Ilsa and Rick talk about the Germans marching into Paris, their love song grows dark and ominous. "And 'The Marseillaise' changes from ironic to clear and resolving as Rick and Renault walk away together," says Daniel Becker. "At that moment, it's almost played as a love theme."

By 1942, the other studios were beginning to catch up, but for years Warner Bros. had had the best music department in the industry. No other studio had two composers the equal of Steiner and Erich Korngold; even their orchestrator, Hugo Friedhofer, would become a noteworthy composer and win his own Academy Award for *The Best Years of Our Lives* in 1946. Steiner and Korngold had both been child prodigies in Vienna. A student of Gustav Mahler, Maximillian Raoul Steiner graduated from the Imperial Academy of Music at thirteen and wrote and conducted his first operetta when he was fourteen.

"But, as good as Steiner was, Korngold was better," says composer Raksin. "His music was of a higher order with a much wider sweep."

Steiner, however, was more important historically. Years before

Korngold came to Hollywood, Steiner was one of the first people to reinsert music into films after talking pictures came in. "His underscoring of *Cimarron* in 1931 even made the newspapers take notice," says Kathryn Kalinak, author of a book on classic film scores. "His *King Kong* in 1933 is one of the first scores where you see the model of loading background music into a movie, seventy out of ninety minutes. In 1939, he wrote three hours and twenty minutes of music for *Gone With the Wind*. By the time Korngold scored his first film in 1935, he didn't have to fight the battles Steiner had won."

If Steiner could not quite match the sweep of Korngold and the blood-stirring fullness of Korngold's scores for *Anthony Adverse* and *The Adventures of Robin Hood, Casablanca* played to Steiner's strengths. "Nobody could write melodies like Steiner," says Kalinak. "Steiner must have dreamed melodies." He could take a borrowed melody—"As Time Goes By"—and color the entire movie with it. And he was a man with some bite.

"Maxie liked all kinds of jokes, including musical jokes," says Raksin. "He was an antic guy. You never knew what he'd do next. When he turned seventy-five, I decided we should give him a party. We started with an intimate couple of hundred people and ended up with over a thousand. Well, what can you give a guy who has got everything? Miklos Rozsa suggested a Haydn manuscript. So we bought it for $1,200. Maxie was at the head table, with Mrs. Steiner, who kept him in line, next to him. Maxie says, 'I know your intentions were of the very best. But I would think you should have gotten something more appropriate.' And our hearts sank. And then he went on. 'Such as a new Cadillac or Marilyn Monroe. On the other hand I don't know what I would have done with either. I haven't driven in some time.' "

In his score for *Casablanca,* Steiner has juiced up the movie by the edgy way his underscoring shifts mood and character, often very quickly. For Ilsa's entrance into Rick's after the flashback, for example, Steiner has written a medley consisting of Ilsa Returns, 33 seconds; "As Time Goes By," 22 seconds; Bitterness, 31 seconds; the noble and stately theme he created for Lazslo, 22 seconds; Agitato No. 1, 9 seconds; Steiner's theme for Ilsa, 32 seconds; "As Time Goes By," 12 seconds; and "The Marseillaise," 7 seconds.

What is not immediately apparent is how rich an underlay of American popular music throbs inside Rick's Café. As conspirators, refugees, Fascists, patriots, and desperate gamblers take the foreground, those songs, subliminally, make the café an outpost of America, an oasis in a foreign land. Looking at the cue sheets, Raksin says, "It's wonderful stuff, the best damn songs." The carpet of background music includes "Crazy Rhythm," "Baby Face," "I'm Just Wild About Harry," "Heaven Can Wait," "Love for Sale," "Avalon," "If I Could Be with You One Hour Tonight," "You Must Have Been a Beautiful Baby," and "It Had to Be You." Often the songs underscore the dramatic content. When Ilsa enters the café for the first time, the band plays "Speak to Me of Love."

The music inside the club effectively serves both foreground and background functions. The customers at Rick's and the audience in the movie theater are intended to listen to Sam. But the singer with the beautiful voice who plays "Tango Della Rose" on her guitar simply allows Laszlo to slip away for a private conversation with Berger, the Norwegian Resistance fighter. Although she was the star of her own radio program and performed three times for President Roosevelt at the White House, Corinna Mura was never more than an interpolation in a movie. Trained by her parents to be a coloratura soprano from the time she learned to talk, Mura ran away from opera as an adolescent. One of her partisans was Edwin Schallert, drama reviewer for the *Los Angeles Times*. Schallert gave Mura a grade of A + and said she always performed brilliantly with the Los Angeles Civic Light Opera. Even though she was under contract to RKO for a while and she would come back to Warner Bros. in 1943 to sing the love song Steiner wrote for *Passage to Marseille*, Mura's success on the stage never translated to movies.

Steiner died in 1971 at the age of eighty-three, cigar smoking and antic to the end. "When Maxie was dying," says Raksin, "with Mrs. Steiner at his bedside, he looked up at all the medicine bottles on the chiffonier and said, 'Look, momma, Medicine Square Garden.' " Fifty years after Steiner wrote it, the Yale students think that only one portion of his score for *Casablanca* is dated—the "Native Music" Steiner created for the scenes in the black market. "Hollywood exoticism," says Ed Harsh, "pretty standard jungle music."

Just as he put his fingers into everything else in *Casablanca,* Hal Wallis also influenced the music. "Wallis was one of only a few producers in that era who had a real sense of what music was," says Professor Kalinak. "He knew enough to write music notes that a composer would listen to. On *Captain Blood,* he wrote Korngold five single-spaced pages of intelligent notes."

However many notes Wallis may have written Steiner on *Casablanca,* only three remain. In a particular scene between Rick and Laszlo, he wants a piano used. In the last reel, the last time Bogart looks off to the Lisbon plane, he wants a dramatic pause in the music and loud motor noises. And, most importantly, in the duel inside Rick's Café between the German officers singing "Watch on the Rhine" and Paul Henreid leading "The Marseillaise":

> On the Marseilles [*sic*], when it is played in the Café, don't do it as though it was played by this small orchestra. Do it with a full scoring orchestra and get some body to it.

Steiner has enlarged the sound so subtly that the Yale composition students did not notice it until their second viewing.

Wallis did have one musical blind spot on *Casablanca.* He never did like Dooley Wilson. Early in July, he asked musical director Leo Forbstein to start looking "for a negro with a good crooning voice to double all of Dooley Wilson's songs." Whether Wallis was talked out of the idea or whether Forbstein couldn't find anyone Wallis liked better, it was Wilson who sang "It Had to Be You," "Shine," and "Knock on Wood" for Rick's patrons. *Variety* singled him out for the great effectiveness with which he sang "As Time Goes By," and the *Hollywood Reporter* said he created "something joyous."* "As Time Goes By" stayed at No. 1 on the Hit Parade for four weeks in the spring of 1943. In any other year, Wilson would have recorded the song and made a great deal of money. But the musicians' union was locked in a long strike with the record companies. So Rudy Vallee's record was rereleased instead.

Wilson had roles in three movies in 1943. *The New York Times* said that he was "frittered away" in *Higher and Higher,* a Frank Sinatra musical; that his presence in a war drama, *Two Tickets to London,* was at least one thing in the movie for which the reviewer was thankful; and that someone should have allowed him to sing in the all-black musical *Stormy Weather.* In 1944, he had another success on Broadway, in *Bloomer Girl,* which ran two years. By 1949 he was a comical butler again in *Come to the Stable.* Two decades after

---

*Woody Allen to the contrary, neither Ingrid Bergman nor Humphrey Bogart ever said, "Play it again, Sam" to Dooley Wilson. Bergman said, "Play it, Sam. Play 'As Time Goes By.' " Bogart said, "If she can stand it, I can. Play it!"

that he had become a movie trivia question—"Who was the black actor who sang 'As Time Goes By' in *Casablanca?*"—that few people answered correctly.

If there are only three notes from Wallis to Steiner on *Casablanca,* there are dozens of notes to the film editor Owen Marks and an additional page of sound-editing notes. "What seems remarkable to us," says the 1980s studio executive Laurence Mark, "is that the producer usurped the director, that the producer was the ultimate authority."

What the studio system provided that does not exist today was a checkrein on the director during production and in postproduction. For better or worse. In the case of *Casablanca,* it was probably for better. In four pages of cutting notes, Wallis usually asks for changes that will make the movie leaner and heighten the tension. He wants a frame to be taken out here, a few feet eliminated there, an unnecessary character trimmed:

> Take out the group of soldiers before the cut of the loading the refugees into the patrol wagon. . . . Trim a little on Rains' line, "And I am prepared to refuse it." . . . Take out two of the last four shots from Ugarte. . . . Lose the long shot of the waiter bringing the bottle and glasses. Cut to Bergman right on her line, "Ask the piano player to come over." . . . Take out that long look of Bergman looking around before she says, "Where is Rick?" . . . You can lose probably five or six feet off the beginning of the shot of Bogart and the girl in the automobile.*

Steiner had written music for the first sequences in the gambling room. Wallis decided to have only the murmur of voices and the sound of the roulette wheel, with a little music seeping through from the main room every time the door was opened.

---

*If Julius Epstein is to be believed, Wallis and Curtiz made one major blunder in the editing. "They told us the ending didn't work and took us into the projection room," says Epstein. "They had the French policemen driving up and Claude Rains telling them, 'Major Strasser has been shot. Round up the usual suspects.' There was no suspense. My brother and I said, 'No, no. You have to cut to Bogart, and then Rains says, "Round up the usual suspects." ' " That a sophisticated producer and director would make such an elementary mistake seems improbable. However, outtakes of the master shot described by Epstein have recently been found.

Immediately after he finished scoring *Casablanca,* Steiner started *Watch on the Rhine,* which Wallis was shooting simultaneously that summer. War or no war, Warner Bros. hadn't yet slowed down. *Watch on the Rhine* finished production on August 22, and a cut was ready for Jack Warner to see ten days later.

Casablanca had many more characters and sets than *Rhine,* and it took Wallis and Curtiz several weeks to complete the film. Almost as soon as *Casablanca* finished shooting on August 3, Owen Marks, a former prizefighter, whose four brothers also worked at Warner Bros., assembled a rough cut of everything but the black-market scenes. After he saw the rough cut, Wallis fine-tuned both the ending and the beginning of *Casablanca.* In addition to writing Bogart's last line, he ordered a new first scene to lead in to the police roundup that had started the film. On August 22, Curtiz found a corner of an unused set on Stage 14 and filmed Jean del Val reading teletype tape into the phone:

> To all officials. Two German couriers carrying important official documents murdered on train from Oran. Murderer and possible accomplices headed for Casablanca. Round up all suspicious characters and search them for stolen documents! Important!

When Curtiz shot that scene, he had to find a new assistant director. Lee Katz had already gone into the army. And, before August turned into September, Francis Scheid had his Army Air Force commission. In a press release Warner Bros. sent to newspapers in February 1943, the studio said it had given 550 technicians, actors, writers, directors, and producers to the armed services, with more leaving every day. Hyperbole aside, a comparison shows that, in early 1943, Warner Bros. led the studios in actors, directors, and writers who had marched off to war. Did some patriotic urgency filter down from above? It may simply be that the scrappy studio had hired more young male players and writers in the first place, but the statistics are interesting. Warners had lost twenty actors to Fox's twelve and ten writers to Columbia's eight. Paramount, the studio that was most resistant to the demands of the Office of War Information, had lost a single writer and no producers or directors.

Except for Bogart, who would have to be brought back to record the new last line—"Louis, I think this is the beginning of a beautiful friendship"—the actors were off to new adventures when Wallis did

FORM 11

WARNER BROS. PICTURES, INC.
BURBANK, CALIFORNIA

INTER-OFFICE COMMUNICATION

TO MR. _____ OWEN MARKS _____   DATE _____ August 7, 1942 _____

FROM MR. _____ WALLIS _____   SUBJECT _____ "CASABLANCA" _____

Attached is copy of the new narration for the opening of the picture.

There are also to be two wild lines made by Bogart. Mike is trying to get Bogart today, but if he does not succeed, will you get Bogart in within the next couple of days.

The two lines to be shot with Bogart, in the event that Mike does not get them, are:

> RICK:
> Luis, I might have known you'd mix your patriotism with a little larceny.

##*#*#*#*#*#*#*

(Alternate line)

> RICK:
> Luis, I think this is the beginning of a beautiful friendship.

##*#*#*#*#*#*#*

Also, I think you had better have the narration made up by some stock actor until I can select the actor who will do it for the picture.

HAL WALLIS

VERBAL MESSAGES CAUSE MISUNDERSTANDING AND DELAYS
(PLEASE PUT THEM IN WRITING)

the final buffing and polishing on *Casablanca*. He wanted a weighty voice similar to the narrator of the *March of Time* shorts to intone: "With the coming of the Second World War, many eyes in imprisoned Europe turned hopefully or desperately toward the freedom of the Americas," and chose a local radio announcer, Lou Marcelle.

Don Siegel was given the assignment of creating a spinning globe and the montage of the refugees crossing the map of the world that accompanies the narration. Siegel had started at Warner Bros. in 1934 as an assistant in the film library at $1 an hour. By 1943, eager to be a director, Siegel was trying to buy himself out of his contract. But Jack Warner knew a good thing when he had it under contract, and the future director of *Invasion of the Body Snatchers* and *Dirty Harry* stayed at Warner Bros. doing montages and directing second-unit action sequences until Warner finally made him a director in 1946.

After Curtiz shot the new scene and Bogart read the new line, *Casablanca* was finished. During the last week of August the movie was shipped off to the Production Code Administration to be appraised. At the end of May, when Joe Breen sent Jack Warner his approval of the script of *Casablanca,* he had added a warning: "You understand, of course, that our final judgment will be based on the finished picture." Breen's response to the finished picture turned out to be unexpected.

"I have never heard him rave about a picture as he did about this one," Hal Wallis wrote to Charles Einfeld on August 28.

Wallis had an ulterior motive in asking Einfeld, who was the head of both publicity and advertising at Warner Bros., to telephone Breen and hear for himself how much Breen liked *Casablanca.* "I thought perhaps that Breen's enthusiasm might inspire you to plan a campaign for *Casablanca* as a really big picture," Wallis wrote.

Wallis's contract had allowed him to choose the writers, actors, and directors for *Casablanca;* his position as the movie's producer had allowed him to overrule his director and bend the movie to his will. But Wallis's control ended when the movie was completed and sent to Jack Warner in Projection Room 5. From then on, it would be Warner and Einfeld who would decide what to do with *Casablanca.*

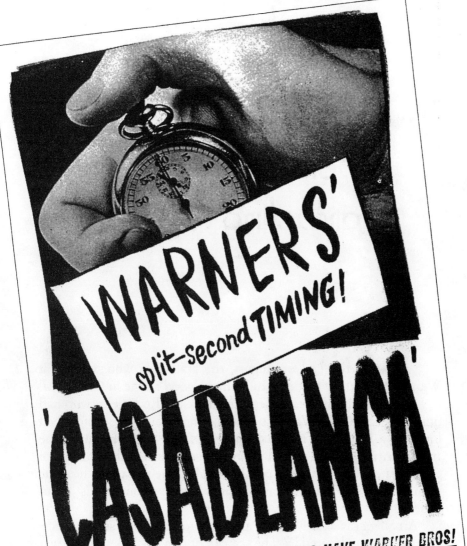

WARNERS'

split-second **TIMING!**

'CASABLANCA'

THE ARMY'S GOT CASABLANCA —<u>AND SO HAVE WARNER BROS!</u>

AND THAT MEANS...

16

Selling the Movie and Selling the War

B y the end of August, the craftsmen who worked at
Warner Bros. knew that the studio had a good movie in *Casablanca*.

"It started in the trailer department," says Rudi Fehr, who had
not yet become Jack Warner's special film editor. "The editors had
lunch at a long table in the commissary. The guy who made the
trailers, Arthur Silver, would always come and sit with us. Most of
the time he'd come in and shake his head. Once in a while, he came
in and said, 'We have a beauty.' *Casablanca* was one of his 'beau-
ties.' "

Art Silver saw *Casablanca* in a rough cut, before the sound effects
and music were layered in. The scarcity of film stock during the war
meant that previews of coming attractions were limited to two
hundred feet, a little over two minutes. Relying heavily on narration,
Silver's two-minute-twelve-second trailer for *Casablanca* sold adventure and a love triangle.

Casablanca, city of hope and despair located in French Morocco
in North Africa—the meeting place of adventurers, fugitives, criminals, refugees lured into this dangerous oasis by the hope of escape

to the Americas. But they're all trapped, for there is no escape. Against this fascinating background is woven the story of an imperishable love and the enthralling saga of six desperate people, each in Casablanca to keep an appointment with destiny.

The portentous narration that was typical of trailers in 1942 seems quaint today, but the purpose of previews hasn't changed. "If you're selling a house, you try to sell the swimming pool first," says Silver. "We sold the adventure. We sold the action, the romance, and the stars."

Bogart was "The most dangerous man in the world's most dangerous city." Bergman was the woman who could not resist him. The plot was left vague, but Silver loaded his trailer with all the action he could find in the movie or the outtakes, including dozens of refugees running from the police, Peter Lorre pulling a gun, and Bogart shooting Conrad Veidt with a snarling "All right, major, you asked for it."

Wallis was never happy to wait on the sidelines, and he tried to shape the trailers as he did the production of his movies. "I had to take the scripts and main titles to his office," says Silver, who hates the trailers that are made today because, "They tell you so much you don't want to see the movie."

Silver always felt uncomfortable standing in Wallis's office and waiting for his reaction. "He was stern. I waited at his desk, and he would look up and say, 'I am not impressed.' He was never a very pat-on-the-back kind of guy. He was an I-am-not-impressed kind of guy."

But it was Jack Warner who had final approval of every trailer as he did of every movie. And, in the darkness of the projection room, Warner was at his best. Director Elia Kazan told *Variety* editor Tom Pryor that Warner had no idea how to read a book or a script but, when he saw a movie, "Jack knew what worked." And Warner was willing to jettison anything that didn't work. "At previews," says sound editor Francis Scheid, "Warner would say, 'Take out the whole sequence. If it doesn't work, throw it away. It doesn't matter how much money it cost.'"

By the time *Casablanca* was released nationally in January 1943, the relationship between Warner and Wallis was severely frayed. Warner demanded the credit for everything that happened at his studio. Wallis felt that the credit for his movies belonged to him, and he liked publicity every bit as much as Warner did. Wallis's files contain a letter written to Jack Warner in June 1937 by the head of publicity, Charles Einfeld. "Much to my amazement, I received the attached wire this morning from Hal Wallis, which is really a burn-up wire because he didn't get any publicity on his return from his vacation," Einfeld wrote. Einfeld said that, if he had known that Wallis was returning, he could easily have gotten the producer's name and picture in the papers and "knowing how this sort of thing pleases him, I would certainly have gone out of my way to have him well covered."

If Jack Warner, Jr., is right and the core of his father's personality was a fear that someone would take advantage of him, Warner found a focus for that fear in the success of the first movies from Hal Wallis Productions. Between September 1942 and October 1943, *Desperate Journey, Now, Voyager, Casablanca, Air Force, This Is the Army, Watch on the Rhine,* and *Princess O'Rourke* followed each other into theaters, to good reviews and lively ticket sales. The only Warner movies among the top fifteen box-office successes of 1943 were Wallis films, *This Is the Army* in third place and *Casablanca* in seventh.

When Wallis questioned the ads on *Casablanca* Warner sent a telegram to Einfeld, telling him to hold firm: "Anyone doesn't like it can buy all Warners holdings 38 million cash exclusive of tax. They then can advertise way they want."

When Wallis courted the press, Warner fumed. In a letter written when *Casablanca* was running wild at the box office and *Air Force* was being prepared for release, Warner berated Wallis for meeting with a reporter from *Life* magazine just forty-eight hours after he had told Jack and Harry that he would refer reporters to the studio publicity department. That letter was never sent. But before the end of 1943 Warner's jealousy was out of control. In November he sent the following telegram:

> To Wallis: Happy you have Epstein working for you again as per L.A. Daily News article 23rd. I resent and won't stand for your continuing take all credit for Watch on Rhine This Is Army Copilot Princess O'Rourke and many other stories. I happened to be one who saw these stories read plays. Bought and turned them over to you. You could have at least said so and I want to be accredited accordingly. You certainly have changed and unnecessarily so.

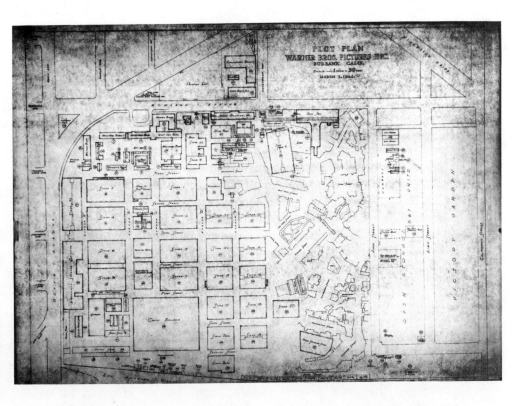

In his return telegram, Wallis tried to placate Warner. He said that he had given Warner due credit, and he blamed the interviewer for omitting the studio chief's name.

Warner refused to accept Wallis's explanation:

> To Wallis: Stop giving me double talk on your publicity. This wire will serve notice on you that I will take legal action if my name has been eliminated from any article or story in any form shape or manner as being in charge production while you were executive producer and executive producer and in charge production since your new contract commenced. So there will be no misunderstanding it will be up to you to prove and see that my name is properly accredited in any publicity.

In a plaintive telegram to Einfeld the same day, Warner wrote: "Sick and tired everyone taking all credit and I become small boy and doing most of work."

Down in the bedrock of his personality, Warner was always the small boy in a world of giant older brothers. Warner's need for recognition tripped him up at the studio—and on the tennis court. "He always poached on his partner," says Solly Baiano, who was hired as a Warners talent scout because he was one of the best tennis players in Hollywood and Jack wanted him for a partner. On Saturday and Sunday afternoons, Warner and Baiano played Ellsworth Vines, Jack Kramer, Frank Sedgeman, and members of local college teams on the court at Warner's Bel-Air mansion. "He liked to play with the best players, and he liked to bet on the games," Baiano says. "A lot of them didn't hit the balls too hard at Jack, but we got into real rough games with good players." Yet, even when it meant losing his bet, Warner was unable to stop himself from running to intercept balls that belonged to his partner. It was Warner's poaching and Wallis's angry resistance that finally ruptured their relationship on March 2, 1944, the night *Casablanca* won the Academy Award as the best movie of 1943.

Casablanca was originally scheduled to be released in the spring of 1943. Throughout the spring and summer of 1942, Warner Bros. had planted the usual announcements of each new actor cast in the movie and the usual phony column items. Hedda Hopper, for example, had reported that Ingrid Bergman was teaching Humphrey Bogart Swedish and "Bogey's so set up with himself he drives out to Bit of Sweden for lunch just so's he can impress the waiters— the big showoff." (That particular restaurant was nearly an hour's drive away from Warner Bros.)

Einfeld, who looked like beefy character actor Edward Arnold, was "consumed with getting publicity," says producer Jack Brodsky, who trained under Einfeld. "If a newspaper or magazine editor wouldn't take a story, Charlie said we had to do one of two things: get down on bended knee and beg or tell the editor that our job was at stake."

The publicity campaign for *Casablanca* really started with Ezra Goodman's "Exit the 'Bogey'-Man" at the end of September. Any newspaper willing to print it could have a feature story on how Humphrey Bogart, "that screen villain of deepest dye," was now a hero. It didn't matter that "Exit the 'Bogey'-Man," like most studio feature stories, was fiction. (Unclear about the movie's plot, Goodman inaccurately describes Bogart waving "a menacing gat at a bunch of Burbank vipers including Conrad Veidt, Peter Lorre, and

The stars of Casablanca *in a studio publicity photograph.*

Claude Rains.") Most newspapers were likely to print such articles unchanged, just as they always ran the photographs the studios sent, using the captions the studios had written.

"We conducted a much more vigorous prerelease campaign in those days," says Arthur Wilde. "When people were under contract, it didn't matter if the papers dropped the name of the movie, because any publicity was worth something. Our big thrust was magazine advertising, which is almost nonexistent now. You'd buy space in the women's magazines way in advance; you knew you would always have some picture that could be advertised. We built stars in the fan magazines. Bogart was picked up by the fan magazines after he married Bacall. Before that, it was just articles about him and Mayo as The Battling Bogarts."

Casablanca was previewed for the first time on September 22. Einfeld was immediately convinced that the studio had a winner, and he set out to convince the New York executives who would be responsible for selling the movie. The day after that first sneak preview, Einfeld sent them a telegram:

> Casablanca really wonderful. . . . The picture is brilliantly directed gorgeously photographed and mounted with production values which will not be duplicated in films for the duration because priorities simply will not allow for any such opulence. . . . Honestly believe this is one of hottest money pictures of the last two or three seasons. Believe me it belongs in the very top bracket.

Einfeld was more prescient than Julius and Philip Epstein. "When we previewed it for the first time, I thought it was a big flop," says Julie Epstein. "We wrote a note to Hal Wallis telling him so. Thereafter, he kept that memo in his desk. Whenever we had an argument with him about anything, he would open his desk, take out that memo and give it to us."

The key tool in selling a movie was the pressbook, an oversized packet stuffed with photographs and advertisements of different sizes, ideas for contests, and feature stories the publicity department had written about the film and the actors. Sent to newspapers, the pressbook always included a glowing review of the movie, with a space for the paper to insert the date and the name of the theater. The press kits that have replaced pressbooks and are sent today to more circumspect and less naïve editors contain relatively factual information about the making of the movie and relatively accurate biographies of the moviemakers. But the prewritten articles have their current counterpart in the electronic press kits that go to television stations, where a local newscaster often splices himself into a studio-created interview with Tom Cruise or Arnold Schwarzenegger.

The twenty-two-page pressbook Warner Bros. prepared on *Casablanca* suggested a five-day newspaper contest with easily solved cryptogram messages, such as "Bogart and Bergman have a date with fate in *Casablanca*." (The contest echoed the ad for the movie: "They had a date with fate! In the City that Rocked the World!") In another contest, the paper could offer free tickets to readers who wrote the best letters about songs that were important to their own romances. For any paper that wanted to tell the story of the movie in pictures as a six-day serial, Warners would provide a Picture Story Mat for 75 cents. The last of the pictures in the Picture Story shows Bergman in Henreid's arms. The caption reads: "The plane was far over the ocean

[SECOND DAY] [CODE KEY: Z for A, A for B, etc.]

CONTEST: Decode the Secret Story of **CASABLANCA** ...the City That Rocked the World!

SGDX VDMS SN BZRZAKZMBZ . . .

SGD QDRS HR GHRSNQX

Here goes more excitement! Just look for the key to the letter A (it might be M, but it isn't) . . . and the rest will just follow. Write in the solved code message below and save this entry with yesterday's until contest ends on (date).
MESSAGE:

(Answer: THEY WENT TO CASABLANCA . . . THE REST IS HISTORY)

and Paul and Ilsa were marveling at the unsuspected nobility of the supposedly hardened Keeper of the Café in *Casablanca*."

The pressbook also contained stories written especially for the women's page of the newspapers. One that appeared in paper after paper concentrated, accurately this time, on Bergman's refusal to pose for leg art or wear makeup. Others had a more tenuous connection with the truth. "Casablanca Blue," the shade of Ingrid Bergman's gowns, was suggested "by the reflection of the white-walled buildings along the coast of North Africa in the deep blue of the Mediterranean." Paul Henreid had adopted the two orphaned granddaughters of his father's head gardener, and they were living in Switzerland until he could bring them to America.

"Not a word of truth, not a word of truth," said Henreid a year before his death.

Nor did Henreid decide to raise chickens to ease the war food

PLAYERS' BIOGRAPHIES • PICTURE FEATURES

She Came, She Saw, She Conquered

When Ingrid Bergman returned to Hollywood for the start of production on "Casablanca," after an absence of almost a year, she chose a very practical but somewhat unusual way for a screen star such as herself to get reacquainted with the film colony.

Miss Bergman, who co-stars with Humphrey Bogart and Paul Henreid in "Casablanca," now at the Strand Theatre, took a sightseeing tour with one of the professional "movie guides."

"Now I know where all the famous people live, who has moved since the last time I was here, and who are the new stars in the business," Miss Bergman explained. "It was very funny, for one of the first houses I was shown was that of David Selznick, to whom I am under contract. I had been a guest at his house just the night before, but the guide told me that I could not get closer than just inside the gate."

Miss Bergman, who lives in Rochester, Minnesota, when not working in a picture, lives very modestly and very quietly while in Hollywood.

Still AP 534; Mat 205—30c

Humphrey Bogart is starred in Warner Bros.' "Casablanca," drama of the city that made history. The picture is now at the Strand.

Imagine Saying 'No' To a Bergman Kiss!

Jack Benny Plays Bit in 'Casablanca'

Your eyes will have to be unusually sharp. But if you look at the right place at the right time you'll see Jack Benny in Warner Bros.' "Casablanca," a picture in which he is not supposed to appear. The picture is now featured at the Strand Theatre.

Benny went stage-hopping at the Burbank studio the other af-

Still C 514; Mat 202—30c

Ingrid Bergman is co-starred with Humphrey Bogart and Paul Henreid in the new Warner Bros. picture, "Casablanca," now at the Strand.

Clothes Make the Man in Casablanca

Of the few Americans who have ever been to the French Moroccan city of Casablanca, it is safe to say that most of them safe in doling out to them a collection of apparel generally approximating that worn in North Africa.

---

problem, as another item claimed. Both the pressbook and the feature stories Warner Bros. sent out on *Casablanca* used the war as a hook or gimmick. Bogart paid a troop of Sea Scouts to collect scrap metal and, in an amazing series of coincidences, he brought a fan letter, written in Swedish, to Bergman to translate and was able to assure a Swedish family that their son was alive. One article, distributed the week the movie opened, was titled "No Ration on Love." Government regulations controlled the materials used to build the sets of *Casablanca,* the article said, but "The material from which kisses are made is not rationed by the O.P.A. or anybody else."

It was Hollywood's ability to sell that made the movie industry so valuable to the war effort. Any industry that could sell dreams was well equipped to sell the ideal war. Lt. James Stewart grinned as he stepped out of the cockpit of his plane in *Winning Your Wings,* and 100,000 young Americans grinned back and enlisted in the air force.

**CARTOON FEATURE PACKS
READER-INTEREST PUNCH**

The above is a particularly popular type of newspaper feature. It can be reprinted for a color-in giveaway to the kids or enlarged from the pressbook for a 40" x 60" display in your lobby or out front.

Order "Cartoon Mat C 201B" — 30c — from Campaign Plan Editor, 321 W. 44 St., N. Y. C.

They were doing more than imitating a movie hero. They were acquiring his invulnerability. James Stewart in the role of naive young senator Jefferson Smith had gone to Washington and defeated all the corrupt politicians. Lt. Stewart would make short work of the Nazis, and anyone who enlisted could join him in the picture. Stewart lived to become a brigadier general in the Air Force Reserve, but thousands of other pilots learned that life is not like the movies.

Selling the war was really no more difficult than selling a film.

Hollywood's press agents used the same tools—sex and adventure. Buy a war bond and win a kiss from Lana Turner. Enlist and help Humphrey Bogart capture a Nazi battalion in *Sahara*. From the beginning, Hollywood's relation to the war was different from that of any other industry. Like the rest of America, the movie industry supplied bodies to die on the beaches of Tarawa and in the Ardennes Forest. But it also provided the men who photographed their deaths, the documentaries that explained why they had to die, the feature films that glorified their sacrifice, and a great deal of money to press on with the war.

When the Treasury Department asked the motion picture industry to spearhead a September 1942 war bond drive with a goal of raising $775 million, it was Charles Einfeld who was in charge of getting one hundred actors on seven separate tours to more than three hundred cities and towns and generating enough publicity to make the drive a success. The movie industry spent nearly a million dollars organizing the "Stars Over America" drive which went $55 million over its quota and raised $838 million for the government.

The Hollywood Victory Committee was formed three days after Pearl Harbor. By the end of the first year of the war, the Victory Committee had sent actors on 6,828 separate appearances at USO camp shows, bond rallies, and other events across the country. The HVC was composed of representatives of all the major guilds, but the publicists were the experts in ballyhoo, showmanship, and getting stars to the right stage at the right time. Before the war was seven months old, Dorothy Lamour, single-handedly, had sold $120 million in war bonds.

In April, to raise money for Army and Navy relief, the Victory Committee sent a trainload of twenty-two celebrities—including Bob Hope, Groucho Marx, Olivia de Havilland, Merle Oberon, Charles Boyer, and Laurel and Hardy—on a thirteen-city Victory Caravan tour. But spending the currency of stardom so lavishly began to seem profligate to the government. By the time *Casablanca* started production in May 1942, Secretary of the Treasury Henry Morgenthau, Jr., was relying so heavily on movie stars to sell war bonds that he announced that, in order to conserve actors for a long war, only one star would be sent to any section of the country at a time.

The government took excellent advantage of the illusions created by Hollywood. Actors were recruited as role models for their fellow Americans. Actors were to make self-discipline popular, influencing ordinary people to car-pool, grow their own vegetables, forego nylon stockings and metallic jewelry, and—since supplies of coffee had already been cut 25 percent—to drink milk. "How you wear your hair and what you serve your dinner guests and where you drive your car is no longer, strictly speaking, your own business," said the Screen Actors Guild magazine.

Actresses were shown doing their own housework—a necessity for most American housewives, since domestic servants were now making much better money in defense plants. And the movie palaces, the suppliers of common dreams, served the purpose of community centers for the war. In 1943, America's movie theaters collected more than two million pounds of scrap metal, plus tons of rubber, grease, and rags. War-bond premieres, free movie days, and lobby booth sales of war bonds and stamps raised more than $1 billion; $12 million more was raised for the Red Cross, Greek War Relief, the USO, and other similar organizations.

The movie industry glamourizes everything it touches as instinctively as a wasp stings the arm on which it lands. Because that glamour provided legitimacy and money to the war effort, the government had good reasons for protecting Hollywood. Early on, the *Hollywood Reporter* was certain that the government would not induct top male stars because of the morale value of their movies and "the hefty income taxes they pour into the Federal coffers." The moguls helped the war effort by paying 75 percent of their huge salaries in taxes. L. B. Mayer, as usual, had had the top salary of anyone in America in 1941, $704,425.60; and the *Hollywood Reporter* estimated that Mayer's state and federal income taxes came to $528,319. (Because of the carefully written tax code, the richest Americans—Carnegies, Fords, Rockefellers, Du Ponts—escaped taxes, since their money did not come from salaries.)

As to morale, on his first trip west after President Roosevelt appointed him to oversee the movie industry, Lowell Mellett urged male stars, creative producers, and the best directors not to enlist. "Your greatest war service will be to stay right here on the job in Hollywood—making pictures," Mellett said. A few weeks later, Brigadier General Lewis Hershey, the director of the draft, announced that men essential to the film industry were eligible for deferments.

One of the most fascinating documents in the archives of the Office of War Information is a letter from Darryl Zanuck warning

Mellett not to let Clark Gable enlist. "In this peculiar business of ours you need only eliminate Clark Gable, Spencer Tracy, Robert Taylor, Tyrone Power, Errol Flynn, Gary Cooper and Mickey Rooney and you would actually wreck the business," Zanuck wrote on January 8, 1942. Zanuck, who had been a reserve officer in the Signal Corps before Pearl Harbor, shaped—and partially drafted—the statement Mellett made in mid-January about Hollywood's creators staying on the job. Zanuck also lobbied for the industry to be given an official classification as a war industry. "It is no exaggeration to say that if 50 percent of those who have applied for commissions or who desire to be of service were given commissions, we would have an industry only half as effective as it is today for the production of feature films," Zanuck wrote to Mellett on January 31.

Gable probably never knew that Zanuck kept him from getting a commission in the Signal Corps. But men who wanted to fight in what was widely seen as The Good War couldn't be blocked indefinitely. By summer, forty-one-year-old Clark Gable—who had earned $357,000 in 1941, third highest in the country behind Mayer and James Cagney's $362,000—had enlisted as a private in the Army Air Corps. In October, he graduated from Officer Candidate School. Unlike James Stewart, Gable spent most of his war on the ground in England, but he did double as a gunner and aerial photographer on five bombing raids.

The buckaroos and swashbucklers—whether actors or directors—had never been left out of anything, and they refused to be left out of World War II. The Screen Actors Guild responded to General Hershey's offer of deferments by spurning his classification. The guild, said a statement by its board of directors, "believes actors and everyone else in the motion picture industry should be subject to the same rules for the draft as the rest of the country."

Most of the actors who enlisted or were drafted ended up doing exactly what they had done in peacetime—making movies. Ronald Reagan is not atypical. "Reagan was too identifiable to be used as an actor," says Owen Crump, whose Air Force photographic unit was responsible for nearly eight hundred training films. "So we used him as a narrator. I made him personnel officer. He was wonderful at it. Warm." Reagan ended the war as adjutant of Crump's unit. Bill Orr was also loosely under Crump, acting on the Army Air Corps's radio network, which aired four morale-building shows a week to the boys in the armed forces.

The directors ended up making movies too, although some—including John Ford, William Wyler, and John Huston—made them under combat conditions. Almost six months to the day after Pearl Harbor, Navy Commander John Ford photographed the Battle of Midway, and was wounded during that first American victory of the Pacific war.

John Huston's commission in the Signal Corps had come while he was making *Across the Pacific*. With his perverse sense of humor, Huston filmed a scene in which he tied Humphrey Bogart to a chair, put Japanese guards at every window and door, and made it impossible for Bogart to escape. Then he walked off the set and left his successor, Vincent Sherman, to find a way to get Bogart out. Ford, Huston, Frank Capra, William Wyler, and John Sturges brought unsettling skills to a war machine whose chief filmmaking interest was such movies as *Camouflage Principles, Concealment of Bivouacs,* and *Passage of Mine Fields.* Hollywood's fictions may have tidied and gentled the war and made it seem more easily winnable, but the War Department was not interested in anything tougher. Huston's documentary, *The Battle of San Pietro,* a study in the futility of war, was distributed over the objections of various generals only because the chief of staff, General George C. Marshall, ordered it shown. One Huston documentary, *Let There Be Light,* examined soldiers whose minds had been broken by their experiences. The War Department was so disturbed by the film that it was labeled top secret and hidden until 1980, when the Vice President of the United States, Walter Mondale, got it released.

Often, Hollywood's heroes and martyrs didn't follow the proper script. While Warners' top star, Errol Flynn, stayed home and won the war single-handedly in *Objective Burma!,* one of the studio's lesser workhorses, Wayne Morris, won four Distinguished Flying Crosses and two Air Medals as a Navy aviator. The first performer to die was comedienne Carole Lombard, in a plane crash on her way home from a bond-selling tour in mid-January, 1942. And Lew Ayres, the popular young Dr. Kildare in half-a-dozen M-G-M films, shocked the country by becoming a conscientious objector. "I told M-G-M a year ahead of time, and they were very nice," says Ayres. "They asked me not to say anything unless I was drafted, and I said, 'Fine.' I was prepared for the big hullabaloo." When Ayres was sent to an internment camp, theaters canceled all bookings for his movies. But he became a symbol of America's tolerance, of the freedom of conscience for which America was fighting. Ayres refused to carry a gun or drive a truck, but he had trained himself to be a medic. Eventually, theaters played his films, and Ayres spent two years in the South Pacific, serving as a medical corpsman in the invasions of Leyte and New Guinea. "I wouldn't trade it for anything," he says.

While thousands of Hollywood's actors, directors, and technicians struggled in one way or another with the realities of World War II, the ones who stayed home would make hundreds of fictions about the war. To no other movie were the caprices of battle and bloodshed as helpful as they were to *Casablanca*. On November 8, 1942, the Allies invaded North Africa. Within days the city of Casablanca fell. *Casablanca* had sold the need for engagement on the side of the Allies in a war against fascism. Now the war sold the movie.

A month earlier, Wallis had sent an anxious memo to Jack Warner, asking if he had had any word from the New York executives. What Benny Kalmenson, Albert Warner, and the others thought about the film in October is not recorded, but they responded to the invasion of North Africa by suggesting that *Casablanca* end with the Allies routing the Nazis. Jack Warner urged them not to tamper with the film:

> It's impossible to change this picture and make sense with story we told originally. Story we want to tell of landing and everything would have to be a complete new picture and would not fit in the present film. It's such a great picture as it is, would be a misrepresentation if we were to come in now with a small tag scene about American troops landing etcetera, which as I have already said is a complete new story in itself. . . . Entire industry envies us with picture having title "Casablanca" ready to release, and feel we should take advantage of this great scoop. Naturally the longer we wait to release it the less important title will be.

What happened next can only be guessed at, since the correspondence from New York is not on file. But the New York salesmen seem to have been insistent, and Warner may have given in. It was Jack Warner's studio, so Wallis scheduled a retake. According to a memo from Wallis to studio manager Tenny Wright on November 11, the retake would involve Claude Rains, Humphrey Bogart, and fifty or sixty extras wearing Free French uniforms. Curtiz would shoot the foggy-night sequence to take place on the deck and in the radio room of a freighter.

The scene may have been a compromise attempt to update the

movie without having the troops storm the beaches. A telegram makes it likely that the studio was going to drag Roosevelt in again, with Bogart and Rains listening to the President's speech announcing the invasion. But Rains had gone home to his farm in Pennsylvania, and, luckily for the movie, Warner Bros. had difficulty getting him an airplane ticket. The priorities of the war delayed Rains's arrival long enough for David O. Selznick to see the film. Whatever Selznick's faults, he knew a good movie when he saw one. He insisted that the studio leave the ending alone. On November 12, from his office in Culver City, Selznick sent the following telegram to Wallis at his office in Burbank:

Dear Hal: Saw "Casablanca" last night. Think it is a swell movie and an all-around job of picture making. Told Jack as forcibly as I could that I thought it would be a terrible mistake to change the ending. And also that I thought the picture ought to be rushed out.

Knowing what they started with, I think the firm of Epstein,

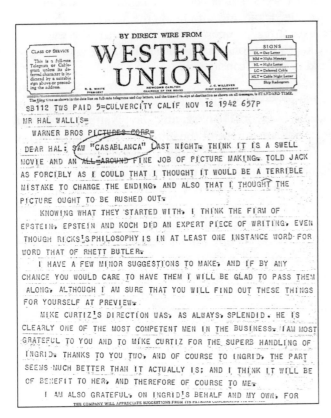

BY DIRECT WIRE FROM

WESTERN UNION

SB112 TWS PAID 5=CULVERCITY CALIF NOV 12 1942 657P

MR HAL WALLIS=

WARNER BROS PICTURES CORP=

DEAR HAL: SAW "CASABLANCA" LAST NIGHT. THINK IT IS A SWELL MOVIE AND AN ALL-AROUND FINE JOB OF PICTURE MAKING. TOLD JACK AS FORCIBLY AS I COULD THAT I THOUGHT IT WOULD BE A TERRIBLE MISTAKE TO CHANGE THE ENDING, AND ALSO THAT I THOUGHT THE PICTURE OUGHT TO BE RUSHED OUT.

KNOWING WHAT THEY STARTED WITH, I THINK THE FIRM OF EPSTEIN, EPSTEIN AND KOCH DID AN EXPERT PIECE OF WRITING, EVEN THOUGH RICKS'S PHILOSOPHY IS IN AT LEAST ONE INSTANCE WORD-FOR WORD THAT OF RHETT BUTLER.

I HAVE A FEW MINOR SUGGESTIONS TO MAKE, AND IF BY ANY CHANCE YOU WOULD CARE TO HAVE THEM I WILL BE GLAD TO PASS THEM ALONG, ALTHOUGH I AM SURE THAT YOU WILL FIND OUT THESE THINGS FOR YOURSELF AT PREVIEW.

MIKE CURTIZ'S DIRECTION WAS, AS ALWAYS, SPLENDID. HE IS CLEARLY ONE OF THE MOST COMPETENT MEN IN THE BUSINESS. I AM MOST GRATEFUL TO YOU AND TO MIKE CURTIZ FOR THE SUPERB HANDLING OF INGRID. THANKS TO YOU TWO, AND OF COURSE TO INGRID, THE PART SEEMS MUCH BETTER THAN IT ACTUALLY IS; AND I THINK IT WILL BE OF BENEFIT TO HER, AND THEREFORE OF COURSE TO ME.

I AM ALSO GRATEFUL, ON INGRID'S BEHALF AND MY OWN, FOR

Epstein and Koch did an expert piece of writing. Even though Rick's philosophy is in at least one instance word for word that of Rhett Butler.

I have a few minor suggestions to make, and if by any chance you would care to have them I will be glad to pass them along. Although I am sure that you will find out these things for yourself at preview.

Mike Curtiz's direction was, as always, splendid. He is clearly one of the most competent men in the business. I am most grateful to you and to Mike Curtiz for the superb handling of Ingrid. Thanks to you two, and of course to Ingrid, the part seems much better than it actually is; and I think it will be of benefit to her, and therefore of course to me.

I am also grateful, on Ingrid's behalf and my own, for Arthur Edeson's superb photography of Ingrid. But then the job of photography on the whole picture is excellent and is to no small extent responsible for the picture's mood.

After "For Whom the Bell Tolls" Ingrid is obviously going to be what I have for so long predicted, one of the great stars of the world. The demand for her services is of course tremendous. In deciding who should have outside pictures with her in the future, and should you and Mike have a really important vehicle for her, the way in which you have kept your promises in regard to her is going to bring you the dividend of special consideration.

Casablanca—unchanged—opened at the Hollywood Theater in New York two weeks later, on Thanksgiving Day. Naturally, Warner Bros. press agents took advantage of the gift the United States Army had given them. One article began, "Until a highly efficient force of United States Rangers, airmen, and infantry landed at Casablanca, in French Morocco, the other day, few Americans had visited that interesting city." The only Americans who knew about the city, said the studio, were the people who had worked on *Casablanca*. Another press release led off with: "Popularity of North African pictures since American troops moved in on the Axis, and *Casablanca* started setting box-office records, has boosted the acting price of camels from 15 dollars a day to 25." In that release the studio was already ordering up camels for *Brazzaville,* the sequel to *Casablanca* that was never made.

That there was a shortage of camels in Hollywood may or may not have been true, but the box-office success of the movie was. It was helped along by another gift from the United States Government. *Casablanca* was released nationally on January 23, 1943, along with Universal's *Mug Town,* starring the Dead End Kids, and RKO Radio's *Cinderella Swings It* with Guy Kibbee. That week, Roosevelt and Winston Churchill were meeting secretly in the city of Casablanca. There was a news blackout until the meeting ended, allowing the story to hit the front pages of the country's newspapers just as *Casablanca* was released.

Casablanca played ten weeks at the Hollywood Theater to total box-office receipts of $225,827.21. Said an interoffice communication from New York on February 8, 1943, "The total, therefore, that the Company realized from this engagement for Film Rental, Theatre Profit, and Rent is $158,208." The records of William Schaefer, who was Jack Warner's secretary for more than forty years, show that *Casablanca* cost $1,039,000 and brought the studio $3,015,000 during its first release in the United States. By 1955, the last date Warner Bros. had comparison figures on its war movies, Warner's gross income from the movie, including ticket sales at theaters abroad, was an astounding $6,819,000. Of all the movies Warners made during the war, *Casablanca* was outgrossed only by *Shine On, Harvest Moon* ($8.2 million) and *This Is the Army* ($10.4 million). The only other movie that came close was *Yankee Doodle Dandy* with $6.5 million. It is interesting, but not surprising, that all of those movies except *Shine On, Harvest Moon* were produced by Hal Wallis and directed by Mike Curtiz.

Casablanca would probably have been a success even without the jolt provided by current history. The movie, shaped during months of defeat, was released into a climate of optimism. In rapid succession in November, the Americans and British invaded North Africa, the U.S. Navy sank twenty-three Japanese ships in the Solomon Islands, and the Russians held the Germans at Stalingrad. With the war news less grim, audiences could savor bittersweet romance, and Rick was the archetype of the individualistic, isolationist American—"I stick my neck out for nobody"—turned interventionist.

In December, Warner Bros. made two announcements. General Charles de Gaulle, leader of the Free French forces, had asked for *Casablanca* to be shown to his staff in London. And a print of the film was being rushed to American troops in North Africa.

De Gaulle's staff may have seen the movie. But the American troops did not. The Office of War Information made certain of that.

17

Controlling Hollywood

———◆———

It was Robert Riskin who barred *Casablanca* from North Africa. Riskin, the screenwriter of Frank Capra's *It Happened One Night, Mr. Deeds Goes to Town,* and *Meet John Doe,* headed the motion-picture division of the overseas branch of the Office of War Information. Riskin was one of two dozen major screenwriters who remained civilians but spent the war as producers, administrators, propagandists, and censors for the OWI and other government bureaus.

When *Casablanca* premiered at the Hollywood Theater in New York City on November 26, 1942, Warner Bros. made sure that the connection with the North African campaign was not overlooked. The movie had ended with Humphrey Bogart and Claude Rains on their way to the Free French garrison at Brazzaville. The premiere began with supporters of the Free French forces of General Charles de Gaulle parading down Fifth Avenue and ended with the singing of the "Marseillaise" and the unfurling of the Free French flag at the

Raymond Massey and Humphrey Bogart in Action in the North Atlantic.

theater. "The occasion took the tone of a patriotic rally rather than the premiere of a timely motion picture," said the *Hollywood Reporter*.

The problem that the OWI had with *Casablanca* was symbolized by Claude Rains's throwing his bottle of Vichy water into the wastepaper basket and going off to join de Gaulle. The United States still had diplomatic relations with France's quasi-independent Vichy government. Hitler allowed Vichy, headed by the French World War I hero Marshal Pétain, to govern southern France while the Germans occupied the northern part of the country. "I blow with the wind. And the prevailing wind happens to be from Vichy," Captain Renault tells Major Strasser. Vichy controlled North Africa. Even after the Allies took Casablanca and Algiers, many French in North Africa were loyal to Pétain; and de Gaulle remained a hot potato. He was disliked by Churchill and Roosevelt, who found him difficult to deal with.

"I saw the picture *Casablanca* and whereas there are no objectionable features in it for general overseas showing, I, nevertheless, am withholding it from shipment to North Africa on the advice of several Frenchmen within our organization who feel that it is bound to create resentment on the part of the natives," Riskin wrote to another OWI official in January 1943. "For your information, the North African situation is completely under our control, inasmuch as the motion picture companies cannot ship to that territory without our assistance."

By the time Riskin used his censorship powers to keep *Casablanca* out of North Africa, the Office of War Information had discovered that controlling Hollywood wasn't going to be easy. The OWI and a sister organization, the Office of Censorship, could keep movies from being shipped abroad—a considerable weapon—but the OWI had no power to keep Hollywood from making whatever pictures it wanted to make. And, despite the OWI's hope that Hollywood would focus on the meaning of the war, what Hollywood chose to make at first was movies using the war as a background for the kinds of heroics that had always been a staple. In *Tarzan Triumphs,* even the jungle animals fought the Nazis. The first War Feature Inventory taken by the OWI showed that between April 15 and September 15, 1942, twenty-eight movies about spies, saboteurs, and fifth columnists had been released and nineteen more spy pictures were already completed, while only two movies had dealt with the issues of the war.

The Office of War Information was America's chief propaganda agency during the Second World War. The OWI was to explain the war to the American people and their Allies, to instill a will to win, and to be the government's liaison with radio, movies, and the press, the country's most important information sources. As the months went by, the OWI, working through the Bureau of Motion Pictures that it set up in Hollywood, would exert more and more pressure on the movie industry. The men who ran the OWI would try to shape films to their own liberal New Deal/One World vision. They would succeed with Warner Bros. and fail with Paramount. Before the war ended, the OWI would read more than fifteen hundred scripts and influence the content of hundreds of films.* The producers, whose movies were regularly banned in Boston, Chicago, and Memphis, and who had voluntarily subjected themselves to the restrictions of their conservative Production Code, quickly accommodated themselves to the restrictions of censorship with a liberal bias. However, despite being headquartered at Hollywood and Vine, the Bureau of Motion Pictures never quite understood what the studios had learned over the decades, that the most effective propaganda is unobtrusive.

During the summer of 1942, while *Casablanca* was in production, there was a honeymoon between patriotic moguls who genuinely wanted to know what they could do to help the war effort and the newly opened Bureau of Motion Pictures. The Bureau sent a manual to the studios which suggested that the moviemakers ask themselves seven questions before starting a new movie.

1. Will this picture help win the war?
2. What war information problem does it seek to clarify, dramatize or interpret?
3. If it is an "escape" picture, will it harm the war effort by creating a false picture of America, her allies, or the world we live in?
4. Does it merely use the war as the basis for a profitable picture, contributing nothing of real significance to the war effort and possibly lessening the effect of other pictures of more importance?

---

* Congressional critics of Roosevelt and the OWI cut the organization's funding in July 1943. Lowell Mellett left, and the Bureau of Motion Pictures was wiped out, but the overseas branch of the OWI, which was headquartered in the same building, took over the bureau's functions.

5. Does it contribute something new to our understanding of the world conflict and the various forces involved, or has the subject already been adequately covered?
6. When the picture reaches its maximum circulation on the screen, will it reflect conditions as they are and fill a need current at that time, or will it be out-dated?
7. Does the picture tell the truth or will the young people of today have reason to say they were misled by propaganda?

As Clayton Koppes and Gregory Black point out in *Hollywood Goes to War,* their incisive study of the effects of the OWI on Hollywood movies during World War II, the manual proclaimed the world view that Vice President Henry Wallace had set forth in his "Century of the Common Man" speech. Against the forces of Satan, we and our thirty Allies were fighting a people's war for democracy everywhere, and if some of our Allies—Chiang Kai-shek's China, Trujillo's Dominican Republic and Somoza's Nicaragua among them—were hardly democratic, it was better to overlook that fact. The enemy was the poisonous doctrine of hate, not the entire German or Japanese people. If American democracy was not yet perfect, movies must still show civilians of all classes, creeds, and colors cheerfully working together and sacrificing together for the common good, while platoons filled with soldiers who had "names of foreign extraction" and an occasional black officer would create the impression of national unity.

The manual divided the subject matter of war movies into six themes:

I. THE ISSUES—Why we fight. What kind of peace will follow victory.
II. THE ENEMY—Whom we fight. The nature of our adversary.
III. THE UNITED NATIONS AND PEOPLES—With whom we are allied in fighting. Our brothers-in-arms.
IV. WORK AND PRODUCTION—How each of us can fight. The war at home.
V. THE HOME FRONT—What we must do. What we must give up to win the fight.
VI. THE FIGHTING FORCES—The job of the fighting man at the Front.

It is the nature of bureaucracy to expand. Each of the themes was further subdivided, and the Bureau of Motion Pictures kept sending out supplements to the manual. Fact Sheet No. 7, for example, was an eight-page warning about the evils of inflation to be inserted into Section V. The moviemakers were asked to dramatize how John Jones, the Average American, "can protect himself, his family and the security of his country by joining with his fellow-Americans in carrying out the President's 7-point counter-inflation program."

Casablanca, like all the movies reviewed by the Bureau of Motion Pictures, was assigned a theme. The major theme of the movie, said the reviewer, was III B (United Nations—Conquered Nations). The minor theme was II C 3 (Enemy—Military). Four members of the Bureau saw *Casablanca* on October 26, 1942, before the invasion of North Africa and the furor over changing the ending. The movie, judged "from the standpoint of the war information program," was given a glowing review. *Casablanca* showed "that personal desires must be subordinated to the task of defeating fascism" and "graphically illustrated the chaos and misery which fascism and the war has brought." In addition, America was shown as "the haven of the oppressed and homeless." By including Rick's background in fighting fascism in Spain and Ethiopia, the film aided audiences "in understanding that our war did not commence with Pearl Harbor, but that the roots of aggression reach far back."

Because all movies were judged from the standpoint of the War Information Program, the OWI often saw films through a distorted and humorless prism. *Sherlock Holmes and the Voice of Terror* was criticized because a Nazi supersaboteur does too much damage, thus showing England as defenseless against Nazi sabotage, while *London Blackout Murders* hurt the war effort by increasing public anxiety about blackouts.

The reviewer of Paramount's Preston Sturges comedy *The Palm Beach Story* was horrified because "America's domestic morals are depicted as incredibly cheap. The daughter of one of the foremost families in America (characterized sympathetically in the film) is the veteran of five marriages, three divorces and two annulments." What was almost worse, the characters were shown "during war time, as fantastically extravagant and irresponsible." Thus, the movie confirmed Axis propaganda that all democratic peoples are decadent. Paramount's *Lucky Jordan,* one of the ubiquitous gang-

ster-turned-patriot films, confirmed another piece of enemy propaganda—that American armed forces are weak, undisciplined, and
reluctant to fight—by showing Alan Ladd as a reluctant draftee and
his sergeant brutally attempting to shape him up.

Watch on the Rhine, which would win most of the critics' awards
for 1943, was criticized as being two years out of date and unnecessary since America, which was portrayed in the movie as a compla-
cent and apathetic country in 1940, was now awake and at war. On
the other hand, Universal's *Pittsburgh* was considered "tops from
every standpoint" by Ulric Bell of the Overseas Branch of OWI.
Pittsburgh, which starred John Wayne and Marlene Dietrich, used
chunks of dialogue straight out of the OWI manual about management and labor pulling together in the steel mills. Another film that
regurgitated OWI propaganda was M-G-M's *Keeper of the Flame,* the
least watchable movie that Katharine Hepburn and Spencer Tracy
made together. The OWI was ecstatic about the movie because, in
its portrait of an American industrialist who planned a Fascist coup,
it raised the question of home-grown fascism. Republican members
of Congress, concerned about movies that seemed intended to help
Roosevelt get reelected in 1944, were less ecstatic. They complained
to Will Hays, the head of the Production Code, about the liberal
propaganda in *Keeper of the Flame, This Is the Army,* and *Mission to
Moscow.* (As to aesthetics, critic James Agee called *Keeper of the
Flame* a roast albatross.)

The problems inherent in wedding movies and propaganda are
illustrated by RKO's *Tender Comrade,* in which Ginger Rogers and
three other women whose husbands have marched off to war live
together and work in the same aircraft factory. In addition to lectur-
ing one of the other women for hoarding lipsticks, Ginger Rogers
explained the Four Freedoms to her infant son. James Agee complained that Rogers's speech "lasted twenty-four hours and five
minutes by my watch." Audiences, too, hated the blatant propaganda. "Ending was awful. TOO MUCH PROPAGANDA," read one
preview card. Another ticket buyer said that, instead of attending a
movie, she felt she had been at a lecture on "why we are fighting this
war." The domestic branch of the OWI was pleased with *Tender
Comrade.* The overseas branch refused it an export visa for the
liberated territories because the women's standard of living was too
high, and their argument over their bacon ration would offend
people who hadn't tasted bacon in years.

Like many of the Warner Bros. war movies, *Keeper of the Flame* and *Tender Comrade* were written by Communists, *Flame* by the upper-class Communist Donald Ogden Stewart and *Comrade* by Dalton Trumbo, one of the Hollywood Ten. *Comrade* was directed by another member of the Ten, Edward Dmytryk. But during the war, with Russia on our side, there was barely a finger's worth of difference between the views of American Communists and American liberals. Both were preaching equality and waving the American flag with gusto. However, equality rarely included women. In *Tender Comrade,* the women did get to make the big speeches about what we were fighting for that were usually delivered by men, but, as Koppes and Black point out, Trumbo wrote standard Hollywood hooey, in which women are still defined by men, live through men, and "will shuffle back to the kitchen" as soon as the men come home.

In most home-front movies, the wives who were left behind waited for men to make them whole again. Most of the films weren't as bad as *Blondie for Victory,* which ridiculed women's attempts to volunteer their services and ended when Blondie conceded that a woman's place is in the home, but most made it clear that no woman was as competent, hard-working, or unselfish as a man. Newspaper and magazine articles played the same tune. *Variety* whined about the "strange quirks of femme psychology that adversely affect the box office." Although they were making good money in defense plants, women refused to part with the money by going to the movies, *Variety* complained. Where men were spreading their money around, women were giving in to tired muscles and fatigue. "Inconsistency, thy name is woman."

Collier's lectured women on how to prepare for a bombing raid. "Suppose you went to bed with cold cream plastered on your face—heck, you'd scare everybody, all the other bombed-out people. Best way was to go to bed with light make-up. Then you put a warm—but attractive—robe beside the bed . . . and put the lipstick and rouge on the bedside table." Even the Hollywood Victory Committee ridiculed the industry's women. Despite their sincerity, the "girls" who belonged to Bundles for Bluejackets and the Volunteer Army Canteen Service were "foolishly being blinded by the glamour of a uniform which they've donned for non-essential activities" and many had joined "because they felt it was the socially smart thing to do," said a press release.

Says Pauline Kael, "Women's lives were affected by the war. You often went to a movie, and it would be full of patriotic speeches or would be saccharine and really repulsive, yet women were working who hadn't worked before, or they had better jobs. Certainly as a young woman your life was affected because men in uniform put a lot of pressure on you. I mean the sexual pressure to satisfy whatever their needs were. If they were in uniform, they often felt you had an obligation to do something for them."

The government didn't force its will on Hollywood. Actress Fay Wray, Robert Riskin's widow, says, "There was an absolute dedication to the concept that this was an important work being done by everyone who was associated in any way with making films. The war was a justified war. And all must be done that could be done to express that or have the world know something about what democracy was and what America was."

The industry needed its foreign markets, but the OWI's greatest weapon was the moguls' desire to help win the war. Movie after movie contained flag-waving speeches because the studio chiefs agreed with the OWI that movies could be a potent morale-building force, while the men who wrote their movies were generally the most liberal of their employees. In April 1942, Warner Bros. had responded to a request from Major Frank Capra with a letter that seems amazing today. "Frankly and sincerely, we consider our whole Warner Bros. setup as another agency of the government, and it is my opinion that all business enterprises should consider themselves in the same way," Charles Einfeld wrote Capra.

It is not surprising that Nelson Poynter, who headed the Bureau of Motion Pictures, told Harry and Jack Warner that he expected them to blaze the trail in Hollywood. A few months earlier, Harry Warner had pledged his support to Lowell Mellett, the man President Roosevelt had appointed to oversee the movie industry, with: "Recent events now call for motion pictures which build and sustain morale. In this cause I dedicate myself and our efforts, and pledge you our fullest support and cooperation." That cooperation would extend to holding back the release of *Princess O'Rourke* for a year. Hal Wallis's film was a well-made romantic comedy about a princess (Olivia de Havilland) from a mythical European country, who falls in love with an ordinary American guy (Robert Cummings). The movie would win Norman Krasna an Academy Award for best original screenplay, but it disturbed the OWI, which felt it implied that the United States was "eager to re-establish monarchs who have lived in luxury and safety while their people fought and suffered under Nazi Occupations, and to perpetuate government by useless, extravagant parasites."

Warner Bros. wrote up justifications for all its movies, emphasizing themes in the OWI manual. Naturally, the studio's perception of *Princess O'Rourke* was quite different. In the category "The American Way of Life, American Youth," the studio wrote: Robert Cummings, a simple commoner, "realizes the dignity and importance of being an ordinary American citizen, refusing to give up his American citizenship to become the husband of a European princess."

Although Hollywood became sensitized to the OWI's concerns and let the bureaucrats win many battles, there was no unconditional surrender by an industry whose first priority was keeping the good will of audiences. When they chose to challenge the OWI, the studios had three weapons. Hollywood's long-standing relationship with the armed services—movies had been glorifying the Army and Navy for years—allowed the studios to get permissions behind the OWI's back. The Office of Censorship, which controlled export to neutral and friendly countries, was usually willing to pass films like *Palm Beach Story* that were politically incorrect in the eyes of the OWI, just so long as they didn't contain military secrets. Most important, the OWI's propaganda often turned into dreary, uncommercial movies.

In the beginning, the OWI tried to get Hollywood to address the serious issues of the war, to cut its output of spy and derring-do films and to tone down its depictions of the Japanese as buck-toothed, repulsive, and treacherous subhumans who deserved to be annihilated.* But there is a virus that affects almost everyone who comes in contact with Hollywood, and the men and women who ran the Bureau of Motion Pictures were no exception. Soon, instead of being content to guide, they were trying to control and create.†

---

* Germany was treated differently. Although Nazis in Hollywood's war movies were cruel and arrogant, the entire German nation was not indicted as irredeemably barbaric. There is no question that racism was a large part of the difference. Fear of the Japanese as the "Yellow Peril" was high in America even before the war.

† The OWI never understood the nuances of the industry. When Frank Capra finished *Prelude to War,* the first of the seven films in his "Why We Fight" series, the OWI refused to let the movie be shown to members of the Academy. Mellett wired the Academy:

Poynter, the thirty-nine-year-old publisher of the St. Petersburg *Times,* who had been appointed to run the Bureau of Motion Pictures by his friend Lowell Mellett, had no particular liking for movies. He saw them not as art but as vehicles for content. "One of the most useful pictures yet made," he said in praising Jack Warner for *Action in the North Atlantic.* In January 1943, Poynter sent a pitch letter to all the major studios suggesting a movie on President Manuel Quezon of the Philippines. The movie could concern Quezon's "visit to the United States, where he discovers a wonderful country and an enlightened non-imperialistic people."

Poynter also tried a bit of screenwriting. He was appalled by *The Desert Song* because of the emphasis on French imperialism in North Africa, and he suggested new speeches that would make it clear that it was not France but only an evil colonial officer who had abused the natives. Warner Bros. agreed to reshoot a few scenes, and Poynter edited the hero's new speech to make it even more explicit. Paramount was considerably less amenable when Poynter suggested that an army chaplain talk about democracy on the march in a speech in *So Proudly We Hail,* one of the few movies about women in combat. In the film, a group of besieged Army nurses in the Philippines in 1942 are saved from the Japs when one of them (Veronica Lake) sacrifices her life. Poynter suggested that the chaplain's Christmas Eve sermon incorporate the idea of the Allied cause as God's will: "The whole concept of Militarism—the doctrine of force which Fascism represents violates the Christ ideal." He wrote dialogue in which the chaplain talked about "the dignity of man which includes a Chinese coolie, a Filipino farmer, or a Malayan coconut picker." Whereas Warner Bros. showed its scripts to the OWI all the time, *So Proudly We Hail* was one of the few Paramount scripts that the bureau got its hands on. Y. Frank Freeman, the conservative Georgia theater owner who ran Paramount, reacted with fury when he learned that Poynter had crossed the invisible line and actually written dialogue for the chaplain.

"Appreciate desire of Col. Capra's Academy friends but suggest in all sincerity that they refrain from embarrassing him and other able directors who had entered the armed services by confusing their present work with their past efforts." Capra complained to his superior, General Frederick H. Osborn, that if there was a ruling against the industry's seeing a product to which they contributed, "it is just another handicap in getting the voluntary cooperation of the studios." Osborn sent a blistering rebuke to Mellett. *Prelude to War* was shown to the Academy and won a 1942 Academy Award.

Both Dennis Morgan's speech in *The Desert Song* and the chaplain's sermon in *So Proudly We Hail* are full of the turgid speechifying that the OWI managed to lard into any number of films. The bureau was most successful in adding "What the War Means" and "How We Can Help the War Effort" material to movies and in deleting offensive lines and characters. It was moderately successful in keeping the studios from making films that might embarrass our Allies or gum up the political works. One of Poynter's early successes was persuading M-G-M to shelve its planned movie version of Rudyard Kipling's *Kim*. And, after the liberation of North Africa, the studios were warned not to make any movies that would deal with the sensitive military or political situation in France. After the warning, Warners dropped *The Life of Charles de Gaulle* and Fox canceled *The Life Story of General Henri Giraud*.

"*Casablanca* was a very political film when it came out," says cinematographer Haskell Wexler. "I was among the first Americans in North Africa. I was nineteen years old and an able seaman in the Merchant Marine. I went into Oran, which was full of French who were German collaborators and sympathetic to Marshal Pétain. Our government was afraid of upsetting the metabolism of the area with local uprisings; they wanted to keep North Africa a colonial empire." Wexler hesitates and then adds, "I suppose enough time has passed so I can say it now. I was doing anti-Fascist work. Oran had a large contingent of Spanish revolutionaries who had escaped from Franco's Spain. I brought them copies of the minefields around Gibraltar."

The OWI was least successful in changing the way that Hollywood routinely attacked a subject. When the movies did change, it was partly because the American experience of the war changed. How Hollywood attempted to deal with World War II and how that was modified from 1942 to 1945 can be seen with a certain amount of clarity by examining Humphrey Bogart's career as a war hero.

In *All Through the Night* Bogart played Gloves Donohue, an ex-gangster turned gambler, who stumbles on a nest of Nazi spies led by Conrad Veidt and foils their plan to blow up a ship in New York harbor. Made in the fall of 1941 and released a month after Pearl Harbor, *All Through the Night* was typical of a dozen or more early war movies in which Hollywood simply grafted old-fashioned Americanism onto its gangster and gambler heroes. In *Mr. Lucky,*

Bogart and Peter Lorre in All Through the Night.

Cary Grant played a crooked gambler and draft dodger who ends up raising money for war relief. In *Lucky Jordan,* Alan Ladd played a swindler and draft dodger who sees the evils of Nazism when an old lady who befriended him is beaten up by Nazi agents. The OWI thought that these movies played into the hands of the enemy by confirming the Axis propaganda that America was populated by criminals. OWI analysts expressed their frustration at the industry they were supposed to guide by writing candid and sarcastic assessments of Hollywood's films. "Hollywood hasn't taken the trouble to distinguish enemy agents from the gangster stereotypes so well known to audiences," one complained about all those spies and saboteurs. "Sometimes they lapse into gutturals toward the end of the film to indicate, one supposes, that they are Nazis. Their objectives and ideologies are seldom given even a passing line."

By the beginning of 1943, as the movies came to grips with the real war, the gangster as patriot and his enemy as spies, Fifth

Columnists, and saboteurs faded away. Another thing that faded away was Warners' use of Bogart as a pinch hitter for George Raft. *All Through the Night* was the last movie in which Bogart inherited a role that Raft refused to play. After talking Bogart into playing the part, his agent, Sam Jaffe, respectfully asked the studio to prepare at least one story in which they had Bogart in mind from the beginning.

In *Across the Pacific,* * which was filmed in March of 1942, Bogart played the other ubiquitous type of early-war movie hero—the secret agent. Already the scene had shifted. The enemy was no longer internal but external. Bogart, as a passenger on a Japanese boat, engaged in clever repartee with Mary Astor and foiled a plot by Sydney Greenstreet to blow up the Panama Canal. (In the first script, Greenstreet intended to blow up Pearl Harbor, but real life forced art to change.) Typical of 1942 movies, the friendly, jive-talking, American-born Japanese boy in *Across the Pacific* is a traitor.

Then came *Casablanca.* In its resonance *Casablanca* is unique. But there were more than a dozen movies in 1943 with the same OWI-labeled theme: "III B United Nations—Conquered Nations." Like *Casablanca,* most of those movies dealt with resistance within countries conquered by the Nazis—from *Assignment in Brittany, Joan of Paris,* and *The Cross of Lorraine* set in France, to *The Moon Is Down* and *Edge of Darkness* in Norway, Fritz Lang's *Hangmen Also Die* in Czechoslovakia and Jean Renoir's *This Land Is Mine,* which took place "somewhere in Europe." Perhaps because the Japanese were seen as monsters or because we spent the first year of the war fighting in the Pacific, movies about the Japanese were almost always combat pictures. The only good Japs were dead Japs, but most of those 1943 melodramas displayed good as well as bad Germans. In an eight-page, single-spaced justification for *Casablanca,* Warners said the film aided international understanding because Carl, the waiter played by S. Z. Sakall, was shown to be an anti-Nazi German.

Casablanca was typical, also, in its insistence on sacrifice. The gangster and secret-agent melodramas had ended with the enemy agents foiled, the heroes unscarred, America victorious, and the Stars and Stripes aloft. The 1943 melodramas were filled with the

---

*Between *All Through the Night* and *Across the Pacific,* Bogart made *The Big Shot,* his goodbye wave to B movies. Once again, he was a gangster who broke out of prison and was killed.

Bogart and Mary Astor in Across the Pacific. *When* The Maltese Falcon *became a surprise hit, Warner Bros. quickly reassembled the cast members and director.*

corruption and chaos of living under the boot or the shadow of the Nazis. The schoolmaster, the widow, or the whole village resists, even though resistance means death. A few of the movies moved back to the battles of the prewar years. In a watered-down screen version of Ernest Hemingway's novel about the Spanish Civil War, *For Whom the Bell Tolls,* the American hero, Gary Cooper, fights for the Loyalists against Franco and the Fascists. By sacrificing his own life, he buys time for his band of guerrillas to escape. In *Watch on the Rhine,* the German hero must leave the comfort and safety of America to return to his underground work and almost certain death in Germany.

In his next two movies, *Action in the North Atlantic,* which played in June 1943, and *Sahara,* which reached theaters a month later, Bogart finally got into combat. It would have been strange if he hadn't, because the combat film blossomed in 1943. The OWI's confidential inventory of December 15, 1942, shows that while only six combat films had been released in the fall of '42, fourteen more were in production or had recently been completed, and scripts were being written on another two dozen.

The OWI had considerable input into both *Action in the North Atlantic,* which was written by John Howard Lawson, another member of the Hollywood Ten, who would go to jail for contempt of Congress, and *Sahara,* which was cowritten by Lawson. Mellett had suggested that a movie be made about the Merchant Marine, and Warner Bros. was the studio that took him up on it. Bogart played Joe Rossi, the first mate, and Raymond Massey was his captain. Their first ship was sunk by a German submarine; their new Liberty ship saved a convoy by ramming and sinking the same U-boat. Warner Bros. framed the movie with the voice of President Roosevelt declaiming: "We shall build a bridge of ships to our Allies over which we shall roll the implements of war."

The Bureau of Motion Pictures objected to several things in Lawson's first script, including a black pantryman who asks why he should fight. Lawson's symbolic solution was to have a white sailor save the mess steward's life, but that didn't solve the BMP's problem with the character. He was still unequal, a pantryman whose job was to serve coffee to the whites. Warners satisfied the bureau by writing the character out, leaving one less role for black actors.

At the time that *Action* was being written, the OWI was making an unsuccessful attempt to become Hollywood's only conduit to the government. If Hollywood had to submit requests for tanks and footage of aerial battles through the bureau, the OWI could better control the pictures being made. Warners agreed to let Poynter serve as a go-between with the Navy, but, when Poynter couldn't get the materials and permissions that the studio needed, Warners went back to its old system and sent the script to the Navy for clearance. Even Warner Bros., the most cooperative of the studios, decided to keep its bread buttered on one side by deference to the armed services although it gave the other side to the OWI to spread.

Action fit almost perfectly into the OWI's ideals. The crew had characters named Pulaski, Goldberg, and O'Hara. The staunch wife who waited at home for Raymond Massey tried never to let him see her cry. The convoy included Soviet, Free French, and Dutch ships. The OWI objected to movies that showed a few Americans easily defeating hordes of Nazis or Japs, and the sailors aboard the Nazi submarine—who spoke ominously and effectively in German— were implacable and efficient. In the end, however, Americans could and did defeat the enemy—with the support of their Allies. The OWI was never able to get Hollywood to eliminate the brash and cocky American heroes that it found so annoying, but it did get the studios to put in scenes of appreciation for the strength and accomplishments of our noble Allies. At the climax of *Action in the North Atlantic,* Russian planes broke through the clouds to escort the Americans to Murmansk, where Russians and Americans greeted each other as comrades.

The combat scenes in *Action in the North Atlantic* are still gripping. The propaganda speeches are not badly done, except when Dane Clark refuses to ship out again after the first ship is sunk—"I want to bounce my kid on my knee"—and is talked into it by shipmates, who point out all the reasons why it is necessary to fight. The OWI encouraged movies to prepare Americans for the deaths that were to come, which translated into many films with graveside ceremonies. In *Action,* Bogart gives a eulogy for a Merchant Marine cadet who has been killed, while in *Passage to Marseille,* Claude Rains speaks the eulogy over Bogart's grave.

As Bogart's first picture since *Casablanca, Action,* which cost more than $2 million, was successful at the box office, and Jack Warner was given a victory flag by the War Shipping Administration. Although critics found the propaganda rather lumpy, the movie would have broken *Yankee Doodle Dandy*'s opening-day record in New York if Warners hadn't kept a thousand free seats at each screening for Merchant Marine sailors. For Bogart, the movie had two consequences. In a not uncommon confusion of star and role, he was dogged by widespread and embarrassing rumors that he was going to join the Merchant Marine. And, a few years later, a notation was made in his FBI file: "Bogart played in the motion picture, Action in the North Atlantic, which was very favorable to Russia, written by John Howard Lawson."

Sahara, which Bogart made on loan-out to Columbia, was one of the subgenre of submarine, lost-patrol, outpost-in-the-jungle films about a small group in tight circumstances. The picture starred Bogart as Sergeant Joe Gunn, the commander of a tank that is trying to reach the British lines. "Humphrey Bogart and several less high-salaried but no less talented soldiers, stranded at an oasis, hold off and then capture a full Nazi batallion," James Agee wrote in *The Nation.* "Anyone who can make that believable, even for so long as you watch it, knows how to make a good war melodrama. *Sahara* is the best one since *Bataan.*"

Even today, Bogart's laconic performance gives a grittiness and authority to a movie that often stops dead for speechifying. In *Sahara,* the equivalent of seamen named O'Hara and Pulaski were various Allies that the tank picked up along the way: several British soldiers, a French Resistance fighter, a Sudanese corporal, and his Italian prisoner. Following OWI guidelines, Italians were treated rather kindly in World War II films, and the prisoner in *Sahara* was typical in having been misled by Mussolini and despising Hitler and fascism.

After reading the script by John Howard Lawson and Zoltan Korda, the OWI persuaded the writers to change the black corporal from a faithful but subservient follower to an equal of the white soldiers. In the film, the Sudanese, played by actor Rex Ingram, chases, tackles and kills a Nazi prisoner who has escaped; he is then shot and killed while trying to return to the oasis.

Although *Casablanca* presented Sam as Rick's friend without help from the Bureau of Motion Pictures, the OWI did fight to expand the image of blacks. In another of the last-stand films, *Bataan,* as in many other combat movies the bureau helped to stir one black man into a band of soda jerks, farmers, and teachers from Iowa, Brooklyn, and Texas fighting a people's war. The black private (Kenneth Spencer) died as stalwartly as the young sailor played by Robert Walker and the sergeant played by Robert Taylor, all of them sacrificing their lives to hold back the Japs for a few extra days. The OWI was also successful in getting Hollywood to cut down the eyeball-rolling, teeth-chattering comic stereotypes of blacks. But, although the OWI persuaded the studios to eliminate black janitors and mess stewards, there were still a lot of Negro butlers left—even in Warner Bros. movies. President Roosevelt's butler waited obsequiously around to see George M. Cohan in *Yankee Doodle Dandy,* while Lucille Watson had a cheerful, silver-polishing butler in *Watch on the Rhine,* and a Negro butler opened the door of the White House to Olivia de Havilland's princess in *Princess O'Rourke.*

James Agee, who could always skewer to the heart, described Fidelia, the role played by Hattie McDaniel in *Since You Went Away,* David O. Selznick's attempt to make a *Gone With the Wind* of the World War II home front, with: "The Hilton cook, satisfying all that anyone could possibly desire of a Negro in these restive times, not only keeps strict union hours on the job she takes when Mrs. Hilton can no longer afford her; when she is done she hustles back to the Hiltons to get in her day's measure of malapropisms, comic relief, mother wit, and free labor." A survey taken by the Writers' War Board late in 1944 examined one hundred movies with Negro themes or characters and described seventy-five as "stereotypical and disparaging" and only twelve as favorable.

Passage to Marseille, released in the spring of 1944, was the last of Bogart's combat films. As early as May 1943, the moguls had started distancing themselves from the war when exhibitors reported that the public was getting bored and wanted musicals and comedies. Again, Harry Warner stood on the opposite side. As reported in *The New York Times,* Warner told theater owners not to be "intimidated or coerced" by "persons who are not wholeheartedly behind our war effort" and told his fellow producers that they had an obligation to inform and would be shirking their duty by making escapist pictures.

Mike Curtiz was concerned that the war wouldn't last long enough for *Passage to Marseille* to be made and released. Just before the movie started production, Curtiz went behind Hal Wallis's back and sent Jack Warner a confidential telegram warning the studio head that, at its scheduled cost of $2 million, *Passage to Marseille* was a bad gamble. As it turned out, *Passage* was a bad movie but not a particularly bad gamble. It cost $2.3 million, brought Warners a little less than that domestically, but gave the studio a nice profit with revenues of $1.6 million outside the United States. The foreign revenues were helped along by the U.S. Government. From the beginning of the war the government had been eager to help Hollywood distribute its movies abroad as an antidote to German propaganda. Within days after North Africa was liberated, American films with French subtitles were flown in on United States bombers to replace German, Italian, and Vichy French films in the 220 theaters in Algeria and French Morocco.

The Warner Bros. file on *Passage to Marseille* shows that the studio had learned some OWI lessons. "It seems to me inadvisable to use the skin color of the negroes in any derogatory sense especially in view of the Japanese fascist propaganda which tries to convince the negroes that this is a war of the colored races against the white," reads one studio note on the script. Although the film is a hymn of praise to de Gaulle's Free French warriors (de Gaulle's stock had risen in the sixteen months since North Africa was liberated), the French officer (Claude Rains) who tells the complicated story of ex-convicts turned patriots carefully hedges about Vichy with: "I try to remember that Marshal Pétain is an old man and in the hands of the barbarians."

Like most of Hollywood's World War II combat films, *Passage to Marseille* glued the war to standard Hollywood melodrama. Only at the very end of the war could a movie, *The Story of G.I. Joe,* dare to look realistically and without histrionics or sentimentality at the men who fought and at the ugly job of fighting. *Passage to Marseille* was a deliberate attempt to duplicate the success of *Casablanca* by reuniting its director, producer, Bogart, Claude Rains, Sydney Greenstreet, and Peter Lorre. Even the theme—cynical and disillusioned hero rejoins the fight—was the same. The movie included a flashback to an idyllic love affair between Humphrey Bogart and Michele Morgan. He remembered how she looked when he first met her, ("You were wearing one of those big floppy hats and a basket on your arm") rather than when he last saw her. This time, Wallis did not have to make compromises. Philip Dorn, Wallis's first choice for the role played by Paul Henreid in *Casablanca,* was the other costar. Casey Robinson wrote the script. James Wong Howe, whom Wallis had tried so hard to get for *Casablanca,* was the cinematographer. And Max Steiner was allowed to write his own—soon-forgotten—love song.

Passage to Marseille is an awful movie, soggy with patriotism, soupy with sentimentality. Bogart plays a crusading French newspaper editor. Unjustly imprisoned on Devil's Island, Bogart escapes with Peter Lorre, Philip Dorn, George Tobias, and Helmut Dantine, duels with Nazi sympathizer Sydney Greenstreet, and becomes a Free French pilot. When Bogart is killed in a bombing raid, his epitaph is a letter he has written to the five-year-old son he has never seen. The treacle and indigestible chunks of propaganda in that epitaph make it clear how much *Casablanca* gained by being made early in the war before the OWI put its weight behind symbolic uplift.

My dear son,

Today you are five years old, and your father has never seen you. But someday, in a better world, he will. I write you of that day. Together we walk hand in hand. We walk and we look, and some of the things we see are wonderful, and some are terrible. On a green stretch of ground are 10,000 graves, and you feel hatred welling up in your heart. This was, but it will never be again. The world has

As these pictures make clear, Warner Bros. was trying to create the same box-office magic with Bogart and Michele Morgan in Passage to Marseille *as they had with Bogart and Bergman in* Casablanca.

been cured since your father treated that deadly abscess on its body with fire and iron, and there were millions of healers who worked with him and made sure there would be no recurrence. That deadly conflict was waged to decide your future. Your friends did not spare themselves and were ruthless to your foes. You are the heir of what your father and your friends won for you with their blood, and from their hands you have received the flag of happiness and freedom.

My son, be the standard bearer of a great age they have made possible. It would be too tragic if the men of good will should ever relax or fail again to build a world where youth may love without fear, and where parents may grow old with their children, and where men will be worthy of each other's faith.

By the time *Passage to Marseille* was released,* Italy had surrendered, the Allies were about to invade France, the end was inevitable

Claude Rains's eulogy over Bogart's grave in Passage to Marseille. *From left to right: Philip Dorn, George Tobias, Rains, Helmut Dantine.*

---

*Warners delayed the release of the movie in the hope that lightning would strike again and the Allies would choose to invade Europe by way of Marseille. They didn't.

despite the fact that another year of bloody fighting remained in the Pacific, and both Hollywood and the country were really tired of the war. In 1943, roughly half of the nominations for major Academy Awards went to films about the war or the home front. For films made in 1945, not a single nomination for picture, actor, actress, supporting actress, or director went to a film that had any relation to the conflict or its effects. Only the supporting-actor nominations for Robert Mitchum in *The Story of G. I. Joe* and J. Carrol Naish in *A Medal for Benny* acknowledged a war that had ended six months before.

To Have and Have Not, which was released in January 1945, was less a war movie than a romantic adventure that used the war as its canvas. Like *Casablanca, To Have and Have Not* took place in a French colony controlled by Vichy in the days after the fall of France and before America's entry into the war. Like *Casablanca,* the new movie required Bogart to move from neutrality to commitment and to help an enemy of the Third Reich escape. The parallels with

Marcel Dalio, Walter Brennan, Bogart, and Lauren Bacall in To Have and Have Not.

Casablanca were not accidental. "I'm glad you're on our side," says the wounded Resistance fighter Bogart has brought to Martinique on his fishing boat. The movie even had Hoagy Carmichael playing piano in the hotel bar that takes the place of Rick's Café. But by 1945 the story of the Free French and Vichy had no urgency or immediacy. It was an exotic, oft-told tale, and Bogart had no need to sacrifice the girl, his boat, or his friend.

Samuel Goldwyn once said that anyone who wanted to send a message should send it by Western Union. During the Second World War, Hollywood, with the help of the OWI, stuffed hundreds of movies with sentences, paragraphs, and pages of messages. The idea of propaganda has always made Americans uncomfortable, but movies are always powerful propaganda for something or other, even if it is only for hairstyles. In 1943, the British Ministry of Labor asked Hollywood to have actresses wear their hair short in future movies. For two years the Ministry, without much success, had been trying to convince female factory workers to change the fashionable upswept curls and pompadours that were too easily caught in machinery. The British government knew that if Veronica Lake cut her hair and Greer Garson wore a boyish bob, the factory workers would change hairstyles within a week, just as undershirt sales had plummeted in 1934 when Clark Gable displayed a bare chest in *It Happened One Night*.

The OWI had a number of messages which it was eager to sell to moviegoers. It is easy to make fun of the OWI's solemn response to such "B" movies as *London Blackout Murders* and *The Gorilla Man* and the agency's confusion of good political content with good art. But the OWI did push and goad Hollywood into portraying a world conflict with more subtlety and depth than the industry would have managed if it had been left alone. Unfortunately, the OWI also asked for dishonesty. The OWI tried to create a celluloid America that did not exist then and does not exist now, a happy land of racial and class equality. The explicit messages of World War II films that preached brotherhood and unity for a better world were seen as propaganda—and accepted or rejected depending on political affiliation and firsthand experience with the war—by all but the very young. Those saccharine messages in movies that wore their patriotism on their sleeves were most fiercely rejected by those who had seen the war up close. In the spring of 1943, an editorial in the soldiers' newspaper, *The Stars and Stripes,* denounced movie flag-waving as "sickening."

The difference in experience of the war between the men who fought it and the men and women who viewed it through Hollywood's prism was wider than the gulf in any other country. When America had been at war for almost two years, James Agee lamented the disease of geography that left most Americans "untouched, virginal, prenatal, while every other considerable population on earth comes of age." Most of America, Agee said, "will emerge from the war almost as if it had never taken place; and not all the lip-service in the world about internationalism will make that different." And because neither the government nor the moviemakers trusted the people, audiences did not even get an honest second-hand picture of the war. The best movies—Army orientation films including Capra's *The Battle of Britain* and *The Battle of Russia*—were rarely shown to civilians whom their tough language and tough images might make uncomfortable. Agee compared *The Battle of Russia* with Goldwyn's *The North Star,* the fictional story of a Russian village and a movie he described as sugared with "romantic juice and the annihilation of any possible reality pouring from every gland."

In praising the bleak and realistic documentaries being made at the same time in England, Agee described them as being totally free of salesmanship. One thing that the OWI and Hollywood had in common was a conviction that the war had to be sold. The other government censors of Hollywood—the Army, Navy, Air Force, and Marines—were also selling sugarcoated reality. All American soldiers, sailors, seabees, and tail gunners were brave; all officers were competent; sergeants, no matter how gruff, were motivated solely by the need to make their charges men enough to survive. And all servicemen, no matter how frightened at the thought of their first battle, rose to the occasion. Of course, some died, but they died cleanly and heroically for democracy.

If Hollywood had not seen its job as keeping up civilian morale (and full theaters) by turning away from unpleasant subjects, films would have been more realistic, but, in the heat of battle, they still would have lacked complexity. It was only after the war that novels like *Catch 22, The Naked and the Dead,* and *From Here to Eternity,* and the movies made from them, began to ask questions about the war. But leaving dialogue and consciously intended ideas aside, movies have always been full of endless unarticulated messages, many of them powerfully expressed through images. And some of the implicit messages in Hollywood's war films probably had more effect than the strident, explicit, intended messages.

In *Sahara,* Bogart's grim-faced competence showed that an enlisted man was capable of being in charge. And men agonized by thirst trusted a black man with the difficult, cramped work of gathering the last drops of water that trickle from the stones of a dry well. At a time when Lena Horne says she was never allowed to touch a white person in a movie because scenes of black performers were snipped out of musicals before the films were sent to states in the south, audiences watched Rex Ingram catch the water in his hands, pour it into cups from which white men would drink, lick his moist palms and cup his hands to catch the next drops.

Using the OWI manual as a guide, Warner Bros. laboriously justified *Casablanca* as demonstrating enemy tactics by dramatizing Nazi control of French North Africa and as promoting international understanding by showing audiences characters of different nationalities: Victor Lazslo (Czechoslovakian), Annina and Jan Brandel (Bulgarian), Rick's bartender (Russian), Mr. and Mrs. Leuchtag (German), resistance fighter Berger and Ilsa Lund (Norwegian), a number of "charming and impetuous" French characters "who have a deep sense of loyalty to their homeland," and several Moroccans who "appear in the background in numerous scenes."

Because many of the roles were stock melodrama characters, audiences in 1942 probably didn't see *Casablanca* as promoting international understanding. But they probably did take from the movie an uneasy feeling about Vichy France, which was certainly not a message that the government wanted to convey at a time when America was cozying up to Vichy. We understand that message, but it is unimportant to us. We simply enjoy the joke when Claude Rains drops his bottle of Vichy water into the wastebasket before he strolls off with Humphrey Bogart. The times dictate the messages to which we pay attention. Today, the regenerating effects of sacrifice are still in the movie and still potent. But the clearest political metaphor we find in the movie was just a joke to audiences in 1942.

"I'm shocked! Shocked to find that gambling is going on here!" Claude Rains says as he pockets his winnings. The eyes we see through in the more cynical and alienated 1990s latch on to Captain Renault's words. In nearly one hundred references in 1990 and 1991, from the *New Republic, Newsday,* the Washington *Post,* and

Daily Variety to the business and sports pages of the Los Angeles *Times* and the Op-Ed columnists of the *New York Times,* the character of Captain Renault has become a metaphor for pervasive hypocrisy.

In magazines and newspapers, his words have been applied to the Japanese stock market scandal, the woman who accused William Kennedy Smith of rape, Saddam Hussein, Clark Clifford's innocence of BCCI's secret ownership of his bank, college athletic directors' indignation over Notre Dame's contract to televise its football games, Hollywood's attempt to torpedo a cable reregulation bill, Nobel Prize–winner Dr. David Baltimore's refusal to accept blame over a faked scientific paper, and to the surprise of Camel cigarettes that Old Joe, its cartoon camel, appeals to children.

No movie can last if it cannot find new things to say to new generations. Captain Renault—the one gray character in a black and white time—would have been amused.

Jack Warner and his trophies, including the Oscar for Best Picture for Casablanca.

18

The Academy Awards

There was no Rick's Café Americain in the real Casablanca, but the city was full of American soldiers when Humphrey Bogart reached North Africa in December 1943. By the end of 1943, the world was beginning to be tamed, and Hollywood stars followed in the wake of the tanks. The Hollywood Victory Committee sent fifty-six actors overseas in 1943 compared to eleven the year before. In December, Bogart went to Morocco and Algiers, Ingrid Bergman to Army bases and hospitals in Alaska.

Bogart and Bergman didn't see each other after *Casablanca* was finished, but their careers and their lives remained parallel. Both had become major stars because of *Casablanca*. Both were about to be nominated for Academy Awards for the first time. And both of their marriages were in trouble.

Bergman would stay married to Petter Lindstrom until Roberto Rossellini came calling five years later, but she already felt strangled by the marriage. She worked as much as possible. The minute she finished a movie, she went off to sell war bonds in Indianapolis or Pittsburgh. In mid-December, as soon as *Gaslight* was completed, Bergman flew to Alaska. The Military Intelligence Division of the War Department noted that she belonged to the Screen Actors

Guild, an organization that was "said to have been identified as a Communist Party group in the Hollywood Movie Colony," but let her go anyway.

Mayo was no Petter Lindstrom. If Bogart wanted to go to North Africa, Mayo would be at his side to keep all other women away. The portrait of Mayo painted in biographies of Bogart is of a jealous alcoholic, a tough woman who turned mean as her career faded and his grew. Afterward Bogart told his next wife, Lauren Bacall, that getting drunk was the only way he could live with Mayo. Many evenings at the house he had nicknamed Sluggy Hollow ended with Mayo's throwing dishes or lamps, and once she stabbed him in the back with a kitchen knife. On the overseas tour, there was some sort of drunken unpleasantness after they reached Italy, and the two of them were shipped back to the United States.

Halfway back to Hollywood, in Drawing Room E on the Santa Fe Chief out of Chicago, Bogart received a telegram from the studio. Could he stop by Warner Bros. before he went home? Director Howard Hawks needed to talk about the new movie he and Bogart were to start in two weeks. On the first day of that new movie, *To Have and Have Not,* Mayo would come to the set to examine her husband's costar. Whether she understood that gawky nineteen-year-old Lauren Bacall would be her nemesis is not recorded. There are never many records of what are perceived as lesser lives.

"Mayo had fought off all the phantom competition like a tigress," Bogart's friend, Nathaniel Benchley, wrote in his memoir of the actor. "Now that the real thing had arrived it was almost as though she sensed the futility of trying to fight any longer." After Bogart married Bacall, Mayo would make drunken late-night telephone calls to one of his friends, asking the woman to have Bogart call her. He never did. One night she said she was dying and wanted to speak to Bogart for the last time. He didn't return that call either, and the next day she was dead.

By the time Bogart and Mayo returned from Italy in February 1944, he had been nominated for best actor and had been named a top box-office star for the first time, No. 7 for 1943 on the Quigley poll of theater owners. Bogart would stay on the list through 1949 but, almost always, in sixth or seventh place, while the decade was dominated by Bing Crosby, Abbott and Costello, and Bob Hope.

In December 1943, as Bogart and Bergman were preparing to go overseas, Jack Warner sent a telegram to his publicity chief Charles

*Bogart and Mayo arriving
at the 1943 Academy
Awards.*

Einfeld: "Start propaganda now for Academy Awards." Warner told Einfeld to concentrate his publicity on Mike Curtiz for best director and *Watch on the Rhine* for best picture.

The 1943 Academy Awards were given out on March 2, 1944, two days after Bogart started work in *To Have and Have Not*. Just after Pearl Harbor, Bette Davis, the first woman president of the Academy of Motion Picture Arts and Sciences, had suggested that, because of the war, the Academy should cancel its usual awards dinner and, instead, hold the Oscar ceremony at a theater to raise money for British War Relief. "You would have thought that I had roasted a sacred cow," Davis said of the Academy's response.* But two years of war had changed attitudes. By March 1944, 6,496 of the industry's 30,000 employees were in the armed services, and the Academy ceremony, shorn of its prewar glamour, was held at Grauman's Chinese Theater with the public allowed to pay their way in for $10 apiece. "All the colorfulness of previous Academy Awards that took place in hotels was gone," *Variety* complained the next day.

---

*Davis, who had been elected president in October 1941, resigned in December over the issue. It wasn't until July 1979 that the Academy would have its second woman president, screenwriter Fay Kanin.

Bogart had been nominated for *Casablanca,* Bergman for *For Whom the Bell Tolls.* And a movie Bergman had made for the Office of War Information, *Swedes in America,* had been nominated as a documentary short. Both *The Song of Bernadette* and *For Whom the Bell Tolls* had a chance of sweeping the awards, predicted *Variety,* although it was most likely that *Bernadette* would win best picture, actress, and screenplay. Paramount's *Bell* and 20th Century–Fox's *Bernadette* were perfectly positioned to win. *Casablanca* had departed from theaters almost a year earlier. Then, as now, movies released in the spring were often barely remembered by the time the awards came around. *The Song of Bernadette,* which had twelve nominations, and *For Whom the Bell Tolls,* which had nine, had been released late in the year, and *Bernadette* was still playing on dozens of screens. In addition, the story of a peasant girl who sees visions of the Virgin Mary was the kind of spiritual uplift that the Academy favored. (The story of a Catholic priest, *Going My Way,* would win as best picture the next year.) Fox signaled the importance of its movie with a four-page trade-paper ad, "The Story of a Masterpiece," printed on special glossy paper and featuring a portrait of Jennifer Jones as Bernadette painted by Norman Rockwell.

Variety, usually an accurate handicapper, assigned the Oscar for best actor to Paul Lukas for *Watch on the Rhine* but gave Bergman a chance of upsetting Jennifer Jones. After Bergman returned from Alaska, the Lindstroms had finally moved to Hollywood, and Petter had begun a residence in neurosurgery at Los Angeles County General Hospital. Living together as an ordinary married couple in the same house in the same city for almost the first time in their marriage increased the strain, and Bergman ran away, as always, into her work. Pia would be eleven when her mother left permanently, but she wrote of the earlier years that her mother "was so busy working that we had only minutes together from day to day."

At night, Bergman was often at the Hollywood Canteen, handing out sandwiches and cigarettes to some of the 1,580,000 young soldiers and sailors who drifted through that recreation center during its first two years. The Hollywood Canteen had been founded by Bette Davis and another liberal Warner Bros. star, John Garfield, and was sponsored by forty-two craft guilds, including both the white musicians union Local 47 and the Negro musicians Local 767. Local 767 had gotten a guarantee from the other guilds that there would be no discrimination. Negro hostesses were not required to dance with white boys nor white hostesses with Negro soldiers, but they must be polite when they turned down requests. When some of the white hostesses chose to dance with Negroes and some of the white soldiers to dance with black girls, there was an attempt by society women on the board to ban mixed dancing. It failed when Davis and Garfield threatened to resign from the board and to withdraw the support of the Screen Actors Guild. A number of Hollywood stars worked one or two nights a week at the Canteen. When Bette Davis put a thank-you ad in *Variety* just before she was reelected president for a third year, Bergman was one of the seventy-five celebrity regulars whom she thanked.

At the studio Bergman was warm and maternal. "Everyone had morning coffee in Ingrid's dressing room before they went to their various jobs on the lot, and she presided," says Dorothy Jeakins, whose costumes for *Joan of Arc* won the first Oscar ever given for costume design. "I was just getting started. I was a nobody, and she accepted me much more than other actresses did. We wore each other's clothes." When Bergman was nominated for *Joan of Arc,* she asked Jeakins to design her gown for the ceremony. "I brought a fitter with me to her house," Jeakins says. "Her daughter peeked in to see her mother, just peeked in. Ingrid said, 'Go away!' She said it in a peremptory way. There was something aloof and very cold about her."

At the age of twenty-six, Pia described the confusions of her childhood and her place on the sideline. " 'That's Ingrid Bergman's daughter,' is the way I was inevitably introduced," she wrote. And: "In the middle of all this stood Mamma, an island in a dark sea. I was separated from her—and from the world. Children—and I was no exception—don't like or want to be different. I ached to be 'normal,' like everyone else."

The third of *Casablanca*'s actors to be nominated for an Oscar was also in Hollywood during the early months of 1944. Claude Rains had inherited the title role in *Mr. Skeffington* when Paul Henreid refused the part. After the success of *Casablanca* and *Now, Voyager,* said Henreid, "I contended it would destroy my career if suddenly I would be the horned husband of Bette Davis."

Jack Warner had rewarded Julius and Philip Epstein for their script of *Casablanca* by making them producers. The promotion gave them the right to eat in the executives' dining room, which, says Julie, "was the equal of any French restaurant in Paris." The Epsteins' first assignment was to produce their screenplay for *Mr.*

Skeffington. From the Epsteins' first script on, the movie ran into trouble with the OWI. The Bureau of Motion Pictures characterized the scripts as "gravely detrimental to the War Information Program." Mr. Skeffington was a Jewish Wall Street broker. The problems began with the fact that, because of his religion, Mr. Skeffington was discriminated against by the society friends of Bette Davis, his vain and unfaithful wife:

> The Jewish question is presented in such a way as to give credence to the Nazi contention that the discrimination for which Americans condemn the fascists, is an integral part of American democracy. Furthermore, the characterization of Skeffington, a Jew, as the richest and most powerful man in Wall Street, lends colour to the Nazi propaganda that Jews control the money interests in all countries. Americans and the values of the American way are misrepresented. The characterization of them as chiefly concerned with money is a further confirmation of Nazi world propaganda about America. And the only Congressman in the story is shown to be completely unfit for his job.

Whether audiences would have confused the social barriers against Jews in America with the confiscation of property and institutionalized murder of Jews in Germany was never tested. For years, the Warner brothers had been braver than the other moguls in touching on Jewish subjects, even if they touched them gingerly. *Disraeli* and *Dr. Ehrlich's Magic Bullet* had Jewish heroes. *The Life of Emile Zola,* which had won Warner Bros. its single Academy Award for best picture in the Academy's fifteen years of presenting awards, was the story of Alfred Dreyfus, a Jewish French Army captain, who was falsely accused of treason to cover up the fact that a non-Jewish officer had committed the crime. However, the word "Jew" was never spoken in *The Life of Emile Zola,* and the Jewish star had had to change his name from Muni Weisenfreund to Paul Muni before he entered the movies, while the star of *Dr. Ehrlich's Magic Bullet* had had to change his name from Emmanuel Goldenberg to Edward G. Robinson.

The OWI suggested that Warner Bros. simply take out anything that implied Mr. Skeffington was Jewish. Warners changed the emphasis of the story enough to win the OWI's approval, but Claude Rains still played a dignified and sympathetic Jew. It was not the first time. Rains had played Haym Salomon, a Jew who lent money to the American Revolution, in a pet Harry Warner project, *Sons of Liberty.* The short subject was made in the prewar years when Hitler was at the height of his power, and Rains said that three actors had refused the role because they were Jewish. He said that since he wasn't Jewish he had no problem accepting the part.

When Rains signed a two-year contract with Warner Bros. after *Casablanca* was released, one of the terms he insisted on was that the studio pay for one first-class round-trip train journey from Stock Grange, his farm in Pennsylvania, to Hollywood each year. As soon as *Mr. Skeffington* was finished, Rains collected a $187.22 check from the studio and boarded the train. He was always jubilant as the train took him home to his soybeans, his Jersey cows, his hogs, and the house whose new wing was built during the War of 1812. The old part was built when American troops were wintering in Valley Forge, and his daughter, Jessica Rains, remembers a two-year search for iron door latches to fit 130-year-old doors. When the age difference between Rains and his wife, Frances, became too strong and the marriage ended in divorce and he sold Stock Grange, Rains grieved as much for the farm as for the marriage. He had planted 25,000 pines, blue spruce, and sycamores, a forest of sycamores. The trees were what he hated parting with the most.

Rains enjoyed acting in movies, but he hated watching himself on the screen, says Frances Rains Feder. Reluctant to be interviewed, she uses her daughter as an intermediary. Rains never saw *Casablanca,* she says, not even when he was nominated for best supporting actor.

On Thursday, March 2, Rains had to wait until nearly the end of the ceremony to learn that his Captain Renault had lost the Oscar to Charles Coburn's performance in *The More the Merrier.* Nominated four times, Rains would lose four times. The next year, his Mr. Skeffington had the bad luck to be matched against Barry Fitzgerald's aging priest in the sweep for *Going My Way,* and two years later his brilliant performance as Ingrid Bergman's husband in *Notorious* had the misfortune of being matched against an armless veteran, nonactor Harold Russell, in *The Best Years of Our Lives.* Then, as today, winning Oscars is an amalgam of luck, timing, benediction for a long career, or reward for a performance that was overlooked a year earlier. It is not that excellence doesn't count, just that a great performance is rarely enough.

The crowded theater smelled of damp fur. It had been raining for ten days, much of the San Fernando Valley was flooded, and the mink coats and jackets that fashion required were soaked because the Academy, which had always held its awards dinners at hotels, hadn't realized that the theater wouldn't provide parking. *Casablanca* had been nominated for eight awards, and, rather quickly, Max Steiner's score lost to *The Song of Bernadette,* Arthur Edeson's cinematography lost to *The Song of Bernadette,* and Owen Marks's film editing lost to *Air Force.* Then came the writing awards. *Variety* had picked *The Song of Bernadette,* but *Casablanca* won. Howard Koch stood alone on the stage of Grauman's Chinese Theater, scarecrow tall and thin and hunched over to talk into a microphone that was much too low for him. The Epsteins, who were in New York writing a play, didn't find out that they had won for nearly twenty-four hours. Says Julie, "One of the wire services made a mistake and said *The Song of Bernadette* had won. It had won everything else." Julie and Phil immediately sent George Seaton a telegram congratulating him.

Then it was Mike Curtiz's turn. According to Wallis, Curtiz

Howard Koch getting his Oscar for Best Screenplay.

accepted his award by saying that he had been always a bridesmaid and never a mother. But neither the *Hollywood Reporter* nor *Variety* reported any such Curtizism. Curtiz had been nominated for *Angels With Dirty Faces* in 1938 and for *Yankee Doodle Dandy,* the movie that would always remain his favorite, in 1942. Genuinely surprised and more subdued than usual, Curtiz said that he had prepared speeches twice before but hadn't bothered to prepare a speech this time.

The award for best picture came next. Today that is the prime Oscar—the one that usually adds $10 million to a movie's ticket sales—and it is given out last. In the 1940s, the four acting awards provided the climax of the ceremony. Humphrey Bogart, who came with Mayo, lost to Paul Lukas, as expected. Mayo was wearing a full-length mink coat. Ingrid Bergman, who was escorted by the owner of her contract, David O. Selznick, wore Persian lamb.

In her autobiography, Bergman said that Selznick had been flabbergasted when he discovered that she didn't own a fur coat. He immediately had his assistant take her shopping for a mink—although she was required to pay for the coat herself. "The fact that

Mike Curtiz, Best Director.

the climate makes a mink coat completely unnecessary has nothing to do with it," she wrote. "When you came to a party, it was the fashion to throw your coat into the ladies' bedroom. The bed was piled high with mink; it groaned under mink coats." When Bergman went to her next party and threw her mink on the bed, she realized that it wasn't as nice as the other coats, since she had been too cheap to buy a really expensive coat. So she sold the coat. "David was very sad again because he thought that I hadn't attained the real status of a movie star in America," Bergman wrote. "The following Christmas he kindly gave me a Persian lamb fur coat which I liked much better, so at least I owned a fur coat and didn't disgrace him." Bergman lost the Oscar to Selznick's other star, Jennifer Jones, and was a good enough actress to feign joy at Jones's victory.

It was *Casablanca*'s award for best picture that severed the last bonds between Jack Warner and Hal Wallis. When the name of the movie was announced, both Warner and Wallis stood up. In his autobiography, Hal Wallis wrote, "I started up the aisle to receive my award. To my astonishment, Jack Warner leapt to his feet, ran to the stage, and received it ahead of me. Almost forty years later, I still haven't recovered from the shock."

That Jack Warner ran to the stage and snatched the Oscar is

Ingrid Bergman and David O. Selznick arriving at the ceremony. She is wearing the Persian lamb coat he gave his star to save himself from embarrassment.

true. That he usurped the award is not so obvious. The Academy had been formed in 1927 by the major studios—with Louis B. Mayer as chief architect—as a company union to forestall real unions. The actors, writers, and directors got their unions anyway, and by 1944 the Academy had turned into a respectable honorary organization. Yet the rules, which changed every year, almost always favored the studio against the individual. Until 1938, for example, the award for scoring a movie went to the music department, not to the composer. Since Max Steiner headed the RKO music department in 1935, he was able to keep his Oscar for the score of *The Informer*. Erich Korngold had no such luck when his score of *Anthony Adverse* won the next year. The award for sound recording went to the studio until 1969.

There were no rules about the award for best picture, but a studio head generally picked up the Oscar, a practice that wouldn't change until 1948. Throughout the thirties, Harry Cohn, L. B. Mayer, and, in 1937, Jack Warner had stood triumphantly at the front of the banquet hall. When the award was claimed by a movie's producer, it was by David O. Selznick, Irving Thalberg, and Darryl F. Zanuck, who also ran their studios.

Once Warner had the Oscar for *Casablanca* in his hands, there was nothing Wallis could do except go back to his seat and listen to Warner joke with Jack Benny, master of ceremonies for the evening. Almost as an afterthought, according to one reporter, Warner thanked Wallis and the movie's stars, although he couldn't quite remember who all of them were.

When Warner stepped down, Wallis had his moment of glory. For the second time, Wallis was given the Thalberg Award, "for the most consistent high quality of production by an individual producer, based on pictures he has personally produced during the preceding year." Today, the Thalberg Award is given for a body of work and is announced in advance. In 1944 it was a surprise, although there were never more than three or four producers in the running for it.

The cool metal of the Thalberg Award didn't cool Wallis's anger. Warner Bros. had won eight awards. Seven of them went to Wallis movies: original screenplay to *Princess O'Rourke,* film editing to *Air Force,* scoring of a musical to *This Is the Army,* best actor to Paul Lukas for *Watch on the Rhine,* and the three major awards to *Casablanca.* The eighth Warner Bros. award, the Thalberg, went to

Wallis himself. Every Wallis movie that was released in 1943 had won at least one award, and Wallis had, single-handedly, tied 20th Century–Fox for first place. But Jack Warner had taken the credit.

Before the night was over, Wallis sent his secretary to Warner's secretary, Bill Schaefer, to ask for the Oscar. The studio's answer was to refuse even to allow Wallis to be photographed with the statue. In defiance of studio rules, Wallis had a private press agent, and on Saturday morning Jack Warner woke to the following headline in the Los Angeles *Times:*

WARNER-WALLIS "RIVALRY"
INTRIGUES AT FILM FETE

The column written by Edwin Schallert, the paper's drama and film critic, began:

Question is being vigorously raised in Hollywood whether J. L. Warner or Hal B. Wallis should have accepted the award tendered for "Casablanca" as the outstanding production at the big Academy shindig.

Last year it was Sidney Franklin, the actual producer of "Mrs. Miniver," who formally took the honors. Sometimes the headman of a studio does it.

Wallis had lit a match. Within an hour, the studio publicity department was smothering the flame. For more than ten years, Charlie Einfeld had been an expert at extinguishing fires. In 1935, when *Black Fury,* one of the studio's movies of social outrage, was threatened by local censorship in Chicago, Einfeld defused the situation by having the leader of the mine workers union, John L. Lewis, complain that the movie was tame compared to the real fights between miners and police and by flying the story's author, a respected Pennsylvania judge, into Chicago for ballast.

Einfeld immediately dictated a telegram for Walter Wanger, the Academy president, to send to Schallert, asking for a retraction. Then Einfeld and his lieutenant, Alex Evelove, drafted a wire for Wallis to send to the columnist. Wallis balked. After telling Evelove that he had not planted the story with Schallert, Wallis insisted that any telegram should be sent by Warner. He told Evelove, "Today's newspaper is tomorrow's toilet paper. The less said the better. If anyone makes a statement it should be JL." But he couldn't help adding, "JL wasn't the executive producer of that picture. I was."

Although Wallis insisted that Sidney Franklin had taken home the statue for *Mrs. Miniver* (and he had probably fed that misinformation to the *Times*), he was wrong. L. B. Mayer had accepted the Oscar. In the end, Wallis gave in and sent the telegram that Einfeld and Evelove had written:

> I have been with Warner Bros. for twenty years and during this time it has been customary here as elsewhere for the studio head to accept the Academy Award for the best production. Naturally I was glad to see Jack Warner accept the award this year for "Casablanca," as he did for "The Life of Emile Zola." I am happy also to have contributed my bit toward the making of that picture. Your comment in your column this morning on rivalry at Warner Bros. is totally unjustified. I would be grateful if you would correct the misleading impression created by it, as well as the impression that we had advance information on the awards.

In his Monday column, Schallert printed Wanger's clarification that "the statuette for outstanding production is always accepted by the head of the studio."

The breach between Wallis and Warner was now irrevocable. One month later, on April 4, Warner Bros. canceled Wallis's contract on a technicality. Wallis was obligated to supply Warners with four movies a year. Although he had made six movies during the first year of his contract, Wallis had only completed two films during the second.

Warner had his studio back, but his rage was too intense for even a pretense of graciousness. Warner Bros. sent out a press release that accused Wallis of negotiating with other studios—which was undoubtedly true—and that credited much of his success to the fact that he had been given the "choicest assignments, including numerous best sellers and Broadway hits." In the studio's portrait of Wallis's career:

> Wallis' departure from Warner Bros. ends an association begun 21 years ago when Jack L. Warner, Vice-President in charge of production, adopted as a protege an ambitious young theatre usher and gave him his first film studio job. Wallis came to Warner Bros. at a salary of $18.00 per week and was last reported as among the

ten top earners in the motion picture industry. His rise from usher to press agent to producer, under Jack Warner's guidance, is one of the real success stories of Hollywood.

Then the studio charged him $7,000 for the projection equipment it had installed in his home years earlier.

Wallis never won another Academy Award for best picture. Warner Bros. didn't win again for twenty-one years. By the time *My Fair Lady* won in 1964, Harry Cohn and L. B. Mayer were dead, the studios were façades, and producers had been taking home the gold statuette for nearly two decades. As it happened, *My Fair Lady* had been personally produced by Jack L. Warner. When Warner claimed his Oscar, he had no need to rush past Wallis. He walked slowly, while Wallis, whose *Becket* had just lost to *My Fair Lady*, stayed in his seat.

19

As Time Went By

—————

The end of studio power came inevitably but slowly. *Casablanca*'s assistant director Lee Katz didn't go back to Warner Bros. at all after the war, even though Mike Curtiz asked him to be the No. 2 man in his film unit. It was already a new era, and Katz became one of the first journeymen production managers, moving from studio to studio and ending up in Europe in 1956, when Hollywood tried to defeat television by aiming its cameras at the foreign landscapes that television couldn't reach. The war had delayed the introduction of television and given the movie studios the gift of half a dozen extra boom years. The studio system could probably have survived and incorporated television, despite local rebellions by leading stars and directors. But, in 1948, the Supreme Court ended the practice of block booking of films and demanded that the studios separate themselves from their theaters. With the once docile stars and directors setting up their own production companies, with television getting more sophisticated each year, and with crushing overhead for their huge, underused lots, the studios

Jack Warner getting the Medal of Merit from General Hap Arnold.

gradually lost most of their function as creators. When Lee Katz came back to Hollywood in 1966, it was as the head of physical production at United Artists, a company without a studio that acted as a sales agent for producers.

During his dozen years abroad Katz worked with Ingrid Bergman once more, on *Aimez-vous Brahms?* She was married to her third husband, Lars Schmidt, by then. "Everyone seems to think, 'What a lucky fellow he is to have worked on *Casablanca*,' " says Katz. "But I certainly never quite appreciated it. I think everybody thought it was a good picture. Nobody thought it was a memorable picture."

There was no magic in *Casablanca* for any of the craftsmen. After a while there was no magic in the movie industry either. When Captain Francis Scheid came back from the war, he returned to his job in the Warner sound department. "In 1972, I took my vacation and told them, 'I'm not coming back,' " says Scheid. "They had brought in guys with long hair and dirty fingernails, all smoking pot. They asked if I was coming back for the cake and the gold watch. I said, 'To hell with the watch.' "

That was five years after Jack Warner sold his Warner Bros. stock to Seven Arts for $32 million, and twenty-five years after the exultant moment when Warner's identification with Warner Bros. and with the heroes of his movies was complete. On March 14, 1947, Warner was awarded the Medal of Merit for his services to the War Department between September 1939 and September 1945. Fewer than two hundred Americans had won the medal since it was created by George Washington in 1782, and Warner was the first from the movie industry. The medal was presented by General Arnold at March Field, where Lieutenant James Stewart had flown in to make *Winning Your Wings;* and the ceremony ended with a flight of P-80s, the Army Air Force's newest planes. The citation said that, in addition to producing over a hundred training and recruitment films, Warner Bros., with a complete disregard of personal gain, had contributed vast sums of money and enabled the armed forces to save vast sums of money.

By the time he sold his studio in 1967, Warner was a dinosaur. All of the founders—except those who died too early—turned into dinosaurs, lumbering behind a culture that had moved beyond them. Warner Bros. became Seven Arts which became Kinney, a parking-lot and funeral-home conglomerate that changed its name to Warner Communications. The Warner Bros. studio in Burbank became The Burbank Studios; to save money the Warner sound-stages and projection rooms were shared with Columbia Pictures; and TBS was written on the water tower.

When Warner died in 1978, at the age of eighty-six after a series of strokes, he had outlived all the other moguls. In 1990, his name went back on the water tower. Warner Bros., now part of Time Warner, Inc., threw a $4.5 million party to celebrate the reclaiming of its studio from Columbia, which had been sold to Sony and had moved to the old M-G-M studios in Culver City. The dinner for Steven Spielberg, Clint Eastwood, Steve Martin, Ruby Keeler, Ronald Reagan, and 995 others took place on Stage 18, which was transformed into Rick's Café Americain. The waiters wore red fezzes, and "As Time Goes By" was played twice, by Hank Mancini and by Quincy Jones.

Time does go by, relentlessly and without much concern for fairness. The writers had rejected the standard Hollywood happy ending, and their own lives had bittersweet endings too. Even though Jack Warner made Julius and Philip Epstein producers after *Casablanca,* the twins moved to Paramount a few years later. Writers had to struggle the hardest for power—in the old Hollywood and the new—but the twins signed a contract to write, produce, and direct. In 1951, when they were exploring locations for *Forever Female,* Phil got a bad case of poison oak. Julie, tramping through a different part of the woods, escaped. Phil was given a new treatment, liquid cortisone. "Massive doses, bottles, of cortisone to drink," says his widow, Lilian Gelsey. It is family belief that the cortisone somehow triggered a raging cancer. Phil died in February 1952, a few weeks after his cancer was diagnosed.

"My brother and I . . ." says Julie today. He starts his sentences with "We," shaping his language to keep his brother alive. When the Boston Public Library wanted to establish a Julius J. Epstein award a few years ago, Julie insisted that it be called the Philip G. and Julius J. Epstein Screenwriting Award. "One of us would start a line of dialogue, and the other would finish it," Julie says. "From the beginning." To comfort himself, Julie tells all the old stories, laughing at the tricks his brother played fifty years ago. But his voice goes dead with reserve when Phil's death is mentioned. Phil was forty-two when he died. Forty years later, Julie's pain has not gone away. Julie taught himself to write alone and won Academy Award nominations for *Pete 'n' Tillie* in 1972 and *Reuben, Reuben* in 1983. Those scripts, and a dozen more, are Julius J. Epstein screenplays, but Philip G. Epstein is written, invisibly, in the margins.

Howard Koch came back from exile eventually, but not to Hollywood. Koch had lost more than a decade, and he came back to upstate New York, where he had been raised. "In the Roosevelt years, we really thought we could change the world," he says. "Would you make a sacrifice for Bush? You live your own life today, and you just hope the politics don't get too bad. You write letters to the *Times,* and they only print about one in six, and you try to be part of the human values that *Casablanca* stood for." During the Reagan years, Koch wrote letters to *The New York Times* protesting American aid to El Salvador; and he wrote a play, *The Trial of Richard Nixon,* which took place in the mind of the former president between his resignation and his pardon by President Gerald Ford. Recently, Koch has put his energy into helping the town of Woodstock save a cornfield from the developers. "That cornfield has a superb view of the Catskill Overlook Mountain, which is our mountain," says Koch.

In the aftermath of *Casablanca,* Hollywood sent for Murray Burnett and Joan Alison. As soon as the picture was released, they were hired by Paramount at $1,000 a week apiece. "More money than I had ever dreamed of," says Burnett, "and sitting in the commissary among the stars lived up to my romantic dreams." But Hollywood wanted things of which Burnett and Alison were incapable. They were asked to write a comedy for Bob Hope. "I said, 'Do you know who we are? We want a melodrama,'" says Burnett. "My agent told me to work on the story for a couple of months and then tell them we couldn't do it. It was probably good advice, but I didn't take it." Said Alison in 1990, "Remember we were not screenwriters. They wanted us to go through all their old scripts that they wanted redone. I'm not a plagiarizer. I couldn't work on anybody else's idea."

It was Hollywood that split them up. "Murray hated Hollywood," said Alison. "I stayed on for a while." Burnett wrote more plays, and one even reached Broadway for a few weeks.* Eventually, he found his niche in radio, creating *Café Istanbul* for Marlene

---

* *Hickory Stick* by Frederick Stephani and Murray Burnett opened on May 8, 1944, at the Mansfield Theater. According to Burnett, Stephani, who also attempted to write a *Casablanca* sequel, latched on to him in Hollywood and offered to help rewrite his play.

Dietrich—"She was a female Rick, no question," says Burnett—and writing, directing, and producing *True Detective Mysteries* for ten years. Burnett lost his suit to get back the rights to his characters, but time and the 1976 copyright act were on his side. Burnett and Alison had copyrighted *Everybody Comes to Rick's* in 1941 and renewed their copyright in 1969. In 1987, they informed Warner Bros. that they would be terminating their agreement when the copyright came up for its last renewal in 1997. In order to protect *Casablanca*'s characters from whatever purposes Burnett might put them to, Warner Bros. gave Burnett and Alison $100,000 apiece and gave Burnett what he had always wanted, the right to have *Everybody Comes to Rick's* produced. The play was presented in London in April 1991. "I advise anyone feeling nostalgic about *Casablanca* simply to rent the movie from their nearest video library," said the *Daily Telegraph. Everybody Comes to Rick's* could never be judged on its own. Most of the reviews were bad, and the play closed in less than a month.

Hal Wallis outlived Jack Warner. And as power moved from studios to independent producers and directors, he thrived, shaping movie careers for Burt Lancaster and Elvis Presley in the 1950s. He would often say that he made a series of Dean Martin and Jerry Lewis movies to finance his prestige pictures, but those movies—*The Rose Tattoo, Come Back, Little Sheba,* and *Becket*—were financial successes, too. He married a young actress, Martha Hyer, collected art, and said farewell to the movie business in 1975 with *Rooster Cogburn,* leaving Los Angeles for the desert, where the skies were still blue. Wallis lived long enough to be cherished as an artifact from the golden age and to be decorated with the order of Commander of the British Empire, an honorary Ph.D. from Northwestern University, and retrospectives of his work in New York, London, and Paris. He always asked the festivals to show *Casablanca,* and he always said, "A producer, to be worthy of the name, must be a creator."

Harold Brent Wallis died in his sleep in 1986 at the age of eighty-eight. At a gala screening of *Casablanca* at a Wallis retrospective in Palm Springs near the end of his life, he turned to his wife and said, "If only we had a Michael Curtiz today." Those were words he had said often in his later years. "If only we had a Michael Curtiz today."

Curtiz had spoken his own cynical epitaph over and over. "It doesn't exist friendship here," he would say. "You make fifty good pictures. Den two bad vuns under you go down de river." Or "The most cruelest city in the world. You are only appreciated so far as you carry the dough into the box office. They throw you into gutter next day." The era of the director was beginning, but Curtiz had no skills in shaping the entirety of a picture, and he was unlucky enough to die before there were film courses at every university and the omnipresent seminars and retrospectives that would keep elder statesman Hal Wallis busy during his ninth decade. Curtiz had been too prolific, and his best work had been done years before his death. He was pidgeonholed as a Hollywood hack, the epitome of a studio director.

There are those who say that Curtiz mellowed as he grew older. Not Samuel Goldwyn, Jr., who produced two of the last five movies Curtiz directed, *The Proud Rebel* (1958) and *The Adventures of Huckleberry Finn* (1960). "He couldn't bear to be out of work," says Goldwyn. "Work was everything. When he left on Saturday, he was waiting to come back to work on Monday. Olivia de Havilland called me up angrily in the middle of the night when we were working on *The Proud Rebel*. She said, 'He was a son of a bitch when I was seventeen, and he's still a son of a bitch.' "

Claude Rains was one of Curtiz's favorite actors. He was one of everybody's favorite actors, but he was too unclassifiable and too short to be a movie star. "What are you going to do about this business of being a midget?" Alfred Hitchcock asked Rains when he cast him in *Notorious*. "You're going to need elevated shoes." Rains's pride was hurt, but he bought the shoes. The older he got, the more frightened Rains became "of the possibility of never working again," says his daughter. "When we were on the farm, he used to wait for the phone to ring."

When, in 1951 at the age of sixty-two, he returned to the stage after seventeen years of making Hollywood movies, Rains could hardly have imagined the result. After his first performance as the Communist leader who accepts martyrdom for the good of the cause in *Darkness at Noon,* he stood alone on the stage weeping. "They wouldn't let me go," he reminisced for that never written autobiography. "They kept me on the stage, bowing and bowing. I was weeping because I didn't expect it. I didn't know the value of the performance. God almighty, it was one of the most wonderful nights any actor ever had in the theater." Rains won reviews he would have been embarrassed to write for himself and took home all of Broadway's major acting awards.

He designed his own gravestone ten years later after an operation that temporarily repaired his damaged liver:

> CLAUDE RAINS
> 1889–1967
> All things once
> Are things forever.
> Soul, once living,
> Lives forever.

If Claude Rains triumphed in his later years, Paul Henreid faded away. Henreid was a good man and a good actor, but things never worked out quite right. During the war, he was Hollywood's heroic European, leader of the resistance in one movie after another. Yet, in a way, he fell victim to the same fate as the minor refugee actors in *Casablanca.* Henreid was part of Hollywood's movie version of the evils of fascism, an account that could have been stamped "Made in Europe." In addition to being stocked with émigré actors, dozens of movies about the Nazis were written and directed by immigrants and émigrés including Bertolt Brecht and Fritz Lang (*Hangmen Also Die*), Billy Wilder (*Five Graves to Cairo*), Jean Renoir (*This Land Is Mine*), Otto Preminger (*Margin for Error*), Michael Curtiz (*Casablanca, Mission to Moscow, Passage to Marseille*), Douglas Sirk (*Hitler's Madman*), and Fritz Kortner (*The Strange Death of Adolf Hitler, The Hitler Gang*). After the war, many of the writers and directors slipped easily into more American subjects. Handicapped by their accents and carrying with them a whiff of foreignness, even the stars among the actors had a harder time.

"I was not part of the Americana, the literature of this country," Henreid told an interviewer in 1977. "I was not a Gary Cooper, who had perhaps fifteen scripts at a time to choose from. I had three, or two, or one—and they were all concoctions." Graylisted by the major studios during the early 1950s, Henreid lost momentum. He directed a number of undistinguished movies, including *Dead Ringer* starring Bette Davis, produced several unmemorable films, and retreated into a dignified old age. "I'm not sorry I took the role," he said of *Casablanca* toward the end of his life, his voice holding little enthusiasm.

"More than anything else, Paul wanted to be on the Oscar show," says Charles Champlin, former arts editor of the Los Angeles *Times*. "I thought it would be wonderful to bring him out in that white suit. He wanted to be a presenter, to have the honor of recognition." Champlin suggested Henreid's name to the Academy several times, but no offer ever came.

Twelve years after *Casablanca,* when Humphrey Bogart was making *Beat the Devil* in Italy, he and Ingrid Bergman met again. By then, the studios no longer had stars to rent. Bette Davis, Errol Flynn, and Bogart had all left Warner Bros., and Bogart's own company was producing *Beat the Devil.* Bergman told the story of her meeting with Bogart several times, in slightly different versions. Didn't she regret ruining her career, Bogart had asked. Bergman was married to Roberto Rossellini then and making unsuccessful movies in Italy. She had answered, "I am a very happy woman and maybe that is just as important as being a box-office success in America."

One can hear the puritan in Bogart needling Bergman with his question and the romantic in Bergman making a grand gesture in her answer. According to Alfred Hitchcock, all of Bergman's movies were grand gestures. "She only wanted to appear in masterpieces," Hitchcock said. "How on earth can anyone know whether a picture is going to turn out to be a masterpiece or not? When she was pleased with a picture she'd just finished, she would think, 'What can I do after this one?' Except for *Joan of Arc,* she could never conceive of anything that was grand enough."

Bergman actually played Joan of Arc three times—for Victor Fleming in 1948, for Rossellini in 1954, and, on Broadway, in Maxwell Anderson's *Joan of Lorraine* in 1946. She had three husbands, four children, and all the lovers she desired; won three Academy Awards and top honors from a dozen other countries; dared to work with the great directors, including Renoir, Rossellini, and Bergman; and ended her movie career with one of her best performances, as the concert pianist in Ingmar Bergman's *Autumn Sonata* who has chosen her career over her daughter. Even the Swedish critics, who were usually cruel to her, praised that performance.

Autumn Sonata, with its parallels to her own life, is Pia Lindstrom's favorite Ingrid Bergman film. "When she was making films in Hollywood, you looked at her and gasped," says Lindstrom. "But

Lauren Bacall, Bogart, and their son, Stephen.

I thought my mother's potential was tapped only after her extraordinary beauty was not the total focus. When she was making *Autumn Sonata* she already had cancer. Had she been healthy and able to go on, she would have made wonderful movies."

If *Casablanca* had a happy ending, it belonged to Humphrey Bogart. "There's nothing as romantic as that movie, is there?" says Lauren Bacall. Until the last year, the end of Bogart's life was equally satisfying. Married to Bacall, the bemused and tentative father of a son and a daughter, winner of an Academy Award for *The African*

Queen, an unforgettable villain in *The Treasure of the Sierra Madre,* in partial control of his fate through his Santana production company and in full control of it at the tiller of his racing yawl *Santana,* he was still Bogart, but Bogart with less need to contest the world. In the end, the years of hard smoking and hard drinking caught up with him, triggering cancer of the esophagus, but, in the end, something catches up with everybody.

Ilsa's note, watered with rain—and Rick's tears?

20

The First Fifty Years

———◆———

Casablanca survived. When Warner Bros. announced a
sequel called *Brazzaville,* starring Humphrey Bogart, Sydney Greenstreet, and Geraldine Fitzgerald as a Red Cross nurse, the studio had
nothing in mind beyond milking a successful movie by gathering
together most of the cast and inventing something to take place in
the same locale with the same characters. But the movie resisted a
sequel, just as it later resisted being turned into a television series,
a play, and a musical. From *To Have and Have Not* to the 1990
Sydney Pollack–Robert Redford movie *Havana,* Hollywood has
reused the elements of *Casablanca,* but the characters, like fish out
of water, have never survived outside the frame of the original
movie.

"The reason it never works, no matter how hard they try, is that
people have in their heads Bogart and Bergman," says Julius Epstein. "The new actors may be better, but they're not Bogart and
Bergman."

In 1951 and again in 1967, Epstein tried to turn the movie into
a Broadway musical. Says Murray Burnett, who created Rick Blaine,
"If your leading man is Rick, there's a large problem. He would

never get up to sing a song about how much he loves Lois."

Even in the first serious attempt at a sequel, in 1943, Rick was no longer the same character, although the untitled story, by Frederick Stephani, started as soon as Renault told his policemen to round up the usual suspects. In the script, that same night—and a year early—American troops invaded Casablanca, and it turned out that both Rick and Renault had been secretly working for the Allied cause. Frederick Faust, a Warner contract writer who wrote western novels under the name of Max Brand, was asked by Hal Wallis to appraise Stephani's story. "The moment Rick becomes, as in Stephani, an agent of the secret police, the interest in his position and character largely evaporates," Faust wrote. "In other words, the hand of Rick is filled with cards, whereas in *Casablanca,* he was walking a tightwire nearly all the way." Stephani's story was rejected. No one else who tried to write a sequel got much further, including Howard Koch. In 1988, Koch suggested a sequel in which Rick's son by Ilsa—she must have gotten pregnant during that dissolve in Rick's apartment—goes to Morocco to find out what happened to his father.

Casablanca, the musical, had several incarnations, none of which got produced, including an Australian version. In 1951 and 1952, a pair of producers worked unsuccessfully first with the Epsteins, then with Alan Jay Lerner and Frederick Loewe. After that, Warner Bros. turned down most producers who asked to buy the rights. By the time Julie Epstein wrote a musical with composer Arthur Schwartz and lyricist Leo Robin in 1967, Jack Warner had sold his studio to Seven Arts. Although Epstein's book was "meticulously faithful" to the movie, according to a Seven Arts memo, the songs seemed ridiculous to the studio. One chorus number had refugees who were lined up for the Lisbon plane wondering if America was a place worth going to, even though, as in the movie, these people had sold their jewels and their bodies to obtain exit visas. Another song from which Seven Arts recoiled was a light patter duet between Rick and Sam. Seven Arts refused to invest, and the musical gathered dust.

If taking away Rick's cynical toughness didn't work, neither did putting him on the air week after week as a North African Mr. Fix-it. In 1955–56, *Casablanca* lasted seven months as an hour-long television series, with Charles McGraw as Rick, Marcel Dalio promoted from coupier to Captain Renault (spelled Renaud), and Clarence Muse finally getting his chance to play Sam. Ludwig Stossel took over S. Z. Sakall's role as headwaiter, while Dan Seymour—who had been described by Warner Bros. as the heaviest actor in Hollywood when he guarded the door to Rick's gambling room in 1942—inherited Sydney Greenstreet's role. The television stories, pedestrian and a bit too heartwarming, inevitably trivialized the movie. In one, Rick protected an Arab orphan. In another, he kept a teenage girl from learning her father was a criminal. In a third, he helped an elderly Englishman find out who had betrayed his son, a British intelligence agent killed by the Gestapo during the war.

The hour adventure series was part of Warner Bros.' first timid exploration of television. "Mr. Warner thought that television was a passing phase," says his editor, Rudi Fehr. "He was kidding himself." Pushed into television by the more visionary or more practical executives in the New York office, Jack Warner approved a single hour, *Warner Brothers Presents,* on ABC. Two shows based on old movies, *Casablanca* and *Kings Row,* and an original western, *Cheyenne,* rotated on Tuesday nights. Jack Warner couldn't hold back the technology that would restructure the empire he and his brothers had built, but he tried—symbolically as well as physically. No home in a Warner Bros. movie was allowed to contain a television set.

"Jack used to say, 'How can anyone watch a big picture on that little box?'" says Bill Orr, who went from being Jack Warner's assistant to being vice president in charge of television.

Kings Row was an immediate failure; *Cheyenne,* which made a star of Clint Walker, was an immediate success. "I chastise myself," says Orr today. "*Casablanca* didn't do that badly except compared to *Cheyenne.* But it never occurred to us that we could do more than one television show, so we took *Casablanca* off the air."

Within three years, Warner Bros. was hugely successful with such western series as *Maverick, Sugarfoot,* and *Colt 45.* Despite the success, television weakened Warner's control of his studio. Says Orr, "I told Jack when *Casablanca,* the first show, was ready to see, and he said, 'We'll run it in Projection Room 2 before lunch.' Well, before lunch something came up, and then he was busy, and about four days later, he said, 'Okay, Bill, now I can run it.' And I said, 'Chief, if you want to see the show, look on television. It's on tonight.' And he said, 'I was supposed to see it.' And I said, 'Chief, television doesn't wait for anybody, including you.'"

For Warner, who was then in his sixties, television was a meta-

Charles McGraw as Rick; Ludwig Stossel in S. Z. Sakall's role as headwaiter; Marcel Dalio promoted from croupier to Captain Renaud (the spelling was changed from "Renault") in the short-lived Warner Bros. television series, Casablanca.

phor for all the things that were taking the fun out of owning a studio. During the early 1950s, Warner Bros. had unsuccessfully used tricks—3-D, CinemaScope, even Abbott and Costello—to try to hold back the tide of moviegoers who were lapping at the shores of television. In 1956, to raise money and against the wishes of his brother Harry, Jack Warner sold *Casablanca* and all the other pre-1948 Warner Bros. movies to United Artists for $21 million.

The movies would eventually become the property of television magnate Ted Turner, who would colorize them. "They said colorizing is a way to bring *Casablanca* to more people, as if color was the same as black-and-white," says Stephen Bogart, Humphrey Bogart's son. Stephen went "reluctantly" to Turner's fiftieth-anniversary homage to *Casablanca* at the Museum of Modern Art in New York in April 1992. "I went to represent the family," Bogart says. "But if you're going to colorize *Casablanca,* why not put arms on the Venus de Milo? At the end of the evening—to a smattering of applause from the Ted Turner–Jane Fonda claque—a representative of the king of Morocco said, 'Wouldn't it be a wonderful thing if we could do a sequel?' *Casablanca 2.*"

In 1956, Warner still had the water tower with his name on it and his special barber down the hall, but Bogart and Flynn, Cagney and Edward G. Robinson, Bette Davis and Ann Sheridan, John Huston and Howard Hawks were gone, and now he had to negotiate with actors and directors on each individual picture. "After he sold the studio, I said to him one day, 'Why did you want to sell the studio?'" says Orr. "He said, 'Too tough.' He used to go every afternoon for a shave, and he said, 'I used to cast a picture from this barber chair. People would pop in and say, What do you think of Clark Gable for so-and-so? Now you have to go through agents. Too tough.'"

The second attempt to make a television series out of *Casablanca* starred David Soul as Rick. The show went on NBC in April 1983, and lasted three weeks. In 1955, *Casablanca* was just another old movie. By 1983, it was one of the three or four movies people always named when they spoke of Hollywood's golden age, and no television show could have succeeded. In 1974, when François Truffaut was approached about remaking *Casablanca,* he said that he shouldn't be intimidated by the idea since *Casablanca* wasn't his favorite Bogart movie; he much preferred *The Big Sleep* and *To Have and Have Not.* "I am aware, however, that American students have created a cult around the film, principally its dialogue, which they know by heart," Truffaut wrote. "There can be no doubt that most actors would feel as intimidated as I do and I cannot imagine Jean-Paul Belmondo or Catherine Deneuve being willing to step into the shoes of Humphrey Bogart and Ingrid Bergman."

Humphrey Bogart died in January 1957. The cult of *Casablanca* was born three months later. If Cyrus Harvey, Jr., was not the father of the phenomenon, he was certainly the midwife. In 1953, Harvey and Bryant Haliday had turned the Brattle Theatre across from Harvard University into an art cinema. Harvey, who had spent much of his Fulbright scholarship year in Paris watching movies at Henri Langlois's Cinémathèque Française, programmed the Brattle with European classics and the early films of Fellini, Antonioni, Truffaut, and Ingmar Bergman, for whom Harvey and Haliday became the American distributors.

"At some point, we thought that we ought to bring in some of the American films that hadn't been shown that much," says Harvey. "And my partner and I both thought that the Bogarts were vastly underrated. I think *Casablanca* was the first one we played. It was my favorite. I thought that Bogart was probably the best American actor who ever lived. And the picture caught on very rapidly. The first time we played it, there was a wonderful reaction. Then the second, third, fourth, and fifth times it took off. The audience began to chant the lines. It was more than just going to the movies. It was sort of partaking in a ritual."

Casablanca played at the Brattle for the first time on April 21, 1957. It was so successful with Harvard students that it was held over for a second week. Then the Bogart festivals began, with six or eight of his movies playing each semester during final-examination weeks. The festivals would culminate with *Casablanca.* It was at Harvard that the relevance of *Casablanca* to a generation that had no relationship to World War II became apparent.

"I was born in 1943," says Todd Gitlin, professor of sociology at the University of California at Berkeley. "But the movie played a very important part in my life. I saw it two to four times a year during the four years I was at Harvard. After I got into politics, which was my sophomore year, I understood *Casablanca* as my personal melodrama. The ritual of watching it was, symbolically for me, the acting out of my own personal rite of passage. Our whole little crowd would go and sit together in the balcony, and when Victor Laszlo said, 'You fought against the Fascists in Spain,' we would cheer. We were a peace group—anti–atom bomb, anti–cold war—and we already understood *Casablanca* as a film that was specially coded for us. I drove to Palo Alto the other day, and I saw a long line of Stanford students waiting to get in to see the film—it was playing at a revival house—and I thought there was hope for the world. I think of the kids as so cynical these days. *Casablanca* requires belief."

One wonders what Humphrey Bogart would have thought of the mystique that began that April in Harvard Square and still envelops him more than thirty years later. Director Vincent Sherman thinks he knows. "Bogie was always a skeptic," says Sherman. "His favorite phrase was 'Let's cut the crap.' I think that if he was asked about the big cult of worship that has developed around him, I think he would be pleased. But I also think he would say, 'Cut the crap, fellows.' "

Bogart's skepticism, his cynicism, and his barely masked bitterness are fuel for the Bogart cult. If he was wearing the acquired persona of the sardonic and dangerous Duke Mantee, as Nunnally Johnson speculated, it was a mantle that fit with little alteration. Bogart was not the Hemingway hero he played in *To Have and Have Not,* not the Hammett detective walking a line he refused to cross in *The Maltese Falcon,* but, even when he did not know he was being observed, Bogart carried their attitudes and their speech patterns, and one can well believe his reading aloud from *The Old Man and the Sea* and saying, "That's how I feel." In the spring of 1943, Bogart refused to make the movie that he would eventually make as *Conflict,* a second-rate film in which he played a wife-killer and Sydney Greenstreet was his nemesis. When Jack Warner called the actor to try to persuade him to play the role, the studio had a stenographer listening in and recording the conversation. In that telephone duel, it was Warner who used words like "herculean," and Bogart who responded in blunt single syllables:

"I'm sorry, Jack; I just can't do it. My stomach will not let me. I am an honest man and I have to be honest with myself in this matter. . . . If you want to get tough with me you can, and I know how tough you can get, but if you do get tough and do the things you say you will, I will feel that I have lost a friend."

Bogart also shared with the Hemingway, Hammett, and Raymond Chandler characters he played a conviction that toughness and manliness required adherence to a moral code. Like Rick, these characters often seem amoral at first because their morality is not necessarily the namby-pamby morality prescribed by society but is based on an often peculiar personal integrity. Bogart seems anguished in that telephone conversation with Warner because, by going back on his word, he is betraying himself. "I am very sorry I ever gave my word to you that I would do it," he told Warner, "for if I had stopped and thought for a minute I would never have agreed to do this picture."

Bogart brought his cynicism to the part of Rick Blaine, says Lauren Bacall, but, she adds, the real connection between the man and the character he played in *Casablanca* was integrity. "The great thing about Bogie that permeated all his parts, the character trait that was so strong, was integrity," says Bacall. "Nobody could buy him. Bogie was his own man. He dealt with things as they were, but he couldn't compromise his own beliefs. In that sense, Rick and Bogie were alike."

Even after he became a star, Bogart's sincerity made him vulnerable. The studios knew that Bogart would lower his price rather than lose a good part. "He was never in a position to ask for a lot of money on a take-it-or-leave-it basis," says Bacall, "because he wanted to do good things and couldn't walk away from excellence." After six weeks of fighting with Warner Bros. over *Conflict*, Bogart gave in because he wanted to make *Passage to Marseille*. And Jack Warner was willing to block the production of that movie indefinitely or to make it with Bogart's French counterpart, Jean Gabin, if Bogart refused to do *Conflict* first.

Different times require different heroes, which makes it all the more amazing that the Bogart cult has spanned thirty-six years. Who seeks out the movies of his contemporaries—Tyrone Power, Robert Taylor, or even Bing Crosby, who was first on the Quigley poll of box-office stars for five years in a row? Only Marilyn Monroe and James Dean, whose uneasy deaths still make a symbolic statement, cast the same psychological net as Bogart.

Why is always more difficult than *Who*. "Bogart has competence," says Billy Wilder. "You felt that, if that big theater where you were watching *Casablanca* caught on fire, Bogart could save you. Gable had that same competence and, nowadays, Mr. Clint Eastwood." But Gable is too heroic for a disillusioned world. Three decades after his death, Bogart still seems modern. "He wore no rose-colored glasses," wrote Mary Astor. "There was something about it all that made him contemptuous and bitter. He related to people as though they had no clothes on—and no skin, for that matter."

Film critic Stanley Kauffmann was born in 1916 and has watched six generations of film heroes. "People never go to see my favorite American film actor of all, Fredric March," says Kauffmann ruefully. "Bogart absolutely encapsulates permissible romance. In this disillusioned, disenchanted world here was a romantic hero we could accept. I think that that disenchantment began with World War I and the emergence of what could be called the Hemingway— the undeluded—generation. And I think that that revulsion with the romances and the lies of the nineteenth century and the twentieth century has persisted. There have been plenty of representatives of the lovely bucolic strain of American life on the screen. Bogart was someone urban—in a sense more jagged and abrasive than Cagney—who you felt was suffering. Cagney was triumphant. Bogart was tough, but he had sensitivity. Certainly, the epitome of everything he stood for was in *Casablanca. I was misinformed.* That's the twentieth century."

The Bogart cult spread from Harvard to other colleges and then to the world beyond the campus. And *Casablanca* was its leading edge. The Club Casablanca in the basement of the Brattle Theatre was only the first of dozens of clubs and restaurants that appropriated the movie's name. By 1977, *Casablanca* was the movie most frequently shown on television. The readers of *TV Guide* said it was also the most popular movie shown on television, while the members of the American Film Institute voted it the third-best American film of all time, behind *Gone With the Wind* and *Citizen Kane.* The British Film Institute went further. In 1983, it called *Casablanca* the best film ever made. Five years later, Sam's piano—the one he played in Paris, not the more valuable piano from Rick's Café—was auctioned by Sotheby's to an anonymous Japanese collector for $154,000. And Bogart as Rick had become the quintessential American outlaw hero, to be parodied and emulated. On the television series *Miami Vice,* a crook tried to corrupt the detective played by Don Johnson with contraband he called their letters of transit; and a real Mafia underboss used the money he skimmed from the hotel and restaurant workers' union to buy a Fort Lauderdale mansion he named Casablanca South and a cabin cruiser he called the Usual Suspects.

The 1972 Woody Allen film, *Play It Again, Sam,* begins with the hopelessly inept Allen watching the closing moments of *Casablanca.* In the movie, and the play from which the movie is derived, Allen is coached by Humphrey Bogart into his own, slightly skewed, manhood. Woody Allen is still surprised that *Casablanca* became the underpinning for his play. Allen says that he has "no special feelings" about *Casablanca* and has "never given it much thought. It's one of thousands of movies I've seen, and the use of Humphrey Bogart in my stage play *Play It Again, Sam* was accidental and arbitrary, undoubtedly inspired by one of the popular posters of him at the time and reinforced by the fact that he was one of a number of standard symbols of macho-romantic movie stars."

Allen may be one of the few people who is willing to believe that his choice of *Casablanca*—or anything else about the movie's permeating of popular culture—was an accident. The Freudians, Jungians, sociologists, deconstructionists, Lacanian psychoanalytic theorists, feminist movie critics, and semiologists, who have examined *Casablanca* in meticulous detail, disagree on the meaning of the film but agree that it has meaning far beyond what was in the conscious minds of Julius and Philip Epstein, Howard Koch, Hal Wallis, and Jack Warner.

The movie has been read as an allegory of America's movement from neutrality to war, with the title "casa blanca"—white house in Spanish—signifying the White House and Rick a reluctant President Roosevelt who finally commits America to the war. Film critic Richard Corliss sees Rick and Renault in Jungian terms, with Rick as the animus and the "radiantly corrupt" Renault as the anima. "Rick can give Renault a sense of values," says Corliss, "and Renault can give Rick a sense of proportion. . . . Or, as they used to say at Schwab's, the two are made for each other." The relationship between Rick and Renault has also been seen as overtly or latently homosexual. Renault's depiction of Rick to Ilsa—"he's the kind of man that, well, if I were a woman and I weren't around, I should be in love with Rick"—has come back to haunt the screenwriters, since Rick turns his back on heterosexual love and chooses male comradeship instead, "a standard case of the repressed homosexuality that underlies most American adventure stories," according to William Donelley's "Love and Death in *Casablanca.*"

"The idea that Rick has been a closet queen all along is lunatic," says psychoanalyst Harvey Greenberg. Greenberg's interpretations of *Casablanca,* like most psychoanalytical interpretations of the movie, begin with the central Oedipal struggle. Renault guesses that Rick can't go home again because he has absconded with church funds or a senator's wife or, perhaps, because he has killed a man. Rick replies that it is combination of all three. Greenberg argues that Rick's exile is symbolic, that "the sacrosanct stolen treasure [is] the wife of a preeminent older man; her husband is the one murdered— and by the love thief. Thus the essence of this 'combination' of offenses is the child's original desire to kill his father and possess his mother." When Rick returns Ilsa to Laszlo at the end of the movie, he is completing his identification with the father and giving up his incestuous claims on the mother.

Rick's killing of Major Strasser has been read two ways. Greenberg sees the killing as an "acceptable displacement" of Rick's Oedipal rage onto a bad father. Literature professor Krin Gabbard and psychiatrist Glen O. Gabbard offer an alternative that "Rick kills the principal enemy of his father surrogate, thereby becoming a man himself." The Gabbards also supply a psychoanalytic analysis of *Casablanca* that follows the ideas of Jacques Lacan. It is based on Rick's toast "Here's looking at you, kid." Rick is the audience's surrogate. The audience looks at Ilsa through Rick. "The possibility that someone or something may be looking at Rick raises the possibility of difference and the possibilities of castration. . . . Significantly, when Rick's looking toast is interrupted in the flashback by Gestapo loudspeakers, Sam (Dooley Wilson) warns him that the Germans will soon be in Paris, "and they'll come lookin' for ya." The invading Nazis represent not only the castrating father but the castrating gaze of the Other as well. The coincidence of the Nazis' arrival with the baffling disappearance of Ilsa leaves Rick as an object in someone else's plot, his previously omniscient gaze reduced to a limited point of view. Similarly, the Oedipal trajectory that leads Rick to the reconciliation with Laszlo and the elimination of Strasser restores him to a sense of origin and identity offered by the father. Rick surrenders Ilsa to Laszlo only after he has completely regained control over the narrative . . ." and thus he once more has the right to say, "Here's looking at you, kid."

The semiologists begin with Umberto Eco's essay "*Casablanca:* Cult Movies and Intertextual Collage," in which the Italian critic calls the film "a hodgepodge of sensational scenes strung together implausibly," a movie that has "glorious incoherence" and is full of so many archetypes that "we reach Homeric depths." Even Eco's followers take issue when he calls the movie a hodgepodge. J. P. Telotte says that the word trivializes *Casablanca,* a film with multiple themes including the desire for freedom and "the lure and fallacy of isolationism as personal and national policy." Telotte concerns himself with the image and substance of thievery in the movie—the theft of Europe by the Nazis, Rick Blaine's stolen love, the stolen Letters of Transit, the stolen wallets and dignity, and, in the end, Rick's stealing from the Nazis the possession they most want, Victor Laszlo. Thus the film gives audiences "the comforting notion that the stolen can eventually be stolen back, that theft—corruption, injustice or simply repression—sets up the very conditions of its own undoing." Another semiologist, literature professor Larry Vonalt, examines the duplicity and betrayals perpetrated by most of *Casablanca*'s characters by examining the movie's double and contradictory visual style of both the *artfully glamorous* and *film noir.*

That *Casablanca* can tolerate these interpretations and a dozen others—from the voiceless woman ("You'll have to do the thinking for both of us") that feminist film critics see in the patriarchal Hollywood cinema to Victor Laszlo as a representative of the patriarchal European father against whom the American colonies rebelled—testifies to the richness of the film.

Billy Wilder puts it another way. "This is the most wonderful claptrap that was ever put on the screen," he says. "Claptrap that you can't get out of your mind. The set was crummy. By God, I've seen Mr. Greenstreet sit in that same wicker chair in fifty pictures before and after, and I knew the parrots that were there. But it worked. It worked absolutely divinely. No matter how sophisticated you are and it's on television and you've seen it 500 times, you turn it on."

"*Casablanca* dramatizes archetypes," says sociologist Gitlin. "The main one is the imperative to move from disengagement and cynicism to commitment. The question is why *Casablanca* does this more effectively than other films. Several other Bogart films of the same period—*Passage to Marseille, To Have and Have Not, Key Largo*—enact exactly the same conversion. But the Rick character does not simply go from disengagement to engagement but from bitter and truculent denial of his past to a recovery and reignition of the past. And that is very moving, partly because it is also associated with Oedipal drama. But there is also a third myth narrative, a story about coming to terms with the past. Rick had this wonderful romance; he also had his passionate commitment. It seems gone forever. But you can get it back. That is a very powerful mythic story, because everybody has lost something, and the past is, by definition, something people have lost. This film enables people to feel that they have redeemed the past and recovered it, and yet without nostalgia. Rick doesn't want to be back in Paris. And the plot is brilliantly constructed so that these three myths are not three separate tales, but one story with three myths rushing down the same channel."

Rick has a surprising cousinship to the heroes of serious American fiction, as described by Leslie Fiedler in *Love and Death in the American Novel*. Like Huckleberry Finn and the heroes of *Moby Dick* and Hemingway and James Fenimore Cooper novels, Rick makes a flight from society to a place where mothers cannot come, accompanied by a male companion "who is presented with varying degrees of ambiguity as helpmate and threat." David O. Selznick was correct in observing Rick's similarity to Rhett Butler, who moved from cynicism about the War Between the States to engagement in the doomed Southern cause and, in the end, turned his back on Scarlett O'Hara. But Rick also has links to Jay Gatsby, and *Casablanca* has echoes of F. Scott Fitzgerald's *The Great Gatsby*. Both have, near their spatial center, a section of calm reverie that is, in a sense, a flashback to a utopian time. In both, love is surrounded by violence, and both Rick and Gatsby hope, wrongly, that they can reach in the present the happiness that was almost theirs in the past.

In novels and on film, Americans are drawn to stories of adolescence and to stories where adult protagonists are filled with an adolescent sensibility. Film critic Richard Schickel thinks that the relevance of *Casablanca* to each new generation comes in part because the film contains carefully coded messages about the journey out of childhood. Schickel sees the Rick of Rick's Café as the late adolescent who has discovered that childhood [the idyl in Paris] "that mixed bag of irresponsible pleasure and protective custody, is forever lost." Lost in nostalgia, he has not yet committed to the adulthood which he will attain at the end of the movie.

In his homage to *Casablanca* on *60 Minutes*, Harry Reasoner described the movie more simply as: "Boy meets girl. Boy loses girl.

Boy gets girl back again. Boy gives up girl for humanity's sake." Certainly it is the movie's two strands, love and politics intertwined like a double string of pearls, that account for much of *Casablanca*'s reverberation and power today. Fifty years ago, screenwriter Howard Koch argued that a flashback to Rick and Ilsa's idyll in Paris would destroy the tension in Rick's Café, while screenwriter Casey Robinson argued that mixing up the love story and the political melodrama in Rick's Café made things a jumble. They were both wrong. The flashback made it clear that Rick had been thrust out of Paradise; and mingling the political and the romantic allowed each story to comment on the other and made Rick's journey from isolation to engagement a double journey.

"Slick shit," says Julius Epstein, looking down from his mountaintop. "Political church," says Howard Koch, standing beside his stream. The movie is both and more, partly because the writers pulled it in two directions. Koch intended to dramatize the necessity for commitment, for the sacrifice of private life to the public good. The myth of sacrifice, self-martyrdom for a worthy cause, is as enticing a fantasy today as it was during World War II. The Epsteins had no idea that the relationship between Claude Rains's "poor corrupt official" and Humphrey Bogart's "I stick my neck out for nobody" isolationist would be read by critic Stanley Kauffmann as: "Rains is Europe and Bogart is America, and they understand each other without saying much about it, and they like each other without admitting it." Or that Pauline Kael, who much prefers *The Maltese Falcon,* would say of the script, "It was the Warners mixture. Warner Bros. had been playing with that mixture for years, and they just seemed to get it right this time."*

Hollywood films have always been rich in archetypes, and whatever the treasures that can be mined from the subtext of *Casablanca,* it is the specifics of the actors, the potent music and the satisfying drama of commitment and renunciation that have a compelling hold on our emotions today. From Bogart's delayed entrance as a disembodied hand scrawling "OK. Rick" on a check, his Rick is an enticingly ambiguous and ambivalent hero. Are his cynicism and isolation real, a façade, or a shield? Is the real Rick Yvonne's callous

---

* That Warner mixture has no relevance to the studio that carries the Warner Bros. name today. House style is nonexistent when studios are differentiated only by how much they are willing to spend for the same scripts and the same actors.

lover, Annina's protector, or the pragmatist who brushes off Ugarte as he would a fly? The movie's first wonder is that Bogart is strong enough to sustain the weight of expectation about the mysterious Rick that has been built up in the audience. If Rick is, metaphorically, America's ambivalence about the war in Europe, which will be resolved by the end of the movie, Bogart undoubtedly brought to *Casablanca* his rage at his own bad marriage and, in his drunken self-pity, was what Michael Wood describes as "a picture of what isolation looks like at its best: proud, bitter, mournful, and tremendously attractive." Because of Bogart, whose persona almost reeks of freedom—freedom from emotional entanglements, freedom to choose to follow a different drummer—Rick's renunciation of Ilsa is sad but exhilarating at the same time. Film critic Andrew Sarris thinks that audiences are actually relieved when Bogart renounces Bergman. "All that she can offer him is an ideal, consuming, ultimately wearying passion," Sarris wrote.

If Bogart's "beautiful friendship" with Claude Rains is not homosexual in any sense, it is a love match of two equals. As Sidney Rosenzweig points out in his book on the films of Michael Curtiz, the relationship of Rick and Renault is similar to the Beatrice-Benedick pattern of sparring hero and heroine that is found in a number of Curtiz movies, including *Captain Blood* and *The Adventures of Robin Hood*. Rick and Renault will have a good time together. Renault is Rick's equally ambiguous double, moving from mocking disengagement to commitment a step or two behind him. Besides, Renault has most of the best lines, and they are deliciously delivered by Claude Rains, with a tiny crust of corruption staining the corner of his lip. The movie's present popularity has been helped enormously by the fact that the funny lines are still funny. Renault's "I'm shocked! Shocked to find that gambling is going on here" is meat and drink to audiences whose cynicism has expressed itself recently in term limits for politicians. And the Pinteresque exchange between Yvonne and Rick—"Where were you last night?" "That's so long ago I don't remember." "Will I see you tonight?" "I never make plans that far ahead"—is still existentialism in miniature.

What Ingrid Bergman brought to the movie—possibly just because the director and screenwriters could not tell her what Ilsa was feeling—was an ambiguity to match Bogart's. Ilsa is, in one standard Hollywood sense, a villain: she deceives and betrays both men. Bergman's combination of the sexual and the inviolate filled out the underwritten role, but Ilsa remains inscrutable. In a recent late-night bull session, two out of six people felt that Bergman really loved Paul Henreid and was play-acting with Bogart to get the Letters of Transit. And one thought that Rick was over his infatuation with Ilsa by the end of the movie. Several theoreticians agree, including film and English professor Leo Braudy, who believes that Rick gives up Ilsa to Laszlo because "he realizes her emotional commitment to Laszlo and the cause" which ends his interest in her. Larry Vonalt goes further: Rick is paying Ilsa back for having abandoned him. "He rejects her just as he believes she had rejected him."

I was in elementary school during World War II; I did my part in the war by rolling tinfoil and rubber bands into balls and bringing them to the Warners Beverly Theater on Saturday mornings. World War II has receded with all its certainties and moral imperatives, leaving muddy flats behind. The world is a cornucopia of grays. I believed the romantic interpretation of *Casablanca* then—love lost for the good of the world—and believe it now. But it is the very ambiguity of *Casablanca* that keeps it current. Part of what draws moviegoers to the movie again and again is their uncertainty about what the movie is saying at the end. The one character in *Casablanca* who is stale and unappealing today is the only main character who lacks ambiguity, Victor Laszlo. Even though Laszlo symbolized all that was heroic and noble in an imperfect world, Paul Henreid wanted to turn down the role because he instinctively understood that being weighed down by perfection is not a recipe for longevity.

The one thing that Hollywood movies—except for an occasional horror film—lack today is ambiguity. Their plots may be confusing, but the cards are on the table from the beginning. Audiences didn't know how they were expected to respond to Bogart or Rains, both of whom had played as many villains as heroes, but the opening credits give the answer when the star is Mel Gibson, Clint Eastwood, or Arnold Schwarzenegger. (Note Schwarzenegger's metamorphosis from killing machine from the future in *The Terminator* to child protector in *Terminator 2* in deference to his salary and status.) When Gibson and Danny Glover bond in the male-buddy *Lethal Weapon* pictures, the Oedipal message is the same as the message given at the end of *Casablanca,* but *Lethal Weapon* and the dozens of other buddy movies shallowly illustrate the end of the Oedipal conflict, while *Casablanca*'s triangle works through it.

Casablanca is not Stephen Bogart's favorite Humphrey Bogart movie. If his favorite movie, *Treasure of the Sierra Madre,* were made today, he says shrewdly, "It would end up being *Indiana Jones.*"

Casablanca's potent blend of romance and idealism—a little corny and mixed with music and the good clean ache of sacrifice and chased down with a double slug of melodrama—is available at the corner video store, but *Casablanca* couldn't be made today. There is too much talk and not enough action. There are too many characters too densely packed, and the plot spins in a hard-to-catch-your-balance circular way instead of walking a straight line. There is no Humphrey Bogart to allow the audience a permissible romance without feeling sappy. And the studio would insist that all the ambiguity be written out in the second draft.

Reference Notes
and Sources

The *Warner Bros. Archives,* School of Cinema-Television, University of Southern California, Los Angeles, CA 90089-2212, contains an enormous amount of information pertaining to the making of individual movies at Warner Bros. during the studio era, as well as contracts and financial and personnel records.

The *Jack Warner Collection,* Archives of Performing Arts, Cinema-Television Library, Doheny Library, University of Southern California, Los Angeles, CA 90089-0184, contains a cornucopia of information about the running of the studio, including memos, notes, telegrams, and speeches.

The *Selznick Archives,* Harry Ranson Humanities Research Center, University of Texas at Austin, TX 78713-7219, houses David O. Selznick's papers and includes material relating to Ingrid Bergman's career while she was under contract to Selznick.

The *Ingrid Bergman Collection* and the *Frank Capra Collection,* Wesleyan Cinema Archives, Wesleyan University, Middletown, CN 06457, house papers that include Ingrid Bergman's acting diary.

Department of Special Collections, University Research Library, University of California at Los Angeles, CA 90024-1575, has a large collection of oral histories of movie-industry figures.

Office of War Information files, Record Group 208, National Records Center, Suitland, MD, contains all the records of the Bureau of Motion Pictures, including correspondence and reviews.

Department of Films, International Museum of Photography, George Eastman House, Rochester, NY 14607, has extensive archival material on cinematography and cinematographers.

The *Schomburg Center for Research in Black Culture,* 515 Lennox Avenue, New York, NY 10037, is part of the New York Public Library system, as is the theater arts library at Lincoln Center. Schomburg contains books and clipping files on African-American figures and problems.

The *Twentieth Century Archives,* Mugar Memorial Library, Boston University, Boston, MA 02215, houses papers of Claude Rains, Bette Davis, Don Siegel, and several other Hollywood figures.

The *Oral History Research* office, Butler Library, Columbia University, New York, NY 10025, contains oral histories of Hal Wallis, Irving Rapper, Paul Henreid, and Otto Preminger among others.

The *William Seymour Theater Collection,* Firestone Library, Princeton University, Princeton, NJ 08544-2098, contained Warner Bros. financial records which have now been moved to USC.

The Margaret Herrick Library, Academy of Motion Picture Arts and Sciences, 333 South La Cienega Boulevard, Beverly Hills, CA 90213, has extensive clipping files, the Production Code Administration records, and possibly the most complete collection of information about Hollywood in any one place.

The American Film Institute Library, 2021 North Western Avenue, Los Angeles, CA 90027, has an eclectic mix of oral histories and transcriptions of seminars with contemporary industry figures.

The *Marta Mierendorff archives,* Max Kade Institute for Austrian-German-Swiss Studies, University of Southern California, Los Angeles, CA 90089, contains records of the film and literary émigrés.

The *Arts and Communications Archives,* Brigham Young University, Provo, UT 84602, has a collection of Max Steiner's scores and papers.

The *Warner Bros. Research Collection,* at the Burbank Public Library, 110 North Glen Oaks, Burbank, CA 91502, has a collection of the costume, architectural, cultural, and historical research Warner Bros. did for its movies.

Key to Abbreviations of Archival References

SC	Special Collections
DSC	Department of Special Collections
OH	Oral History
PCA	Production Code Administration files, Margaret Herrick Library, Academy of Motion Picture Arts and Sciences
CSF	Casablanca Story File—The Casablanca Story File is the record of all the extant memos, notes, and telegrams pertaining to the making of *Casablanca.*
WBA	Warner Bros. Archives
JWC	Jack Warner Collection
SA	Selznick Archives
IBC	Ingrid Bergman Collection
DSC/URL/UCLA	Department of Special Collections/University Research Library/University of California at Los Angeles
OWI	Office of War Information files
DF/IMP/GEH	Department of Film/International Museum of Photography/George Eastman House
SCRBC	Schomburg Center for Research in Black Culture
TCA	The Twentieth Century Archives
OHRO/CU	The Oral History Research office/Columbia University
WSTC	The William Seymour Theater Collection
MHL/AMPAS	Margaret Herrick Library/Academy of Motion Picture Arts and Sciences
AFIL	American Film Institute Library
MMA	Marta Mierendorff Archives
ACA	Arts and Communications Archives
WBRC/BPL	Warner Bros. Research Collection/Burbank Public Library
NSB/WBS	New Storage Building on the Warner Bros. Studio lot in Burbank, CA. Some material remains on the studio lot but is not generally available.

In these notes, books are cited by the author's name and title only; full listings can be found in the bibliography. The words identifying a note are taken from the beginning of the section of the text to which they refer.

Chapter One

PAGE

3 *Casablanca* ended production . . . *Casablanca* Daily Production Report, WBA.

4 *"You are Maria . . ."* Ingrid Bergman's acting diary written in Swedish and translated by Harriet Alvord, p. 75 right, IBC. This book is not a diary in the usual sense of the word, since entries were made at intervals and cover several months at a time. There is no way to tell how long Bergman waited before she wrote about *Casablanca.*

4 *"that of a tigress . . ."* Paul Henreid, *Ladies Man,* p. 131.

5 *Its final cost . . .* "Comparison of Negative Costs and Gross Incomes on productions released from 9/1/41 to 8/31/46," William Schaefer Collection, JWC.

6 *"But to be at the Brattle . . ."* Cyrus Harvey, Jr., interviewed by author.

6 *"That was wonderful . . ."* Philip Dunne, interviewed by author.

7 *"There is no reason . . ."* Memo from Wallis to Curtiz, Mar. 31, 1942, CSF/WBA.

7 *"She was surprised . . ."* Pia Lindstrom, interviewed by author.

7-8 *"Bogie would say . . . "* Lauren Bacall, interviewed by author.

8 *Songwriter Harry Warren . . .* Harry Warren, interviewed by author.

8 *Sam Marx, did want . . .* Sam Marx, interviewed by author.

9 *By July 22 . . .* Los Angeles *Times,* July 22, 1942, Part I, p. 1.

9 *"Because there was nothing . . ."* *Warner Club News,* May 1943, p. 4. JWC.

9 *But in 1942 the unions . . .* *Variety,* Oct. 8, 1942, and Oct. 9, 1942.

10 *Hal Wallis wrote . . .* Julius Epstein and Howard Koch, interviewed by author. Also Casey Robinson, interviewed by Joel Greenberg in an oral history, reprinted in *Backstory,* Pat McGilligan, ed., p. 308. Wallis always claimed authorship of the line and no one connected with the picture ever disputed it.

12 *runaway leader . . .* *Variety,* Jan. 5, 1944. Both *For Whom the Bell Tolls* and *The Song of Bernadette* were released so late in the year that *Variety's* figures for box office receipts were estimates.

12 *"a picture which makes . . ."* Bosley Crowther, *New York Times,* Nov. 27, 1942, p. 27.

12 *"Splendid anti-Axis propaganda"* . . . *Variety,* Dec. 2, 1942.

12 *"an exciting film . . ."* John T. McManus, *PM,* Nov. 27, 1942, p. 22.

12 *A poll of 439 critics . . .* *Film Daily Yearbook,* 1944, p. 105.

13 *"The 'Casablanca' kind"* . . . Manny Farber, *The New Republic,* Dec. 4, 1942, p. 793.

13 *"pretty tolerable . . ."* David Lardner, *The New Yorker,* Nov. 28, 1942, p. 77.

13 *"Apparently* Casablanca . . ." James Agee, *The Nation,* Feb. 20, 1943. (Agee's reviews are reprinted in *Agee on Film.*)

13 *"Casablanca is still . . ."* Ibid., Dec. 25, 1943, p. 769.

13 *"I've got almost a mystical feeling . . ."* Howard Koch, interviewed by author.

Chapter Two

16 *"Fiefdoms . . ."* Billy Wilder, interviewed by author.

16 *a thirty-five-year-old reader* . . . Stephen Karnot contract files, WBA.

17 *"Excellent melodrama . . ."* Stephen Karnot synopsis, Dec. 11, 1941, CSF/WBA.

18 *"But it was Irene Lee . . ."* Julius Epstein, interviewed by author.

18 *an unpublished memoir by* . . . Johnny O'Steen, *Were These "Golden Years"?* pp. 110–11, unpublished manuscript at Theater Arts Library, URL/UCLA.

18 *"When* Casablanca *came out . . ."* Irene Lee Diamond, interviewed by author.

18 *In a thirty-three-page contract* . . . Hal Wallis contract files, WBA.

20 *"By the time . . ."* Neal Gabler, *An Empire of Their Own,* p. 152.

20 *By 1937,* Fortune *magazine* . . . *Fortune,* Dec. 1937, p. 111.

20 *"My uncle was . . ."* Jack Warner, Jr., interviewed by author.

21 *"Harry was a solid . . ."* Lee Katz, interviewed by author.

21 *"I have been watching . . ."* Memo from Jack Warner to Henry Blanke and all producers, Jan. 9, 1942, JWC.

21 *Once, when a picture* . . . Carlisle Jones in an undated studio press release, JWC; Doc Solomon also repeated the story himself over the years.

22 *"My dressing room . . ."* Letter from Errol Flynn to T. C. Wright, Aug. 12, 1944, JWC.

23 *"Bogart will just have to . . ."* Telegram from Jack Warner to Steve Trilling, May 17, 1943, JWC.

23 *"I'm a bad boy . . ."* Telegram from Warner to Trilling, Jan. 9, 1943, JWC.

23 *"They were passed . . ."* Bill Orr, interviewed by author.

23 *"Part of his job . . ."* Richard Brooks, interviewed by author.

23 *"M-G-M didn't encourage . . ."* Ring Lardner, Jr., interviewed by author.

25 *His grandson, Gregory* . . . Gregory Orr, interviewed by author.

25 *"I have never owned a dog or cat . . ."* Jack Warner with Dean Jennings, *My First Hundred Years in Hollywood,* p. 114.

26 *"I think a psychiatrist . . ."* Jack Warner, Jr., interviewed by author.

26 *"He was scared of actors . . ."* Geraldine Fitzgerald, interviewed by author.

26 *"He was always . . ."* Lauren Bacall, interviewed by author.

26 *"Abdul was like . . ."* Bill Schaefer, interviewed by author.

26 *"He was terribly upset . . ."* Jack Warner, Jr., interviewed by author.

28 *"I can't understand . . ."* Memo from Warner to Curtiz, July 15, 1942, CSF/WBA.

28 *Keeping control of his directors* . . . Telegram from Warner to Trilling, Dec. 4, 1943, JWC.

28 *Hal Wallis's secretary let* . . . Memo from Paul Nathan to Jack Warner, Feb. 4, 1942, CSF/WBA.

28 *"We'd stay until 1:30 A.M. . . ."* Rudi Fehr, interviewed by author.

28 *"He smelled a good picture . . ."* Owen Crump, interviewed by author.

28 *"If you were able . . ."* Henry Blanke, p. 63, OH, 1969, DSC/URL/UCLA.

28 *"hasn't done a picture . . ."* Memo from Wallis to Jack Warner, Apr. 13, 1942, CSF/WBA, responding to Warner's memo of Apr. 4, 1942.

29 *"Today the whole industry . . ."* Daniel Melnick, interviewed by author.

29 *"A certain amount of murkiness . . ."* Laurence Mark, interviewed by author.

29 *"I saw the dailies . . ."* Memo from Wallis to Curtiz, July 9, 1942, CSF/WBA.

30 *"a very obvious imitation . . ."* Memo from Robert Lord to Irene Lee, Dec. 23, 1941, CSF/WBA.

30 *"This story should . . ."* Memo from Jerry Wald to Irene Lee, Dec. 23, 1941, CSF/WBA.

30 *"that other prime necessity . . ." Fortune,* Dec. 1937.

31 *"There's no individual producer . . ."* Tom Pryor, interviewed by author.

31 *"Hal was exceedingly disciplined . . ."* Charles Higham, interviewed by author.

31 *The messenger boys . . .* Stuart Jerome, *Those Crazy Wonderful Years When We Ran Warner Bros.,* pp. 260–61.

31 *"There were two Hal Wallises" . . .* Julius Epstein, interviewed by author.

32 *"He was a very cool . . ."* Dennis Morgan, interviewed by author.

32 *"Having pretty babes . . ."* Owen Crump, interviewed by author.

32 *"I was making . . ."* Irene Lee Diamond, interviewed by author.

Chapter Three

SCRIPT MATERIAL USED IN THIS CHAPTER

The following scripts and script material quoted and referred to in this chapter can be found in the *Casablanca* files at the Warner Bros. Archives at the University of Southern California:

> *Everybody Comes to Rick's,* the stage play by Murray Burnett and Joan Alison on which *Casablanca* was based.
>
> The "PART 1 TEMP." script of April 2, 1942, by Julius and Philip Epstein.
>
> A complete script, titled "FINAL PART 1," dated May 11, 1942.
>
> A "FINAL REVISED SCRIPT" dated June 1, 1942, which was by no means final.
>
> In addition, the scripts of April 2, May 11, and June 1 contain many dated, revised pages written later.

The nineteen pages of "Suggestions for Revised Story" written by Howard Koch and referred to in this chapter are held by author. Other scripts and script materials are cited at the head of the notes for Chapter Nine and Chapter Thirteen.

36 *"But it's not . . ."* Murray Burnett, interviewed by author.

36 *"The play provided . . ."* Howard Koch, "The Making of America's Favorite Movie: Here's Looking at You, *Casablanca,*" *New York* magazine, Apr. 30, 1973, p. 74.

36 *"Koch took credit . . ."* Murray Burnett, interviewed by author.

37 *"Having read . . ."* Howard Koch, Los Angeles *Times,* June 1, 1991, F, 2.

37 *Koch has been apologetic . . .* Howard Koch, interviewed by author.

37 *"All I saw was . . ."* Ibid.

37 *"I went through . . ."* Howard Koch, *Casablanca,* p. 21.

39 *The process of finding* . . . Memo from Paul Nathan to Hal Wallis, Dec. 30, 1941, CSF/WBA.

39 *"I don't believe . . ."* Memo from Robert Buckner to Hal Wallis, Jan. 6, 1942, CSF/WBA.

39 *"The present material . . ."* Letter from Joseph Breen to Jack Warner, June 18, 1942, CSF/WBA.

39 *"the possibility of . . ."* Memo from Aeneas MacKenzie to Paul Nathan, Jan. 3, 1942, CSF/WBA.

40 *"I'm Julian Blumberg . . ."* Julius Epstein, interviewed by author.

40 *"One day a frightened . . ."* Budd Schulberg, *What Makes Sammy Run?*, p. 28.

42 *Cagney agreed* . . . James Cagney, *Cagney by Cagney*, p. 105.

42 *"The Epstein boys . . ."* Memo from Raoul Walsh, Feb. 13, 1942, *Desperate Journey* story file, WBA.

42 *wisecracking competition* . . . Alvah Bessie, *Inquisition in Eden*, p. 36.

42 *"Our publicity department . . ."* Julius Epstein, interviewed by author.

42 *"One day as . . ."* Ibid.

43 *"Julie does care . . ."* Leslie Epstein, interviewed by author.

43 *Koch wrote that* . . . Howard Koch, *Casablanca*, p. 19.

43 *"We never sat . . ."* Julius Epstein, interviewed by author.

43 *Koch sent Julie* . . . Letter from Howard Koch to Julius Epstein, Apr. 1, 1985, courtesy of Julius Epstein.

44 *Warner suggested that* . . . Memo from Jack Warner to Roy Obringer, Feb. 24, 1942, CSF/WBA.

45 *"Attached is my . . ."* Memo from Hal Wallis to Mike Curtiz, Mar. 30, 1942, CSF/WBA.

45 *"It is assuming . . ."* Daniel Melnick, interviewed by author.

46 *"That first part . . ."* Julius Epstein, interviewed by author.

46 *"Once we knew . . ."* Ibid.

46 *and begged for another* . . . Trilling to Wallis, May 4, 1942, JWC.

47 *"an actor like Bogart . . ."* Laurence Mark, interviewed by author.

47 *"falling in love . . ."* Casey Robinson interviewed by Joel Greenberg for an American Film Institute oral history in 1974, reprinted in part in Pat McGilligan's *Backstory*, p. 307.

47 *"While we handle . . ."* Letter from Julius and Philip Epstein to Hal Wallis, early March, 1942, CSF/WBA.

49 *"My brother and I . . ."* Julius Epstein, interviewed by author.

50 *"The major work . . ."* Howard Koch, interviewed by author.

52 *In their authoritative study* . . . Larry Ceplair and Steven Englund, *The Inquisition in Hollywood*, pp. 437–38.

52 *"My cousins and I . . ."* Leslie Epstein, interviewed by author.

53 *an exhaustive Ph.D.* . . . Christine Ann Colgan, "Warner Bros.' Crusade Against the Third Reich: A Study of Anti-Nazi Activism and Film Production, 1933–1941," Ph.D. dissertation, Doheny Library, University of Southern California.

53 *"I had inherited . . ."* Murray Burnett, interviewed by author.

55 *"Murray came over . . ."* Joan Alison, interviewed by author.

55 *they had submitted three* . . . Warner Bros. submission files, story department, Warner Bros. studio.

55 *"Joan nourished me . . ."* Murray Burnett, interviewed by author.

55 *"Murray's concept . . ."* Joan Alison, interviewed by author.

56 *"Warner Bros. was like . . ."* Julius Epstein, interviewed by author.

56 *"a family . . ."* Howard Koch and Julius Epstein, both interviewed by author.

56 *"Everybody stakes out . . ."* Jack Brodsky, interviewed by author.

57 *"My brother and I . . ."* Julius Epstein, interviewed by author.

59 *"She was moaning . . ."* Ibid.

59 *On May 6, Wallis . . .* Memo from Wallis to Curtiz, May 6, 1942, CSF/WBA.

59 *"I think this . . ."* Memo from Wallis to Koch, May 11, 1942, CSF/WBA.

59 *"Although the Epstein . . ."* Memo from Koch to Wallis, May 11, 1942, CSF/WBA.

Chapter Four

63 *top "money getter".* . . On Dec. 17, 1941, *Variety* listed Curtiz as seventh on the list of the "10 top money directors" for 1941, and on Jan. 5, 1944, *Variety* pronounced Curtiz Warner Bros.' top "money getter."

64 *Their friendship began* . . . Sam Goldwyn, Jr., interviewed by author.

64 *On Saturday, April 2* . . . Scott McQueen, "Dr. X: A Technicolor Landmark," *American Cinematographer,* June 1986, p. 37.

64 *"Wallis was deeply . . ."* Charles Higham, interviewed by author.

64 *"I saw last night's . . ."* Memo from Wallis to Curtiz, June 4, 1942, CSF/WBA.

64 *"Hal was never . . ."* John Meredyth Lucas, interviewed by author.

65 *with his right hand* . . . John Meredyth Lucas, interviewed by author; also a Warner Bros. press release written by Ken Whitmore in spring 1942.

65 *"I think flirting . . ."* Jack Warner, Jr., interviewed by author.

66 *3.5 billion* . . . Ticket sales figures provided by Art Murphy, financial analyst for *Variety.*

66 *"with the exception . . ."* Undated draft of studio's "War News," Warner Bros. Studio War Effort box, JWC. Also *Hollywood Reporter,* Dec. 11, 1941, and Dec. 12, 1941.

67 *"When I first . . ."* Rudi Fehr, interviewed by author.

67 *"will work too great . . ."* Telegram from Harry and Jack Warner to Franklin Roosevelt, May 20, 1940, JWC.

67 *After a Ku Klux* . . . *Variety,* Oct. 22, 1941.

68 *"United we survive . . ."* June 5, 1940, box 56, folder 18, JWC.

68 *"Americanism is my . . ."* *Warner Club News,* Oct. 1940, p. 3, JWC.

68 *"Through the . . ."* *Warner Club News,* Nov. 1940, p. 8, JWC.

68 *a job Harry Warner* . . . Johnny O'Steen, *Were These "Golden Years?,"* p. 163.

69 *In a government survey* . . . U.S. Bureau of Intelligence, Office of Facts and Figures, "Pacific Coast Attitudes toward the Japanese Problem," Feb. 28, 1942.

69 *how few Japanese* . . . *Variety,* Dec. 3, 1941.

69 *"A little indignation . . ."* Mary Astor, *A Life on Film,* p. 168.

70 *Betty Grable was* . . . *New York Times,* Feb. 15, 1942, VIII, 5.

70 *"Oh, it was . . ."* *Fortune,* April 1942, p. 95.

70 *"on wooden benches . . ."* *Hackensack* (N.J.) *Record,* Jan. 3, 1942.

71 *a three-page account* . . . "Hollywood Blackout," an undated studio press release, WB Studio War Effort Box, box 59, folder 2, JWC.

72 *"I was 4F . . ."* Arthur Wilde, interviewed by author.

72 *"Until World War II . . ."* C. E. Carle, p. 39, 1969, OH, DSC/URL/UCLA.

72 *"National Hardware Week . . ."* Arthur Wilde, interviewed by author.

73 *"Today the press . . ."* Jack Brodsky, interviewed by author.

74 *There was never any chance* . . . Reagan's position during those six months can be traced through his contract files and the *Desperate Journey* production file, both at WBA.

74 *Reagan, Sheridan, Morgan* . . . *Hollywood Reporter,* Jan. 8, 1942.

74 *"Mr. Wallis will . . ."* Memos from Paul Nathan, Jan. 5, 1942, CSF/WBA.

75 *"I thought it was . . ."* Vincent Sherman, interviewed by author.

75 *"the happiest of happy . . ."* Andrew Sarris, *The American Cinema: Directors and Directions: 1929–1968,* p. 176.

76 *"if something worked . . ."* Julius Epstein, interviewed by author.

76 *"I would never . . ."* Daniel Melnick, interviewed by author.

76 *"You will talk . . ."* Memo from Wright to Weyl, May 14, 1942, CSF/WBA.

77 *And Wright refused* . . . Memos from Wallis to Tenny Wright and from Wright to Wallis, both Apr. 22, 1942, CSF/WBA.

77 *"Michael Cimino . . ."* Lee Katz, interviewed by author.

77 *"He will be . . ."* Telegram from Warner to Steve Trilling, May 19, 1943, JWC.

77 *"The continuous re-writing* . . . Memo from Warner, Oct. 22, 1943, JWC.

78 *"A third of the words . . ."* Telegram from Warner to Trilling, Nov. 30, 1943, JWC.

78 *Orry-Kelly, Warners'* . . . Orry-Kelly contract files, Jan. 22, 1942, WBA.

78 *R. J. Obringer* . . . Curtiz contract files, WBA.

78 *Helmut Dantine owed* . . . Aug. 19, 1944, Box D, Trilling Files, JWC.

78 *And Warner instructed* . . . Morris Levison to Warner, Aug. 17, 1944, JWC.

78 *"I have a poster . . ."* Jack Warner, Jr., interviewed by author.

78 *"The thoughtless waste . . ."* Harry M. Warner speeches and interviews folder, JWC.

79 *"I noticed today . . ."* Letter from Jack Warner to Peter Lorre, Sept. 27, 1943, JWC.

79 *"A single sheet . . ."* Warner Bros. Studio War Effort box, JWC.

79 *"Without them we . . ."* *Warner Club News,* Mar. 1942, p. 8, JWC.

Chapter Five

81 *In January of 1942* . . . Personnel list of Jan. 7, 1942, WBA.

81 *"Metro sprinkled stardust . . ."* Bill Orr, interviewed by author.

83 *"like a marvelous . . ."* Katharine Hepburn, *Me,* pp. 221, 225.

83 *"If you belonged to M-G-M . . ."* Geraldine Fitzgerald, interviewed by author.

83 *"As far as organization . . ."* Jean Burt Reilly, OH, 1962, DSC/URL/UCLA.

83 *"consciously or unconsciously"* . . . Nunnally Johnson, *The Letters of Nunnally Johnson,* p. 243.

84 *"she was totally incapable . . ."* Humphrey Bogart as told to Kate Holliday, *McCall's,* July 1949.

85 *"He felt about the sea . . ."* Lauren Bacall, interviewed by author.

85 *"any script that . . ."* Dennis Morgan, interviewed by author.

86 *"You told me once to let . . ."* Memo from Bogart to Wallis, May 4, 1940, *High Sierra* story files, WBA.

86 *Even before he made . . .* Bogart contract files, WBA.

86 *"I remember," says film critic . . .* Pauline Kael, interviewed by author.

87 *"Are you kidding . . ."* Memo from Bogart to Trilling, Mar. 17, 1941, cited in *Inside Warner Bros.* (1935–1951), Rudy Behlmer, ed., p. 143.

87 *"Bogart had formulated . . ."* Geraldine Fitzgerald, interviewed by author.

87 *"It was a very bad script"* . . . Dennis Morgan, interviewed by author.

87 *"particularly guilty"* . . . Lee Katz, interviewed by author.

87 *"it is not an important . . ."* Letter from George Raft to Warner, June 6, 1941, *Maltese Falcon* story file, WBA.

88 *"Will you please figure on . . ."* Memo from Wallis to Steve Trilling, Feb. 14, 1942, CSF/WBA.

88 *Six weeks later, Jack . . .* Memo from Warner to Wallis, Apr. 2, 1942, CSF/WBA.

88 *They didn't believe . . .* Geraldine Fitzgerald, interviewed by author.

88 *"We will not make stars . . ."* Telegram from Warner to Trilling, Nov. 21, 1943, JWC.

89 *"the rental of Humphrey Bogart" . . .* Nov. 26, 1937, Bogart contract files, WBA.

89 *"Jack said they would come . . ."* Bill Orr, interviewed by author.

89 *"See what you can do . . ."* Telegram from Warner to Trilling, Glazer, Jan. 6, 1943, JWC.

90 *"doesn't give the effect . . ."* Graham Greene, *The Spectator,* Jan. 1940, p. 108.

90 *"I was praised (as usual) . . ."* Ingrid Bergman's acting diary, p. 75 left, May–August 1942, IBC.

90 *"Ingrid had a . . ."* Fay Wray, interviewed by author.

90 *"having a home . . ."* Letter from Bergman to Ruth Roberts, Jan. 12, 1942, quoted in *Ingrid Bergman: My Story,* pp. 138–39.

91 *One of her chief memories . . .* Ingrid Bergman and Alan Burgess, *Ingrid Bergman: My Story,* p. 145; also John Kobal, *People Will Talk,* p. 464.

91 *"Success," she wrote . . .* Ingrid Bergman's acting diary, p. 74 left, August 1941, IBC.

92 *"I am so fed up . . ."* Ingrid Bergman and Alan Burgess, *Ingrid Bergman: My Story,* p. 140.

92 *"would be ideal" . . .* Memo from Wallis to Trilling, Mar. 30, 1942, CSF/WBA.

92 *Wallis telephoned Selznick . . .* "Vehicles suggested for Miss Bergman," SA; also memo from Wallis to Curtiz, Apr. 1, 1942, CSF/WBA.

92 *"Knowing that I wanted . . ."* Hal Wallis and Charles Higham, *Starmaker,* p. 86.

92 *"Wallis said to us . . ."* Julius Epstein, interviewed by author.

93 *"If this should be true . . ."* Confidential memo from David O. Selznick to Dan O'Shea, Mar. 17, 1942, SA.

94 *"fantastic speech"* . . . Laurence Leamer, *As Time Goes By,* p. 34.

94 *"an agent at heart . . ."* Hal Wallis and Charles Higham, *Starmaker,* p. 86.

94 *"David became virtually . . ."* David Thomson, interviewed by author.

94 *Between January and April . . .* "Vehicles suggested for Miss Bergman," SA.

94 *"seems very eager"* . . . Memo to Dan O'Shea, Apr. 4, 1942, SA.

95 *"I think we should strike . . ."* Memo from Selznick to O'Shea, Apr. 6, 1942, SA.

95 *"That was a time when . . ."* David Thomson, interviewed by author.

95 *"so fed up with Rochester"* . . . Telegram from Kay Brown to O'Shea, Apr. 22, 1942, SA.

95 *"I was warm and cold . . ."* Letter from Bergman to Roberts quoted in *Ingrid Bergman: My Story*, p. 144.

95 *Wallis's choice for the third starring role* . . . Memo from Wallis to Steve Trilling, Mar. 26, 1942, *Watch on the Rhine* story file, WBA. Also see memos from Trilling to Wallis, Apr. 14, 1942 and Wallis to Curtiz, Apr. 22, 1942, CSF/WBA.

96 *"I saw the script . . ."* Paul Henreid, interviewed by author.

97 *"Bogart was straightforward . . ."* Ingrid Bergman's acting diary, p. 75, May–August 1942, IBC.

97 *"a bit of a ham"*. . . Memo from Steve Trilling to Wallis, May 1, 1942, CSF/WBA.

97 *"Mr. Bogie was nobody"* . . . Paul Henreid, interviewed by author.

97 *According to Henreid's autobiography* . . . Paul Henreid, *Ladies Man*, pp. 38–41.

99 *"The part is played with . . ."* Brooks Atkinson, *New York Times*, Dec. 31, 1940, p. 19.

99 *"Then my agent . . ."* Paul Henreid, interviewed by author.

99 *"Casablanca set Paul Henreid . . ."* Pauline Kael, interviewed by author.

99 *"self idolatry"* . . . Irving Rapper interviewed by Charles Higham, OH, Jan. 3, 1972, OHRO/CU.

100 *He complained to the studio* . . . Paul Henreid contract files, WBA.

100 *In 1972, he was still* . . . P. D. Knecht to Jenny T. Christopher, Jan. 7, 1972, Paul Henreid contract files, WBA.

100 *"I will always have the girl"* . . . Paul Henreid, interviewed by author.

100 *But neither the contract* . . . Paul Henreid contract files, WBA.

100 *"Within the next year . . ."* Louella Parsons, Los Angeles *Examiner*, Dec. 25, 1942, I, 19.

Chapter Six

102 *In January, 1942* . . . Memo from Paul Nathan to Wallis, Jan. 13, 1942, *Watch on the Rhine* story file, WBA.

103 *Henreid and Charles Boyer* . . . *Watch on the Rhine* story file, WBA.

104 *Early in May* . . . Memo from Wallis to Curtiz, May 8, 1942, CSF/WBA.

105 *Film Conservation Committee* . . . *Hollywood Reporter*, June 12, 1942, May 14, 1942, and July 13, 1942.

105 *"We built two versions . . ."* John Beckman, interviewed by author.

106 *"A Leaf from the Book* . . . Studio release, June 1942, box 56, folder 6, JWC.

107 *"He had next to his . . ."* Ring Lardner, Jr., interviewed by author.

108 *Because so many* . . . *Hollywood Reporter*, Mar. 23, 1942.

108 *Women who showed signs* . . . Los Angeles *Times*, Mar. 30, 1942, Part II, p. 1.

108 *"When I left . . ."* Irene Lee Diamond, interviewed by author.

108 *Wigs, for example . . .* Memos from T. C. Wright to all producers, unit managers, and directors, May 18, 1943, Aug. 2, 1943, JWC.

108 *Frugal as always . . .* Memo from T. C. Wright to Fred Messinger, Sept. 17, 1943, JWC.

109 *"To the Point of . . ."* Hollywood Reporter, June 25, 1942.

109 *"Negatives are as good . . ."* Letter from Jack Warner to Max Milder, Oct. 14, 1942, JWC.

109 *"Jack took me with him"* . . . Owen Crump, interviewed by author.

110 *"For your information . . ."* Undated June 1942 letter from Jack Warner to Max Milder, JWC.

110 *"Jack thought it was . . ."* Owen Crump, interviewed by author.
Footnote, *"I felt his son . . ."* Bill Schaefer, interviewed by author.

111 *"It is with deep . . ."* Letter from Hal Wallis to Jack Warner, Aug. 2, 1942, JWC.

111 *During the making of . . .* Warner Bros. Studio War Effort box, JWC.

112 *"the first important . . ."* Unidentified sheet in Casablanca publicity file, WBA.

112 *"in strict accordance . . ."* Hollywood News sent out weekly by the publicity department, Vol. V, No. 28, Jan. 18–25, Casablanca publicity file, WBA.

112 *"I supplemented my income . . ."* Bob William, interviewed by author.

112 *"We'd photograph him with . . ."* Arthur Wilde, interviewed by author.

112 *"it would tend to . . ."* Hollywood Reporter, Dec. 17, 1941.

113 *"labor, class or other . . ."* Statement of information, June 4, 1942, from the Chief Postal Censor of the Office of Censorship, JWC.

113 *"to eliminate all scenes . . ."* Hollywood Reporter, June 16, 1942.

113 *"The American motion picture . . ."* Open letter from Roosevelt to all publications, printed Dec. 24, 1941.

114 *"First, complete indoctrination . . ."* Bruce Catton, The War Lords of Washington, p. 64.

115 *"Will this picture help . . ."* OWI Manual, Summer 1942, OWI.

115 *The studio said* The Gorilla Man . . . Files in the NSB/WBS.

Chapter Seven

In this and succeeding chapters, information about *Casablanca*'s changing schedule, about which scenes were being shot on what days, and about which actors were on the set and what stages were being used most often comes from the movie's daily production files and daily camera reports. Occasionally the information comes from memos and other material in the *Casablanca* story file. All are at the Warner Bros. Archives.

117 *his wife worked best* . . . Laurence Leamer, As Time Goes By, p. 71.

118 *"In my whole life . . ."* James Bacon, Made in Hollywood, p. 60.

118 *"Picture the sweetheart . . ."* Bosley Crowther, New York Times, Jan. 21, 1940, IX, 5.

118 *"When she was . . ."* Art Buchwald, interviewed by author.

118 *He warned Lauren Bacall* . . . Lauren Bacall, By Myself, p. 155.

119 *"I never saw Bogart . . ."* Meta Carpenter, interviewed by author.

119 *"He has very set . . ."* Ezra Goodman, *Bogey: The Good-Bad Guy,* p. 134; this book is based on extensive, in-depth interviews by Goodman in 1953–1954; the interviews were for a *Time* cover story about Bogart in which little of Goodman's material was used.

119 *"His manner is wry . . ."* Final shooting script.

119 *"I had lunch with . . ."* Geraldine Fitzgerald, interviewed by author.

119 *"There was distance . . ."* Dan Seymour, interviewed by author.

120 *"Almost nobody . . ."* Lee Katz, interviewed by author.

120 *Bogart was too drunk . . .* T. C. Wright to Obringer, Dec. 26, 1944; Eric Stacey to Wright, Dec. 26, 1944; and Bogart legal files, WBA.

121 *"We had a few days . . ."* Vincent Sherman, interviewed by author.

121 *"Bogie was very unhappy . . ."* Francis Scheid, interviewed by author.

121 *"I kissed him but . . ."* There are various versions of this quote. One can be found in the frame-by-frame picture book, *Casablanca,* edited by Richard J. Anobile, p. 6, another in Ingrid Bergman and Alan Burgess's *Ingrid Bergman: My Story,* p. 146.

121 *"He was always . . ."* Lee Katz, interviewed by author.

122 *he also left behind . . .* Original declaration of paternity and financial agreement, District Court Landstrasse, Dept. I, Vienna, Oct. 30, 1923.

122 *a heartbreaking letter . . .* Letter from Mathilda Foerester to Jack Warner, July 15, 1933, Curtiz folder, WBA.

122 *"When they were married . . ."* John Meredyth Lucas, interviewed by author.

123 *"Bogart would say . . ."* Francis Scheid, interviewed by author.

123 *"If he was stuck . . ."* Paul Stader, interviewed by author.

123 *"When we had a story . . ."* Julius Epstein, interviewed by author.

123 *"He spoke five languages . . ."* John Meredyth Lucas, interviewed by author.

123 *"Next time I send . . ."* Vincent Price, interviewed by author.

123 *"The next time . . ."* John Qualen, *Classic Images,* no. 95, May 1983.

123 *the poor white trash . . .* Lee Katz, interviewed by author.

124 *"There're more words milling . . ."* Pete Martin, *Saturday Evening Post*, Aug. 2, 1947, p. 23.

124 *"approximately, like Gertrude Stein" . . .* In an article by Mary Morris, *PM,* Sept. 17, 1944, M13.

124 *a bully . . .* Philip Dunne, interviewed by author.

124 *"In almost every scene . . ."* Memo from Wallis to Curtiz, Mar. 27, 1940, Rudy Behlmer, ed., *Inside Warner Bros. (1935–1951),* p. 112.

124 *"He kept saying, 'Move . . .'"* Fay Wray, interviewed by author.

124 *"She had one line . . ."* Lee Katz, interviewed by author.

125 *she turned down* Mildred Pierce . . . Whitney Stine, *"I'd Love to Kiss You . . . ,"* p. 211.

125 *"Mike kept insulting . . ."* John Meredyth Lucas, interviewed by author.

125 *"I think he resented . . ."* Lauren Bacall, interviewed by author.

126 *"I greatly enjoyed Mike . . ."* Ingrid Bergman's acting diary, p. 75, IBC.

126 *"With Bergman, he oozed . . ."* Francis Scheid, interviewed by author.

126 *"Mike called Bergman . . ."* Lee Katz, interviewed by author.

126 *"devil up" . . .* Bill Orr, interviewed by author.

126 *"He was not crude . . ."* Fay Wray, interviewed by author.

126 *"Curtiz was a miserable . . ."* Francis Scheid, interviewed by author.

128 *"The major portion . . ."* Memo from Hal Wallis to George Groves, May 26, 1942, CSF/WBA.

129 *"Why didn't the mixer . . ."* Francis Scheid, interviewed by author.

130 *"A high-ball a day . . ."* *Warner Club News,* March, 1942, p. 8, JWC.

130 *"a single dollar of profit"* . . . Account of meeting on Dec. 23, 1942, JWC.

131 *"The middle register . . ."* Francis Scheid, interviewed by author.

131 *"The face is quite . . ."* Pauline Kael, interviewed by author.

132 *"So that when I met . . ."* Richard J. Anobile, ed., *Casablanca,* p. 6.

132 *"I've always gotten out . . ."* Undated clipping by Alice Pardoe West, *Stanford-Examiner* (Mass.), Bette Davis scrapbooks, TCA.

132 *a mutual friend, Mel Baker* . . . Nathaniel Benchley, *Humphrey Bogart,* pp. 104–105.

132 *"I have a personal phobia . . ."* Ezra Goodman, *Bogey: The Good-Bad Guy,* p. 48.

132 *"What the women liked . . ."* Whitney Stine, *"I'd Love to Kiss You . . ."* pp. 134, 136.

132 *"I honestly can't explain . . ."* Pauline Kael, interviewed by author.

132 *"She was like a rose"* . . . Stanley Kauffmann, interviewed by author.

133 *"I spent weeks testing . . ."* Taped interview with Arthur Edeson by George Pratt, Apr. 15, 1958, DF/IMP/GEH.

133 *"Arthur Edeson's photography . . ."* Kevin Brownlow, *The Parade's Gone By,* p. 256.

134 *"The principal factors . . ."* Edeson in George Pratt interview.

134 *"The photography bears out . . ."* Haskell Wexler, interviewed by author.

134 *"superb photography . . ."* Telegram, Selznick to Wallis, Nov. 12, 1942, CSF/WBA.

134 *"I understand that . . ."* Memo from Wallis to Edeson, May 26, 1942, CSF/WBA.

136 *"a suggesting of . . ."* Edeson in George Pratt interview, Apr. 15, 1958, DF/IMP/GEH. Edeson also discussed his lighting techniques in an oral history done for the American Society of Cinematographers.

136 *"I am anxious to . . ."* Memo from Wallis to Edeson, June 2, 1942, CSF/WBA.

136 *"They wanted it kind of . . ."* Francis Scheid, interviewed by author.

136 *"He cried, but he knew . . ."* Lee Katz, interviewed by author.

136 *"Wallis's memo . . ."* Haskell Wexler, interviewed by author.

136 *"We had a very poor day . . ."* Wallis to Groves, May 26, 1942, CSF/WBA.

136 *"All the pictures I worked on . . ."* Francis Scheid, interviewed by author.

Chapter Eight

139 *"by air mail . . ."* Warner to Wilk, Feb. 2, 1942, box 59, folder 17, JWC.

139 *"I personally want to okay . . ."* Warner to Phil Friedman, Mar. 12, 1943, JWC.

139 *He decided to change* . . . Memos from Wallis to Trilling, Feb. 5, 1942 and Feb. 9, 1942; memo from Trilling to Wallis, Feb. 7, 1942, CSF/WBA.

139 *"endeared themselves . . ."* *The Negro Actor,* July 15, 1939, SCRBC.

139 *"My father said . . ."* Lena Horne, interviewed by author.

141 *"inevitable colored . . ."* Theodore Strauss, *New York Times,* July 2, 1942, p. 25.

142 *"Dear Mike:/The test . . ."* Memo from Wallis to Curtiz, Apr. 22, 1942, CSF/JWA.

142 *Curtiz found . . . Casablanca* Production file tests, Apr. 20, 1942.

142 *"Clarence Muse . . ."* Katherine Dunham, interviewed by author.

144 *"I was absolutely . . ."* Ibid.

144 *"a show which is . . ."* Daily Worker, Oct. 31, 1940.

144 *"sweet" and "dear" . . .* Lena Horne, interviewed by author.

144 *the Roosevelt Administration . . . New York Times,* Feb. 7, 1943, II, 3.

144 *In May 1942 . . .* Dooley Wilson contract files, WBA.

145 *Claude Rains had to . . .* The information in this paragraph comes from the contract files of the actors referred to, WBA.

146 *Bette Davis always thought . . .* Whitney Stine, *Mother Goddam,* p. 167; also an unpublished interview with Davis for a Rains biography.

146 *"You son-of-a-bitch . . ."* Claude Rains in 30 hours of unpublished taped interviews owned by Jessica Rains.

146 *"That voice was . . ."* Stanley Kauffmann, interviewed by author.

147 *"He didn't go . . ."* Jessica Rains, interviewed by author.

147 *"When we walked . . ."* Ibid.

148 *one of the "Twenty Hopes" . . .* S. R. Littlewood, *The Referee,* date on clipping missing.

148 *"To my favorite . . ."* Rains's copies of Shaw's plays are at TCA.

148 *"Women always served . . ."* Paul Henreid interviewed by Charles Higham, OH, 1972, OHRO/CU.

148 *"We told Wallis . . ."* Julius Epstein, interviewed by author.

149 *"bare, cold, and brown" . . .* Unpublished taped Rains interviews.

149 *80 tons of hay . . .* Claude Rains's 1941 income tax returns.

149 *"When he talked . . ."* Leonid Kinskey, interviewed by author.

151 *"We spend a good portion . . ."* Hedda Hopper, Los Angeles *Times,* Sept. 28, Part III, p. 1, 1947.

151 *"You can get rid . . ."* Unpublished taped Rains interviews.

151 *"Veidt, I think . . ."* Memo from Shumlin to Wallis, Apr. 13, 1942, *Watch on the Rhine* story file, WBA.

152 *"Veidt would never . . ."* Patricia Battle, interviewed by author.

153 *"Connie must have . . ."* Robby Lantz, interviewed by author.

153 *In late May, Warner . . .* Conrad Veidt contract files, WBA.

153 *"just short of . . ."* Hollywood Reporter, May 25, 1942.

153 *fifteen hundred or 5 percent . . .* Hollywood Reporter, Mar. 17, 1942; *Variety,* Feb. 23, 1944.

153 *On April 29, a month . . .* "Tentative Cast" list, Apr. 29, 1942, CSF/WBA.

154 *he was willing to . . .* Memo from Wallis to Trilling, May 15, 1942, CSF/WBA.

154 *"To some acute . . ."* Stanley Kauffmann, interviewed by author.

155 *The story Greenstreet told . . .* Brooklyn *Daily Eagle,* Oct. 16, 1932.

155 *"Someone, perhaps . . ."* John Anderson, New York *Evening Post,* Jan. 6, 1927.

155 *"Greenstreet was made . . ."* Pauline Kael, interviewed by author.

156 *"This is an . . ."* Stanley Kauffmann, interviewed by author.

157 *"I am a young man"* . . . Release sent out by Columbia, July 25, 1934.

158 *"Peter Lorre's American . . ."* Andre Sennwald, *New York Times,* Mar. 31, 1935.

158 *"Gothic tales"* . . . Vincent Price, interviewed by author.

158 *"Oh yes"* . . . . Sam Arkoff, interviewed by author.

158 *"Even as Mr. Moto . . ."* Billy Wilder, interviewed by author.

158 *"At lunch one . . ."* Amanda Dunne, interviewed by author.

158-59 *"Peter said, 'That's . . .' "* Victor Sherman, interviewed by author.

Chapter Nine

Much of the script material referred to in this chapter is cited at the head of the notes to Chapter Three. The major additional piece of script material in this chapter is Casey Robinson's "Notes on Screenplay Casablanca," May 20, 1942, which can be found in the *Casablanca* story file at the Warner Bros. Archives.

162 *Joe Breen had read* . . . Letter from Breen to Warner, May 19, 1942; copies in Production Code Administration files, MHL/AMPAS and CSF/WBA.

162 *It had been written* . . . The creators of the Code were Daniel A. Lord, S.J., and Martin Quigley, the publisher of the *Motion Picture Herald.*

163 *"Specifically, we . . ."* Letter from Breen to Warner, May 21, 1942; copies in PCA and CSF/WBA.

163 *A month later* . . . Letter from Breen to Warner, June 18, 1942; copies in PCA and CSF/WBA.

163 *"The sanctity of . . ."* The Motion Picture Production Code formally adopted in March 1930, PCA.

164 *After a meeting* . . . Letter from Breen to Warner, June 5, 1942, PCA and CSF/WBA.

164 *"quite definite reference . . ."* Ibid.

164 *Production Code Certificate* . . . PCA.

166 *Carl Schaefer, was* . . . Memo from Schaefer to Warner, May 22, 1942, CSF/WBA.

166 *"We didn't want . . ."* Carl Schaefer, interviewed by author.

166 *"Allah, Allah . . ."* Memo from Wallis to Curtiz, May 25, 1942, CSF/WBA.

167 *"Hal was a great . . ."* Irene Lee Diamond, interviewed by author.

167 *"sketchy, interesting lighting"* . . . Wallis to Curtiz, June 15, 1942, *"the general lighting . . ."* Wallis to Curtiz, June 12, 1942, CSF/WBA.

167 *"with just the clothes . . ."* Memo from Wallis to Curtiz, May 21, 1942, CSF/WBA.

167 *"His contribution . . ."* Whitney Stine, *Mother Goddam,* pp. 181–82.

168 *Wallis had tried* . . . Virginia Olds to Selznick, May 28, 1942, SA.

168 *"In order for her to look . . ."* Selznick notes on Bergman costume tests, May 27, 1942, SA.

169 *Bergman assured Selznick* . . . Through Virginia Olds, May 28, 1942, SA.

169 *"fugitive leader . . ."* Paul Henried, *Ladies Man,* p. 121.

169 *Lee Katz wrote* . . . Memo from Katz to Wallis, May 27, 1942, CSF/WBA.

169 *"If we want . . ."* Memo from Wallis to Curtiz, May 27, 1942, CSF/WBA.

170 *"Picturesque North Africa"* . . . General Research Record, *Casablanca* files, WBA.

170 *the bible* . . . WBRC/BPL.

170 *"While I know . . ."* Wallis to Curtiz, June 4, 1942, CSF/WBA.

171 *"We used to drink . . ."* Leonid Kinskey, interviewed by author.

172 Casablanca *was his major example* . . . Trilling to all producers, Feb. 11, 1943, JWC.

174 *"He wouldn't pay . . ."* Casey Robinson in an oral history told to Joel Greenberg, reprinted in *Backstory,* ed. Pat McGilligan, p. 295.

174 *Wallis had asked the writer* . . . Memo from Robinson to Wallis, May 5, 1942, *Now, Voyager* story file, WBA.

178 *"Remember that Casey . . ."* Robert Blees, interviewed by author.

178 *"There was one gimmick . . ."* Casey Robinson, *Backstory,* ed. Pat McGilligan, p. 307.

179 *Wallis sent Curtiz* . . . Wallis to Curtiz, Apr. 16, 1942, CSF/WBA.

179 *"Only one line . . ."* Julius Epstein, interviewed by author.

179 *"I was wrong . . ."* Howard Koch, interviewed by author.

Chapter Ten

182 *"For the Love of . . ."* Undated advertisements from *Variety* and *Hollywood Reporter.*

182 *"In Europe, if . . ."* Pete Martin, *Saturday Evening Post,* Aug. 2, 1947, p. 66.

182 *"His camera movement . . ."* Lee Katz, interviewed by author.

183 *"Mike had an . . ."* John Meredyth Lucas, interviewed by author.

183 *Hal Wallis told* . . . Charles Higham, interviewed by author.

183 *"I think that . . ."* Billy Wilder, interviewed by author.

184 *"I don't understand . . ."* Memo from Wallis to Curtiz, Aug. 28, 1935, *Captain Blood* story file, WBA.

184 *"All he [Curtiz] . . ."* Memo from Warner to Wallis, Mar. 10, 1936, *Charge of the Light Brigade* story file, WBA.

184 *"There is one . . ."* Memo from Wallis to Blanke, Dec. 3, 1937, *The Adventures of Robin Hood* story file, WBA.

184 *Curtiz is responsible* . . . The material in this paragraph comes from an analysis of the available script materials.

184 *"Curtiz, of course . . ."* Leonid Kinskey, interviewed by author.

185 *"Once," says Lee* . . . Lee Katz, interviewed by author.

185 *Curtiz would brush him* . . . Howard Koch, interviewed by author.

185 *Peter Lorre once* . . . Ezra Goodman, *Bogey: The Good-Bad Guy,* p. 135.

185 *"Mike used to say . . ."* John Meredyth Lucas, interviewed by author.

185 *Curtiz told Hedda* . . . Hedda Hopper, Los Angeles *Times,* July 7, 1942, Part I, p. 9.

185-6 *"Alex was violently . . ."* John Meredyth Lucas, interviewed by author.

186 *"There is no point . . ."* Memo from Wallis to Curtiz, May 25, 1942, CSF/WBA.

186 *Wallis agreed . . .* Sakall and *Casablanca* Contract files; also memos from Wallis to Katz—May 27, 1942, Wright to Wallis—May 28, 1942, and Kumin to Wallis—June 2, 1942, CSF/WBA.

187 *"The transition . . ."* Memo from Wallis to Curtiz, May 28, 1942, CSF/WBA.

187 *But, on the afternoon . . . Casablanca* Daily Production Report, WBA/USC.

187 *"We were in New . . ."* John Meredyth Lucas, interviewed by author.

188 *Claude Rains usually . . .* Unpublished tapes of interviews with Claude Rains.

188 *"terribly tense" . . .* Ibid.

188 *"a great, great . . ."* Geraldine Fitzgerald, interviewed by author.

188 *"He was one of . . ."* Leonid Kinskey, interviewed by author.

188 *"The dog cost them . . ."* Lenke Kardos, interviewed by author.

189 *"very sweet and nice . . ."* Richard J. Anobile, ed., *Casablanca,* p. 6.

189 *"Finest and most . . ."* Interview with Mary Morris, *PM,* Sept. 17, 1944, M12.

189 *Curtiz was also . . .* Lee Katz and Frances Scheid, interviewed by author.

189 *Warner sent a telegram . . .* Warner to Wallis, Curtiz, and Trilling, May 25, 1942, CSF/WBA.

190 *"what not to do . . ."* Unpublished taped Rains interviews.

190 *"My father only . . ."* Jessica Rains, interviewed by author.

190 *"He thought the way . . ."* Lauren Bacall, interviewed by author.

190 *"They were furious . . ."* Lee Katz, interviewed by author.

190 *"is fifty per cent . . ."* Pete Martin, *Saturday Evening Post,* Aug. 2, 1947, p. 63.

191 *Warners claimed that only . . .* Profit-loss statement, Aug. 31, 1953, Curtiz folder, WBA.

191 *"I never dreamed . . ."* Curtiz to Warner, Jan. 15, 1954, Curtiz folder, WBA.

192 *"I thought these . . ."* Ibid.

192 *"Mike found out . . ."* John Meredyth Lucas, interviewed by author.

Chapter Eleven

195 *"I must say Ingrid . . ."* Lee Katz, interviewed by author.

196 *"I made many friends . . ."* Ingrid Bergman's acting diary, p. 75, IBC.

196 *"The glow that comes . . ."* Howard Koch, interviewed by author.

196 *"She always looked . . ."* Jean Burt, OH, 1962, DSC/URL/UCLA.

197 *" 'Trooper' is a lousy . . ."* Leonard Nimoy, interviewed by author.

197 *"And that was during . . ."* Jean Burt, OH, 1962, DSC/URL/UCLA.

197 *"I never visited . . ."* Petter Lindstrom in a telephone conversation with author.

198 *"evil man" . . .* Ezra Goodman, *Bogey: The Good-Bad Guy,* p. 99; this book is based on extensive, in-depth interviews Goodman made in 1953 and 1954; the interviews were for a *Time* cover story in which he used little of his material.

198 *"Bogey thinks of . . ."* Nathaniel Benchley, *Humphrey Bogart,* p. 5.

198 *"He was a real . . ."* Tom Pryor, interviewed by author.

198 *"There was something . . ."* Ezra Goodman, *Bogey: The Good-Bad Guy,* p. 55.

198 *"Exit the 'Bogey'-Man . . ."* Warner Bros. publicity, Vol. V, No. 11, Sept. 21–28, 1942, WBA.

198 *"Bogart was the kind . . ."* Richard Brooks, interviewed by author.

198 *"Teasing . . ."* Ezra Goodman, *Bogey: The Good-Bad Guy,* p. 136.

198 *"He had manners . . ."* Philip Dunne, interviewed by author.
199 *"We are at a total . . ."* Letter from Roy Obringer to Bogart, June 7, 1952, JWC.
199 *"I was to take . . ."* Arthur Wilde, interviewed by author.
199 *"I was over there . . ."* Richard Brooks, interviewed by author.
200 John Huston said that . . . John Huston, *An Open Book*, p. 114.
200 *"Steve Taggart did not . . ."* Richard Brooks, *The Producer*, pp. 184, 206, 211–12.
200 *Bogart thought it was* . . . Richard Brooks, interviewed by author.
201 *"Let's make it . . ."* Ibid.
201 *In her autobiography* . . . Lauren Bacall, *By Myself*, 227–60.
201 *"there were no . . ."* Pia Lindstrom, interviewed by author.
201 *"Elliot and his wife . . ."* Frances Williams, interviewed by author.
202 *"We waited 'til . . ."* Unit publicist Ken Whitmore's notes on *Casablanca*.
202 *In his autobiography* . . . Paul Henreid, *Ladies' Man*, pp. 126–27.
203 *"When she was younger . . ."* Gregory Orr, interviewed by author.
203 *"sweet" and protective* . . . Joy Page, a recluse for many years was interviewed through her son, Gregory Orr; also Bill Orr, interviewed by author.
203 *Lorre told Ezra* . . . Ezra Goodman, *Bogey: The Good-Bad Guy*, p. 133.
204 *"I couldn't keep up* . . ." James Wong Howe, interviewed by Charles Higham, OH, June 11, 1971, OHRO/CU.
204 *Encouraged by John* . . . Mary Astor, *A Life on Film*, pp. 162–63.
205 *Bogart used to make money* . . . Nathaniel Benchley, *Humphrey Bogart*, p. 53.
205 *"He wouldn't have a chance* . . . Ezra Goodman, *Bogey: The Good-Bad Guy*, pp. 88–89.
205 *"We knew we were . . ."* Richard Brooks, interviewed by author.
205 *"I enjoy chess because . . ."* Ezra Goodman, *Bogey: The Good-Bad Guy*, p. 39.
205 *The postcard on* . . . The postcard was part of a collection of autograph dealer Joseph M. Maddalena, Beverly Hills, California.
205 *"My father loved . . ."* Jessica Rains, interviewed by author.
206 *"Bogart never missed . . ."* Meta Carpenter, interviewed by author.
206 *"He was completely . . ."* Lee Katz, interviewed by author.
206 *"the real pros . . ."* Jean Burt, OH, 1962, DSC/URL/UCLA.

Chapter Twelve

210 *"Naked in four . . ."* Paul Henreid, interviewed by author.
210 *"And so the story . . ."* Lotte Palfi Andor in a draft of her memoirs. They were published as *Die Fremden Jahre: Errinerungen An Deutschland*.
212 *And in 1943* . . . Dantine File, MHL/AMPAS.
212 *she was a flyttfagel* . . . Laurence Leamer, *As Time Goes By*, p. 44.
212 *"If you think . . ."* Pauline Kael, interviewed by author.
214 *"nation of poets . . ."* Lotte Palfi Andor in a draft of her memoirs.
214 *"We went through . . ."* Warner Bros. press release, from Alex Evelove, Hollywood news, Vol. V, No. 21, *Casablanca* file 683, WBA.
214 *"I have such a small . . ."* Curt Bois, interviewed by author.
215 *"For the rest of . . ."* Billy Wilder, interviewed by author.

216 *"America was called . . ."* Lotte Palfi Andor in a draft of her memoirs.

216 *It was Jack Warner . . .* Lenke Kardos, interviewed by author; also telegram from Warner to Obringer, Oct. 24, 1944, JWC.

216 *"to see me coming . . ."* Lenke Kardos, Sakall's sister-in-law, interviewed by author.

217 *"Since that excellent . . ."* New York Times, Oct. 5, 1936.

217 *"He draws no crowds . . ."* Szoke Sakall, *The Story of Cuddles,* translated by Paul Tabori, p. 192.

217 *"Everything happened as . . ."* Ibid., p. 198.

217 *"He had lived . . ."* Lenke Kardos, interviewed by author.

218 *"I ain't got no . . ."* Leonid Kinskey, interviewed by author.

218 *"visualized the famous . . ."* Ibid.

218 *"Serves the unprosperous . . ."* Bertolt Brecht, "Hollywood Elegies," *Poems 1913–1956,* p. 380.

218 *When Ingrid Bergman . . .* Laurence Leamer, *As Time Goes By,* p. 107.

218 *"I can't understand . . ."* Marta Feuchtwanger in a four-volume 1976 oral history, Vol. 3, p. 1328, DSC/URL/UCLA.

219 *"From one day . . ."* Meta Cordy, interviewed by author.

219 *"they are desperately . . ."* Letter from C. Dieterle, Aug. 15, 1938, MMA.

219 *"We signed to assure . . ."* Julie Epstein, interviewed by author.

219 *"I was there when . . ."* Lupita Tovar, interviewed by author.

220 *Kohner asked Ernst . . .* Frederick Kohner, *The Magician of Sunset Boulevard,* pp. 109–12.

220 *According to the . . .* The Deutsches Film Museum mounted a show at the Academy of Motion Picture Arts and Sciences—From Babelsberg to Hollywood—citing these figures; Jan Christopher Horak, interviewed by author, disagrees in the appendix to his Ph.D. diss. "Fluchtpunkt Hollywood; Eine Dokumentation zur Filmemigration nach 1933," Munster: MAkS, 1986.

221 *From the money that . . .* Charlotte Dieterle's 1942 European Film Fund list, MMA.

221 *"One could stay . . ."* Interview with Zilzer in a commemorative book about his work by the Deutsche Kinemathek Berlin for the 33rd Berlinale in 1983.

221 *"But 1950 was an . . ."* Ilka Gruning's form, MMA.

222 *"But, madame . . ."* Curt Bois, interviewed by author.

222 *"To the Actor . . ."* Bertolt Brecht, "To the Actor P.L. in Exile," Feb. 1, 1950, *Poems 1913–1956,* p. 418.

222 *"as bait . . ."* Letter from Steve Trilling to Jack Warner, July 24, 1943, JWC.

223 *"Lorre's carefully . . ."* Vincent Canby, *New York Times,* Aug. 1, 1984, III, 21.

223 *"That's what made . . ."* Nicola Bautzer, interviewed by author.

223 *"I played a Frenchie . . ."* Commemorative book on Wolfgang Zilzer written for the 33rd Berlinale in 1983.

224 *When he was honored . . .* Ibid.

224 *"I am not acting . . ."* Dantine File, MHL/AMPAS.

224 *"Following my arrival . . ."* Lotte Palfi Andor in a draft of her memoirs.

225 *"Lotte knew she . . ."* Peter Almond, interviewed by author.

225 *"I was not there . . ."* Billy Wilder, interviewed by author.

225 *"Our image of . . ."* Pauline Kael, interviewed by author.

225 *"Certainly* Casablanca's *. . ."* Anthony Heilbut, interviewed by author.

Chapter Thirteen

The full citations for the following items of script material can be found at the head of the notes on Chapter Three: *Everybody Comes to Rick's,* Howard Koch's "Suggestions for Revised Story," and the PART I REV. FINAL script of June 1. This chapter also refers to the PART II TO END TEMP. script of May 21, a revised version of the last third of the picture, and the Cutter's Script, both of which can be found in the *Casablanca* script files at the Warner Bros. Archives, and Lenore Coffee's six-page "suggested story line" and a three-page outline of the third act by the Epsteins, which are in the possession of the author. The tracing of various versions of speeches, scenes, and endings has been done by the author through an analysis of the extant material.

227 *"an exceptional dose . . ."* Los Angeles *Times,* June 27, 1942, Part I, p. 2.

227 *"The pages were colored . . ."* Carl Stucke, interviewed by author.

228 *"But Hal came down . . ."* Lee Katz, interviewed by author.

228 *"the only dramatic . . ."* Memo from Wally Kline to Wallis, Jan. 5, 1942, CSF/WBA.

229 *Both Koch and Epstein . . .* Howard Koch and Julius Epstein, interviewed by author.

229 *"MISCELLANEOUS NOTES . . ."* Robinson's "Notes on Screenplay Casablanca," p. 6, May 20, 1942; these notes are discussed in detail in Chapter Nine.

230 *"One of them . . ."* Leslie Epstein, interviewed by author.

232 *"play it in-between" . . .* Ingrid Bergman and Alan Burgess, *My Story,* p. 145.

232 *"there is a little . . ."* Richard J. Anobile, ed., *Casablanca,* p. 6.

232 *"didn't dare to look . . ."* Ingrid Bergman and Alan Burgess, *My Story,* p. 145.

232 *"I wasn't there . . ."* Lauren Bacall, interviewed by author.

232 *"We never had . . ."* Howard Koch, interviewed by author.

233 *another revision of . . .* Al Alleborn to T. C. Wright, June 26, 1942, daily production files, WBA.

233 *"Dear Mike . . ."* Memo from Wallis to Curtiz, July 6, 1942, CSF/WBA.

234 *"Wallis was not . . ."* Charles Higham, interviewed by author.

235 *"During the day . . ."* Alleborn to T. C. Wright, July 18, 1942, Daily Production file, WBA.

235 *"He was only . . ."* Geraldine Fitzgerald, interviewed by author.

235 *"He didn't have a . . ."* James Wong Howe interviewed by Charles Higham, OH, June 11, 1971, OHRO/CU.

235 *Wilder said that . . .* Ezra Goodman, *Bogey: The Good-Bad Guy,* pp. 98–99.

236 *Bogart kept arguing with . . .* Richard Brooks, interviewed by author.

237 *Bergman has talked . . .* Richard J. Anobile, ed., *Casablanca,* p. 6.

237 *camera reports for July 18 . . .* A separate file of camera reports in the WBA shows that both versions of Bogart's "confession" to Laszlo were shot on the morning of July 18.

237 *"We were not allowed . . ."* Lee Katz, interviewed by author.

238 *"the stuff will . . ."* Memo from Wallis to Curtiz, July 22, 1942, CSF/WBA.

238 *"Political church . . ."* Howard Koch, interviewed by author.

Chapter Fourteen

Much of the information in this chapter comes through the Freedom of Information Act (FOIA). The government kept files on Peter Lorre, Humphrey Bogart, Ingrid Bergman, and Conrad Veidt, as it did on thousands of Americans. Much of this information was collected by the FBI.

242 *"racist statement . . ."* Memo from Bessie to Jerry Wald, Dec. 2, 1944, JWC.

243 *"I had done three . . ."* Howard Koch, interviewed by author.

243 *"There's no reason . . ."* Telegram from Jack Warner to Ambassador Davies, Jan. 15, 1943, JWC.

244 *"I didn't know anything . . ."* Lena Horne, interviewed by author.

244 *"John Huston and I . . ."* Philip Dunne, interviewed by author.

245 *"We went to Washington . . ."* Bogart on a radio program, station WIP, Philadelphia, Oct. 29, 1947, 10 P.M.

245 *"I went to Washington . . ."* News Chronicle (London), Dec. 15, 1947.

245 *"Although the script . . ."* Letter from Breen to Warner, Dec. 30, 1938, PCA and Confessions of a Nazi Spy story file, WBA.

246 *"Hitler and his . . ."* Karl Lishka, PCA.

246 *"Harry Warner in particular . . ."* Donald Ogden Stewart, By a Stroke of Luck, p. 231.

246 *"Jack and Harry Warner . . ."* Sonja Biberman, interviewed by author.

246 *"any of the Jewish or . . ."* Letter from Joseph Hazan to Jack Warner, Jan. 27, 1939, JWC.

246 *"sacred treatment . . ."* James Agee, The Nation, May 22, 1943, p. 749.

247 *"to Warner Bros.' continued . . ."* Time, Aug. 16, 1943, p. 94.

248 *Warner told the committee . . .* Prepared statement by Harry M. Warner delivered to the subcommittee of the Senate Committee on Interstate Commerce, Sept. 25, 1941, Harry M. Warner speeches and interviews folder, JWC.

248 *The OSS . . .* CIA document, 100-304299-8, FOIA, released March 1992.

248 *HUAC member J. Parnell . . .* Bergman FBI file, FOIA.

248 *Henreid's plane trip . . .* Paul Henreid, Ladies Man, pp. 191–94.

249 *"It takes particular . . ."* Philip Dunne, interviewed by author.

249 *"We played the same . . ."* Julius Epstein, interviewed by author.

250 *"my seven little dwarfs . . ."* Letters from Capra to Lucille Capra, Feb. 1942, Frank Capra Collection, Wesleyan Cinema Archives, Wesleyan University.

250 *"were larded with . . ."* Frank Capra, The Name Above the Title, p. 335.

250 *"I was never political . . ."* Curt Bois, interviewed by author.

250 *"I hedged and didn't . . ."* Unpublished taped Rains interviews.

Chapter Fifteen

253 *"It struck a chord"* . . . Murray Burnett, interviewed by author.

254 *" 'As Time Goes By' . . ."* Ann Sothern, interviewed by author.

254 *Hal Wallis pushed Leo* . . . Memo from Wallis's office to Forbstein, July 11, 1942, CSF/WBA.

254 *"None of us likes . . ."* David Raksin, interviewed by author.

254 *"He told me he . . ."* Al Bender, interviewed by author.

255 *Steiner told an interviewer* . . . Mark Schubart, *PM,* Aug. 2, 1943, or Aug. 21, 1943, date on clipping unclear.

255 *"We should be able . . ."* Letter from Warner to Forbstein, Apr. 16, 1943, JWC.

255 *"The song is a main . . ."* Yale graduate students Arthur Bloom, John Rogers, Ed Harsh, Joe Rubenstein, and Lee Heuermann presented their written analyses of music to the author; Daniel Becker was interviewed by the author.

256 *Hupfeld tried* . . . Stuart Stewart to Trilling, Sept. 22, 1943, JWC.

256 *"I always thought . . ."* Margaret Scannell Wooley, interviewed by author.

257 *"His mother, a pianist . . ."* Letter from Harold G. Rader to author, Sept. 11, 1990.

257 *"And the 'Marseillaise' . . ."* Daniel Becker, interviewed by author.

257 *"But, as good as . . ."* David Raksin, interviewed by author.

258 *"His underscoring . . ."* Kathryn Kalinak, interviewed by author.

258 *"Maxie liked all kinds . . ."* David Raksin, interviewed by author.

258 *For Ilsa's entrance into* . . . *Casablanca* music cue sheets, WBA.

259 *"It's wonderful stuff . . ."* David Raksin, interviewed by author.

259 *Schallert gave Mura* . . . Edwin Schallert, Los Angeles *Times,* June 9, 1942, Part II, p. 8, June 13, 1942, Part I, p. 8.

259 *"When Maxie was dying . . ."* David Raksin, interviewed by author.

259 *"Wallis was one . . ."* Kathryn Kalinak, interviewed by author.

260 *only three remain* . . . Hal Wallis, music notes, Sept. 2, 1942, CSF/WBA.

260 *"for a negro with . . ."* Memo from Wallis to Forbstein, July 3, 1942, CSF/WBA.

260 Variety *singled him* . . . *Variety,* Dec. 2, 1942; *Hollywood Reporter,* Dec. 8, 1942.

260 The New York Times *said* . . . *Two Tickets to London* July 3, 1943; *Stormy Weather,* July 22, 1942; *Higher and Higher,* Jan. 22, 1944.

261 *"What seems remarkable . . ."* Laurence Mark, interviewed by author.

261 *"Take out the group . . ."* Hal Wallis, cutting notes, Reel #2, Sept. 2, 1942, CSF/WBA.

262 *In a press release Warner* . . . Special to the *Independent,* Feb. 24, 1943, JWC.

262 *a comparison shows that* . . . Report from Beetson, Feb. 18, 1943, JWC.

264 *Siegel was trying* . . . Bill Schaefer to Obringer, Feb. 23, 1944, Siegel contract files, WBA.

264 *"You understand, of course . . ."* Letter from Breen to Warner, May 27, 1942, CSF/WBA, and PCA.

264 *"I have never heard . . ."* Memo from Wallis to Einfeld, Aug. 28, 1942, CSF/WBA.

264 *"I thought perhaps . . ."* Ibid.

Chapter Sixteen

266 *"It started in . . ."* Rudi Fehr, interviewed by author.

266 *"Casablanca, city of . . ." Casablanca* trailer courtesy of Ronald Haver, curator of film, Los Angeles County Museum of Art.

267 *"If you're selling . . ."* Art Silver, interviewed by author.

267 *Director Elia Kazan . . .* Tom Pryor, interviewed by author.

267 *"At previews . . ."* Francis Scheid, interviewed by author.

268 *"Much to my amazement . . ."* Letter from Einfeld to Warner, June 29, 1937, Wallis file, WBA.

268 *"Anyone doesn't like . . ."* Warner to Einfeld, Jan. 9, 1943, JWC.

268 *In a letter . . .* Warner to Wallis, Feb. 17, 1943, Hal Wallis contract file, WBA.

268 *"To Wallis: Happy . . ."* Warner to Wallis, Nov. 28, 1943, JWC.

269 *In his return . . .* A copy of this telegram from Wallis to Warner, Nov. 30, 1943, is embedded in the material Warner sent to Einfeld the same day, JWC.

269 *"To Wallis: Stop giving . . ."* Telegram from Warner to Wallis, Nov. 30, 1943, JWC.

269 *"Sick and tired . . ."* Telegram from Warner to Einfeld, Nov. 30, 1943, JWC.

270 *"He always poached . . ."* Solly Baiano, interviewed by author.

270 *"Bogey's so set . . ."* Hedda Hopper, Los Angeles *Times,* July 11, 1942, Part I, p. 7.

270 *"Consumed with . . ."* Jack Brodsky, interviewed by author.

270 *"that screen villain . . ."* Ezra Goodman, "Exit the 'Bogey'-Man," Warner Bros. Publicity, Vol. V, No. 11, Sept. 21–28, 1942, WBA.

271 *"We conducted a much . . ."* Arthur Wilde, interviewed by author.

272 *"Casablanca really wonderful . . ."* Telegram from Einfeld to Kalmenson, Kalmine, Schneider, Blumenstock, Schless, and Hummel, Sept. 23, 1942, JWC.

272 *"When we previewed . . ."* Julius Epstein, interviewed by author.

272 *The twenty-two-page pressbook . . .* The pressbook is at the Warner Bros. Archives.

273 *"Not a word . . ."* Paul Henreid, interviewed by author.

276 *The Hollywood Victory Committee . . . Film Daily Yearbook 1943,* pp. 157–58.

277 *"How you wear your . . ." Screen Actor,* a publication of the Screen Actors Guild, June, 1942, p. 7.

277 *"the hefty income . . ." Hollywood Reporter,* Jan. 27, 1942.

277 *"Your greatest war . . ." Hollywood Reporter,* Jan. 15, 1942.

278 *"In this peculiar . . ."* Letter from Zanuck to Mellett, Jan. 8, 1942, Darryl Zanuck file, Box 1443, OWI.

278 *"It is no exaggeration . . ."* Letter from Zanuck to Mellett, Jan. 31, 1942, OWI.

278 *"believes actors and . . ." Hollywood Reporter,* Feb. 10, 1942.

278 *"Reagan was too . . ."* Owen Crump, interviewed by author.

279 *"I told M-G-M . . ."* Lew Ayres, interviewed by author.

280 *Wallis had sent an anxious . . .* Memo from Wallis to Warner, Oct. 9, 1942, JWC.

280 *"it's impossible . . ."* Telegram from Warner to Kalmenson and other New York executives, Nov. 10, 1942, CSF/WBA.

280 *the retake would involve* . . . Memo from Wallis to Wright, Nov. 11, 1942, CSF/WBA.

281 *A telegram makes it* . . . Telegram from Wallis to Jacob Wilk, Nov. 11, 1942, CSF/WBA.

281 *Dear Hal: Saw "Casablanca"* . . . Telegram from Selznick to Wallis, Nov. 12, 1942, CSF/WBA.

282 *One article began* . . . These articles are in the *Casablanca* publicity files, WBA.

283 *"The total, therefore . . ."* Schneider to H. M., Jack, and Albert Warner, Feb. 8, 1943, JWC.

283 *The records of William* . . . Statistics on negative cost and studio grosses, The William Schaefer Collection, JWC.

Chapter Seventeen

284 *The premiere began* . . . Casablanca Pressbook, WBA, and *Hollywood Reporter,* Nov. 27, 1942.

286 *"The occasion took . . ."* *Hollywood Reporter,* Nov. 27, 1942.

286 *"I saw the picture . . ."* Robert Riskin to Ulric Bell, Jan. 8, 1943, box 3510, OWI.

286 *The first War Feature* . . . Report from Dorothy B. Jones to Nelson Poynter, Sept. 22, 1942, box 1435, OWI.

287 *1) Will this picture* . . . Government Information Manual for the Motion Picture Industry, summer 1942, box 15, OWI.

288 *the manual proclaimed* . . . Clayton Koppes and Gregory Black, *Hollywood Goes to War,* pp. 67–69.

289 *"can protect himself . . ."* Fact Sheet No. 7, Trilling files, JWC.

289 *"from the standpoint of . . ."* *Casablanca* feature review by Lillian Bergquist, box 1438, OWI.

289 Sherlock Holmes . . . Box 1438, OWI.

289 London Blackout Murders . . . The comments on *London Blackout Murders, The Palm Beach Story,* and *Lucky Jordan* are contained in a report on movies confirming Nazi propaganda, box 1438, OWI.

289 *"America's domestic morals . . ."* Review by William Roberts, box 1435, OWI

289 *Paramount's* Lucky Jordan . . . Ibid.

290 Watch on the Rhine, *which* . . . Ibid.

290 *"tops from every . . ."* Ulric Bell to Robert Riskin, Dec. 9, 1942, box 3510, OWI.

290 *Republican members of Congress* . . . *New York Times,* Oct. 10, 1943, p. 40.

290 *As to aesthetics* . . . James Agee, *The Nation,* Oct. 30, 1943. (Agee's reviews are reprinted in *Agee on Film.*)

290 *"lasted twenty-four hours . . ."* Ibid., May 6, 1944, p. 549.

290 *"Ending was awful . . ."* Koppes and Black, *Hollywood Goes to War,* pp. 165–69.

291 *"strange quirks of femme . . ."* *Variety,* Oct. 1, 1942.

291 *"Suppose you went to . . ."* Jim Marshall, *Collier's,* Jan. 17, 1942, p. 11.

291 *"foolishly being blinded . . ."* "Movie War Effort," Public Relations Committee of the Motion Picture Industry, box 59, folder 22, JWC.

292 *"Women's lives were affected . . ."* Pauline Kael, interviewed by author.

292 *"There was an absolute . . ."* Fay Wray, interviewed by author.
292 *"Frankly and sincerely . . ."* Letter from Einfeld to Capra, undated but responding to a Capra letter written Apr. 18, 1942, Frank Capra Collection, Wesleyan Cinema Archives, Wesleyan University.
292 *It is not surprising . . .* Koppes and Black, *Hollywood Goes to War,* p. 70.
292 *"Recent events now call . . ."* Harry Warner to Mellett, Jan. 5, 1942, Warner Bros. file box 1443, OWI.
293 *"eager to re-establish . . ."* Review of Sept. 22, 1943, *Princess O'Rourke* folder, OWI.
293 *"realizes the dignity . . ."* NSB/WBS.
294 *"One of the most useful . . ."* Telegram from Poynter to Jack Warner, May 18, 1943, NSB/WBS.
294 *"visit to the United . . ."* Box 1438, OWI.
294 *He was appalled . . .* Correspondence between Warner Bros. and the OWI regarding *The Desert Song* can be found in the Trilling files of the JWC— letters from Poynter to Trilling on Dec. 24, 1942, and Mar. 2, 1943, and from Robert Buckner to Poynter on Mar. 3, 1943, and from Trilling to Poynter on Feb. 27, 1943.
294 *"The whole concept . . ."* Nov. 25, 1942, box 3511, OWI.
295 *One of Poynter's early . . .* Poynter's weekly logs, Sept. 14, 1942, to Oct. 17, 1942, box 3510, OWI.
295 *Warners dropped* The Life . . . *New York Times,* Jan. 31, 1943, II, 3.
295 *"Casablanca was a very . . ."* Haskell Wexler, interviewed by author.
296 *"Hollywood hasn't taken . . ."* "Interpretation of Statistics on Feature Length Films," released by the Motion Picture Industry, Dec. 1, 1941–July 1, 1942, box 1556, OWI
297 *After talking Bogart into . . .* Sam Jaffe to Trilling, Aug. 4, 1941, quoted in Rudy Behlmer, ed., *Inside Warner Bros.,* p. 156.
297 *In an eight-page . . .* Justifications for *Casablanca,* NSB/WBS.
298 *The OWI's confidential . . .* "Inventory of Feature-Length Films Directly Related to the War," Dec. 15, 1942, box 1435, OWI.
299 *The Bureau of Motion Pictures . . .* Reviews of *Torpedoed* and *Action in the North Atlantic,* box 3505, OWI.
300 *"Bogart played in the . . ."* Bogart Freedom of Information Act files.
300 *"Humphrey Bogart and several . . ."* James Agee, *The Nation,* Oct. 23, 1943, p. 480.
301 *"The Hilton Cook . . ."* James Agee, *The Nation,* July 29, 1944, p. 137.
302 *"stereotypical and disparaging" . . .* A copy of this Writer's War Board survey done by the Bureau of Applied Social Research at Columbia University is at the SCRBC.
302 *"intimidated or coerced . . ."* New York Times, May 19, 1943, p. 16.
302 *Curtiz went behind Hal Wallis's back . . .* Curtiz to Warner, July 27, 1943, Trilling files, JWC.
302 *Within days after North . . .* Hollywood Reporter, Nov. 10, 1942.
302 *"It seems to me inadvisable . . ."* Passage to Marseille story file, WBA.
307 *In 1943, the British Ministry . . .* New York Times, Feb. 23, 1943, p. 16.
308 *"untouched, virginal, prenatal . . ."* James Agee, *The Nation,* Oct. 30, 1943.
309 *"charming and impetuous . . ."* Justifications for *Casablanca,* NSB/WBS.

Chapter Eighteen

313 *"said to have been . . ."* Bergman Department of the Army file, Dec. 30, 1943, Freedom of Information Act.

313 *Afterward Bogart told* . . . Lauren Bacall, *By Myself,* p. 98.

313 *Bogart received a telegram* . . . Trilling to Bogart, Feb. 12, 1944, JWC.

313 *"Mayo had fought off . . ."* Nathaniel Benchley, *Humphrey Bogart,* p. 136.

314 *"Start propaganda now . . ."* Warner to Einfeld, Dec. 1, 1943, JWC.

314 *"You would have thought . . ."* Whitney Stine, *"I'd Love to Kiss You . . ."* p. 197.

314 *"All the colorfulness . . ."* Variety, Mar. 3, 1944.

315 *Both* The Song of Bernadette . . . *Variety,* Feb. 23, 1944.

315 *"The Story of a Masterpiece"* . . . *Variety,* Dec. 24, 1943.

315 *"was so busy working that . . ."* Pia Lindstrom, "My Mother, Ingrid Bergman," *Good Housekeeping,* October, 1964, p. 83.

315 *At night, Bergman* . . . Much information about the Hollywood Canteen can be found in Scrapbook 45, Bette Davis Collection, TCA.

316 *"Everyone had morning . . ."* Dorothy Jeakins, interviewed by author.

316 *"That's Ingrid Bergman's . . ."* Pia Lindstrom, "My Mother, Ingrid Bergman," *Good Housekeeping,* October, 1964, p. 82.

316 *"I contended it would . . ."* Paul Henreid, interviewed by author.

316 *"was the equal of any . . ."* Julius Epstein, interviewed by author.

317 *"gravely detrimental to . . ."* Confidential script analysis, *Mr. Skeffington file,* OWI.

317 *The OWI suggested* . . . Warren H. Pierce to James J. Geller, Oct. 22, 1943, OWI comments on Overseas Pictures box, JWC.

318 *Rains said that three* . . . Unpublished taped interviews with Claude Rains.

318 *Rains grieved as much* . . . Ibid.

318 *Rains enjoyed acting* . . . Frances Rains Feder, interviewed by author through Jessica Rains.

319 *"One of the wire services . . ."* Julius Epstein and Lilian Epstein Gelsey, interviewed by author.

320 *In her autobiography* . . . Ingrid Bergman, and Alan Burgess, *Ingrid Bergman: My Story,* pp. 172–73.

321 *"I started up the aisle . . ."* Hal Wallis and Charles Higham, *Starmaker,* p. 92.

322 *Almost as an afterthought* . . . Jimmy Starr, Los Angeles *Herald,* Mar. 3, 1944.

323 *Before the night was over* . . . Alex Evelove, Mar. 4, 1944, typed notes dictated to himself on the events on March 2–4, WBA.

323 *Warner-Wallis "Rivalry"* . . . Los Angeles *Times,* Mar. 4, 1944, Part I, p. 7.

323 *"Today's newspaper is . . ."* Alex Evelove, Mar. 4, 1944, notes dictated to himself, WBA.

324 *"I have been with . . ."* Telegram from Wallis to Schallert, Mar. 4, 1944, WBA.

324 *"the statuette for . . ."* Los Angeles *Times,* Mar. 6, 1944, Part I, p. 10.

324 *"choicest assignments, including . . ."* Studio press release, Apr. 4, 1944, WBA.

Chapter Nineteen

328 *"Everyone seems to think . . ."* Lee Katz, interviewed by author.

328 *"In 1972 . . ."* Francis Scheid, interviewed by author.

329 *"Massive doses . . ."* Lilian Gelsey, interviewed by author.

329 *"My brother and I . . ."* Julius Epstein, interviewed by author.

330 *"In the Roosevelt years . . ."* Howard Koch, interviewed by author.

330 *"More money than . . ."* Murray Burnett, interviewed by author.

330 *"Remember we were not . . ."* Joan Alison, interviewed by author.

331 *"She was a female . . ."* Murray Burnett, interviewed by author.

331 *"I advise anyone . . ."* Daily Telegraph (London), Apr. 12, 1991.

331 *"If only we had . . ."* Charles Higham, interviewed by author.

331 *"It doesn't exist . . ."* New York Mirror, May 12, 1948.

332 *"The most cruelest . . ."* PM, Sept. 17, 1944, M13.

332 *"He couldn't bear . . ."* Samuel Goldwyn, Jr., interviewed by author.

332 *"What are you going to do . . ."* Unpublished taped interviews with Claude Rains.

332 *"When we were . . ."* Jessica Rains, interviewed by author.

332 *"They wouldn't let me go . . ."* Unpublished Rains taped interviews.

333 *"I was not part . . ."* Mary Beth Crain, Los Angeles Times, Aug. 21, 1977, Calendar, p. 33.

334 *"More than anything . . ."* Charles Champlin, interviewed by author.

334 *"I am a very happy . . ."* Richard J. Anobile, ed., Casablanca, p. 7.

334 *"She only wanted . . ."* François Truffaut, Hitchcock, p. 139.

334 *"When she was making . . ."* Pia Lindstrom, interviewed by author.

335 *"There's nothing as romantic . . ."* Lauren Bacall, interviewed by author.

Chapter Twenty

338 *When Warner Bros. announced . . .* Schallert, Los Angeles Times, Jan. 18, 1943, Part I, p. 11.

338 *"The reason it never works . . ."* Julius Epstein, interviewed by author.

338 *"If your leading man . . ."* Murray Burnett, interviewed by author.

339 *Even in the first serious . . .* Synopsis of Frederick Stephani's original story, Casablanca files, WBA.

339 *"The moment Rick becomes . . ."* Frederick Faust to Hal Wallis, spring 1943, reprinted in Inside Warner Bros., Rudy Behlmer, ed., p. 219.

339 *In 1988, Koch suggested . . .* Howard Koch proposal, Jim Bernet to John Schulman, Aug. 8, 1988, Warner Bros. legal files, Warner Bros. studio.

339 *"meticulously faithful . . ."* Howard Price to Kenneth Hyman, undated, basement, Stage 15, Warner Bros. studio.

340 *"Mr. Warner thought . . ."* Rudi Fehr, interviewed by author.

340 *"Jack used to say . . ."* Bill Orr, interviewed by author.

342 *"They said colorizing . . ."* Stephen Bogart, interviewed by author.

342 *"After he sold . . ."* Bill Orr, interviewed by author.

343 *"I am aware . . ."* Truffaut to Simon Benzakein, Mar. 10, 1974, François Truffaut: Correspondence 1945–1984, p. 401.

343 *"At some point . . ."* Cyrus Harvey, Jr., interviewed by author.

343 *"I was born . . ."* Todd Gitlin, interviewed by author.

344 *"Bogie was always . . ."* Vincent Sherman, Oral History, pp. 140–41, AFIL.

344 *"I'm sorry, Jack . . ."* Transcript of telephone conversation between Bogart and Warner that took place on May 6, 1943, between 4 and 4:30 P.M., JWC.

345 *Bogart brought his cynicism . . .* Lauren Bacall, interviewed by author.

345 *"He was never . . ."* Lauren Bacall, *By Myself,* p. 211.

345 *"Bogart has competence . . ."* Billy Wilder, interviewed by author.

346 *"He wore no . . ."* Mary Astor, *A Life on Film,* p. 166.

346 *"People never go . . ."* Stanley Kauffmann, interviewed by author.

346 *a real Mafia underboss . . .* Marguerite Del Giudice, "Philip Leonetti: The Mobster Who Could Bring Down the Mob," *New York Times Magazine,* June 3, 1991, p. 36.

347 *"no special feelings . . ."* Letter from Woody Allen to author, Aug. 20, 1990.

347 *"Rick can give . . ."* Richard Corliss, *Casablanca: Script and Legend,* by Howard Koch, p. 188.

347 *"a standard case . . ."* William Donelley, "Love and Death in *Casablanca,"* *Persistence of Vision: A Collection of Film Criticism,* Joseph McBride, ed., p. 103.

348 *"The idea that . . ."* Harvey Greenberg, *The Movies on Your Mind,* pp. 103, 88.

348 *"Rick kills . . ."* Krin and Glen O. Gabbard, "Play It Again, Sigmund," *Journal of Popular Film and Television,* Vol. 18, Spring 1990, pp. 7–17.

349 *"a hodgepodge . . ."* Umberto Eco, *"Casablanca:* Cult Movies and Intertextual Collage," *Sub-Stance* 47, 1985, pp. 3–12.

349 *"the lure . . ."* J. P. Telotte, *"Casablanca* and the Larcenous Cult Film," *The Cult Film Experience,* J. P. Telotte, ed., p. 45.

349 *Another semiologist . . .* Larry Vonalt, "Looking Both Ways in *Casablanca,"* *The Cult Film Experience,* J. P. Telotte, ed., pp. 55–65.

349 *"This is the most wonderful . . ."* Billy Wilder, interviewed by author.

349 *"Casablanca dramatizes . . ."* Todd Gitlin, interviewed by author.

350 *"who is presented . . ."* Leslie Fiedler, *Love and Death in the American Novel,* p. 181.

350 *"that mixed bag of irresponsible . . ."* Richard Schickel, *Schickel on Film,* p. 217.

350 *"Boy meets girl . . ."* "The Greatest Movie Ever Made," *60 Minutes;* CBS News, Nov. 15, 1981.

351 *"Rains is Europe . . ."* Stanley Kauffmann, interviewed by author.

351 *"It was the Warners . . ."* Pauline Kael, interviewed by author.

352 *"a picture of what . . ."* Michael Wood, *America in the Movies,* p. 25.

352 *"All that she . . ."* Andrew Sarris, *Village Voice,* Jan. 8, 1970.

352 *the Beatrice-Benedick pattern . . .* Sidney Rosenzweig, *Casablanca and Other Major Films of Michael Curtiz,* p. 80.

353 *"he realizes her . . ."* Leo Braudy, *The World in a Frame; What We See in Films,* p. 204.

353 *"He rejects her . . ."* Larry Vonalt, "Looking Both Ways in *Casablanca,"* *The Cult Film Experience,* J. P. Telotte, ed., p. 64.

354 *"It would end up . . ."* Stephen Bogart, interviewed by author.

Bibliography

———◆———

This is a selected bibliography. It includes all books referred to in the text, but it does not include any of the archival material, newspaper articles, government documents, interviews, or other primary sources which are cited in the Reference Notes and Sources. The only periodical material cited here are those articles also cited in the Reference Notes and Sources that I thought might be of special interest to readers of this book. I have included books not referred to in the text that I found particularly useful or feel a reader interested in following up on some of the issues discussed in this book might find of interest.

Agee, James. *Agee on Film.* New York: McDowell, Obolensky, 1958.

Alicoate, Jack, ed. *The Film Daily Year Book of Motion Pictures.* Vols. 1942, 1943, 1944, and 1945. New York: *The Film Daily,* 1942, 1943, 1944, and 1945.

Andor, Lotte Palfi. *Die Fremden Jahre: Erinnerungen An Deutschland.* Berlin: Fischer Taschenbuch, Wolfgang Benz, 1991.

Anobile, Richard J., ed. Casablanca: *The Film Classics Library.* New York: Darien House/Avon, 1974.

Astor, Mary. *A Life on Film.* New York: Delacorte, 1971.

Bacon, James. *Made in Hollywood.* Chicago: Contemporary Books, 1977.

Bacall, Lauren. *Lauren Bacall by Myself.* New York: Alfred A. Knopf, 1979.

Basinger, Jeanine. *The World War II Combat Film: Anatomy of a Genre.* New York: Columbia University Press, 1986.

Behlmer, Rudy. *America's Favorite Movies: Behind the Scenes.* New York: Frederick Ungar, 1982.

———, comp., ed., and annotated by. *Inside Warner Bros. (1935–1951).* New York: Viking Press, 1985.

Benchley, Nathaniel. *Humphrey Bogart.* Boston: Little, Brown, 1975.

Bergman, Ingrid, and Alan Burgess. *Ingrid Bergman: My Story.* New York: Delacorte, 1980; New York: Dell, 1981.

Bessie, Alvah. *Inquisition in Eden.* New York: Macmillan, 1965.

Bogart, Humphrey. "I'm No Communist." *Photoplay,* March 1948, 52 + .

———, as told to Kate Holliday. "My Mother: I Never Really Loved Her." *McCall's,* July 1949.

Braudy, Leo. *The World in a Frame: What We See in Films.* New York: Doubleday, 1976.

Brecht, Bertolt. *Poems 1913–1956.* Ed. John Willet and Ralph Manheim with Erick Fried. New York: Methuen, 1976.

Brooks, Richard. *The Producer.* New York: Simon and Schuster, 1951.

Brownlow, Kevin. *The Parade's Gone By . . .* New York: Alfred A. Knopf, 1968.

Buckley, Gail Lumet. *The Hornes: An American Family.* New York: Alfred A. Knopf, 1986.

Cagney, James. *Cagney by Cagney.* New York: Doubleday, 1976; New York: Pocket Books, 1977.

Capra, Frank. *The Name Above the Title.* New York: Macmillan, 1971.

Catton, Bruce. *The War Lords of Washington.* New York: Harcourt, Brace, 1948.

Ceplair, Larry, and Steven Englund. *The Inquisition in Hollywood: Politics in the Film Community, 1920–1960.* Garden City, NY: Anchor Press/Doubleday, 1980.

Colgan, Christine Ann. "Warner Bros.' Crusade Against the Third Reich: A Study of Anti-Nazi Activism and Film Production, 1933–1941." Ph.D. diss. Doheny Library, University of Southern California.

Corliss, Richard. "Analysis of the Film." Casablanca: *Script and Legend.* Comp. Howard Koch. Woodstock, NY: The Overlook Press, 1973. 182–98.

Cripps, Thomas. *Slow Fade to Black: The Negro in American Film, 1900–1942.* New York: Oxford University Press, 1977.

Deming, Barbara. *Running Away from Myself: A Dream Portrait of America Drawn from the Films of the Forties.* New York: Grossman, 1969.

Donnelly, William. "Love and Death in *Casablanca.*" *Persistence of Vision: A Collection of Film Criticism.* Ed. Joseph McBride. Madison, WI: Wisconsin Film Society Press, 1968. 103–7.

Dunne, Philip. *Take Two: A Life in Movies and Politics.* New York: McGraw-Hill, 1980.

Eco, Umberto. "*Casablanca:* Cult Movies and Intertextual Collage." *Sub-Stance* 47, 1985, 3–12.

Erens, Patricia. *The Jew in American Cinema.* Bloomington, IN: Indiana University Press, 1984.

Fiedler, Leslie. *Love and Death in the American Novel.* Rev. ed. New York: Scarborough, 1982.

Freedland, Michael. *The Warner Brothers.* London: Harrap, 1983.

Fussell, Paul. *Wartime: Understanding and Behavior in the Second World War.* New York: Oxford University Press, 1989.

Gabbard, Krin, and Glen O. Gabbard, M.D. "Play It Again, Sigmund: Psychoanalysis and the Classical Hollywood Text." *Journal of Popular Film and Television* 18, Spring 1990, 7–17.

Gabler, Neal. *An Empire of Their Own: How The Jews Invented Hollywood.* New York: Crown, 1988.

Goodman, Ezra. *Bogey: The Good-Bad Guy.* New York: Lyle Stuart, 1965.

———. *The Fifty Year Decline and Fall of Hollywood.* New York: Simon and Schuster, 1961.

Greenberg, Harvey R., M.D. *The Movies on Your Mind.* New York: Saturday Review/Dutton, 1975.

Heilbut, Anthony. *Exiled in Paradise: German Refugee Artists and Intellectuals in America from the 1930's to the Present.* New York: Viking, 1983.

Henreid, Paul, with Julius Fast. *Ladies Man.* New York: St. Martin's Press, 1984.

Hepburn, Katharine. *The Making of the African Queen: Or How I Went to Africa with Bogart, Bacall and Huston and Almost Lost My Mind.* New York: Alfred A. Knopf, 1987.

———. *Me: Stories of My Life.* New York: Alfred A. Knopf, 1991.

Horak, Jan Christopher. "Anti-Nazi Filme Der Deutsch Sprachigen Emigration, 1939–1945." Ph.D. diss. Munster, Germany: MAkS Publikation, 1984.

———. "Fluchtpunkt Hollywood: Eine Dokumentation zur Filmemigration nach 1933." Appendix to Ph.D. diss., published separately. 2nd ed. Munster, Germany: MAkS Publikation, 1986.

Huston, John. *An Open Book.* New York: Alfred A. Knopf, 1980.

Hyams, Joe. *Bogie: The Biography of Humphrey Bogart.* New York: New American Library, 1966.

Jerome, Stuart. *Those Crazy Wonderful Years When We Ran Warner Bros.* Secaucus, NJ: Lyle Stuart, 1983.

Johnson, Nunnally. *The Letters of Nunnally Johnson.* Ed. Dorris Johnson and Ellen Leventhal. New York: Knopf 1981.

Kane, Kathryn. *Visions of War: Hollywood Combat Films of World War II.* Studies in Cinema 9. Ann Arbor: UMI Research Press, 1982.

Katz, Ephraim. *The Film Encyclopedia.* New York: G.P. Putnam's Sons, 1979.

Kobal, John. *People Will Talk.* New York: Alfred A. Knopf, 1986.

Koch, Howard, comp. Casablanca: *Script and Legend.* Woodstock, NY: The Overlook Press, 1973.

———. "The Making of America's Favorite Movie: Here's Looking at You, Casablanca." *New York,* April 30, 1973, 74–78.

Kohner, Frederick. *The Magician of Sunset Boulevard: The Improbable Life of Paul Kohner, Hollywood Agent.* Palos Verdes, CA: Morgan Press, 1977.

Koppes, Clayton R., and Gregory D. Black. *Hollywood Goes to War: How Politics, Profits and Propaganda Shaped World War II War Movies.* New York: The Free Press/Macmillan, 1987; Berkeley: University of California Press, 1990.

Lardner, Ring, Jr. *The Lardners: My Family Remembered.* New York: Harper and Row, 1976.

Leab, Daniel J. *From Sambo to Superspade: The Black Experience in Motion Pictures.* Boston: Houghton Mifflin, 1975.

Leamer, Laurence. *As Time Goes By: The Life of Ingrid Bergman.* New York: Harper and Row, 1986.

Lindstrom, Pia, as told to George Christy. "My Mother, Ingrid Bergman." *Good Housekeeping,* Oct. 1964, 80+.

Lingeman, Richard R. *Don't You Know There's a War On?: The American Home Front, 1941–45.* New York: Putnam, 1970.

McGilligan, Pat, ed. *Backstory: Interviews with Screenwriters of Hollywood's Golden Age.* Berkeley: University of California Press, 1986.

McQueen, Scott. "Dr. X.: A Technicolor Landmark." *American Cinematographer,* June 1986, 34–42.

Mordden, Ethan. *The Hollywood Studios: House Style in the Golden Age of the Movies.* New York: Alfred A. Knopf, 1988.

Mosley, Leonard. *Zanuck: The Rise and Fall of Hollywood's Last Tycoon.* Boston: Little, Brown & Co., 1984.

Navasky, Victor. *Naming Names.* New York: Viking, 1980.

Niven, David. *Bring on the Empty Horses.* New York: G. P. Putnam's Sons, 1975.

Null, Gary. *Black Hollywood: The Negro in Motion Pictures.* Secaucus, NJ: Citadel, 1975.

O'Steen, Johnny, *Were These "Golden Years"?: 50 Years of Warner Bros., Hollywood and Much More.* Ms. Theater Arts Library, University of California at Los Angeles.

Rosenzweig, Sidney. Casablanca *and Other Major Films of Michael Curtiz.* Studies in Cinema 14. Ann Arbor, MI: UMI Research Press, 1982.

Rosten, Leo C. *Hollywood: The Movie Colony, The Movie Makers.* New York: Harcourt, Brace, 1941.

Sakall, Szoke. *The Story of Cuddles.* Translated by Paul Tabori. London: Cassell, 1954.

Sampson, Henry T. *Blacks in Blackface: A Source Book on Early Black Musical Shows.* Metuchen, NJ: The Scarecrow Press, 1980.

Sarris, Andrew. *The American Cinema: Directors and Directions: 1929–1968.* New York: Dutton, 1968.

Schatz, Thomas. *The Genius of the System: Hollywood Filmmaking in the Studio Era.* New York: Pantheon, 1988.

Schickel, Richard. *Schickel on Film: Encounters—Critical and Personal—with Movie Immortals.* New York: William Morrow, 1989.

Schickel, Richard. "Some Nights in Casablanca." *Favorite Movies: Critics Choice.* Ed. Philip Nobile. New York: Macmillan, 1973. 114–25.

Schulberg, Budd. *What Makes Sammy Run?* Anniversary ed. New York: Random House, 1990.

Schumach, Murray. *The Face on the Cutting Room Floor: The Story of Movie and Television Censorship.* New York: William Morrow, 1964.

Schwartz, Nancy Lynn. *The Hollywood Writer's Wars.* Completed by Sheila Schwartz. New York: Alfred A. Knopf, 1982.

Sennett, Ted. *Warner Bros. Presents: The Most Exciting Years—From* The Jazz Singer *to* White Heat. Memphis, Tenn.: Castle Books, 1971.

Silke, James R. *"Here's Looking at You, Kid": 50 Years of Fighting, Working and Dreaming at Warner Bros.* Boston: Little, Brown, 1976.

Smith, Jessie Carney. *Images of Blacks in American Culture.* New York: Greenwood Press, 1988.

Steele, Joseph Henry. *Ingrid Bergman: An Intimate Portrait.* New York: David McKay, 1959.

Stewart, Donald Ogden. *By a Stroke of Luck!* London: Paddington Press, 1975.

Stine, Whitney. *"I'd Love to Kiss You . . .": Conversations With Bette Davis.* New York: Pocket Books, 1990.

———, with a running commentary by Bette Davis. *Mother Goddam: The Story of the Career of Bette Davis.* New York: Hawthorn Books, 1974.

Taylor, John Russell. *Strangers in Paradise: The Hollywood Émigrés 1933–1950.* New York: Holt, Rinehart and Winston, 1983.

Telotte, J. P. *"Casablanca and the Larcenous Cult Film." The Cult Film Experience: Beyond All Reason.* Ed. J. P. Telotte. Austin: University of Texas Press, 1991.

Thomas, Bob. *Clown Prince of Hollywood: The Antic Life and Times of Jack L. Warner.* New York: McGraw-Hill, 1990.

Thomson, David. *A Biographical Dictionary of Film.* New York: William Morrow, 1976.

Truffaut, Francois. *Francois Truffaut: Correspondence 1945–1984.* Ed. Gilles Jacob and Claude de Givray. Trans. Gilbert Adair. New York: The Noonday Press/ Farrar, Straus and Giroux, 1990.

———. *Truffaut on Hitchcock.* New York: Simon and Schuster, 1967.

Viertel, Salka. *The Kindness of Strangers.* New York: Holt, Rinehart & Winston, 1969.

Vonalt, Larry. "Looking Both Ways in *Casablanca." The Cult Film Experience: Beyond All Reason.* Ed. J. P. Telotte. Austin: University of Texas Press, 1991.

Wallis, Hal, with Charles Higham. *Starmaker: The Autobiography of Hal Wallis.* New York: Macmillan, 1980.

"Warner Bros." *Fortune,* Dec. 1937, 110–13 +

Warner, Jack, with Dean Jennings. *My First Hundred Years in Hollywood.* New York: Random House, 1964.

Warner, Jack, Jr. *Bijou Dreams; a Novel.* New York: Crown, 1982. Rpt. as *The Dream Factory.* London: Sphere, 1985.

Wilson, Arthur, comp. and ed. *The Warner Bros. Golden Anniversary Book.* New York: A Dell Special, published by Film and Venture Corp., 1973.

White, David Manning, and Richard Averson. *The Celluoid Weapon: Social Comment in the American Film.* Boston: Beacon Press, 1972.

Wood, Michael. *America in the Movies: Or Santa Maria, It Had Slipped My Mind.* New York: Basic Books, 1975.

Youngkin, Stephen D., James Bigwood, and Raymond G. Cabana, Jr. *The Films of Peter Lorre.* Secaucus, NJ: Citadel, 1982.

Index